UNLIMITED HEARTBREAK

THE INSIDE STORY OF LIMERICK HURLING

HENRY MARTIN

The Collins Press

First published in 2009 by
The Collins Press
West Link Park
Doughcloyne
Wilton
Cork

British Library Cataloguing in Publication Data

Martin, Henry.
Unlimited heartbreak : the inside story of Limerick hurling.
1. Hurling (Game)—Ireland—Limerick (County)—History.
2. Hurling players—Ireland—Limerick (County)—Interviews.
I. Title
796.3'5'094194-dc22
ISBN-13: 9781848890145

Typesetting by Carrigboy Typesetting Services
Typeset in Baskerville
Printed in Spain by GraphyCems

Front cover: A dejected Dave Clarke after Limerick's shock defeat by Clare in the 1995 Munster senior hurling final. *Back cover (left):* The Limerick Team that beat Kilkenny in the 1940 All-Ireland final. *Back row (l–r):* Mick Hickey, Jim McCarthy, Tommy Cooke, Paddy Scanlon, Tony Herbert, Jim Roche, Paddy McMahon, John Mackey, Paddy Mackey, Timmy Ryan, Dave Hurley, Jackie Power, Martin 'Robbie' Lawlor. *Front row (l–r):* Paddy Clohessy, Mick Mackey, Mick Kennedy, Ned Chawke, Dick Stokes, Peter Cregan. *Back cover (right):* The official programme for the 1940 All-Ireland final where Limerick achieved a minor and senior double.

CONTENTS

❧

HENRY MARTIN played underage with Galbally in Limerick in the 1980s and still plays club football. He also hurled for Garryspillane when the hurling in Galbally was disbanded, winning a county senior hurling medal in 2005. He has been a GAA referee since 2002. A graduate of the University of Limerick and primary school teacher, he wrote a weekly GAA column in the *Limerick Leader* and random snippets for other publications. He now writes for *Hurling World* and the website An Fear Rua.

PICTURE CREDITS

☙

The author and publishers wish to thank the following who have kindly given permission for reproduction of the photographs on the following pages. If any photographs are incorrectly attributed we apologise for this and will be glad to make corrections in any future editions.

Gerry Piggott: pages 3, 5, 13, 23, 25, 29, 111.

Jim Ryan: pages 7, 10, 19.

Christy Murphy: pages 9, 35, 139.

James Lundon: pages 11, 12, 17, 27, 28, 48–49, 53.

Cora Moroney *nee* Mackey: page 15.

Vera Mulcahy *nee* Mackey: page 21.

Gerard Cussen: page 24.

Dermot Kelly: page 31.

Patrickswell GAA: page 43.

Ned Rea: pages 56–57, 67.

Sportsfile: pages 63, 87, 123, 191, 193, 287.

Sean Curtin: page 69.

Mike Weekes: pages 73, 81.

Frank Burke: pages 99, 103, 312–13.

Richard Moloney: pages 125, 131, 133.

Matt Rea: page 127.

Mike Hartnett: pages 143, 147, 282, 283.

John Kiely: page 151.

Irish Examiner: pages 181, 382–383.

John McCarthy: page 189 (both).

Hogan Stand: page 197.

Inpho: pages 211, 228–229, 235, 291, 295, 259, 321.

Tom Ryan: pages 225, 266–267.

Peter O'Byrne: page 275.

Limerick Leader: page 317.

Flann Howard: page 357.

Carmel Ryan: pages 368–369.

Denis O'Brien: pages 372–373, 385.

Tomas and Marie Ryan: pages 376–377.

Henry Martin: page 381.

ACKNOWLEDGEMENTS

ⓒ♥

It all began on the morning of Wednesday 25 November 1998, in the canteen in UL. A group of GAA obsessed final year students were sitting at one of the tables taking our turn to have our daily 'free' read of the *Examiner* bought by Brendan Coleman of Youghal, then a Cork senior hurler. In an article criticising the involvement of UL in club competitions entitled, 'Here's hoping Doonbeg beat the tar out of UL', Diarmuid O'Flynn mentioned my own club Galbally.

There was a fierce rivalry between UL and Galbally at the time. The UL footballers had spent the best part of a year whinging that Galbally were too physical in the 1997 Limerick county final, so Galbally came back and beat them playing fluent football at Cappamore in the 1998 championship. UL were also critical of the sideline antics of Johnny Wallace, a legend in Galbally and Limerick football circles and a former Limerick selector. Wallace had been involved in an altercation with Dave Mahedy in the tunnel at the Gaelic Grounds during half time in the 1997 final.

Séamus Kearney of Kilbehenny, a proud Galtee Gaels man who played hurling with me for Galbally said in his distinguished accent, 'Christ lad, you will have to write a letter to the sports editor about that article.' I replied, 'Sure, I can't put two words together.' Next Coleman piped up, 'Quinn will give you a hand with it.' An idea was conceived, the temperature was hot and I didn't need much encouragement. Mikey 'Sporty' Kelly, Ciarán Favier, Keenan Mullane, Mark McManus and Frank Connolly were also sitting around the table. Their promptings could only be compared to adding petrol to a fire.

Karl Quinn was from Tulla, County Clare, a 'mature' student who wasn't with us that morning due to his allergy toward early mornings. He did a little bit of cosmetic surgery on the letter and the rest is history. My letter was printed, followed by a series of tit-for-tat letters between myself and some UL footballers and their families, all of which were printed in the *Examiner* in subsequent weeks. Needless to say, I was an endangered species around the university for a few months!

Almost eleven years later, in a bizarre sequence of events, the then fresh-faced 21-year-old student with limited writing skills has somehow become a 32-year-old author. It was not without the help of many people who helped this book to come to fruition. Everywhere I went, the people couldn't have been more helpful and facilitated me in every way that they possibly could have in terms of putting me in touch with others. This applies to the 100+ interviewees who appear throughout the book and also those who provided the photographs.

James Lundon was, in many ways, my right hand man, and pestered me to keep at it when energy levels were sapping. I cannot speak highly enough of the role he played in proofreading the book and being permanently available at the other side of the phone. We fought and argued incessantly regarding the content but somehow are still talking. Without him, the book would never have seen the light of day. The infinite number of red correction marks are a testament to that! He put his life on hold at certain stages to proofread the book and offer advice. As a programme collector, he was in a position to offer many relevant artefacts. His quest to add to his programme collection is ongoing, and he will always be willing to speak to any readers with rare programmes.

My mother Mary Teresa (Terri), sister Siobhán, brother Johnny, Des Hayes and Jamie Keaty also assisted with various parts of the proofreading and to them I am very grateful. Thanks to my uncle Christy Murphy of the Cuchulainn Lounge in Patrickswell who did everything possible to help me, and also to my aunt Milly Hanly who makes a great cup of tea. Thanks to Jack Dillon and Tommy Sheehan, passionate hurling men who trained me at underage level with Galbally, and helped foster my passion for the game of hurling.

A huge thanks is also due to Pat O'Dwyer of Bruff, a great servant to underage GAA in Limerick for many years, who provided me with many old videotapes of the *Sunday Game* and provided valuable advice in terms of happenings from bygone days. Thanks also to MacDara McDonnacha of TG4, John McCarthy of Patrickswell, John Power of Kilkenny and Willie Ryan of Ballybrown for assisting me with video footage.

A special thanks is due to Liam Cahill of *An Fear Rua – The GAA Unplugged* who was a massive influence on me as a writer long before I began writing this book, and who has always taken the time and effort to try and smooth some of my rough edges. In modern society, internet journalism is eating into the market traditionally held by the print media. It's an honour to have received so much advice from someone at the blue chip end of that spectrum. Frank Burke of *Hurling World* and also Jackie Cahill were extremely generous with their advice and offered excellent guidance and assistance. All three have been through the mill themselves, having compiled successful books of their own and that sort of experience is invaluable.

Thanks also to the following people who helped me along the way and steered me in the right direction: my old work colleagues Pat O'Riordan and Willie Ryan, Orla O'Donovan, Francis Byrnes, Hugh Hynes, Liam O'Brien, Bosco Ryan, Ian McLoughlin, Cathal Ryan, Chris Madden, John Lyons, John Liston, Jamie Hennessy, Padraig Sweeney, Mike Meade, Noel Tobin, Liam O'Sullivan, Danny Deady, Tim O'Connor, Michael S. Martin and Johnny Cummins.

Many thanks to those at The Collins Press who were very thorough and professional at all times. Many thanks also to Aonghus Meaney for his editing skills.

I sincerely hope you enjoy the read.

HENRY MARTIN

PROLOGUE

❧

1973 All-Ireland final day . . .
Micheál O'Hehir: Twenty-four points to seventeen. One goal and twenty-one points to Limerick, one fourteen . . .

And Limerick are the champions, and just look, just look at it.

Well, after a wait since nineteen hundred and forty we have Limerick the All-Ireland champions, the worthy All-Ireland champions after a truly memorable game. The day was atrocious, it's pouring rain still, but just look here in the centre of the field where everyone seems to have gathered, every Limerick player being carried shoulder high and I think if Limerick men had an extra pair of shoulders they'd put Richie Bennis up there on top and just in under him they'd put Éamonn Cregan, and not far away they'd put Ned Rea and, ah look, you could go through the whole lot of them. John Foley, Éamonn Grimes, the whole lot of them, shades of all decency you might say, shades of the past have come to Croke Park today, as Limerick after so long have won this title. Nineteen forty, well, it's thirty-three years ago, and here we are, the team that two years ago almost beat Tipperary in Killarney and everybody said that when they were beaten the following year that that was the end of Limerick. But back they've come and what a brilliant performance they have put up today. And let nobody take away from this victory. True, Kilkenny were short some of their stars, but the way Limerick played, stars or no stars, Limerick are the worthy champions of this day, this September Sunday in 1973.

Here comes the hush. Who cares about presidents' speeches when you have won the All-Ireland after thirty-three years of waiting? Wait 'til you hear the silence when Éamonn Grimes comes up on the podium.

President: Agus anois, agus anois, ba mhaith liomsa an chorn seo a bhronnú ar chaptaen Luimní, Éamonn Grimes.

Micheál O'Hehir: And now Éamonn Grimes at the microphone. You don't have to be a president, just a captain to get silence.

Éamonn Grimes: A uachtarán, a cathaoirligh, a dhaoine uaisle, is mór an onóir domsa, a bheith anseo inniu mar captaen an fhoireann iontach seo. Ba mhaith liom buíochas a ghabhail do gach duine a cabhraigh linn chun an chorn seo a rugadh thar n-ais go dtí Contae Luímní. Ba mhaith liom freisin bualadh bos a ghabháil do Contae Chill Chainnaigh a d'imríodar go h-an mhaith ar fad. Mr President, reverend fathers, ladies and gentlemen, it's a great privilege for me as captain of this great Limerick team to bring the McCarthy Cup back to Limerick for the first time in thirty-three years. In doing so I'd like to thank each and everyone that helped to bring it back, and I'd like to pay a special tribute to Kilkenny for a very sporting game. Now three cheers for Kilkenny . . . hip hip hurray, hip hip hurray, hip hip hurray. And also three cheers for yourselves . . . hip hip hurray, hip hip hurray, hip hip hurray.

Micheál O'Hehir: There you have it, one of the most exciting scenes that has ever been my privilege or anyone else's privilege to see in Croke Park or anywhere else. The whole county of Limerick seemed to erupt in glorious victory for a glorious hurling team. And as somebody wrote somewhere during the week, gone will be the talk of the Mackeys – not that they weren't and aren't great – now the children will talk of the Bennises, they'll talk of the Hartigans, they'll talk of the Cregans, with the same reverence with which they have spoken of the Mackeys, the Ryans and all the others of the great glorious hurling past of Limerick. Well, the Limerick crowd, I don't think they'll let the Limerick team go down into the crowd or maybe they will. The crowd are going back down now (heaven help the steps) and in a matter of seconds they are going to go up in the air again and they'll be up in the air for the next month I'd say after this.

ONE

࿊

PRE-1940–1960: LOST GLORIES

By 1940 Limerick had won the All-Ireland hurling title six times, but since then the Liam McCarthy Cup has only been brought back to Shannonside once, when, in 1973, Limerick defeated Kilkenny, with whom they had established a certain rivalry.

In 1897, a Kilfinane selection defeated a Tullaroan selection by 3-4 to 2-4 at Tipperary to bring Limerick its first title. Limerick won All-Ireland semi-finals in both 1911 and 1912, over Galway and Antrim respectively. But in 1911 they refused to contest the final due to the state of the pitch and in 1912 they were defeated by Cork in a delayed Munster championship match and it was Cork who took their place in the All-Ireland final. Kilkenny would have been Limerick's opponents in both finals and, indeed, went on to win the title on each occasion.

A sequence of outstanding clashes between Limerick and Kilkenny commenced in 1933, with the sides meeting in four All-Ireland finals in seven years. Kilkenny were victorious in 1933 by 1-7 to 0-6, and again in 1935 by 2-5 to 2-4. That 1935 final is best known for a shot by Mick Mackey that was saved towards the end of the game. Mackey went for goal from a free when a point would have drawn the final. Limerick secured the silverware in 1936 with a comprehensive 5-6 to 1-5 demolition of the Cats, and won again in 1940, this time by 3-7 to 1-7.

Éamonn Cregan recalls stories told to him by his father, who played for Limerick in the 1930s:

My father maintained that the greatest hurler he ever saw was Lory Meagher; he played against him on three occasions in All-Ireland finals. He saw both Ring and Mackey playing but in his opinion Lory Meagher was the greatest player of all. He didn't say Mackey went for goal deliberately in 1935, I think it might have been a mis-hit shot. In those days ground hurling was the main way of playing. Even if you look at the hurleys, they have a very narrow bas. One of the famous things he always said was . . . never put your hand where your hurley should be.

Limerick also won titles in 1918, 1921 and 1934. In the 1918 final, played on 26 January 1919, a Newcastlewest selection beat a Wexford selection by 9-5 to 1-3, while in the 1921 final – played on 4 March 1923 – a Faughs side (Dublin) were beaten by 8–5 to 3-2. Timmy Ryan (Good Boy) captained Limerick to victory in 1934 when they beat Dublin 5-2 to 2-6 in a replay at Croke Park, the first game finishing Limerick 2-7 Dublin 3-4. In what was truly a golden era for Limerick hurling, a remarkable five League titles in a row were won between 1934 and 1938. Limerick also won four consecutive Munster titles from 1933 to 1936 and went thirty-one games without defeat in this period.

Tommy Cooke, the only survivor from the 1940 starting team, recalls the era:

Limerick were beaten in Thurles in the 1939 Munster final by Cork by a disputed goal, and Cork went on to play in what was known as the thunder and lightning All-Ireland final. Kilkenny won by a point and Langton came on as Kilkenny captain and hurled all around him. For the Oireachtas tournament in 1939 I was picked to go up to Dublin with Limerick. The Central Council decided that they wouldn't play Cork against Kilkenny a second time, and thought that Limerick would be a better attraction.

So we went up to play Kilkenny at Croke Park. I milked cows that morning, went to the creamery in Gormanstown, and went to Mass in Knockainey. When I came home, I ate my breakfast and a car called and took me up to Croke Park. And when we got to Barrys Hotel in Dublin, where we used to tog out, we were told Limerick were short five of their best team, and most of the subs were started. We were left with only a couple of subs but we beat Kilkenny, the All-Ireland champions. The Oireachtas match was played a month after the All-Ireland final, and they had their full team. Paddy Clohessy was a great friend of mine and he said to me going out on the field, 'Keep those feckers out from you now and give them plenty of timber.' And that's how we beat Kilkenny, because even now if you leave them in near you, especially the forwards, they will hold the back of your hurley, the back of your jersey, or they will obstruct you every way they can, in the hope that you will hit back by swinging the hurley and hitting them a

The Limerick team that beat Dublin in the 1934 All-Ireland final.
Back row (l–r): Dave Conway, Jack Keane, Paddy Mackey, Pat O'Reilly, Mick Ryan, Jim Roche, Jackie O'Connell, Paddy Scanlon, Anthony Mackey, Garrett Howard, Timmy Ryan, Pat Ryan, Tommy McCarthy, Willie Hannon, Ned Cregan, Christy O'Brien, Mick Mackey, Paddy Clohessy and W. P. Clifford. *Centre row (l–r):* Mick Neville, Denny Lanigan, Mickey Cross, John Mackey, Bob McConkey, Mick Kennedy, Jimmy Close, Dave Clohessy, Liam Scanlon. *Front row (l–r):* Mick Hickey, Mickey Condon, Dan Flanagan, Peter Browne (trainer).

skelp. They will make sure the referee sees you doing it and give them a free, so they get half their scores by aggravating. I played twice in Croke Park and we beat Kilkenny both times.

We were hardly trained at all. I used to leave home in the evening, Stephen Gleeson from Fedamore used to call up in his car for me. We would go down by Fedamore then to pick up Paddy Clohessy. He could be saving hay and we often went in and gave him a hand to finish up. We'd go into the training afterwards, but it might be over when we would get there. When it got nearer the All-Ireland final they used have the backs playing the forwards in training. And that's about the best way a team can train and learn to play. The present trainers aren't training them at all, they are only getting them fit. That's not very good when they aren't able to take touch pucks [line balls] or frees or anything like that consistently. Mick Mackey was a great man to take frees, but the only thing about Mick Mackey was that he was always going for goals. He could rise the ball in the middle of three or four Cork men. And they would all be pulling left and right on him.

And he would walk out through them and would hit one or two of them a belt of a shoulder and knock them. The Cork fellas used to make out that he used to put the ball under his jersey. Mackey ruined hurling actually, over his soloing. Christy Ring did a bit of soloing too but he only did it off and on. Mackey was doing it the whole time.

After training, we used to come up to the hotel in Catherine Street, belonging to Sadliers. The Ahane players wouldn't come after training, they used to go to some place in William Street called Ryans. They also togged out there when they were hurling in the club championship in Limerick. They refused to go to Sadliers because Mickey Fitzgibbon, who was treasurer of the county board at that time, didn't get on so well with them. Paddy Clohessy and Mick Mackey weren't talking to each other at the time of the All-Ireland in 1940. Croom and Fedamore used to have war when they would meet in the championship. It was the same with Fedamore and Ahane. Clohessy wouldn't play with Limerick in 1938 because of rows in club games. He fell out with Jim Roche of Croom and fell out with the Mackeys as well. They were nearly afraid of him.

I used to take the touch pucks and I used sky them off to the other side of the field where Dick Stokes and Jackie Power were. Mick Mackey used to be roaring at me to give him the ball but Mackey was always well marked, and by hitting it across to the other side we used to get scores a lot quicker than if I hit it to Mackey. I hurled against Jack Lynch for half an hour the first day in 1940. We drew that match and in the replay, Jim Young was selected on me. He was a lot harder player to mark than Jack Lynch. I found Lynch a soft hurler because I could shoulder him and outrun him for the ball. He didn't score off me and neither did Jim Young when he was on me. I hurled against Waterford then twice that year and their forward that I was marking never scored either. We met Galway in the semi-final and I kept their forward scoreless. In the final I was marking Jack Gargan – his father hurled with Kilkenny years before – and he got no score either. As far as I can remember nobody scored off me in 1940.

The night before the final we went to Shelbourne Park. Our trainer that time used to train greyhounds for a vet inside in Limerick and he took a greyhound called Erin's Champion and ran him that night. We backed him and he won at 2/1 and it made our night. In the final, Terry Leahy got away from Paddy Clohessy once in the first half of the final and I saw him getting away and I ran like hell after him, but

Timmy Ryan (kneeling) kisses the bishop's ring prior to the 1934 All-Ireland final.

I didn't get as far as him and he scored the goal. That was the only goal that Kilkenny got against us. There was no reception for us in Dublin when we won the All-Ireland. There was no Limerickmen's Association in Dublin that time. We got our dinner after the match and maybe there was a few speeches, or whatever, but you had to go out in the city then after that and buy your own drink. Paddy Clohessy and myself finished the night in the Kilkenny hotel with the Kilkenny players, and it was grand to go into them after beating them. They gave us a great reception, but I'd hate to be in Dublin the morning after being beaten in an All-Ireland final. And we had two girls with us, one of them was my sister and the other was her friend and they had to pay to go into the sideline to see the match because I only got four tickets to the All-Ireland. I had broken my nose earlier that year playing hurling against Bruff and Dr McDonald in Limerick operated on it. He asked me was there any chance of a couple of tickets for himself and his wife so I gave him two of the tickets I got. My father and mother then went up to the All-Ireland as well and I gave them the other two. I couldn't get any more tickets.

Having made an impression in the Oireachtas final of 1939, a young Tony Herbert, who started the earlier games in the 1940 championship, was called into the fray as a substitute in the All-Ireland final:

I had been on the Oireachtas team in 1939. We played Kilkenny in that game and I came on at centre field with Timmy Ryan. Jimmy Kelly and Jimmy Walsh were at midfield for Kilkenny and I was marking Jimmy Kelly. In the 1940 All-Ireland final I came on at half-time. Paddy Clohessy shouted for me to come in. I came in at half-forward and Jackie Power went to centre-back. Paddy Phelan, the Kilkenny left-half-back, was beating Power. I went in on Paddy Phelan then. Straight away, I took a ball off his hurley and let it in to John Mackey and he put it over the bar. Paddy Phelan turned around and said, 'It's time for me to give it up now; you are too young for me and too fast for me.'

The Mackey brothers did not play in the Cork game in 1941 due to a bereavement, and Paddy Clohessy was also missing. Tommy Cooke gives an account of his years from 1940 onwards:

We went up to Cork in 1941 and they beat us all the way home. That year Paddy Scanlan was working in Galway – he was our goalie – and it was Galway race week and he didn't want to go to Cork at all that day. The county board officers went to Galway and brought him away and held him inside in Limerick for the Saturday night. In 1940 every time there was a stop in the game, Robbie Lawlor [trainer] used have a bottle of whiskey and poitín and would give him [Scanlan] an auld skelp of it every so often to keep him going. Paddy Clohessy would get a skelp of it and so would Timmy Ryan. There was none of that in 1941. I was sick the week of the Waterford game in 1942. I told Jackie O'Connell, the secretary, that I wouldn't be able to play. He said to travel to Cork anyway, that the car would call for me. They were short of players and I had to tog out to be a sub on the sideline. Paddy Clohessy wasn't picked at all when the team was named. On the day they wanted him to play but he wouldn't. He said he would play in the next round against Cork if they beat Waterford. They didn't pick him that day either and Cork beat them in Limerick. The selectors played

The Limerick senior hurlers on the boat to the US in 1936. This Limerick side were unbeaten in 31 games over a 22-month period from October 1933 to August 1935. This included six games against both Cork and Dublin, four each against Clare, Galway and Tipperary. The only draw was a league game against Cork at Croom in March 1935. This amazing record has never been equalled in the history of hurling.

two of the Cregans against Waterford and they did well and were picked again against Cork. Myself and Clohessy were dropped. I didn't play with them any more; I was busy with horses and wanted to concentrate more on them.

There was heartbreak throughout the 1940s as Limerick lost five Munster finals. Fr Liam Ryan, who captained the 1955 Munster championship winning team, assesses what happened after the 1940 senior and minor double:

You would imagine that in 1940 between winning the minor and the senior that it was the beginning of an era. In fact, what happened was that the senior team were a very old team. They should have won the Munster championship in 1944 but the goalkeeper let them down in the drawn Munster final. In the replay Christy Ring got a very dubious goal to win the match. In 1945 they should have beaten Tipperary but in those times their biggest problem was beating Cork. They beat Tipperary three years in a row in the first round in the mid to late 1940s, only to lose to Cork each year. By 1945 and 1946 that Limerick team had grown old. Apart from Dick Stokes, most of the 1940 team were ageing and that's what I would view as the reason for the decline.

John Mulcahy, who played for Limerick in the 1940s, agrees:

Paddy McCarthy was really the only one who made it from that minor team. When I went onto the team, the old players were starting to move off and you had nothing ready to come in, the minors hadn't the experience. None of the minors were picked until 1946; they kept on the old players too long. So you were dealing with a weak period again. Some attempt should have been made to bring them through earlier.

Mick Rainsford believes the 1944 drawn game with Cork would have been won but for the goalkeeper:

The goalkeeper left in six goals, and in the replay they selected Dinny Malone from Fedamore in goals, the man who should have started the drawn game. I believe that if Malone started the drawn game, there would have been no need for a replay.

Fr Liam Ryan remembers being at a function in 1995:

Noel Walsh, then chairman of the Munster Council, decided that he would have a function to host the Munster finalists of twenty-five years and fifty years previously. The Limerick and Tipperary teams of 1945 were hosted. It struck me at the time that there were only three or four of the Limerick team of 1945 still alive fifty years later, which suggests that they were very much a mature team at that time. In contrast, about ten of the Tipperary team were alive.

John Mulcahy scored two goals against Kilkenny in the League final of 1947, and has his own views on the 1947 Munster final:

Paddy McCarthy from Newcastlewest, who captained the 1940 minor team, was to play. He was an army man in Galway and they sent him the price of a hackney to come down. He spent the money on drink and thumbed down for the match. A priest met him on the road thumbing, but passed him out and reported him to Canon Punch. He was in Thurles in plenty of time for the match but Canon Punch wouldn't pick him on account of him thumbing. Mick Herbert

The Limerick team which won the Oireachtas in 1939. *Back row (l–r):* [first two players are unknown], Paddy Scanlan, Mick Mackey, Johnsie Donoghue, Dan Givens, John Mackey, Timmy Ryan, Willie Lee. *Front row (l–r):* Tommy Cooke, John Foley, Mick McCarthy, Paddy Mackey, Peter Cregan, Jackie Power, Tony Herbert.

hopped up on a chair in the dressing room and said, 'Canon Punch, whatever grievance you have with Paddy McCarthy, we want the best team on the field,' to which the canon replied, 'If Paddy McCarthy is playing, I will dissociate myself from the GAA.' He bested us and he put on Johnsie Donoghue from his own parish, Mungret, and he scored a goal for Cork. Donoghue was coming out the wing with the ball, and a Cork player hit him. He turned back with the ball in his hand and threw it up to hit it, and stuck it inside in his own net. Poor Donoghue wasn't on the League final team and never hurled afterwards. And Paddy McCarthy wouldn't play ever again.

Mulcahy has a particular grievance regarding the following year's championship exit:

In the 1948 championship we beat Tipperary again and lost to Cork in the semi-final. I got the two goals against Cork and my name never appeared in the paper for scoring them, because that time when the ball would be in the net we had players who would run in after it

The Limerick Team that beat Kilkenny in the 1940 All-Ireland final.
Back row (l–r): Mick Hickey, Jim McCarthy, Tommy Cooke, Paddy Scanlon, Tony Herbert, Jim Roche, Paddy McMahon, John Mackey, Paddy Mackey, Timmy Ryan, Dave Hurley, Jackie Power, Martin 'Robbie' Lawlor. *Front row (l–r):* Paddy Clohessy, Mick Mackey, Mick Kennedy, Ned Chawke, Dick Stokes, Peter Cregan.

and would be belting it again. That gave plenty of time for the photographers outside to take photographs.

In 1949 Canon Punch, the Limerick County Board chairman, took steps to quell the dominance of Ahane, the unbeatable force in Limerick club hurling. Up to then, a junior club hurler could represent his own club at that level and another club at senior level. Canon Punch ended this practice and also controversially decided to allow Croom and Young Irelands to join together in an attempt to create a team that would end the dominance of the now weakened Ahane. He had a great dislike of Ahane, but most particularly Mick Mackey because of the profile that Mackey enjoyed at the time.

John Mulcahy did not play in 1949 due to the controversial ruling:

Myself, Paddy Creamer and Jimmy Butler Coffey played for Ahane as well as our own club Cappamore, and Canon Punch brought in the rule to stop us playing with them. He then allowed Croom and Young Irelands in the city to join up and yet deprived us of playing with

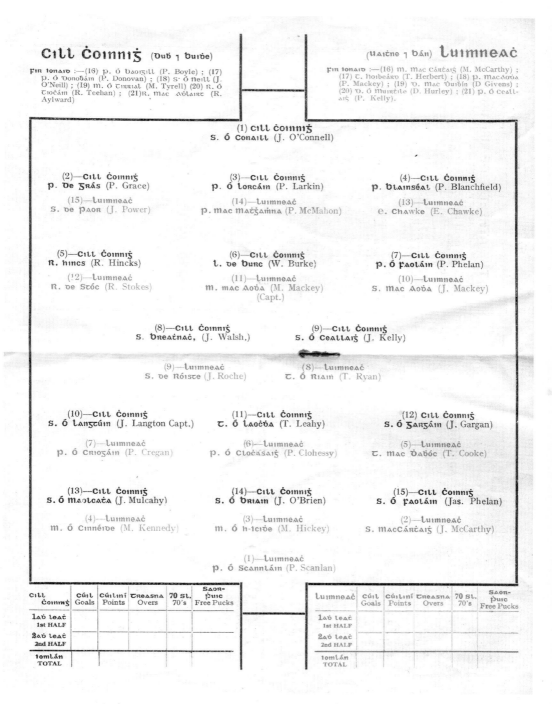

Cill Coinnig (Dub ┐ buide)

Fir ionaid :—(16) p. ó baoigill (P. Boyle) ; (17) p. ó Donobáin (P. Donovan) ; (18) s· ó neill (J. O'Neill) ; (19) m. ó Tirrial (M. Tyrell) (20) R. ó Tiocáin (R. Teehan) ; (21)R. mac adlairt (R. Aylward)

Luimneac (Uaitne ┐ bán)

Fir ionaid :—(16) m. mac cártaig (M. McCarthy) ; (17) T. hoibeárd (T. Herbert) ; (18) p. macaoda (P. Mackey) ; (19) d. mac duibín (D Givens) (20) d. ó muinéile (D. Hurley) ; (21) p. ó Ceallaig (P. Kelly).

(1) Cill Coinnig
S. Ó Conaill (J. O'Connell)

(2)—Cill Coinnig	(3)—Cill Coinnig	(4)—Cill Coinnig
p. De Grás (P. Grace)	p. ó Lorcáin (P. Larkin)	p. blainséal (P. Blanchfield)
(15)—Luimneac	(14)—Luimneac	(13)—Luimneac
S. De paor (J. Power)	p. mac matgamna (P. McMahon)	e. Chawke (E. Chawke)

(5)—Cill Coinnig	(6)—Cill Coinnig	(7)—Cill Coinnig
R. hincs (R. Hincks)	l. De burc (W. Burke)	p. ó faoláin (P. Phelan)
(12)—Luimneac	(11)—Luimneac	(10)—Luimneac
R. De stóc (R. Stokes)	m. mac aoda (M. Mackey) (Capt.)	S. mac aoda (J. Mackey)

(8)—Cill Coinnig	(9)—Cill Coinnig
S. breacnac, (J. Walsh,)	S. ó Ceallaig (J. Kelly)
(9)—Luimneac	(8)—Luimneac
S. De Róiste (J. Roche)	T. ó Riain (T. Ryan)

(10)—Cill Coinnig	(11)—Cill Coinnig	(12) Cill Coinnig
S. ó Langtúin (J. Langton Capt.)	T. ó Laochda (T. Leahy)	S. ó Gargáin (J. Gargan)
(7)—Luimneac	(6)—Luimneac	(5)—Luimneac
p. ó Criogáin (P. Cregan)	p. ó Clocásaig (P. Clohessy)	T. mac dabóc (T. Cooke)

(13)—Cill Coinnig	(14)—Cill Coinnig	(15)—Cill Coinnig
S. ó maolcata (J. Mulcahy)	S. ó briain (J. O'Brien)	S. ó faoláin (Jas. Phelan)
(4)—Luimneac	(3)—Luimneac	(2)—Luimneac
m. ó Cinnéide (M. Kennedy)	m. ó h-icide (M. Hickey)	S. maccártaig (J. McCarthy)

(1)—Luimneac
p. ó Scanntáin (P. Scanlan)

Cill Coinnig	Cúil Goals	Cúilíní Points	Treasna Overs	70 Sl. 70's	Saor-puic Free Pucks
1ad leac 1st HALF					
2ad leac 2nd HALF					
iomlán TOTAL					

Luimneac	Cúil Goals	Cúilíní Points	Treasna Overs	70 Sl. 70's	Saor-puic Free Pucks
1ad leac 1st HALF					
2ad leac 2nd HALF					
iomlán TOTAL					

The team listings from the official programme for the 1940 All-Ireland final.

cLÁR OIFIZeAMAIL

I bPáIRC An CRÓCAIZ, 1-9-40
AR A 3.15 p.m.

CRAOÓ IOMÁNA nA h-éIReAnn

cILL ĊOInnIZ
(KILKENNY)

v.

LuImneAĊ
(LIMERICK)

ReIċeóIR :— S. S. CALLAnAIn

CRAOÓ IOMÁnA nA mIonÚR

LuImneAĊ v. AOnċRuIm
(LIMERICK)   (ANTRIM)

ReIċeóIR :— An DOCċÚIR S. SċIúbAIRċ   AR A 1.45 A ĊLOZ

LuAĊ 2ṗ.

Padraig Ó Caoim

Rúnaíóe.

AR AĠAIÓ LInn

Cló-OIṗIZ UÍ ĊAOILċe, Cċa., bAILe ÁċA CLIAċ

The official programme for the 1940 All-Ireland final where Limerick
achieved a minor and senior double.

An action shot from the 1940 All-Ireland final. Pictured are No. 12 Dick Stokes, No. 14 Paddy McMahon (with cap), Jackie Power beside him partially hidden, John Mackey in front of goal, Ned Chawke under crossbar and Jim Roche outfield behind John Mackey on 21-yard line. Timmy Ryan (with 3 marked on togs) and Mick Mackey (just in front of him) are also in the picture.

Ahane. We refused to turn out with Limerick over that decision and were suspended for the year because of our protest.

Fr Liam Ryan has clear memories of the 1949 championship:

Limerick were very unlucky in 1949. They met Tipperary in Cork. Jackie Power got a goal to level the match in the last five minutes that was disallowed. Con Murphy of Cork was refereeing that game. Even though Con played full-back himself, he was very severe on the backs and the full-back line. He actually was the making of Jimmy Kennedy of Tipperary, who was very accurate from frees. He got more frees from Con Murphy than he ever got from any other referee. Con

Murphy's refereeing cost Limerick that match that day. Had Limerick won that match who knows what way it would have gone. Tipperary went on to win a three-in-a-row.

Fr Ryan outlines the motives behind Canon Punch's controversial changes in the county:

There was only one senior team in east Limerick, Ahane, and they had the pick from all the junior teams in the division . . . Canon Punch was chairman of the county board and he had a great dislike of Ahane, who had won several championships in succession. He thought that Limerick hurling would go nowhere until he removed Ahane as county champions. In 1949, Canon Punch allowed Croom and Young Irelands to join and introduced divisional teams – City Gaels, East Geraldines, Western Gaels, and Emmets – which prevented Ahane from picking hurlers from junior clubs. That was a reason for the long-term decline of Ahane; they were confined to picking players from their own parish and many of their established stars had finished up also.

Jimmy Butler Coffey, however, could see benefit in the changes:

Canon Punch was a very curious man with very curious ideas. It wasn't a question of stopping Ahane, but he thought it would be better for the county. I always maintained that it was up to other teams to beat Ahane.

Ahane met the Croom/Young Irelands combination in a 1949 championship game best known for an incident in which Mick Herbert almost lost his life. His brother Tony, who had departed Limerick a couple of years after the 1940 All-Ireland success and who went on to win two Leinster championships with Dublin and Railway Cups with Leinster, had planned to go to the match:

I wasn't at the game. I was in Dublin at the time and was due to go down to Limerick with another former Limerick hurler, Dan Givens from Ahane, the father of Irish soccer international Don. Givens couldn't start the car. It was a good job because we would all be in jail, because when that incident happened we would all have gone in like a flash.

John Mulcahy recalls being there:

It wasn't a rough game and Mick Herbert was never as clean as he was that day. He was only walking up to a row between Tom Cregan

(*L–r*) Mick and John Mackey pose for a photograph before a Limerick game in the early 1930s.

and his brother Seán Herbert when it happened. The row was nothing serious. Joe Cregan ran in from the sideline with a hurley and before Mick Herbert reached the row he was struck on the head from behind and knocked out cold. There was no row or anything. It was a very serious incident, his head was the shape of a rugby ball. I went in to the field to see it. He was taken to hospital and when we were going home we called in to see him. We couldn't get in and they were saying the rosary on the steps going in. They thought he was gone. He was that bad.

Éamonn Cregan was very young when the incident occurred but remembers being told that there was 'a hushed silence among the crowd when Herbert fell because they thought he was dead'.

Mick Rainsford was in attendance:

That game between Ahane and Croom was postponed until after the Munster hurling final that year, and I believe that if Limerick had reached the All-Ireland final it would have been postponed until after that. The reason was that there was trouble expected in that game, and they didn't want any trouble in a club game interfering with the chances of the county team. A lot of supporters who wouldn't normally have gone to those games went because of that expectation of trouble. It was internal bleeding that Herbert had, and if he was bleeding externally I don't think the game would have been finished. There were three or four people holding him down prior to the arrival of the first aid men. I can't say if he lost consciousness after that. It was always said that the first aid men who took him to the hospital weren't allowed back into the Gaelic Grounds because they knew how seriously he was injured, and word might have spread on to the field. I believe that if the Ahane players knew how seriously he was injured, they wouldn't have finished the game. It finished Limerick hurling because we lost four great players who never represented Limerick afterwards – Joe and Tom Cregan of Croom and Mick Herbert and Jackie Power of Ahane.

John Mulcahy feels the incident could easily have been prevented:

It was the breaking up of the Limerick team. Players wouldn't hurl with one another for the county. The Cregans were good players for Croom and good for Limerick as well. The man at fault for that was Paddy Clohessy, the referee. If he had picked up the ball at half-time

cumann lúit cleap zaeveal

Clár Oiṗiseaṁail (Official Programme) - Luaċ 3ᴅ.

What a pride and glory it is to witness the stirring scenes associated with a well-played, cleanly and keenly contested Gaelic match, especially in Hurling; to feel the thrills coursing through one's veins as the springy ash Camans crash in the air above and on the sod below; and to realise that here is being enacted before our excited and admiring gaze, a vivid symbol of the long ago; a sure reminder that Knocknagow is not dead; and a striking and soul-stirring guarantee that by Shannon, Suir and Lee, and by hillside and glenside throughout the province, the virile manhood and traditions of our race are keeping a firm hold on their hard-won inheritance.

Seán Mac Cápṫaiṡ, b.e., *Chairman, at Munster Convention, 1940.*

1940

munSTER

championships

SENIOR AND MINOR HURLING FINALS

AT THURLES

SUNDAY, JULY 28th, 1940

SENIOR HURLING FINAL

CORCAIṠ	v.	Luimneaċ
(CORK)		(LIMERICK)

3.45 p.m., Summer Time. Referee—D. Ryan, Kerry.

MINOR HURLING—Luimneaċ v. Cláiɴ

2.30 p.m., Summer Time. Referee—W. O'Donnell, Tipperary.

Admission to Field - 1s.; Stand (1s.), Sideline (2s.) extra

S. Mac Cápṫaiṡ   Rúnaɴᴅe

The official programme for the 1940 drawn Munster final.

or looked for the ball, it would never have happened. When the half-time whistle went, Seán Herbert and Tom Cregan were arguing as to which club owned the ball. It was only a simple argument. Mick Herbert was no angel at the best of times but he did nothing wrong that day. He was only walking over to the row when Joe Cregan came in from the sideline.

Tony Herbert recalls the media attention – and has strong views on Canon Punch:

It was on the news that evening that one of the players in the game, a county star, was critically injured and was taken to hospital. It was all over the papers afterwards because Joe Cregan got jail. Mickey Roberts was the man looking after him in Limerick, and he stopped the bleeding in the skull, which was cracked, and fixed it up. The bleeding started again. They took him to the Richmond hospital in Dublin and a top neurosurgeon operated on him. The operation took five hours, and they closed off the ward for a whole fortnight. That incident finished Limerick hurling. Seán played for a while afterwards. Canon Punch was the cause of it all. They never recognised him and they didn't ever have anything named after him. He was a vicious man and was very prejudiced. He finished Limerick hurling, Jackie Power didn't play any more, John Mackey didn't play. It brought a gloom over the whole parish, because Mick was in hospital.

Fr Liam Ryan believes the effect lasted a number of years:

Limerick hurling went downhill after that rapidly. In 1950, 1951, 1952, 1953, 1954 a lot of players picked for Limerick for League matches didn't even turn up.

Jimmy Butler Coffey agrees:

It was a very serious incident and shouldn't have happened, it's as simple as that. Nothing happened again in Limerick until Cappamore won the county final in 1954. Limerick hurling fell apart, you had no unity in the county. The real heart went out of the team.

Dermot Kelly says the county board was also split:

The dispute split hurling in Limerick. Apart from the Mick Herbert thing, there was also a split in the county board, one element would be on one side of the dressing room and another element would be on

Timmy Ryan poses with fans before playing his last game for Limerick in 1945.
This picture was taken by Gerry Piggott.

the other side. It was well known that there was definitely a split, and Canon Punch would definitely be central to that. I remember when I was a young lad seeing him hitting people on the sideline with an umbrella. There was no spirit and no unity there. If that hadn't happened in 1949 and if we had the two Herberts, who weren't that old in 1955, it would have been a fantastic team. Hurling in the city was dead.

Éamonn Cregan has heard an alternative view, however:

I always remember Jackie Power saying that the Mick Herbert incident wasn't the reason Limerick hurling went down, but that it was because Limerick lost to Tipperary that year. The incident did have an effect though. We were born in the city and you never saw a young fella walking with a hurley in the city in the 1950s, because we had an inferiority complex. Why I had an inferiority complex I don't know, we played hurling in the People's Park and we played hurling in the Bombin Field. You were an oddity if you walked down O'Connell Street with a hurley in your hand. I assume that came from what happened in that match. In Cork they walked freely around with hurleys in their hand.

Fr Liam Ryan says that selecting the Limerick team in 1955 was akin to 'clearing out the old':

They put out a very young team. There was also a myth then relating to a new rule that had come in called the 'non-stop' rule. Previously when a man went down injured, the whole game stopped. In 1954 a rule came in that the play shouldn't stop if a player was injured, he simply went to the sideline. The myth was that somehow you needed young men to last the hour, which was total nonsense. For one reason or another Limerick put out a very young team in 1955 and not many of the men who had been there in the previous five years had survived. Four or five did but that was all, it was practically a clean sweep. Of the experienced men Dermot Kelly was at most twenty-five, Gerry Fitzgerald from Rathkeale would have been the oldest at nearly thirty, Paddy Enright was next in line. Seven or eight of the team were certainly no more than twenty.

Dermot Kelly says the selectors in 1955 had no choice but to pick new players:

When all else fails throw the hurley! Tipperary's Seán Ryan (*left*) throws his hurley at John Mackey (*right*) in 1945 watched by Paddy Fitzgerald of Askeaton (*second from left*).

I played against Waterford in 1954 and Limerick scored only one point in that Munster championship match. About ten minutes before the beginning of the match with Clare in 1953 we were missing about four players who hadn't turned up. The final score in that game was 10-8 to 1-1. Why was the 1955 team so young? What could you pick from a team that could only score one point?

Indeed, in two years of championship hurling, Limerick scored a grand total of 1-2. 'I made up for that in 1955 though,' laughs Kelly, who scored 1-12 in the 1955 Munster final against Clare. He concedes, however, that there was an element of fortune in his scoring spree:

We togged out before the game in Sadliers, a place where there was very little room. I would have been friendly with Mick Mackey and remember saying to him, 'Mick, what about the frees?' He mentioned Vivian Cobbe, Ralph Prendergast or one of the Ryans. I wasn't mentioned at all. The match started then and Clare scored a few points; the next thing we got a free and nobody moved towards it. They were shocked. I said to myself, 'I'll take it,' and I think I hit the spire in St John's Cathedral, and I took all the frees after that. It was our speed and the heat that beat them. All of our players were flyers. Clare couldn't cope with the speed of our fellows because it was one of the first games of the non-stop ruling.

In later years, I used to sing a lot. One time, the priests were trying to put a roof on the church in Corofin, County Clare, and they asked me to sing for them in a concert to raise money. We went into the pub afterwards and in the middle of the night there was a candle lit in the pub. I was chatting to a Clare man, and he turned to a friend of his who was in the corner. 'Mick, Mick, do you know this fella?', and the friend didn't so he went on about the 1955 match, and Mick said, 'I know you now, you hoor, and I want to tell you one thing: you were never any good before that match and you were never any good after.' Any time I went singing in Clare afterwards I used to tell that story.

Fr Liam Ryan captained the team that year:

I was captain simply because the system at the time, and the system that still prevails, is that the county champions, if they have someone on the team, automatically provide the captain. I was only nineteen and the Munster final was my first time playing a championship match with Limerick, so I was in awe of others who had been around a while. Someone like Dermot Kelly probably should have been captain. I was certainly not a captain who led the team or anyone who inspired them or anything like that, it was the very opposite.

I don't think the captain should automatically come from the county champions. Anthony Daly was a very successful captain, and the board, the players, all accepted him even though his club weren't county champions. All the captain does on a GAA field is call the toss of the coin, and lead the team around the pitch. After that he has no duties and it's up to the sideline to make changes and all that. Being the captain in rugby means much more.

Dermot Kelly believes the 1955 team signalled the re-emergence of Limerick:

I saw players from earlier years like Paddy Clohessy and Paddy McMahon crying in our dressing room after the match. You have to give credit to the junior All-Ireland win in 1954. One of the best hurlers I ever saw was Mick O'Shea from Treaty Sarsfields who was on that junior team. He was the nearest thing to what Mick Mackey was. He was a sprinter, built like a rock. He was unbelievable. He would have been the best player in 1955 but he suffered a knee injury and he never really recovered from it.

The Limerick team that beat Tipperary in the 1947 Munster Championship at Páirc Uí Chaoimh. *Back row (l–r):* Mick Herbert, Mick Ryan, John Mackey, Thomas O'Brien, Jim Sadlier, Derry McCarthy, Toddy O'Brien, Timmy Ryan. *Front row (l–r):* Jackie Power, Seán Herbert, Peter Cregan, Owen O'Riordan, Johnsie O'Donoghue, Paddy Fitzgerald (Askeaton), Paddy Fitzgerald (St Patrick's), Gerry Piggott.

Already in Munster Clare had beaten Tipperary and Cork, who between them had shared the previous six All-Ireland titles. Fr Liam Ryan feels they took Limerick for granted in the Munster final:

In 1955 Clare thought they had only to tog out as they had beaten Cork who were going for a four-in-a-row. Clare would have given a better match to Wexford. We led Wexford at half-time but faded. Clare had beaten Wexford in the Oireachtas, and would have been confident of beating them again.

Fr Liam Ryan believes there were far too many people picking the team:

'Mackeys Greyhounds' was a name created by some journalists [for the Limerick team], but Mackey was only one of eleven selectors. There was no manager in those days. Mick Mackey I suppose, because of his prestige, would have looked like a manager but he was only one selector and had no authority. He was one of eleven! It was crazy. The chairman, treasurer and secretary of the county board were selectors.

Cumann Lúit-cleas gaedeal

Munster Hurling Final, '49

AT CORK ATHLETIC GROUNDS
ON SUNDAY, JULY 17TH.

Minor - 2 p.m. (S.T.)-

Tiobrad-Árann   V.   **An Clár**
TIPPERARY   CLARE

Referee - C. Conway, Cork.

Senior - 3.30 p.m. (S.T.)

Tiobrad-Árann   V.

Tipperary   **Luimneac**

Limerick

REFEREE - CON MURPHY, CORK.

Admission to Field, 1/-; Juveniles, 6d.; Enclosure
(Direct), 2/-; Stand, 1/- extra from enclosure;
Sideline (Direct), 3/-.
NO TRANSFER FROM FIELD OR ENCLOSURE TO SIDELINE.
GATES OPEN 12 NOON.

SPECIAL TRAINS

will leave Horse & Jockey, 7.20 a.m. (and all stations);
Thurles, 7.35 a.m. Kingsbridge, 8.20 a.m.; Templemore, 10.21; Thurles, 10.38; Cashel, 7.30;
Ardmayle, 7.43; Gooldscross, 8.13; Dundrum, 8.21.

An official poster advertising the 1949 Munster final.

Limerick 1947 National Hurling League Winners. *Back row (l–r):* Canon Edmund Punch (selector), Paddy Fitzgerald (St Patrick's), Jim Sadlier (Young Irelands), Thomas O'Brien (Ahane), John Barry (Kildimo), Paddy Clohessy (selector), Mick Ryan (Young Irelands Dublin), Mick Herbert (Ahane), Jackie Power (Ahane), Pat O'Reilly (selector). *Front row (l–r):* Denis Flanagan (Knockaderry), Mick Dooley (South Liberties), John Mulcahy (Cappamore), Paddy Collopy (St Patrick's), Seán Herbert (Ahane), Dick Stokes (UCD), Paddy Fitzgerald (Askeaton), Tom Cregan (Croom).

The four divisions had one selector each, the county champions had two, and the last two were probably board officers as well. Cappamore were the county champions and the selectors were Jimmy Butler Coffey and Paddy Creamer.

Jimmy Butler Coffey agrees:

There were too many selectors. It was hard to work with eleven. If you wanted to make a change you had to consult with too many people. Wexford made a great change in the semi-final, they moved Ned Wheeler onto Séamus Ryan who was having a great game on Padge Keogh. I said to Mackey, 'Look at this,' when Wheeler was moved onto Séamus, and he said, 'What can we do? There are too many others to go to.' We couldn't make the change on our own. It was even very hard for me to force Séamus onto the team at the start of the championship because he was too young. When they saw him playing they decided he was worth his place. It wasn't his hurling at all, it was just that he was too young. The older players were gone past it, and we went for young players, there were a lot of young players worth trying.

Dermot Kelly feels inexperience cost Limerick the Wexford game:

None of the 1955 team had ever been on the Croke Park pitch before and we were ahead at half-time but we didn't have the firepower. I remember Billy Rackard telling me that they didn't know any of our names. Séamus Ryan would have been the best centre-back that ever played except that he only got out from the priests' college to play for a couple of weeks in the summer.

Kelly also believes that Limerick should have qualified directly for the All-Ireland final after winning Munster:

In 1955 I believe that it should have been Antrim we met in the semi-final, but Antrim were so bad they pulled out and the GAA probably said that this Limerick crowd are no good and they felt they would have no All-Ireland, so they set it up that Galway and Wexford would meet in the final.

Vivian Cobbe, who came through from the 1954 junior winning team, recalls the training methods in 1955:

For the junior All-Ireland, we took every match as it came. I didn't play in the Munster championship. I don't think we trained at all. For the seniors in 1955, we trained the Monday, Tuesday and Wednesday before the match and that was it; apart from that it was training with the clubs. Limerick played Waterford in the first round in 1955, and a trial game took place before the Munster final where the older players were given a chance to get their place if they were good enough.

Fr Liam Ryan outlines the training:

There were no methods; you went into the Gaelic Grounds and spread out over the field and pucked the ball up and down on the ground mainly. And there were no tactics; we did some sprints and some rounds of the field and that was it. We played backs and forwards but very little if I recall.

Jim Quaid, who was also on the junior team of 1954, believes the Clare victory in 1955 was not a shock:

A Limerick team that played in the 1947/1948 National league. *Back row (l–r):* Canon Edmund Punch, Con Birrane (Doon), Dick Sadlier (Young Irelands Limerick), Paddy Collopy (St Patrick's), Thomas O'Brien (Ahane), Mick Ryan (Young Irelands Dublin), Toddy O'Brien (St Patrick's), John Barry (Kildimo), Mick Herbert (Ahane), Jackie Power (Ahane). *Front row (l–r):* Paddy Fitzgerald (St Patrick's), Seán Herbert (Ahane), John Mulcahy (Cappamore), Paddy Fitzgerald (Askeaton), Johnsie Donoghue (Mungret), Tom Cregan (Croom).

Six of us were picked off the 1954 junior team to play with the seniors. We were outsiders for the Munster final in 1955, but we played Clare in the League in Ennis earlier that year and we did everything except beat them. In 1956 Cork beat us in the Munster final. We were completely on top and Vivian Cobbe missed two goals in the first five minutes, and I went off injured at half-time. I was on Gerald Murphy. We left that behind us.

Dermot Kelly was not at his best in 1956:

I had hamstring trouble and before the Clare game in 1956 I went into Barrington's and this fella put in a syringe and drew out congealed blood and put me in plaster. I played in the Munster championship about three weeks later but was very weak.

Fr Liam Ryan recalls the nightmare of 1956 against Cork:

cRAOb 1omÁna — na muman

AN CLÁR

— v. —

Luimneac

1 Luimneac

Dia Domnais 10ad Iuil, 1955.

Clár Oifiseamail

Luac - - - 6p.

KEY PRINTING WORKS, WILLIAM ST., LIMERICK

The official programme for the 1955 Munster final.

The presentation of the Munster trophy to Liam Ryan, captain of Mackey's
Greyhounds, in 1955. He remains the youngest ever Munster championship
winning captain watched by his Cappamore clubmate and Limerick selector
Jimmy Butler Coffey (*extreme left*).

We were seven points up with about ten minutes left and Christy
Ring got three famous goals. They weren't all great goals; one of them
was, but they were goals and there's no such thing as a bad goal. Cork
went on to be beaten in the All-Ireland final by Wexford. Limerick
would probably have been beaten too had we beaten Cork. The
tragedy of that Munster final was that it was a very old Cork team;
they were on their last legs in 1956 and they didn't win another
Munster championship for ten years.

Dermot Kelly recalls some banter with Ring about the three goals:

We had a goalkeepers' exhibition in Monaleen some years later.
Mick Mackey was at it, and Ring was the referee. I challenged Ring
about the three goals. I told him he threw one of them in off the

ground. Mick Cunneen was in goals and there was chicken wire in the goals. Cunneen put up his hurley and it got caught in the chicken wire so he couldn't stop it; another one ricocheted in and the third one was a great goal.

We lost to Tipperary in the 1958 championship, but we never had the benefit of having the two Ryan brothers in training full-time because they were in Maynooth and Ralph Prendergast went to America. The thing kind of broke up. Tom McGarry got suspended. McGarry was an excellent player but he was also playing handball and soccer and rugby.

The 1958 League final was the last hurrah for 'Mackey's Greyhounds' when Wexford beat them in a thriller at Croke Park. Jim Quaid recalls the quality of the game:

One of the journalists in the daily papers said that it was the best League final ever played, one of the greatest games of hurling ever seen. My brother Jack wasn't on the team at all; we played a challenge game against Kilkenny a week before and he broke his finger.

Dermot Kelly made the unusual transition to corner-back:

I had gone over on an ankle against Waterford a year earlier, and I always had trouble with it since. The day of the League final I was captain of the team and couldn't play, but they said I would have to play. The team photo shows that I had a bandage around my boot.

I used to play centre-back by then but I went in corner-back that day and I was marking Martin Codd. The ball broke out near the sideline and I ran over to it and I couldn't turn. Mick Mackey came over and I said, 'Mick, I can't turn on my ankle.' When we went in at half-time I said, 'Let me in full-back for the second half,' and I finished the game full-back and held Tim Flood scoreless in the second half. The reason I was corner-back was because I couldn't run.

The injury to Kelly and the other defections undoubtedly cost Limerick the 1958 championship game against Tipperary and more besides. There was hope for the future, though, because Limerick claimed another junior All-Ireland title in 1957, and in 1958 the Limerick minors also claimed the All-Ireland crown. Con O'Connell was on the team:

I was corner-back on the 1958 team. I was a sub the year before and we were well beaten by Jimmy Doyle's Tipperary who went on to

Dermot Kelly (*front left*) cleverly tries to evade the oncoming Billy Rackard (*front right*) in the 1955 All-Ireland semi-final between Limerick and Wexford at Croke Park, as Liam Ryan (*back left*) and Mick Morrissey (*back right*) look on.

win the All-Ireland. We beat Tipperary nicely in the first round in 1958. We played Clare then, and they drew with us the first day but we beat them well the second day.

John McDonagh was a minor in 1958 and captained the team in 1959:

When we beat Antrim in the semi-final in Croke Park, it was the first time I was ever there. We had a big, strong, physical minor team with John Bresnihan full-back. In the early part of the first half of the All-Ireland final he got a bang on the shoulder from a Galway man and broke his collarbone. He had to go off and we had to rearrange our defence under the watchful eye of Fr McNamee. I went in full-back for Bresnihan. That was the year they were building the new Hogan Stand, and the presentation was made to Paddy Cobbe on the far side in the Cusack Stand.

Phil Bennis missed out on the success:

I was sent off in the first match, and I didn't get back on the team for the rest of the year. I wasn't even on the panel. It was a bit disappointing. That time if there was six from west Limerick they would only go in with the four they would fit in the car.

The influence of Canon Punch, the chairman with the dictatorial style, was not to be understated. Gerry Bennis was acquainted with him in later years:

He wouldn't live in today's world. Everyone was used to strictness back then but it's different now. One day I was talking to him outside Thurles after Limerick had been well beaten. Someone walked past and roared at the canon, 'The only medal you ever won was a rugby medal.' The canon had a stick with him and he put it around his neck and pulled him back to him! I remember one year an issue of the *Pioneer* magazine contained a photo of a rugby player. Canon Punch refused to allow that particular issue to be sold in Raheen church.

Canon Punch, a strong supporter of 'the ban', once said: 'The GAA was founded the year I was born, but the year the ban is lifted I will be attending its funeral.' In 2001 Pádraig S. Ó Riain, who soldiered with Punch in the old days, voted against the opening of Croke Park to other codes. There is no doubt but that the canon would have been proud.

TWO

ೞ

1961–1972: NEW GENERATION

Dermot Kelly remembers:

We had no facilities for hurling in the city at that time so we trained in Bombin Field which is Caledonian Park, a soccer field. I was up there training young lads one day and I was picking teams to play a match, to play into the soccer goals. This small, young lad came up wanting to play and I said to him, 'What are you doing here, you are too small.' He really wanted to play and he insisted on playing, and eventually he wore me down so I said, 'Go down and stand in goals so.'

In time, that small, young lad would develop into the greatest modern day Limerick hurler since the Mackey era. His name was Éamonn Cregan.

Cregan recalls his early hurling days:

I originally started playing with Limerick at under-12 level in a game against Galway at the Gaelic Grounds. Pa O'Brien of St Patrick's was my centre field partner. I played minor for three years, coming on as a sub in 1961 and in 1963 we went all the way to the All-Ireland minor final, losing to Wexford, having beaten Tipperary in the Munster final. Limerick went on again in 1965 and lost the final to Dublin. That would have been backboned by that year's Limerick CBS Harty Cup team.

Limerick CBS won four Harty Cup titles in a row, 1964 to 1967, and Cregan believes that the input of two men in particular was incalculable:

It just happened that a group of players came together at the one particular time. There would have been far better Harty Cup teams prior to our team in 1964, but the two main reasons for winning would have been Brother Burke and Jim Hennessy. Jim Hennessy had trained Thurles CBS to win the 1956 Harty Cup and trained Ennis CBS to win it in 1962. He came to Limerick in 1963 and trained the Harty winning teams. Both of those people were instrumental in teaching Limerick how to win. That carried through to minor with Limerick and we won the minor final against Tipperary in 1963. We went on to beat Tipp in the under-21 semi-final in 1966 and also at senior level that year. While Tipperary beat us in the Munster final in 1971, they didn't beat us in a championship match after that until 1988. We were lucky in that other players outside the Harty Cup teams, such as Richie Bennis, were in that age group too.

Tony Roche was on the 1963 minor team and scored 0-6 in the All-Ireland final from midfield. He tells a remarkable tale from the All-Ireland semi-final which may be best described as an urban legend:

When we played Roscommon in the All-Ireland semi-final at the Gaelic Grounds we were winning so easily that the Roscommon secretary came into the dressing room and asked us to mix the teams so that we would have a decent match in the second half. I played centre field for Roscommon in the second half and I was marking Éamonn Cregan, having partnered him at midfield for Limerick in the first half. The previous year we were playing Galway in the Gaelic Grounds in the first round of the Munster championship and Fr McNamee stalled the game before the throw-in. He told the referee not to throw in the ball, that I was being taken off. I was being suspended because my photo was on *The Kerryman* newspaper having played for Castleisland in rugby. Fr McNamee was from Glenroe and as far as I know he was principal of St Munchins at the time. For the 1963 All-Ireland final, we went up the night before the game and stayed in the Manor hotel. We were so cocky that we thought we were unbeatable. The newspapers had us blown up as the best team ever.

Éamonn Grimes was on both the 1963 and 1965 teams:

We were conscious in 1963 that we had a good balanced team with a good number of South [Division] players, and felt we could go somewhere. The 1963 team were a better team than the 1965 team who lost the All-Ireland final to Dublin. They proved that by playing very important roles in later years with their clubs and with the Limerick senior hurlers.

In 1962 the Limerick seniors faced reigning All-Ireland champions Tipperary in the Munster championship and lost heavily after a replay. Owen O'Neill Senior was on the team:

Michael Tuohy (*left*) fights a rearguard action along with Jim O'Brien (*centre*) against Cork full-forward Andrew O'Flynn (*right*) in a national League game at the Cork Athletic Ground on 19 February 1967.

In the drawn game we had Tipperary on the rack, we were coming from behind and had drawn level. Momentum was with us, but Jimmy Smyth blew the final whistle about four minutes early. They got their second wind in the replay. My recollection is that all we did was physical training between the draw and the replay. We had a game of backs and forwards one night, and the backs leaked five goals in about ten minutes and Mick Mackey decided to call it to a halt. There was no more ball work before the replay. Tipperary had their eye in and had their game plan and we never got off the ground. Tipperary beat Waterford by a cricket score in the Munster final, so I feel we would have won Munster.

Smyth restarted the game after the early final whistle but selector Rory Kiely believes the loss of momentum proved costly:

I became a selector that year representing the county champions, Western Gaels, who I was actually playing with at the time. We weren't too happy when he blew it up early but there was nothing we could do; that was the way it happened.

Nevertheless, Limerick were being noticed and the drawn game was the incarnation of Babs Keating's well documented fear of the Shannonsiders:

Tipperary have very good reason to fear Limerick and that goes back to 1962 when Limerick drew with what turned out to be one of the great Tipperary teams in the first round of the championship in Cork. Tipperary won the replay handy but could have been beaten the first day. The next encounter was in 1966, when there would have been an expectation that we were going for the three-in-a-row. Two Sundays before Limerick played Cork in the 1966 Munster semi-final, we opened the Newcastlewest field. Having been knocked out by Limerick in the championship, we beat them by about fourteen points. I am not casting a shadow over that Limerick team, but as it transpired they weren't good enough to win a Munster championship and progress, unlike the team that won the League in 1971. They should have beaten us in the Munster final in Killarney that year because I think the back line was superior.

Éamonn Grimes offers a different view:

I first played senior in 1966. Éamonn Cregan had a fantastic game against Tipperary and I think he scored 3-5 off Mickey Burns, who was playing his last game. Brother Burke had taken over at that time and he made a huge change when he switched Tom Bluett from corner-back to corner-forward on John Doyle. It was a huge change, and it worked and we won pretty well. I was on the best hurler I ever played on, Len Gaynor. I sat my Leaving Certificate the following morning. I was taken off the same day. First I was on Gaynor and then I went in on Maher; it was out of the frying pan into the fire. I believe that the 1966 team was the best Limerick team that I ever played on. We were beaten by Cork by 2-6 to 1-7 in the semi-final. Séamus Quaid had a crash going to the match but still played.

Limerick faced Cork in Killarney without the injured Phil Bennis on a day when the half-forward line contained three Éamonns: Cregan, Carey and Grimes. Many believe that Quaid should not have started because the accident had left him shaken. The game was lost in controversial circumstances when a goal was disallowed and a free in awarded. Bernie Hartigan was credited with the goal, but Tom Bluett is in no doubt:

Bernie Hartigan soloed in from out the field and Jerry Sullivan gave him a flick coming in. The referee blew the whistle but nobody heard it. Bernie let fly on the ball, and Paddy Barry, the Cork goalie, blocked it with his hurley. I was standing there and pulled on it and sent it to the net. I had always been a corner-back. Nobody said anything to me about changing and one day they were playing Waterford in Limerick in the League and I was picked at corner-forward. I was on Jimmy Byrne and I got 2-2 off him and was in the forwards forever more.

Bernie Hartigan has his own views on the game – and the goal:

I scored the goal, and it was disallowed. We were better than Cork but the referee didn't do us any favours on the day. The Tipp team we beat in the first round could have won six or seven All-Irelands in the 1960s. They lost a few games they should have won: Waterford caught them in Limerick in 1963, we caught them in 1966 and Wexford caught them in 1968. They always seemed to get caught.

Richie Bennis believes the absence of his brother Phil proved costly:

Phil cut his finger at work the Friday before the game. Seánie Barry went to town on the replacement, Eddie Prenderville. We definitely would have beaten Cork if Phil was playing. He could always get the better of Seánie Barry. He could stop a good forward; he mightn't have been a great hurler himself, but he was a great man at stopping a forward from hurling.

Éamonn Grimes was not the only young hurler to cut his teeth in the early and mid-1960s. Éamonn Cregan made his championship debut in 1965 at midfield against Waterford marking Larry Guinan, having made his League debut in 1964. Mickey Graham and the Bennis brothers also emerged, as did Bernie Hartigan, the South Liberties native and founder member of new city club, Old Christians, who were closely aligned to Limerick CBS. From the South Division Jim O'Brien, Ned Rea and Mossie Dowling were making an impact. Rea, who became a Limerick senior hurler by virtue of his performance for Emmets in the 1963 county final, was born in Glenroe but moved to Effin at a young age:

I recall watching my neighbours passing my house with hurleys on the way to the local hurling field in Effin. When I was nine or ten I was allowed to join them, and I have fond memories of Andy Dillon giving me my first hurley. I remember travelling to games in Ned Burke's cattle truck, which was cleaned out for us. When it came to going to secondary school, my mother promised me a hurley and ball if I would sit the entrance exam for St Munchin's. My regret about St Munchin's is that we didn't compete in the Harty Cup, because we had a side good enough to beat Limerick CBS. I rate the 1966 team as the best Limerick side I ever played on.

Apart from 1966, Limerick did not make any significant impact in the decade, as Phil Bennis recalls:

Limerick hadn't a settled fifteen throughout the 1960s, they were chopping and changing the team a lot. Players like Paddy Cobbe, Pat Murphy (Old Christians), Éamonn Carey (Patrickswell) should have been on the team the whole time and were only in and out. It was only in 1970 that they started trying to keep a settled team together. We should have won a lot more and in 1966 we should have won the All-Ireland. We were very inconsistent but the selectors lost a lot of matches that time. Players weren't allowed to gain confidence and the selectors were always making changes and taking off players that shouldn't have been taken off.

Bernie Hartigan, meanwhile, feels that the opposition were of a high standard at the time:

We didn't build on 1966 but were coming up against good teams. Clare beat us well in 1967. They had a super team that time and were good enough to win an All-Ireland but they were inconsistent, would have one great game and then flop. Cork beat us in 1968 and in 1970, and Tipperary beat us in 1969. There was no second chance. It was do or die. We started to get to the League finals then; we won the one in 1971 and were unlucky in 1972. In 1972 I remember Éamonn Grimes missed a sitter of a goal chance at a vital stage, and we lost by three points.

Richie Bennis believes politics played its part:

We were not unlucky; there was too much chopping and changing. There was fierce politics in hurling that time. They got rid of players too young and it was an annual championship outing for a while because of the knockout system. Bernie Savage, for example, never got the run he deserved. He was a great goal poacher.

Éamonn Cregan believes that leadership shown by some key players was instrumental in the upturn in fortunes in the 1970s:

From 1967 to October 1969 we were a disgrace. When I trained for the 1965 championship match against Waterford, we had only four players training. Tony O'Brien was a deep thinker at the time along with Jim Hogan and Bernie Hartigan. They met the county board and wanted better, so we started winter training. The results of the winter training were reaching League finals of 1970 to 1974, the Munster finals of 1971 to 1976 and the All-Ireland finals of 1973 and 1974.

Bernie Hartigan agrees:

We would have got together with Joe McGrath to arrange things. A commission into improving Limerick hurling was set up and I recall several meetings with the county board around that time. When I started with Limerick in 1962, we had only two weeks' training ahead of the championship. We had no training for the League games; we just turned up for the games. There was very little done apart from when Noel Drumgoole and Brother Burke were involved. I am convinced that if there were more preparations in the 1960s we would have won a lot more.

When Joe McGrath arrived on the scene in late 1969 he brought a degree of professionalism. Crucially though, while McGrath was ahead of his time in many respects, he had no role in team selection. This ultimately resulted in defeat and cost McGrath his job.

Bernie Hartigan was an admirer of the Down man:

Joe McGrath would be more akin with the modern managers and was often looking for things. I remember him going into the Gaelic Grounds one night and demanding two sliotars for every hurler. Now there are buckets of sliotars. Prior to that, the trainer might have a couple of sliotars in his pocket. He wanted all sorts of equipment. I remember looking at the faces of the county board officials and it was like a death sentence to them.

In the 1970 League final Limerick were beaten 2-17 to 0-7 by Cork, but Mickey Graham did not feature:

I had played in 1968 and was gone for two years. Tom Boland was a selector at the time and I remember they played Galway in a challenge game at Kilmallock and they picked players up along the road the same night. I never even got a run. Claughaun were playing a football match the next weekend, and Limerick were playing Galway in another challenge game. Tom Boland told me to be there and I said I was going playing football. That was the end of me for two years. They played Cork in the League final in 1970 and were well beaten. I remember saying to my club-mate Mick Tynan, who was a selector with Limerick, 'Am I as bad as some of them fellas?' 'You are not,' he said. 'Why am I not being picked?' I asked. He replied: 'Will you play? I thought you didn't want to play.'

Graham returned to the panel for the 1970 championship and Limerick drew with Clare in the first round at Thurles. Four players were sent off in the replay, two from each side, but Limerick pulled through and Graham got his place for the next round against Cork. He scored 2-2 but, as in the League final, the Rebels were victorious. It was the end of the road for stalwarts like John McDonagh, P. J. Keane and Tom Bluett. Wearing the number 2 jersey gave a huge sense of pride to McDonagh; his son Stephen would eventually inherit the jersey and wear it with the same ferocious pride:

I trained for one winter under Joe McGrath and he was very thorough. He brought this type of collective training that was new to the county board and new to the Gaelic Grounds. If anything, it shook up the county board and maybe they weren't that happy with his methods, yet he built the foundation of the team that won the All-Ireland. I was a bit annoyed around that time because we trained hard through the winter and they cut the panel very quickly and got rid of guys who had all the work done in preparing themselves. That 1970 team was a good team that trained a lot over the winter.

You tend to stay away from controversies as a player because they tend to distract you when you are trying to hurl. There was one incident when we were playing Waterford and they picked the team during the week and I was on it. I went to the match with Tommy Casey. About half an hour before the throw-in we were preparing in the dressing room and we went out for a puck around, and I noticed that there was another player wearing number 2. I was number 2 as well and there were sixteen players on the pitch and the sixteenth player was Michael O'Loughlin. You would joke about it now. I was picked, but nobody told me I wasn't playing, but Declan Moylan came in and grabbed me by the sleeve and took me off and said there was a mix up. Politics crept in but I kept my head down and steered away from the controversies. I regarded it as a fierce honour to put on the green jersey. I still have the hurley and jersey I won the All-Ireland minor medal with in 1958. If you saw the jersey – how small and simple and insignificant it was – it's too many of those things they have today. That honour of the jersey seems to have slipped away from a lot of players today.

Limerick returned to the National League final in 1971 and beat Tipperary in Páirc Uí Chaoimh when Richie Bennis scored a late winner. It was the first League victory since 1947. They went on to beat Cork in the championship for the first time since 1940 but lost to Tipperary in Killarney in the Munster final, the day of the dry ball. Mickey Graham has fond memories of 1971:

My happiest day was winning that League. It was the only title that had been won in years; it was always going to be brilliant. The 1971 Cork match was one of the greatest hurling matches I ever played in – unbelievable hurling, non-stop to the very end. In the Munster final, we knew something happened at the time of the dry ball incident. They were cuter than us on and off the field. If we got the 21-yard free, we wouldn't have had anyone onto the field fast enough with a dry ball. They knew how to win, we didn't.

Babs did a lot of damage in the second half. I held Mick Roche for about half an hour, not through hurling but by just tormenting him. Eventually he calmed down and started to hurl and forgot about me, played his own game, and there wasn't a hurler in Ireland who would mark Roche at that time. We were good enough to win an All-Ireland if we were cute enough. I think we would have beaten Kilkenny. Limerick hadn't been at that level of hurling, and on and off the field we didn't have the savvy and knowing how to win. Winning is a habit.

Babs Keating believes winning the League cost Limerick a Munster title in 1971:

Limerick had beaten us in the League final in Cork two months before that. It was probably Limerick's undoing. I have always said that if Limerick hadn't won that League final, that they would have beaten us in the Munster final. Joe [McGrath] lived beside me in Limerick and to be fair to him, he had an awful lot of good ideas. I was actually only having a go at Joe after the match, and unfortunately a reporter picked it up. What happened was that I said, 'Only for you Joe, there's no way we would have a new dry ball.' I was ball-hopping him that for all of his organisation and planning, we were one step ahead of him. He had a lot of mod cons to be fair to him, and would have been a perfectionist regarding balls. He had ideas that the generations before him didn't have in terms of match day plans.

Joe discussed all those with me, and as it transpired Donie Nealon did happen to be at the back of the goals when I was taking the free. John Flanagan had been fouled and he hit the ball away. The ball didn't come back and wasn't going to be returned, so I would have been given a new ball anyway. It's as simple as that. It was a replacement ball, there was no such thing as changing the ball. The story became a legend and the fact that I scored the goal added insult to injury. That was one of the best games of hurling ever played, there was eighty minutes of tension in that.

Pat Hartigan believes Limerick needed to win silverware:

It was a massive honour to win the League because we were so long without any success. We played Tipperary three times in that League and won each match by a point. Limerick were at a stage where we had to go for the League. Having lost in 1970 we couldn't afford to lose another. I don't think winning the League was to our detriment, because we were still better than Tipperary in Killarney. Twice in that match we were eight points ahead, it was a wet day, there were a lot of issues. I think the 1971 team was arguably the best team Limerick had. We went on to beat Kilkenny by eight points in an Oireachtas semi-final and they had their full team and we went on to beat Wexford in the final.

That Oireachtas win was the first title since Tommy Cooke's day. Joe McGrath, appointed trainer following success with Claughaun, believes the Munster final loss cost Limerick more silverware:

I remember Mick Dunne was with the *Irish Independent* and RTÉ and he asked me at one stage what my plans were for Limerick and my reply was to win every trophy that could be won within a five-year period. That's exactly what happened. During the period of my stay

Parading the League trophy in 1971. *Back row (l–r):* Mick Tynan (Claughaun), Con Shanahan (Croom), Davy Bourke (Garryspillane) *Front row (l–r):* Richard Bennis (Patrickswell), Tony O'Brien (Captain) (Patrickswell), Rory Kiely (Feenagh/Kilmeedy).

with Limerick, they won the Oireachtas competition, and that's the only medal Christy Ring never won. The plan was simple: a five-year plan where we would look at four headings – skill, teamwork, physical fitness and positive attitude.

For skill, you take the skills of hurling and you break them down and there are approximately ten basic skills in the game, give or take. What made Ring different from everyone else was that most others had four or five that they used extremely well; Ring had them all and that was the difference. I set about improving that aspect of the Limerick hurlers, but you have to have time.

Limerick won one All-Ireland, but they should have won three or four. They were beaten by Tipperary in 1971 and that team on the day should have beaten Tipperary well; a lot of things went against us. Frank Murphy disallowed the goal because Éamonn Grimes had been hit after he had struck the ball. Murphy should have given the advantage. If Limerick won that Munster final, they would have won at least three All-Irelands; they were good enough to do it.

When you are coaching you have to coach your players not only to beat the opposition but also to beat the umpires, linesmen and the referee because they all make mistakes. I always took notes of every game – who played, if they played well or not, what they did wrong and how we could improve them for the future. We had the makings of a great panel of players, and at the beginning of every year they were getting better and all they needed to do was keep the focus and keep it simple.

Willie Moore, the goalscorer, has no idea why it was disallowed:

Frank Murphy actually gave a free in. The ball hit the net and the whistle blew and I assumed that it was a free out for some reason; I wasn't fully sure. It probably did cost us the game, looking back on it.

Richie Bennis believes the dry ball had no impact:

We had beaten Cork for the first time since 1940 in the Munster championship. We had shaken the Cork monkey off our backs and were very confident approaching the Tipperary game. We were well ahead at half-time. The dry ball had no bearing on the game whatsoever. The biggest problem was that Jackie Power, who was a gentleman and a very shrewd man, Mick Mackey and one of the Herberts came into the dressing room at half-time. I had never spoken to Mick Mackey prior to that. They weren't selectors, they just came into the dressing room. They more or less told us we had the game won, instead of giving us a fong up in the arse, and telling us we needed to do more. It was John Flanagan who scored the winning point for them that day. He was nearly falling and Tony O'Brien hit him a flake of a shoulder, and it actually steadied him and he drove it over the bar. We had a chance of drawing after that, a shot from an awkward angle and it went wide. I was devastated to lose in 1971; I cried for the first time ever after a match. I didn't come home at all. I stayed in Killarney for a week. I drank out of sorrow, there was no singing and roaring I can tell you.

His brother Phil believes a crucial switch needed to be made:

Pat Hartigan should have followed Babs Keating in the second half.
Hartigan had Keating beaten in the first half and didn't follow him
and Keating came into the game. I don't know how we lost that match
because we were well ahead.

*In 1972 Limerick lost the League final to Cork by 3-14 to 2-14 and in the
championship were defeated by Clare in Ennis with a totally restructured team;
only five played in the same position as in the League final. Full-back Pat
Hartigan was moved to centre-back and a rookie, Donal Manning, was named
at full-back. Mickey Graham gave a five-star display in the League final at
wing-back but was switched to the forwards for the Clare game:*

That League was my best match ever for Limerick and the reason
we lost was that I was the only one who hurled [laughs]. Centre field
was my favourite position but I played everywhere from wing-back to
corner-forward. I didn't care once I was on the team. The selectors
were doing a lot of messing around with the team around the time.
They were never happy with Jim O'Donnell for some reason and they
weren't happy with Pat at full-back. They had it in their head the
whole time that Pat Hartigan was playing too much ball at full-back.
It was a team nobody would put out. They ate us in Ennis. Grimes
wouldn't come off. In the second half Rory Kiely went in and asked
him to come off but Grimes refused.

Rory Kiely gives his own version of events:

We were favourites to win in Ennis. It's very hard to beat Clare
there. Éamonn Grimes had a bad game, and we decided we were
going to take him off. I had to go into him and tell him that we were
thinking of taking him off and giving Donie Flynn a run. The very
minute I went in to him, he ran up the field and wouldn't come off. It
looked very bad but that was the way it was done that time, you had to
go in to the field to take someone off. There was a post mortem at the
next county board meeting. Joe McGrath used to speak a lot to the
press at the time, and Matt Connell who was chairman of the city
board said, 'The trainer said before the match that Limerick had a
psychological advantage. I don't know what a psychological advantage
is, but coming home from the match they didn't have a hurling
advantage anyway.'

Grimes feels the knockout system did not help Limerick in those days:

If we had the qualifier system then there would have been a lot more seen of Limerick. I had thirteen wides against Clare in Ennis in 1972 and on another day could have been the next Dermot Kelly, but unfortunately it didn't work out.

Seán Foley feels that preparations were inadequate:

The Clare game in 1972 was a shock, it was generally a case of just going down to play the match and, as the saying goes, the rest is history. And did we play poorly on that day! That 1971 team was a good team, and we felt that we should be winning things, expectations were higher. We were absolutely shocked and our fans were more disappointed. There was a bizarre thing that day prior to the game: one group of players went to one hotel and another group went to another hotel thinking it was the right hotel. That was the preparation at that stage.

That wasn't Joe McGrath's fault. He came out at the wrong side of '72. Joe was a great trainer and broke any divisions between players from different clubs. They were wearing the Limerick jersey and that was it. That was very important. Only for Joe McGrath I may not have been on the 1973 team because I was considering going to England working. I was almost gone, the bags were packed and nobody rang me only Joe McGrath, even though he wouldn't have known me that well personally. That was in late 1972. I would have been gone only for him. It's ironic that he was the man who kept me, yet I was there and he was gone. Tony O'Brien only retired in 1972. He was a gallant hurler and I heard at that time that he retired because he felt there were too many good young hurlers coming through.

Denis Barrett was a selector in 1972 and explains the changes for the Clare game:

We thought we would find new players and try different players in different positions and treated it like a League game and experimented. We were sure we would fill vacancies that we thought should be filled. We thought we were doing the right thing and that it was a move in the right direction. It proved afterwards to be a move in the wrong road. I'm not sure if there was enough pressure put on Grimes to go off. We were not tough enough at that time.

The match was late starting and there were words in the dressing room before the match over timekeeping. Some players were caught in traffic because there was such a big crowd and weren't in time for the match. There's no excuse for a player being delayed. We couldn't send out the team onto the field because we were waiting for the players to arrive. It was a bad start.

Richie Bennis was a major doubt before the game:

I was injured the week before playing a junior football match. I broke the thumb because I was trying to catch a football and I wasn't able to! I took the plaster off the morning of the match between Limerick and Clare. I wasn't right, because I should have been in a plaster for another few weeks. I would have played if I had been started, even with a plaster on me. I loved hurling. I wasn't able to play, I went in as a sub and it was the greatest mistake going. It was madness because I wasn't able to handle a hurley.

The game was a disaster. I remember meeting Micheál Ó Muircheartaigh in the hotel after the match, and he couldn't believe it. He said we would have been regarded as favourites for that year's All-Ireland.

Bennis was introduced following an injury to Mickey Cregan, whose Limerick career ended soon afterwards:

I went to challenge Séamus Durack and he bent down and I landed on my AC [shoulder] joint. It put me out for a couple of months. When I returned, we were playing Patrickswell in a club game. Phil Bennis pulled and connected with my small finger and broke it. It never recovered properly and that finished my inter-county career.

Pat Hartigan says Joe McGrath had laid the foundation for success:

Éamonn Grimes was a fantastic player and should never have been considered for being taken off in that game, and I am not saying that because he was a fellow South Liberties man. Joe McGrath fell on his sword after that game. I believe Limerick winning the All-Ireland was not a consequence of Joe McGrath being sacked because I think we would have won it anyway. We had a lot of success under Joe McGrath in 1971. I won League and Oireachtas medals. We didn't lose the Munster final in 1971 or in Ennis in 1972 because Joe McGrath was manager; we lost because the wrong team was picked in 1972.

The Limerick team that beat Kilkenny in the 1972 League semi-final. *Back row (l–r):*
Bernie Hartigan (Old Christians), Jim O'Brien (Bruree), Pat Hartigan (South Liberties),
Jim Allis (Doon), Willie Moore (Doon), Éamonn Cregan (Claughaun), Tony O'Brien
(Patrickswell), Mickey Cregan (Claughaun). *Front row (l–r):* Seán Foley (Patrickswell),

Éamonn Grimes (South Liberties), Richard Bennis (Patrickswell), Mickey Graham (Claughaun), Jim Hogan (Adare & Claughaun), Phil Bennis (Patrickswell), Donie Flynn (Cappamore & Killeedy).

Hartigan adds that playing Clare in Ennis was a mistake:

We took Clare for granted, and there was no reason to take them for granted, because we were very lucky to get over them in 1971. You were limiting the crowd to 12,000 by having the game in Ennis in 1972, whereas Thurles could hold 40,000 or 50,000. Ennis was a hostile ground, and that hostility was reflected in the way that Clare played down there.

Richie Bennis agrees:

It was Limerick politics again of course, agreeing to toss on the venue. Nobody to this day ever came out of Ennis with a win. Limerick teams never came out of Ennis. Galway didn't come out of there in 2007 with Ger Loughnane in charge. Waterford didn't come out of there in the 2005 qualifiers. Cork footballers were beaten down there in 1997 and were lucky to get a draw there in 1996. It's a graveyard for teams. And it was a stupid mistake to go down there.

Joe McGrath, however, is dismissive of such theories:

They talk about graveyards and all that, but that's another Biddy Earley story. Clare blamed Biddy Earley for their lack of success for many years and she had nothing to do with it. People blame going to Ennis for beating Limerick but it had nothing to do with it. If the best Limerick team had been fielded that day they would have beaten Clare out the gate. I was confident of playing any opposition, because the spirit, teamwork, physical fitness and attitude of the opposition of that time weren't great. I was confident we could improve in those areas, and on our day I felt we could take any team.

In the present day, management make the decisions and have total control. In those days I was the coach, the selectors picked the team and I had no say whatsoever on the team they put out. I was purely a coach. I would not have been afraid to take that Limerick panel anywhere. Clare or any other team, in Ennis or any other venue, held no fears for me. The problem was that the team was totally rearranged with individuals put in places that they never played before and with new faces who had never played before. The team wasn't a patch on itself, and I could see things that I would never do. It could have been political, but when you go out to win matches you go out with the best team in the places where they play best. I would not have been afraid to take them anywhere because I was so proud of them and they were so talented, they hadn't even reached 50 per cent of their potential.

Superstition or not, tossing for home advantage was often done for financial reasons, as gate receipts from a home game could be substantial. This raises the issue, of course, of whether financial considerations should be allowed to take precedence over the interests of the team.

THREE

ଔ

1973: PROMISED LAND

In late 1972 Joe McGrath was sensationally axed as trainer and replaced by Mick Cregan. Many queried the decision, and in early 1973 the county board issued the following statement:

Regarding the appointment of Mick Cregan as trainer of the county hurling team, the officials and selectors met as instructed by the county board. The decision to have Joe McGrath replaced was arrived at after lengthy deliberation by the selectors who, having considered the poor performance of the team during the early portion of 1972, considered that a change of trainer might help.

Clearly the board had no regrets about removing McGrath – but some of the players were far from happy. Jim Hogan, Bernie Hartigan, Pat Hartigan, Éamonn Grimes and Joe Grimes all declared themselves unavailable for selection. They missed one League game, a draw against Tipperary on 11 February, but were back for the next one, against Cork on 4 March.

Mickey Cregan outlines Joe McGrath's impact:

Joe McGrath was in Claughaun, a very positive guy and had a lot to offer when compared to what went before him. He was a modern-day thinker, he had attended coaching courses and may have been involved in them when Joe Lennon ran them in the late 1960s and early 1970s and brought all that down to Limerick. He was involved with Molex, an American company as a general manager, so he was an able individual. So he stepped in and trained and coached and upset people in the county board, I would think, because suddenly we had boots and sliotars and hurleys that we never had before.

The responsibility for raising cash would have fallen back on Tom Boland, the county secretary at that time. Suddenly the bills started coming in and Tom Boland had to deal with them. Joe brought lights

Éamonn Grimes (*left*) and Éamonn Cregan (*right*) prior to a shinty international in 1973. Shinty is a scottish game similar to hurling.

to the Gaelic Grounds, and brought modern training methods into an era when it wasn't there.

Pat Hartigan says McGrath had made changes in terms of preparation, some of which 'wouldn't have gone down well with those in the county board who were used to the old ways'. His brother Bernie believes the switches in the team were the reason for the downfall:

When we were beaten in 1971 in Killarney the selectors made a lot of switches. I don't think any player ended up in the position they had started in. There was complete panic after half-time. We were eight points ahead and Tipperary got a few scores and they [the selectors] started chopping and changing. None of that was down to Joe McGrath. In all our games there would have been a lull at a certain point and we would come back hard into it again. It wasn't his fault that we lost in 1972 either, there were too many changes. Taking Pat out of full-back and putting in a raw recruit for his first game wasn't Joe's fault.

When he was removed there was a bit of a coup and a bit of a strike and a few of us didn't hurl for a while. I remember playing away with the footballers. That time you could play both easily enough because the matches were staggered and training wasn't as intense. It was Jackie O'Connell who eventually gathered the dissenters together one night. Jackie was a good negotiator, and it was solved, but without us getting any sort of satisfaction either. Joe wasn't treated properly.

Mickey Cregan explains how he got the job:

Rory Kiely and Jackie Power came to my door one night in October. I was surprised to see them, because I was out of the loop at that stage. They asked me to become the trainer. I was in the army, a qualified army physical training instructor. I presume they were aware of this, but they knew it by the time they were finished anyway. I said, 'OK, provided that I am totally in charge of the physical preparation of the team and nobody interferes with that.' They agreed to that, and as far as I was concerned, that was the end of it.

Joe had an awful lot to offer and what happened between him and the county board and others after that, I don't know, nor was I too interested. It wasn't my function. I was asked to take over an appointment. It was a straightforward thing. I couldn't play any more, my finger was broken and that was the end of that. There was a certain amount of difficulty in Claughaun because Éamonn and myself were there along with Joe McGrath and Jim Hogan. The boys went on strike but that was all right, they put their case and they came back into the fold.

It was awkward for a while when the lads were on strike. They had a meeting with the management, and possibly Rory Kiely. The chairman was involved and they were requesting that Joe McGrath be brought back and the management didn't accept it. I travelled to a few matches while this rumpus was going on. It was going on for a while. The job of the management was to select a panel and on 6 January we went into training in the Gaelic Grounds with the new panel minus those who didn't accept it.

The main beneficiaries of the strike were Séamus Horgan, Liam O'Donoghue and Frankie Nolan, who became regulars in the absence of others. Goalkeeper Jim Hogan, captain in 1972, was the biggest casualty, losing his place permanently.

Richie Bennis believes that both McGrath and Cregan had much to offer:

Joe McGrath was hard done by, but we wouldn't have won the All-Ireland unless Mickey Cregan came on the scene. At the same time we wouldn't have won the All-Ireland either in 1973 but for Joe McGrath, because he had brought professionalism into the situation.

Tom Ryan offers his view:

A couple of things happened around the time. You had the South Liberties factor; they had come up from junior and brought a new image to the senior championship. Joe McGrath had come in then and was supported and proposed mostly by Claughaun and Éamonn Cregan. He brought a freshness, new voice, new ideas, he was a very progressive man thinking-wise and that had an impetus on the team and the training was changed from the traditional slog to a lot of drills. He was always in the middle of players, talking to them and lifting them up and his psychology definitely brought Limerick onto the 1973 All-Ireland.

At that time the Limerick team was beginning to make an impact. Winning the League and the breakthrough in 1973 was something that really and truly happened because of that. By the end of 1972, there was a split in the camp about McGrath. Some players wanted him and more players didn't want him. Joe McGrath was shafted by the county board and by player influence and player power. And at that time you had different pockets of power. Joe McGrath was a gentleman, a great character, and a very innovative individual. I was never very close to Joe McGrath but I could see very well that he was a man before his time. He was too much of a gentleman to deal with dissenters, and we have them in Limerick today, and we had them in Limerick that time.

The winning of the All-Ireland in 1973 was when the players on strike went up into the stand the day of the Tipperary game in the League. They actually went up into the stand and Limerick had to play with a depleted team. Tipperary were lucky to get a draw when Len Gaynor levelled the game with a long-range free. They were

The Limerick team that beat Kilkenny 1-21 to 1-14 in the 1973 All-Ireland final. *Back row (l–r):* Richard Bennis (Patrickswell), Liam O'Donoghue (Mungret), Jim O'Brien (Bruree), Pat Hartigan (South Liberties), Joe McKenna (South Liberties), Éamonn

Cregan (Claughaun), Willie Moore (Doon), Ned Rea (Faughs). *Front row (l–r):* Seán Foley (Patrickswell), Mossie Dowling (Kilmallock), Bernie Hartigan (Old Christians), Éamonn Grimes (South Liberties), Phil Bennis (Patrickswell), Frankie Nolan (Patrickswell), Séamus Horgan (Tournafulla).

down from the stand for the next game. That broke the strike very fast because the players knew that the team could cope without them. Mickey Cregan, who was also a very good trainer, replaced McGrath. He did a very good job as trainer; it was different training again, he went back to the knuckle down training. It was hard training. You expect that, he was an army lieutenant at that time. He took over the team and won the All-Ireland. I believe that the seeds of that All-Ireland were set on the day that the dissenters came back. It meant that they knew they could be done without.

Mossie Dowling compares the training regimes of McGrath and Cregan:

I was only just back on the panel after a couple of years out when Joe got the bullet. Joe was the fittest man on the field; when we were inside doing the training, Joe would be out in front. That time in the Gaelic Grounds there was only a couple of lights and the smart boys – Richie and Phil and a few more – would duck out in the dark for a while, and join back in then again. A few fools would stay training, and McGrath was out in front and didn't know any different.

Mickey Cregan came in as trainer and there was no hiding, the smart boys got caught. But still, when we would be sprinting they would try and sneak a few yards always, but if Mickey spotted you doing it he would crucify you. Mickey had played with the boys, so knew who was dodging and who wasn't. I reckon that only for the change we wouldn't have won the All-Ireland. Mickey was an army man, and nobody was getting away with anything when he was around. If he said do ten rounds, you did ten rounds, not nine and a half.

The selectors in 1973 were Dick Stokes, Jackie Power, Seán Cunningham, Denis Barrett and Jim Quaid. Some believe Joe McGrath was removed because people like Stokes and Power were keen to take over what was now a promising team. Denis Barrett reiterates the point about expenses:

Around that time, we went over to London to play Tipperary in a tournament game. Joe would often buy gear out of the blue and the county board couldn't keep paying for it and weren't happy. If he had his way, the team would have a new jersey, new shorts or something new every time they went out. He knew some guy in London and bought a lot of gear there when we were over. We would never have enough sliotars for training only for Joe McGrath. He was excellent, a great trainer, and we wouldn't have won an All-Ireland in 1973 only for him.

Another great help was Fr McCarthy, who brought in this thing about having a meal after training. That was a great improvement and a great way of getting fellas to come to training.

Éamonn Grimes identifies other influential characters:

J. P. McManus and Declan Moylan got on board with regard to getting us meals, and Steve Foley in the Shannon Arms was a great patron to Limerick GAA at the time. J. P. and Declan started to get a fund together. I would say we were one of the first teams to do so. There was a great camaraderie that time going to training; there was a feel good factor playing for Limerick.

Speaking of the 1973 campaign, Tom Ryan feels Limerick, for once, were fortunate:

We were lucky and we did get the breaks in 1973. We must also look at 1973 in its entirety. We were lucky to beat Clare, and in the Munster final in Thurles we came back from an impossible situation. We got the rub of the green with the decision at the end and we still don't know if it was a point or not. The next day was against London; it was played in Ennis and we were a shambles and were lucky to beat them. London were missing one of the Cuddys, one of their best players who was on his honeymoon. In the final we met a depleted Kilkenny and we got a result that day. Thank God for that. There have been too many days that we didn't have the luck. It was a milestone. I believe that the Limerick team should have developed on from that.

Éamonn Cregan reminds us that while Kilkenny were missing players, Limerick were also without a star man:

I don't care what people say, whether they were short four players or not. We were short Mickey Graham, the forgotten man of that team; he had his leg broken in the League final against Wexford.

Graham's own view is forthright:

I was the forgotten man of 1973 all right, they forgot about me when they were going on the holiday after winning the All-Ireland. There weren't too many county board officials left at home though. I got a belt from behind in the League final, I was in the act of tapping the ball into an empty net, I got a belt in the leg and I just went to put the leg under me and the leg went, three bones broken.

I always slag the boys, I tell them that if I didn't get injured they would never have won the All-Ireland. We were all over Wexford and were two points in front. Instead of getting a goal, the ball was cleared and Tony Doran stuck it to the net at the other end and we were one behind instead of five in front. So they decided to stop the f*** acting and they put Pat Hartigan back in full-back.

Someone came up with the bright idea then of trying Rea full-forward in the championship. Sure, Rea frightened the life out of Tadhgie Murphy, the Tipperary goalie, in the Munster final; he spent most of his time sitting on top of him inside in the back of the net. They would have left Rea at full-back if we won the League. We wouldn't have won the All-Ireland. Instead they put Pat in full-back, and brought Willie Moore back from the forwards to corner-back where he had always hurled. Tony Doran going to town on Ned Rea was the thing that won it.

Limerick lost the League final by 4-13 to 3-7. As in 1972, the selectors made drastic alterations to the championship team, but this time they were the correct changes. Willie Conway from Bruff was recalled but, as Denis Barrett explains, failed to apply himself:

We were after dropping Conway from the panel for the League final and were beaten well. After that bad beating, we were playing Tipperary in a challenge game down in Killarney and Stokes said, 'Tinkers, tailors, soldiers or sailors, whoever they are we will bring them in if they can hurl.' We brought in a few and Conway was one of them. He blew the hand off Francis Loughnane in the first clash and that suited Stokes, and more so Jackie Power. He more or less had got his place but then he started missing training. There was no way I could stay calling for him and making excuses for him. Jack O'Dwyer from Pallasgreen was also a good hurler. He played in the Clare game but got injured and he didn't make it back when we had the settled team.

Limerick narrowly defeated Clare in Thurles, 3-11 to 3-9. Richie Bennis believes an injury to Pat Hartigan in that game actually helped Limerick:

Pat Hartigan got injured and he was marking Noel Casey. Casey was beating Hartigan. Jim Allis came in for the last twenty minutes. He had no hurling but he was as strong as a horse, and he horsed Noel Casey out of it.

Ned Rea could have been forgiven for thinking he was another forgotten man in 1973. Having been involved in the 1966 side, he moved to Dublin, and had the unique distinction of playing in county finals in three different counties – Limerick with Emmets, Cork with UCC and Dublin with Faughs. He won a number of Dublin league and championship titles and was recalled to the Limerick panel in 1972. He watched the Clare game from the bank in 1973, having been dropped after conceding 2-2 to Tony Doran in the League final:

I was full-back in the League final against Wexford and the reason for that was that I came in there when the South Liberties boys were on strike and I stayed there. I hated playing full-back; corner-back was my favourite position. Tony Doran was a hard man to mark, a great man to catch a high ball. I was brought down for a challenge match against Waterford prior to the Munster final, and they were going to play me full-back, which I wasn't happy about. To be called back was a big surprise. My grandmother was in the hospital so I went in to see her and Jim O'Donnell was driving. Rory Kiely was there as well as he was after being gored by a bull. When I came down from my grandmother, John Whelan and Jackie Power were there, they were on their way into Limerick. Before I came down they were talking about me playing full-forward and Rory said to Jackie, 'Why don't you ask him yourself would he like to play full-forward?' He had seen big men in there like Tony Doran and Roger Ryan and big players create more space. He asked me, and I said, 'I wouldn't mind, it would be very unlikely anyone will score off me in there.' I scored 2-1 against Waterford and was called back into training. I was playing at full-forward in training and when I got the taste of a chance of playing in the Munster final, I went hell for leather. I was on Pat Hartigan in the training games and wasn't holding back so Power called me in behind the goals one night and said, 'You are on the team for the final, keep it to yourself, but we want Hartigan on the team as well.'

Denis Barrett explains the logic behind the switch:

We had a selectors' meeting and we decided we would have to find a big full-forward. I was working in Kilmallock and I met John Fitzgerald who was the secretary of the South board at the time. I said to him that I had an idea for the full-forward position, and he asked me who it was, and when I said Ned Rea he told me to forget it. I said that I was going to propose him that night at a meeting. The rest is history and when I came back to John Fitzgerald after the Waterford game he agreed that it wasn't a bad idea after all.

Rory Kiely was also involved:

I had known about the change and was alone in bed thinking to myself that it's a bit unfair on Rea coming all the way down from Dublin thinking that he would be playing in the backs and ending up at full-forward. On the night of the match, Jim O'Donnell came in to see me and said that Rea was upstairs visiting his grandmother. When John Whelan and Jackie Power came in, I suggested that they ask Rea first.

The Munster final has gone down in Limerick folklore, with a late Richie Bennis 70 sealing victory. Some in Tipperary claimed that Richie's effort went wide, and even that an umpire had been struck. Babs Keating had a quiet word with Bennis as he steadied himself:

The comment was a harmless slag to try and put him off. I couldn't in my heart tell you if it was a point or not. If you were to ask me to put my house on it, I couldn't tell you. To be fair I was in line with the ball and I didn't dispute it, it was that close, but it was high over the top of the posts. I could not tell either way. The big dispute about that incident was the awarding of the 70. That's why Len Gaynor got involved with the umpire afterwards. For the 70, Gaynor and the Tipperary backs were adamant that the ball went wide before the goalie touched it. In his urgency to puck the ball out, he stepped behind the line and stopped the ball. I couldn't tell you either way, I was too far out but that's how Gaynor got involved with the umpire that day.

Limerick owe Joe McGrath an awful lot for 1973 because it was he that brought them together. Go back to early '73 when Joe McGrath was gone. You had two camps in Limerick; you had the camp that supported Joe McGrath and the camp that didn't support him and they were nearly split 50:50 at the time. The players who ousted Joe McGrath had to prove their point, and the other players that held firm had to prove a point too. I remember Limerick playing Tipperary in a League game with only half a team. I still contend that there was a better Limerick team in 1971 than in 1973. In 1973, in the final, Limerick got the breaks that they didn't get in 1971, but they were a better team in 1971. But at the end of the day justice was done because that team deserved to win an All-Ireland. I don't believe that

Éamonn Grimes proudly delivers his victory speech from the Hogan Stand in 1973.

the Limerick team would have won an All-Ireland only for the injuries to Kilkenny though.

Captain Éamonn Grimes recalls the climax in Thurles:

We had ambitions of winning the All-Ireland in 1973 and I remember coming off the field the day of the League final and thinking 'here we go again'. We were just coming right, and then we lost Mickey Graham. It was devastating. If everybody had the heart that Mickey Graham had then, and still has to this day, we weren't going to go far wrong.

I will never forget that Munster final. I felt that day that there was a vacuum, a cloud over Thurles. It was heavy, the hair would stand on the back of your neck. If you couldn't hurl in Thurles you couldn't hurl any place. If I had a say in the running of the Munster championship, I would play every hurling game in Thurles and divide the gate receipts between all the counties. There is a great atmosphere there and the access to it is good.

I was captain and I went over to Seán Foley who was taking the frees from that distance all day. I said to Seán, 'All we need is . . .' and Seán replied, 'I can't. I am knackered.' There was only one other player you could turn to – Richie – who never shirked a challenge and stood over it confidently, as he did in the 1971 League final in Cork. Just as the free was being taken, Babs had the famous few words with him, and the more he spoke to Richie the nearer the centre of the posts the ball was going. I would say Babs would have been better off if he never spoke to Richie. When the final whistle went, the vacuum that was there disappeared and suddenly there was air.

Seán Foley claims the credit for Richie Bennis becoming a folk hero:

A lot of people wouldn't be aware that on that day I was detailed to take the 70s. This was a vital one and Richie was more assured than I was. As I was thinking about taking it, he came up and took it. As I have reminded him many times since, there would have been no doubt about it being a point if I had taken it. It would have been straight over the bar. He took all the glory on that one. It was outstanding. A number of us were quite young, but a lot of fellas had been trying longer and harder. To beat Tipperary in Thurles was something else, Tipperary were still the kingpins at the time.

To this day there is speculation that Babs Keating offered Richie Bennis money to miss the 70:

If he did offer me money I'd have taken it [laughs]. And I'd have taken his hand and all off with it. Babs didn't offer me anything in 1973. I don't even remember what was said. It wasn't anything important anyway. It's very like what Mackey said to Ring, there's a lot made of all these things.

Bennis was no stranger to scoring long-range winning points in finals against Tipperary, having done the same in the League final of 1971. After scoring in Thurles, he and Seán Foley celebrated wildly Limerick's first Munster success in eighteen years:

It was a case of having to score the point if we wanted to win the Munster final. I didn't see the umpire being struck because we were engulfed in the celebrations. I'm not going to say it was wide [laughs]. RTÉ and Micheál Ó Muircheartaigh have proven that the ball was over the bar. It was definitely a point, in fairness. Mickey Cregan was training us and he said to me that he never saw me run as fast in my life as I did in the immediate celebrations. It was unbelievable, an unbelievable feeling.

Séamus Horgan did not take the puck-outs in the second half:

I hurt my shoulder before the Munster final and they didn't play me in Ennis against London. The Munster final was a special day, winning by a point with the last puck of the game. I thought we were gone when John Flanagan put them in front near the end. I hurt my shoulder and had thought I wouldn't make the game, but I got through it. I had been with a physio the week before and was lucky enough to make it. When we were walking down through Thurles after the match I couldn't even lift my hand over my head.

When Pat Hartigan took over the puck-outs there was a tactical element in his approach:

I was aiming to try and hit the ball as long as possible and keep it away from Mick Roche, to drag him around the place. It worked well and we won. That Munster final was a special day.

Ned Rea also had a role in the last 70, saving a few vital seconds as the game entered the melting pot:

There was the famous incident near the end with Tadhgie Murphy. The ball was out in the half-forward line and I was waiting for the puck-out and he was waiting for the ball to come back in to puck it out. I reckoned that if I hit the ball into him that he would have let it run behind the goals and delayed more time, so I just picked it up and went in and handed it to him. He had no choice then but to puck it out and there was a lot of speculation about what I said but I don't recall saying anything.

As it transpired afterwards the winning point from the 70 was the last puck of the game. We will never know if securing that few seconds made a difference, but we were a point down and saving time was my reason for doing that. My biggest memory is Micheál O'Hehir's commentary saying, 'Blow the whistle, referee.' To me those are the most magical minutes of all time, listening to that commentary.

When I was a young boy, to go to a Munster final was an honour, and to play in one was great; you could say for the rest of your life that you played in the famous Munster final. To actually go and win it then was fantastic. I played midfield and half-forward for the club up in Dublin so it was no big deal for me, but the Tipperary players thought it was a big joke that I wouldn't manage at full-forward at all. Cregan was delighted with me there and so was Frankie [Nolan]; all they wanted was space, because there was loads of loose ball breaking.

I never saw the cup after the game; I got a cut over the eye and I had to go to the hospital for stitches. I ended up in Haulie Gleeson's house. I never got back to the hotel afterwards and I didn't see the boys again until the following week in Ennis against London. I don't know if they trained during the week, but if they did I wasn't there. I remember almost getting stuck in traffic on the way down to the game and nearly missed the start of that London game.

Limerick defeated London in the All-Ireland semi-final by 1-15 to 0-7. Jim Hogan replaced Séamus Horgan in goals, and a unique situation arose when brothers Ned and Gerry Rea marked one another. Gerry was at full-back for London:

To be honest I wouldn't have foreseen it, because I wouldn't have expected London to beat Galway. On the day it was good humoured between us; there was no point in getting heavy with him because he was too big for me! We gave them a fright, and it was great to see them going on and winning the All-Ireland.

Ned agrees:

There was no needle between myself and Gerry, but it was very unusual. It wasn't publicised as much at the time as maybe it should have been. It was a rare thing to happen, I don't think it has happened since that two brothers have marked each other in an All-Ireland semi-final.

Limerick were to face Kilkenny in the All-Ireland final, their first since 1940. Excitement was building, but Ned Rea was based in Dublin and so was somewhat removed:

As a player a lot of it passes you by, it happens so fast. The previous May we were beaten in the League final, and then in September you are winning the big one. It wasn't a bad thing being in Dublin because I missed all the hype, but then missing the hype you are missing a great part of it as well. I was travelling up and down with Jim O'Donnell. Jim O'Donnell and Andy Dunworth played with Faughs, though Jim

Ned Rea and his grandfather Tom O'Brien with the McCarthy Cup at the O'Brien house in 1973. Mike O'Brien, a current Limerick hurler and a first cousin of Rea, now resides here.

hadn't started at that stage. The night the team was picked for the final we were staying at the Shannon Arms hotel. And all I could say was that I'd prefer to be put on than taken off. As it happened, Jim wasn't put on, they put on Tom Ryan for Bernie Hartigan. In fairness Bernie should never have been taken off. He was taken off in the 1974 final again, which was wrong also. We weren't going to lose anyway in 1973 and we weren't going to win in 1974.

The training sessions leading up to the final were fantastic, and the crowds were unbelievable. On the night of the last training session before the final, the crowd gave us a standing ovation as we left the field. And you are thinking, 'Jesus we have got to win this.' That night we got our tickets for the match, and the following day I went out to my uncle's in Glenroe. My grandfather was there, and he always had a picture of the 1940 team up on the fireplace. I remember saying to him, 'You will have a new picture next week,' and I did get him a new one, and we did change it. It was very emotional, because he was big into hurling and going to the games in Thurles with his sons who are my uncles. It was very emotional leaving him that day and you would be saying, 'I have to do this for his sake.'

When we won I brought the cup back to Glenroe and my grandfather slept with it by his bedside overnight and I have a great picture of the two of us with the cup taken outside the front gate. It's in Effin now; my mother likes to have it because of the connection, and she is ninety-one now and still very sharp.

Jim O'Donnell was an outstanding centre-back for Limerick in the early 1970s but broke his leg and never recovered his pace. He was replaced in both the League and Munster finals. The Limerick selectors were aware of the threat Kilkenny's Pat Delaney posed and switched Éamonn Cregan. Denis Barrett was one of those selectors:

We spoke about putting Cregan back centre-back for weeks upon end. It was going to be an awful big switch but it was one that we really thought would be a very good switch and it was. But when you win an All-Ireland every switch is a good one. It was massive to win the All-Ireland. I was the youngest of the selectors at the time, and I never thought I would see Limerick win an All-Ireland let alone be a selector on a winning team.

Some saw the switch as dramatic, but for Cregan it was nothing new:

Some of the Limerick players and supporters celebrate the All-Ireland success at the Cuchulainn Lounge in Patrickswell in 1973. *(L–r):* Catherine Fenton, Gerry Bennis, Mick Tynan, Seán Foley, Willie Foley, Richard Bennis, Éamonn Grimes, Noel Morrissey, Phil Bennis, Frankie Nolan, Josephine Piggott.

I had played at centre-back as far back as 1968 with Claughaun against Adare. I was used to the position, and it was no great move to go back if you were playing centre field or half-forward. I maintain that Tony Wall was the greatest centre-back that I saw because of his ability to stop the ball going past. The whole function of a centre-back is to control his area and make the ball go forward. You have to cover your wings all right but you don't live on the wings. When I was asked to play there I said to the selectors, 'Ye are the selectors, ye make the decision.'

I felt sorry for Jim O'Donnell; he was the centre-back and that was a tough one, but it was their job to pick the team. They picked it and I did the job. At the time I was more interested in finishing the training session we were in the middle of than thinking about the move. I had to watch Delaney then and see how he played the game and adjusted my game accordingly. We didn't have any stars in the final, everyone played above themselves and it was a team effort from start to finish.

Cregan's achievement is unique in that he was one of the best forwards in the country at the time. He gave a five-star defensive display against one of the toughest opponents, Pat Delaney. Bear in mind that Cregan went on to score 2-7 in the 1980 All-Ireland final. Richie Bennis gives his views on the switch:

He was a great centre-back. I used to play centre-forward for Patrickswell and I knew how good Cregan was. I was playing great stuff with the club and they put Cregan back there to mark me; that's how he became a centre-back. There wouldn't have been any other player they could have played at centre-back, except maybe Seán Foley. Seán was a great hurler but was never really a centre-back because he was mad for going up the field that time, and a centre-back can't do that. If Cregan wasn't centre-back in the All-Ireland we wouldn't have won the match. Yet if he was playing centre-back in the Munster final we wouldn't have won that match either because he scored two goals.

He can thank Ned Rea for those two goals though. We wouldn't have won the Munster final only for Ned Rea. And I would also say that because of his physical presence alone, he was the one man that contributed most to us winning the All-Ireland. He was able to hurl as well and people didn't realise it, he was able to use the ball when he got it. He wasn't just a mullocker. He mullocked when it suited but he also hurled when it was needed. It was massive to win the All-Ireland.

Éamonn Grimes feels it was Limerick's day regardless of who Kilkenny were missing:

When we went up to play that match, whether there was one Eddie Keher or ten Eddie Kehers playing, we were going to win. We were just primed. Mick Lipper, the bus driver, was the mayor of Limerick at the time and drove us up the night before. The following morning we went to Mass, and soon after, the bus left for Croke Park. There was a headcount and I was missing and they had to come back for me. I had gone to Mass, and we were so relaxed about the whole thing that I went up to my room and fell asleep. When we went out onto the pitch, I couldn't see anyone beating us. From 1966 up we should have won a hell of a lot more and that was our big chance. It was nice.

We had fantastic selectors and they have to be recognised. They made one huge tactical decision in putting Éamonn Cregan back on Pat Delaney. I was at centre field and my job at that stage was to play catch-up and chase back after Delaney and put pressure on him if he got past Éamonn. In fairness Éamonn had a fantastic game and I hardly had to worry about Delaney. One of the most consistent hurlers over the years had to be Jim O'Brien. Pat Hartigan could have been still hurling today had he not got the eye injury. The physique of the man, he was a colossus. Willie Moore was a sweeper. The game was so intense that I gave a pass that was meant for Bernie Hartigan at one stage and I didn't realise he had just been replaced by Tom Ryan.

Pat Hartigan had a conversation with Jackie Power:

Jackie said to me afterwards that the All-Ireland final would become a great armchair memory in years to come. People identify us with 1973, the fact that it was [just] one; if we had won two, we might not have been associated with either of them. My own two girls are conscious that I was part of that. They can identify with what it was like for us to have won it.

Eddie Keher, who missed out on the game, gives a Kilkenny perspective:

Limerick had been knocking on the door during the 1970s. We were getting very familiar with the players, such as Pat Hartigan and Éamonn Cregan, who had been making the All-Star teams. We were becoming very familiar with their capability, and we were playing against them in games and they were building a team of great ability.

Eventually they got together a great balanced team, a good spine in the team and great individual players then. You had Hartigan, Seán Foley and you had Éamonn Grimes and Richie Bennis in the centre of the field and Frankie Nolan. They were as near as you could get to a balanced team with the skill in the right areas and the strength in the right places. It was no surprise to us that they beat Tipperary and got through to the All-Ireland final.

I wasn't aware that Éamonn Cregan was such a good defender. I had played with him with the All-Stars and he was a fantastic forward to play with. It was a very big surprise and it was a brave move from the selectors because they were removing the most lethal forward in the game at the time from their attack. We had no prior knowledge of it until we saw the team selected; it raised a lot of eyebrows and we weren't sure if it was a decoy or not. It was very much a reality on the day and very effective.

We were struggling from the start of the game. The talk around Kilkenny was that the 1973 Leinster final against Wexford was the peak performance of that particular team, and from then on it was all downhill. I don't think Limerick were going to be stopped, and it wasn't so much the weakened team that had the effect but the playing pattern of the team. The team had come together as knowing each other's play very well and playing to a pattern. The players who came in were excellent – the likes of Claus Dunne and Brian Cody.

I think Kilkenny were struggling from the start because Limerick hit them with a power of hurling. One of the deciding factors was the great save by Séamus Horgan from Mick Crotty. To my mind, Kilkenny heads dropped after that, they thought they weren't going to be able to do it from there. A goal might not necessarily have changed the result, but Limerick really went on to victory from that point.

Phil Bennis enjoyed playing against Keher:

I always beat Eddie Keher. I had a great record on him, he rarely scored from play off me and I marked him several times. Claus Dunne scored all his frees in Keher's absence. Mickey Cregan was the first man to come in and do a bit of coaching. The team was never coached up to that, we just went out and hurled. Cregan got on well with Dick Stokes and Jackie Power and even though he was the trainer he did a bit of coaching as well. Mickey would always tell the selectors how positive the attitude of the players was. It was the first hard training that we had ever done. Before that we were jumping over stools and doing things like that. Maybe Mickey didn't vary it, but we did it and we did it hard. The attitude of the Limerick team was good in 1973.

Mossie Dowling of Kilmallock has no doubt who scored the goal in the 1-21 to 1-14 victory:

I scored the famous pushover try in the final. Ned Rea always tried to claim it, and I always say to him, 'How can you claim it? You didn't

(*L–r*) Mike Weekes, Joe McKenna, Pat Hartigan and Brother Gregory in
Carrickmacross, County Monaghan, with the McCarthy Cup.

even know where the ball was!' I hit the ball into Skehan, and he saved
it, and I followed it in and picked the ball up. The boys came in
behind me and pushed and the momentum carried me into the net. I
had the ball in my hand crossing the line, and once I was across the
line I threw it out of my hand. It was like Ginger McLoughlin's
famous try in Twickenham.

When we played in the 1973 Munster final, we all played in our
own gear; everyone was wearing different togs and socks. In 1973
when we won the All-Ireland, they made a concession to us: they told
us we could keep the jerseys. That time we got togs and socks – it was
a big treat.

*There is a legend told about the goal in Mossie Dowling's home territory.
When Kilmallock lost the All-Ireland club final to Sarsfields in 1993, Pat
Barrett scored their only goal and the team were drowning their sorrows in
Paddy McAuliffe's pub in Kilmallock the following night. Mossie Dowling was
also present. One of the players, Dermot Hanley, asked the house: 'Tell me, who*

was the first Kilmallock man to score a goal in Croke Park?' There was silence. Mossie was putting the chest out, waiting to be named. Then came the answer from Dermot: 'Pat Barrett yesterday, because Mossie Dowling scored a try.' The place erupted.

Willie Moore was not too worried about the quality of the goal:

It flogged rain all day. And the pushover try . . . they all count. The rules were different that time, you could charge the goalie that time and drive him back into the net. My attitude to 1973 was not to win it, but to make sure not to lose it. My real focus was on not losing it.

Frankie Nolan believes winning the Munster final was key:

There was more tension in the Munster final than in the All-Ireland final. Getting the 1955 thing off our backs was the biggest thing. The biggest difference in 1973 was putting Ned Rea at full-forward for the Munster final. It was ideal for me, they were all watching him, and Cregan and myself were free to pick up the pieces. I was in the corner and there was no need of standing on the end line for the 70 because it was the last puck of the game. So I stood out the field a small bit and as the ball went over the bar, I threw the hurley up into the air. It was definitely a point. Why would I be throwing the hurley in the air if the ball was going wide? They robbed us in 1971, so it was about time they paid us back in 1973; it wasn't as if we were taking Munster titles off Tipperary every year.

In the All-Ireland final, every single player fought for every single ball, and that doesn't happen every day. We hooked and blocked and tipped the ball away and never gave up. The crowd kept us going. At the time it was a relief to win it, but the sad part about it is that we didn't win one since. If we had one All-Ireland since from the ones we lost, we would be delighted.

Getting the first score in both of the 1973 and 1974 finals meant that I was awake from the very start and wasn't dreaming or looking out into the stand like some of the players in subsequent All-Irelands were. I was ready for every touch of the ball, and there was no waving at the crowd. The motto from Jackie Power and Dick Stokes was: teamwork. As I say to Richie, I got plenty of handy frees for him to tap over the bar.

Éamonn Grimes describes what it felt like to lift the McCarthy Cup:

It was a unique experience. It was thirty-three years prior to that when Limerick had won and coincidentally when we won the Harty Cup in '63/64 it had also been thirty-three years since the last victory. We were in the Crofton Airport Hotel after the All-Ireland, and supporters slept wherever the body took them. That time you would watch a video of the match and it was unbelievable. I didn't drink at the time, and I would say 70 per cent or 80 per cent of the team didn't drink either.

We are a mad sporting county and still are. Apart from the Dublin footballers, and perhaps Cork, we are there or thereabouts as regards passion from the supporters. I would hate to have been a garda trying to stop our supporters invading Croke Park. My father was a rugby man who won a Bateman Cup with Old Crescent in 1927. He had been badly troubled for a long time with the right hip, and was unable to walk without a stick. Such was the emotion at the end that he walked down from the stand and forgot all about the stick. It just goes to show the excitement.

Jim O'Brien was standing beside Grimes as he raised the cup:

Bringing an All-Ireland medal back to Bruree was a big thing, and we didn't know what was happening for a while. It's hard to beat Kilkenny twice, so it was a big achievement to beat them once. It was great to win in 1973 because 1971 had been a big disappointment with the dry ball. That day I was going back into the goals concentrating on the game and getting things ready for the free, and didn't know anything about it until afterwards. It was great to be on the right side of a result for a change.

All the corner-forwards were cute at the time. When you were playing corner-back you had to keep the head down and mind your own corner, because all the corner-forwards were great to get scores with half a chance. I had enough to do with my own corner.

Seán Foley also savoured the occasion:

It was an amazing experience going up to Croke Park for your first All-Ireland. Even though we had played Munster finals, Croke Park was a different scene. Incredible scenes. We weren't sure what would happen right up to the very end, two fast goals and that could have changed everything. The pitch was very heavy in the second half. It was a good team, we were a loyal bunch of players. The week after we won the All-Ireland I had to go to America with work. Someone told me I was lucky to have missed it.

Joe McKenna had been Limerick based since 1970 and joined South Liberties in 1972. He did not even play in the National League with Limerick in 1972/3, yet ended the year with an All-Ireland medal:

I played with Offaly right up to the end of the League. My first match with Limerick was against Clare in the championship. I didn't play in the Munster final or All-Ireland semi-final and for the All-Ireland final I came in when Cregan went back centre-back. When you win the All-Ireland at twenty-two, you think you are going to win many more. That time it was our first win; obviously there was a lot of celebrating done but we got back into it and to me the edge never returned although personally I played better hurling in 1974.

Jim Quaid pays no heed to those who focus on the absence of the Kilkenny players:

We won the 1973 All-Ireland anyway, whoever was or wasn't missing. Limerick won and the name is on the cup and everything else is history.

Liam O'Donoghue offers an interesting insight into the training methods of the time:

They talk about players being fitter today, and modern fitness and all that, but to go forty minutes either side of half-time, no problem at all, we mustn't have been too bad. We were very fit because we were doing a lot of that work. I trained under Mickey Cregan, Tim Crowe, John Sheehan and Dave Mahedy when I was playing. They say that fitness levels are way higher now than they were back then but I don't agree. We had Mickey Cregan in 1973 and after a day's work you would be afraid of going in and facing it, and you definitely wouldn't be having a cup of tea beforehand. I think the 1973 Munster final in particular shows you how fit we were, that we could play eighty minutes on one of the hottest days of championship hurling and you saw the score; it was a fabulous game.

Mickey Cregan elaborates:

It was very hard training, typical army style, boot and bollock with a bit of carrot and stick and the idea was to gel the players into one group, and improve morale. If you and I are equal in skill and I am first to the ball there is nothing you can do about it any more. I run around you, and leave you trailing behind me. It's that simple. The only way you can beat me is to out-think me and if you do get to the ball first I am behind you and I will stop you from playing, and you are nullified. You can't function in any game now unless you are supremely fit.

I did a six-month course in The Curragh, the first time in my life I was ever properly fit. I was able to run 5 miles and was still fresh enough to sprint. By keeping them in a group, everyone moved at the same level, even if it meant consciously holding back the harder runners to bring the weaker guys up to the level.

The group rarely fail if the morale is high. In the games in training it was competitive. Nobody wanted to go in marking Jim O'Brien in training because they would get nothing off him; it could cost them their place. He was hard as steel, he had deceptive pace and was physically very strong.

Éamonn Grimes was a strong character [laughs]. He had fixed views on a lot of things. You need people like that in leadership roles. You need a man to stand out. In addition to that he was a champion sprinter in school, and he ran all day in the 1973 final. Éamonn was a magnificent athlete. Mossie Dowling was the fastest of them all. We had six or seven sprinters on the team; all the midfield and forwards could run except Ned Rea and Richie Bennis. It would take a blackthorn stick to get Andy Dunworth going. The backs were in the second division in terms of their ability to move quickly but were very effective nonetheless.

Fr Liam Ryan, the captain of the 1955 Munster championship winning team, was determined not to miss the final:

I was in America in 1973 and I missed the Munster final. I was friendly with a lot of the Holy Ghost fathers and they invited me down to Brazil. I said I might get to Brazil again, which incidentally I didn't, but I might never get to see Limerick win an All-Ireland again. I came home for a week and I was glad I did.

J. P. McManus, a long-term benefactor and loyal supporter of Limerick hurling, was in the dressing room afterwards, as Pat Hartigan explains:

J. P. was the chairman of South Liberties, and a club-mate of Éamonn Grimes, Joe McKenna and myself. He was, and still is, a huge GAA supporter and found his way into the dressing room through the window. He was the only person to get into the dressing room that day that I can remember. He had to come in through the window because the doors were blocked. Once we saw him putting his head in through the window, we opened it up and dragged him through it. We certainly weren't going to leave him outside! A lot of other people tried to get in when they saw him getting in but they weren't so lucky and were locked out.

In torrential September rain, Limerick won their first All-Ireland for thirty-three years. And nearly forty years later, the county is still awaiting its next one. Five finals have been lost in that time, with glorious opportunities to claim the top prize particularly in 1974, 1980, 1994 and 1996.

FOUR

C3

1974–1979: FALLEN HEROES

In 1974 Limerick lost the League final comprehensively to Cork, but beat Waterford and Clare to win the Munster championship. Clare were beaten easily in the final, but in the Waterford game Limerick had been 3-11 to 1-10 down with twelve minutes remaining.

Kilkenny were once again their opponents in the All-Ireland final. Limerick surged into an early 0-6 to 0-1 lead but were undone by two rapid-fire Kilkenny goals in ninety seconds. Séamus Horgan was the goalkeeper:

We were well beaten, we didn't play well on the day. The goals were a killer blow. It was a wet day and for the third goal, the ball hit the ground and it just glided along the surface under me, it didn't hop or anything. I was so sure I was going to take it up. It would have been worse if we hadn't won the All-Ireland the year earlier. If we had got one All-Ireland from the two in both the 1980s and the '90s you would take them too.

Donie Flynn became involved with the under-21 team in the 1970s:

We had good solid teams each year but unfortunately we came up against Cork teams of great talent with Jimmy Barry-Murphy, Tom Cashman, Johnny Crowley, Diarmuid McCurtain and many others. I believe that an excellent opportunity was lost to promote and advance hurling in Limerick city at that time. The hub of something great was there and with the reduced input from the Christian Brothers, decline set in.

There were a number of reasons why Limerick failed to retain their title in 1974. The celebrations took their toll on the players. Preparations were interrupted because Mickey Cregan was away on overseas duty with the army and the team holiday was very late in the spring of 1974. The appetite and desire to win among the players had diminished having reached the promised land. Two local factors also had an effect: the decision to throw South Liberties out of the 1974 county championship, and the row between Tom Ryan and Richie Bennis in a club game.

Bernie Hartigan feels the row had an effect in the 1974 final, his last in a Limerick jersey:

We started well in the 1974 final and were flying it but they got two quick goals. Pat [Hartigan] was blown up for a foul that wasn't and they [Kilkenny] got a goal from the free and were back in the game, after we had all the hurling done. Richie Bennis and Tom Ryan were put off in a club game not long before the All-Ireland. That row didn't do any good for the team; people were saying afterwards that we would have been better off if they got three or four months.

I didn't hurl any more after the 1974 All-Ireland. I was a hammer thrower and a discus thrower. I did a lot of athletics for a good few years after that but played very little club hurling. Being taken off in both All-Ireland finals was a disappointment. I was just after scoring a point in 1973; it wasn't my happiest game but I was still doing as well as anyone. It's water under the bridge now.

Phil Bennis also retired after the final. He had lost his place on the team:

I pulled out after 1974; I should have been on the team. Rory Kiely approached the selectors to play me because Eddie Keher was on the team and I always had a good record against him. I had a good record in the League that year against him as well. I came in at half-time for Tom Ryan and it was a pity we lost that. It was a match we should have won, we were five points up. They didn't do the training they should have done. Mickey Cregan had an awful job pushing them and pushing them. The attitude was wrong in 1974. We threw it away. If the attitude was as right in 1974 as it was in 1973, we would have won the All-Ireland that year. And it is Limerick's story for years and years. Attitude! You have to have the right attitude.

Some suggest the row between Richie Bennis and Tom Ryan was due to the fact that Phil Bennis and Tom were competing for the same place on the Limerick team. The feeling was that Richie wanted to undermine Tom in an attempt to get Phil back on the team, but Tom refutes this:

After the Munster final in 1974 myself and Richie got involved and were put off in a city championship game played at the Gaelic

Mike Weekes (*right*) in conversation with Canon Edmund Punch in 1974.

Grounds. That was a nasty bit of work. We were marking one another and a big row broke out. Nobody knows Richie better than me because we marked one another for twenty years in club matches between Ballybrown and Patrickswell. I would be centre-back and he would be centre-forward. He was the same Richie then that he is now; it had nothing to do with Phil or anything like that.

It only developed late on; there was nothing in the game before that. I was probably blamed for the incident myself, but it showed the intensity of club hurling at the time. I wasn't thinking of Limerick that night; I was playing for Ballybrown and Patrickswell were hammering us. They were rubbing salt into our wounds, and Richie would be very good at that, until he tried his case with me, that is. That was different then, he broke the rules and I did what I had to do. Rory Kiely was chairman and I said as I walked off the field that night that it was all fair in love and war. At that time I knew leaving the Gaelic Grounds that night, whatever Richie got, I would get the same. They could do without me, but they could hardly do without him. I was in a plea bargaining situation at that stage.

Richie Bennis gives his account:

That time you got a month's suspension and it happened exactly a month before the All-Ireland final in 1974. I was going through with the ball; we had Ballybrown well beaten and I suppose I was swanning and acting the bollox a bit in fairness. Well, Tom drew a flake and he nearly broke my hand. I thought it was gone. So I just turned around and let go. There was a free for all then and that was it. We were blamed for starting the row. Nobody had any explanation for it. I never took anything off the field, I don't believe in that. Keep it between the white lines whatever happens. It was unreal. There was big headlines on the national papers and everything.

We were suspended for a month and got back the Saturday night before the final. If we missed the All-Ireland through suspension there would have been war. We might have been better off [laughs]; they might have won it. That's what Christy Murphy, the chairman of the city board, used to say: 'If I suspended ye for longer we might have won the f***ing thing.'

Tom Ryan had earned the nickname 'Timber Tom' in the 1970s. Mossie Dowling explains:

Tom Ryan would spare nobody. He hated the sight of Richie Bennis and Éamonn Cregan in club games so it was no surprise that the row happened. In another match Tom was marking Cregan. Cregan put his hand up and caught the ball, and turned around and gave a smart comment to Tom. Tom said to him, 'Put up your hand for the next one,' and Cregan replied, 'You won't stop me anyway.' After the next ball came between them, Cregan was on his way to the Regional with a broken finger, and Tom was saying, 'I told you not to put up your hand.' But, to be fair to Tom, he would always tell you what he was going to do to you.

Pat Hartigan outlines another controversy that took its toll in 1974:

I often felt that Bernie [Hartigan] was a victim of circumstances and he scored an important point in 1973, I could see no reason to take him off and we hadn't a great panel and I didn't think there was anyone better on the subs to replace him. In any event, you needed strength and endurance in both finals and there was nobody better to give you that. If anyone had that, Bernie had it. I thought taking him off in both finals was totally unnecessary.

1974 was a special year, because we had laid the ghosts of Clare to rest in the Munster final. I wouldn't say that we took it easy in 1974. I got injured in the Munster final; I had five weeks with no training before the All-Ireland final. There was a rumpus with the county board because Liberties wanted to get a championship game with Doon postponed to allow me to recover. The county board, having said they would call off the fixture, went ahead and played the match. South Liberties didn't show up and were thrown out of the county championship, so that rolled over into the Limerick camp. Doon got the walkover in the East final and that certainly didn't help the spirit in 1974. To win an All-Ireland you want everything going well. In 1973 everyone played well and five or six played blinders, but in 1974 ten played well and five fell below their level.

You had two discrepancies – the South Liberties situation and the Tom/Richie situation – and with that you had the Patrickswell boys who didn't like what went on with Tom. I was hurling with the Doon players, Willie Moore, Jim O'Donnell and Jim Allis, and we had no problem with them. However, there were county board guys close to the team, and the fact that we were thrown out didn't rest easy with us in their presence. The county board threw us out and I think the

Munster Council subsequently backed that. I was in hospital and I was convinced the match was off. I am not going to say that Liberties weren't right in hindsight not to play the game, but as it happened I wasn't going to be able to play for Liberties anyway because I was out injured for a few weeks.

Not surprisingly, after Limerick won the All-Ireland in 1973 for the first time in thirty-three years, the team celebrated long and hard. This was bound to have an effect for the following campaign, as Mossie Dowling outlines:

After the All-Ireland final we were celebrating for twelve months afterwards, non-stop everywhere, the carry on was ridiculous. It was night out after night out. After thirty-three years I suppose every club wanted a bit of you. Everyone wanted a part of you going into a pub. Five or six of the players would go with the cup wherever it went.

Éamonn Grimes, as captain, felt the burden more than most:

I have to say that the celebrations lasted too long. At that time every club had a dinner dance. Paddy Ryan was manager in the Parkway at the time and it was the only place that would hold 400–500 people. I remember being there thirteen out of fourteen nights at one stage. Then the cup had to go to every club, every parish and every school. As captain, the demands were greater and it was draining on a body; you just couldn't keep it up. For a finish I had to delegate. But having said that, it was a lovely feeling being the captain of a successful team, and I would take it back all over again, and so would many more.

I thought it was an achievement to even get to the All-Ireland final [in 1974] considering everything that had happened and where the cup was taken from January on. And there had to be celebrations, not having won it since 1940. A year earlier, Séamus Horgan made a fantastic save in the final, but it didn't happen in 1974. Whatever was with us in 1973 there was nothing going to stop us, but that wasn't the case in 1974. I suppose on top of that, Kilkenny had a point to prove.

Eddie Keher feels Kilkenny had to deliver in 1974:

We were under a lot of pressure in 1974 in the sense that supporters were saying we now had our full team and would beat Limerick. It's something I don't agree with at all. No matter who was out there, Limerick would have beaten them in 1973. One of the goals in 1974 was fortunate. We were starting to apply pressure then, and that was the start of it and once we got started there was no stopping us.

I think that Limerick had done it, had a great All-Ireland win, a wonderful achievement and that team was probably fêted and lauded around the county, having been the first to have won it for so long and it was going to be very hard to get back with the attitude to win the next year, and we were obviously a hungrier team. That was a wonderful Limerick team, and our team of that era was also very strong. We had a great bunch of players together and Limerick were the same, so it was a toss of a coin between the teams. The hunger that the respective teams had decided both finals.

Tom Ryan feels the evenness of the teams was not reflected on the scoreboard in either final:

The game I would look at to compare the two teams was the Whitson tournament in Wembley in 1974. That was one of the best hurling games I ever participated in. It was a draw at full-time. They played five minutes a-side extra time and Kilkenny won narrowly. It was a fantastic game of hurling, a true reflection of the parity between the teams.

Mickey Cregan found it difficult to train the team in 1974:

I went overseas in October 1973 and came back in April 1974 to find the lads were still in San Francisco. Getting them moving again wasn't easy. They became too close. Soccer managers get fired, but it's the players that aren't performing. Alex Ferguson has got rid of big name players. You can bring an ordinary guy up to a high level of performance quite easily but he has to be with the group. If you have guys slipping away for pints, they have to be gotten rid of. They undermine the whole purpose of unity. After victories, unless there is strong management in place, celebrations can get out of hand.

We won the League and the Oireachtas in 1971; suddenly people become invincible and become All-Stars. 'Who is going to tell me what to do?' That had a lot to do with losing in Ennis in 1972. That's what happened also after 1973 – we had six or seven All-Stars, they were off to the States on holidays, sure, they were coming down from the high of the trip. What chance had they? I think it was appalling to have a trip so late in the year even if it was the done thing at the time. Everything should stop on 31 December, back to training.

We trained very hard in 1974 but it was after the Munster final. They were mentally exhausted. I pushed them too hard too late, but I had no choice because the work wasn't done. It was a chance that didn't work but you couldn't go out with a whimper. The momentum had gone by 1975 and 1976. We were going, going, gone.

Willie Moore's inter-county days finished soon after:

There was too much recreation looking back on it, but we did get to the final at the same time. It's very hard to put two All-Irelands together, the surprise element is gone and teams are waiting in the long grass and Kilkenny, of all teams, with all their players available, were always going to be tough. I was more or less eased out of it after 1974. They went for change and I wasn't too disappointed, I got more out of it than I ever expected to get.

Éamonn Cregan feels that, having tasted success, the players were satisfied with their lot and were not prepared to push on:

The All-Ireland success was part of a five-year plan, a culmination of effort over the previous five years. We got to finals and lost them, but in the process we learned how to win. Those League games seasoned the team, and put the team through high intensity matches, so that by the time the 1973 final came a lot of the team were twenty-seven or so and knew how to win it. The 1971 League was one step in that process. After 1973 we didn't want to win any more. We wanted to win but the heart wasn't there. We reached a pedestal and were prepared to settle for lower standards.

In 1974 we had players training who didn't put 100 per cent in and they hid. That malaise spread through the team, and if players thought they could get away without putting it in, they tried it and then the next player tried it. And then, six weeks before the All-Ireland final, the trainer told us that we hadn't trained properly and we made a big effort with six weeks to go. But we weren't at the same peak as we were in 1973. But we still won Munster easily, we got away with winning. Prior to the 1974 Munster final against Clare I had food poisoning for three weeks. It didn't go away and I didn't know if I would last. Before the game I took a drop of brandy to settle the stomach. I never drank in my life. After the game and when the match was over it was a case of going straight to the toilet. Unfortunately it made me weak that summer and nobody knew it except the Limerick

Captains Seán Foley (Limerick) on the left and Nicky Orr (Kilkenny) on the
right pose for a photograph with referee John Moloney prior to the toss
in the 1974 All-Ireland final.

players. I was marking Noel Casey in that game and if he knew, he
would have run through me.

A mistake was made in 1973 and 1974: instead of promoting the
game and getting every guy hurling we went off and we celebrated.
The mistake was made by the county board.

Ned Rea was not impressed either with the effort put in:

I was amazed with the attitudes of some of the players in 1974, I
mean we should have been going hell for leather for another one. We
were doing all right, We won the Munster championship, and we
scored twelve goals in two consecutive Munster finals in 1973 and
1974. I was down for two goals but I think I got three. We were
straight into the All-Ireland and I remember in training one night –
being a senior player and one of the oldest – stopping them at the city

end left hand corner and saying we have got to cop ourselves on and start taking this seriously.

I was very disappointed with the attitude of some of the players. Limerick hadn't got to a Munster final from 1956 to 1971 and, all of a sudden, we got to an All-Ireland final and we hadn't been in an All-Ireland final since 1940 and we won it. All of a sudden, we had a chance of making it two and you don't get those chances every day in Limerick. You might in Kilkenny or Cork but not in Limerick, and when you get them you have to take them. If I had a choice I would have preferred to have lost 1973 and won 1974. I think we would have appreciated it more having lost one first; you are on an upward curve, the other way we were in decline.

Tom Ryan believes the signs were there from an early stage in 1974:

I thought we were better in 1974, the team was playing better and a couple of players had come on the team and we had matured a bit. We didn't do justice to ourselves in the 1974 All-Ireland final and it was decline after that. The decline was caused by dissent, by nobody taking the thing by the scruff of the neck.

When you are at that level you can't have players pulling in different directions. Different factions were beginning to form through 1974, you had a lot of roguery going. You had factions between three clubs, Patrickswell, Claughaun and South Liberties. They held the whip hand.

We lacked leadership on and off the field. Jackie Power and Dick Stokes had a rough time and found the players hard to handle in 1974. Things got very strained. It got so bad they had to call a convention of the players early in the year. We were called into the Shannon Arms one Sunday for a day. This was a kind of open, talk out your mind type of session. Whoever thought it up, it was a good idea. The factions and relations had become so strained that they decided they would have an open meeting.

However, that was the day Limerick hurling really went downhill. Looking at it and listening to the comments, it was pathetic really to hear players who had won All-Ireland medals the year before complaining about training being too hard. We were in the blame game then. Every player was wrong except themselves.

At that time they definitely had enough of Mickey Cregan. Mickey was a good, tough trainer, which he needed to be. If you are a player and that goes against you, you can turn sour and can bring your pals along and go on a half strike, or down tools in an unofficial sort of way. The Cork strikes didn't start today or yesterday, but a lot of players don't even want to remember them. Push it to one side, and pretend that never happened; but it did happen and there's no denying it.

Matt Ruth played in the 1974 final but was off the panel soon after. Richie Bennis believes Limerick lost a good talent:

Matt Ruth went down and won two All-Irelands afterwards with Kilkenny so he must have been a very good hurler. He wasn't appreciated. He was with Old Christians, and they were always knocked out early on in the championship, so he was never in the limelight where he could be seen. He was teaching in Limerick CBS so Old Christians were the club associated with the school.

Denis Barrett says changes made during the game just did not work out:

Matt Ruth was a good forward but didn't do the trick on the day. Taking off Bernie Hartigan was the only problem we had as selectors when I was involved. We couldn't agree on that. I couldn't see that he had done anything wrong. At that stage in the final we were looking for speed, and we introduced Paddy Kelly who had the speed, but it didn't work out on the day. We probably wouldn't have pulled it back in 1974 but with two pucks of the ball you don't know.

Following the 1974 defeat, Limerick's fortunes dipped; they lost the Munster finals of 1975 and 1976 to Cork. Indeed, in the All-Ireland and League finals of 1974 and the Munster finals of 1975 and 1976, Limerick were beaten by an aggregate total of forty-eight points. Tipperary, Clare and Waterford were not at their best in 1975 and 1976, though Clare picked it up in 1977 and 1978 under Justin McCarthy, and beat Limerick in both those years in the Munster championship. In 1979 Limerick reached the Munster final again. Joe McKenna recalls the period:

By the time we got to 1976 we were changing players, and there was a valley period for 1976 and 1977. We started to improve in 1978 and we got to the semi-final of the League. We were building again and in 1979 we did well in the League and were doing well in the championship up to Pat Hartigan's injury.

Éamonn Cregan does not have fond memories of 1975 or 1976:

We drew with Tipp in Thurles in 1975 and won the replay. I suffered a hamstring injury that year and didn't know what it was. Nobody knew how to treat it. I was marking Willie Walsh and after ten minutes the hamstring went, and I said I couldn't run any more and they put me in full-forward. We had won the All-Ireland and were on a downward turn. We went down to the second division of the League that year and we just weren't up for the Cork game in 1975. The game in 1976 was peculiar in that the players would have picked a different team to the selectors. I remember going through the game and for twenty-two minutes didn't touch the ball because it was going over my head wide, wide, wide. Cork were ahead by about ten points at half-time, and the team was changed to what the players felt it should be with a full-back line of Pat Heffernan, Mike Barron and Jim O'Brien, with Pat Hartigan going out to centre-back. The second half was a different game, but we were leaking in too many places. We still came to within four points of them at one stage.

In 2007 after Limerick had beaten Tipperary in the League at Nenagh, Micheál Ó Muircheartaigh asked Richie Bennis about the last time he played. Richie told him it was 1975, that he was dropped soon after. 'You never forget those things,' he added. Bennis outlines the circumstances:

I played in the Munster final against Cork in 1975 and was corner-forward that day but I was dropped from the panel completely after that. It was a shock to the system. In 1976 I would only have been thirty-one and that wasn't old that time. In 1978 they brought me back, and I togged out as a sub but I was never brought on. I made an unmerciful effort. I remember playing at centre-forward against South Liberties. I was on Pat Hartigan and wanted to prove a point, which is a great thing for any man to do. I bate the s**t out of him. The following week on the paper I was called the forgotten man of Limerick hurling.

John Mulcahy was a selector at the time and disagreed with the decision to drop Bennis:

Politics are a big thing in Limerick hurling. In 1943 when I was playing, two Cappamore men got a Limerick jersey and played a League game even though they wouldn't be fit for the local team. That was the only day they were on, but they were always able to pick up a soft ticket for an All-Ireland because they wore the Limerick jersey. Richie Bennis nearly won the All-Ireland in 1973 on his own but two years after, they dropped him without trying him properly anywhere else. I was a selector that time and couldn't hold him on the team. In my first year as a selector, prominent players were trying to influence team selection and had no authority to do that. Some selectors were genuine but a lot of them were going as selectors just to get their name in the paper; there was no sincerity there. Once they got their name in the paper; you wouldn't see them any more at a club match.

Liam O'Donoghue comments:

In 1975 there was a bit of swapping around, players were leaving the panel and new players were coming in. Cork were beginning to become a bogey team for us. Down through the next couple of years, right up to 1980 we had a problem with Cork. The day we played Cork in Páirc Uí Chaoimh in 1976, Cregan got four goals and Mick Malone gave Tom Ryan a bit of a roasting. I was brought back to mark Mick in the last twenty-five minutes. That was the end of Tom and the start of my career as a wing-back.

Tom Ryan says the venue for the game was an issue:

We went to Cork in 1976, but it was a mistake going down there. It was a total new environment for us; we hadn't been there. Things went wrong that day for us; Cork got the run on us and gave us a bit of a hammering.

Páirc Uí Chaoimh, opened in 1976, is the only GAA stadium where the perimeter is completely uniform in a bowl-type structure. This increases the noise from the crowd and creates an intimidating atmosphere, as Pat Hartigan explains:

Cork had lost the All-Ireland semi-final in 1975 to Galway. They came back in 1976 where the supporters in the new stadium were worth five extra players to them, and it resembled a cauldron.

Mossie Dowling has strong views on 1976:

I was dropped in 1974. Politics! If I was on the team in 1974, I would have been captain because Kilmallock were county champions. They wanted their own man as captain so I had to get the bullet. It wasn't because I was hurling badly, because I didn't play in the games. I was out in San Francisco and I had two games out there against the All-Stars and I was man of the match in the second game. In 1975, I was called back again. Kilmallock didn't have many players, considering we were champions in 1973, 1974 and 1975. Jackie McCarthy became a Limerick player in 1981 when he was in his thirties and nearly finished hurling. He should have been on in the 1970s.

Kilmallock challenged the Limerick senior team to a match in 1974 or 1975 and they refused to play us. We played the Cork under-21s that time; Christy Ring was the trainer and we beat them by eighteen or nineteen points, and they won the All-Ireland easily enough.

I came on as a sub in 1976 in Cork and they beat us, and I told the selectors to shove it at that stage. Éamonn Cregan had too much of a say that time. In general, the big names all had too much of a say. Player power was around that time as much as it is now, except that in those days they kept it a lot quieter. If your face doesn't fit you are totally out.

They put me on in 1976 when the match was over, but Limerick got three goals after I went in. They had this tactic in training before the game where the midfielders would bat down the ball to the half-forwards. We were training in St Patrick's field, and they had two players on McKenna and O'Donoghue. It went fine for a while and the half-forwards were scoring. Next thing they put Jackie McCarthy and myself in there and we knew the tactic, so all we were doing was flicking the ball away. Whoever was training us that day threw a ball at McCarthy and myself and told us to puck around on our own, that we were only spoiling their plan. I said, 'Do you think the Cork fellas are eejits?' And the plan worked in the match for the first puck-out, but after that the Cork players copped it and started flicking it away the same as we were doing.

Phil Bennis has his own ideas on how Limerick lost to Clare in 1977:

We should have won but Éamonn Cregan refused to accept that he was full-forward and kept going out the field. Séamus Durack was allowed to play almost like a full-back. We would have won if Éamonn accepted authority and stayed inside. He didn't and was nearly taken off at half-time.

Mike Fitzgerald was a minor selector throughout the 1970s and there was sterling work being done to ensure that talent was nurtured to replace those who were retiring post-1973:

The minors were hammered in 1971 by 10-17 to 1-5 [by Clare in the Munster championship] and we set about improving things. I was there consistently as a selector from 1972 to 1977, working with different people such as 'the Jap' [J. P. Ryan], Seán Heffernan, Seán O'Connor and Éamonn Cregan. The minor team improved dramatically; we were in a few Munster finals. Players like Tommy Quaid, 'Bomber' Carroll, Paddy Kelly, Mike Barron, Dom Punch, Dave Punch, Seán Herbert, Pa Foley, Ger Moloney, Ollie O'Connor, Mossie Carroll and Jimmy Carroll all came from those minor teams and went on to represent the Limerick seniors. It's the first time in Limerick that I believe that there was organised training for the minor championship. I believe it was very scant prior to that, maybe a trial, very old-fashioned preparation, even when they got to finals. It was post-1971 that there was an upsurge in preparation.

Pat Heffernan was on the minor team of 1963 but subsequently emigrated to London. He was back in the Limerick squad from 1975 onwards:

We came up against some excellent Cork teams. We had a great team in 1975 and 1976, but we were in hard luck that the Cork three-in-a-row team was emerging. In 1976, Éamonn Cregan scored 4-1 and we still lost badly. You would expect that with any forward scoring 4-1 that you would be in with a chance. Clare were coming then in 1977 and 1978 and they had one of the best half-back lines in the country – Ger Loughnane, Seán Stack and Seán Hehir.

Pat Hartigan was a centre-back by then but was far more comfortable at full-back:

I had a run at centre-back in the second half of 1976, and in the championships of 1977 and 1978. Some say you have more control of the game at centre-back but I disagree. I preferred full-back. I felt I had more control of the game at full-back. I think you can contribute more because generally speaking the ball has to come into you. Once I covered an imaginary semi-circle I was in control, whereas at centre-back they can draw you away and find a way around you. In 1979 Clare tried to draw me out from full-back, and I only went half way so

Clare didn't know whether to go back in or to draw me out further. There weren't many goals scored when I was full-back.

In 1979 Limerick were shaping up well – until disaster struck. They had beaten Waterford and Clare comfortably in high scoring games, and were training for the Munster final against Cork when Pat Hartigan suffered a horrific eye injury that ended his career:

We were playing backs and forwards and I had been injured the previous week against Clare so I was late for training. I was supposed to have been getting some physio at the South Liberties grounds whose team were due to be training too. That session was cancelled, so I decided to head into the Gaelic Grounds where Limerick were training. There was a twelve-a-side match, and it was a windy night and I was on Éamonn Cregan. I said to Éamonn that I was going out the field and he said that if I was going he was going with me. A ball came across and I just cleared it and one of the lads pulled with me and the ball spun up and hit me in the eye. I knew I was in trouble immediately. When I came out of hospital I got eye guards, which weren't much help. It was only after that incident that facial protection became an issue.

I trained for the Munster final against Cork. I had come out of hospital on the Thursday week before the final, and I went to the Gaelic Grounds with Noel Drumgoole. We were pucking away and next thing he took a shot and missed it and I was still waiting for the ball. I knew then that I wasn't going to make it. I don't have any judgement of distance or depth and I couldn't recognise how near or far away the ball was from me. I said that it's not going to work, and I only had sight in one eye. I went to a lot of specialists worldwide and failed to get any improvement. I have a small bit of peripheral vision. I see outlines and that's about it.

Cork were a great team, they won five Munster titles and three All-Ireland titles. Once Cork started to wane, Limerick began to come good. We may not have beaten Cork in 1979, even if I was playing, because Cork won well in the end. When I lost out, Jim O'Brien came out of retirement, which was unfair on him because he hadn't hurled with Limerick at that level that year. Joe Grimes was the other option. I feel it was a monumental mistake not trying to work with Joe, who had been on the panel, and if it didn't work out, Jim could have been used as a backup.

I think my injury was a bigger problem for Limerick in 1980, 1981 and 1982 than it was in 1979. The team was beginning to gel by then. I was only twenty-eight when I got injured on 21 June 1979, I wouldn't have been twenty-nine until August. 1980 and 1981 would have suited me; things were beginning to gel, and we had some of the greatest players still remaining from 1973.

If the 1980 team won the All-Ireland, which they should have won, they would have gone on to win a lot. It would have broken my heart to play in and lose the final in 1980. We had endured so much heartbreak from 1975 to 1979, to come back strongly from that by winning Munster in 1980 only to lose the All-Ireland final would have killed me. If we were told in '73 and '74 that we had Galway and Offaly left to play in the championship, we would say that we would win both All-Irelands. If we don't win both, we will definitely win one, but we lost both. The All-Irelands of 1980 and 1981 were definitely there to be won, we had a real hunger gotten back. By 1979 we were doing everything to win an All-Ireland. The drive in 1979 was phenomenal. We knew what it was like to lose a final and how difficult it was to get back there. Cork were beginning to slide and Clare were really nowhere. Galway were starting to build momentum.

If I had been full-back in 1980 it would have released Leonard Enright to centre field where he played very well in 1975. He was a fast, lively player and liked freedom. Even though he played very well at full-back it always looked to me in 1980 as if he didn't enjoy it there and there was a lot of pressure on him. If I made a mistake I took it in my stride, but if Leonard made one, everyone would have been saying he shouldn't be playing there in the first place.

Éamonn Cregan believes the planning for the 1979 Munster final left a lot to be desired:

On the Tuesday night before the '79 final management announced that Pat wouldn't play because of the eye injury. The match was lost in the dressing room that night. It was a crazy decision. The announcement should have been made three weeks earlier, the team would have accepted it and then if the announcement was subsequently made that he was available, it was a tremendous boost. If not, then we had already accepted it and we were going to go ahead without him.

The travel arrangements for the game were crazy as well. We were supposed to be in Thurles in Hayes' hotel at 12.30 but we were stuck in traffic outside in Holycross. There were four cars with nine players stuck in traffic for two and a half hours prior to that Munster final in 1979. Éamonn Grimes, Tommy Quaid, Joe McKenna and myself had to run a mile and a half to get into the stadium to be in time to play the match.

Jimmy Barry-Murphy acknowledges Hartigan's loss to hurling:

Ray Cummins was a huge player for us around that time, and with Pat out injured it was a massive psychological blow for them. In Cork, Pat would have had massive respect and he would undoubtedly have backboned Limerick for years to come. He was a massive loss to Limerick and to hurling in general. We were always aware of his stature as a full-back. I think they had no chance when Pat was gone. We were all devastated for Pat, he was such a popular figure in the game. It would have affected us as well in preparation for the game because nobody wants to see a fellow player's career ended like that.

George Ryan, who refereed the 1979 Munster final, agrees:

Pat Hartigan was one of the top players at the time, was a huge loss to Limerick and they suffered in subsequent years by not having him. I was a firm believer of being up with the play at all times, and his clearances didn't make life easy for a referee. It was possible to predict where the clearances from most players would land, but Hartigan could be under pressure from three or four players and still manage to drive the ball 100 yards downfield, meaning that catching up with play was difficult.

Éamonn Cregan was one of the best players Limerick had in the 1970s, and he accepted every decision gracefully and I would regard him very highly. His undoubted class was proven by the fact that he excelled in the backs and the forwards at the highest level.

Limerick played in six Munster finals in the 1970s, winning only two. While most of those who played in the 1975 and 1976 finals had All-Ireland senior medals, the team was in transition in many ways. Indeed, by late 1979, Seán Foley, Éamonn Grimes and Éamonn Cregan were the only survivors from the team that beat Tipperary in the League final of 1971.

FIVE

ㅇ웅

1980–1981: BORN AGAIN

Despite Hartigan's injury, 1980 promised new beginnings for Limerick. Unlike the build-up to the 1979 Munster final, the players had time to accept that they would be without one of their leaders on the field.

In one of the shrewdest moves in the history of Limerick hurling, Leonard Enright was moved to full-back. A versatile player, Enright was sub-goalie on the 1971 League-winning panel, and throughout the 1970s made several appearances in defence and midfield for Limerick, while much of his club hurling with Patrickswell was played in his favoured position of centre field. He recalls Noel Drumgoole asking him to wear the number 3 shirt for the first time:

He asked me one night if I would play full-back. I said I would, that to have a Limerick jersey on my back, I was prepared to play anywhere.

Enright admits, however, that it took time to adjust to the new role:

I had nothing to lose, and over time I settled in. If I made a mistake in the first year, the management were blamed for playing me there; it was their fault, not mine. But it didn't take too long before all that changed and suddenly it became my fault [laughs].

There was an emphasis on bringing through new blood at the time. John Flanagan had represented Limerick at minor level in the early 1970s and, following an impressive championship with his club Feoghanagh in 1979, was called into the Limerick senior panel:

My first match was against Clare in Tulla in February 1980. There was fierce pressure on the team to deliver because they had a few bad League results prior to that and there was even talk of relegation. We were expected to win and we lost that as well.

Flanagan, a farmer and a physical hurler, would become a key player for Limerick over the next few seasons. Also called up was sub-goalkeeper Séamus O'Sullivan, whose club Tournafulla reached the county senior final in 1979:

We were defeated by Patrickswell, which was disappointing, but almost immediately afterwards I was drafted onto the Limerick panel.

Jimmy Carroll had returned from the US and would become a key player at midfield. He recalls a statement of defiance from Noel Drumgoole early in the season:

I remember at the first training session, in his distinct Dublin accent, he said to us, 'I am here to get ye to Croke Park next September.' Drumgoole was a great man, very influential in the dressing room, never used a swear word, and brought a whole new life to it. If we were to give credit to any one man it would be him.

Carroll recalls in particular the physical preparation:

We brought in Tim Crowe as trainer, he was an All-Ireland champion runner. We used to use the facilities in Thomond College and the training was so different that we loved it. And that's what made it. We couldn't wait to go training. We started off in November doing 300-m and 400-m runs and then we would have a break from that and we would go running on the riverbank. We used also do the three-and-a-half- or four-mile run down by the river at Thomond College. We used to do it in groups of three or four and that was tough enough if you did it a few times and you knew if you were fit enough or not.

Over a period of time we then worked on our sprinting. Paddy Kelly was a serious sprinter, a serious athlete and the name of the game was to beat Paddy. If you beat Paddy, you knew you were good enough. I think I achieved it one night in a 200-m sprint. It was like winning an All-Ireland but I nearly collapsed; I thought I was going to die after it. It was our first time using the Thomond College facilities. It was new to us and we were treated like gods inside there. We thought we owned the place and it made us feel good.

Carroll acknowledges, however, that he needed to work on his hurling if he was to succeed, and gives great credit to Éamonn Cregan:

Éamonn Cregan was a class act, probably the best player I ever played with. He was full of discipline, and I remember arriving at the Gaelic Grounds with two different socks one night and a gearbag that wasn't very posh looking. I went onto the field anyway and who was I pucking the ball across to only Éamonn. I was giving it as good as I

The Limerick players are marked absent after P. J. Molloy scores the
second goal against Limerick in the 1980 All-Ireland final. (L–r): Frank Burke,
Bernie Forde, P. J. Molloy.

was getting it, but there was a bit of a ping off my hurley and the hoop
was half off. Then we did running. I was fit at the time. I used to train
on my own twice a week in Cratloe hills, and it always stood to me.

I was training with Cregan this night anyway and I ran him off the
field. And he came out after me after training and I was putting my
gear into the boot of the car. And he says, 'Have you any real interest
in playing with Limerick?' I said, 'Why do you say that?' and he said,
'First of all, you came in with two socks that aren't the same,' and of
course I answered, 'I have a pair at home that are the same.' He didn't
particularly like that, but he had a good sense of humour as well, and
he said, 'Look, throw away that stick of a hurley, here's a proper hurley
for you, go home and bang a ball off the wall and keep at it for a few
days because you can't strike a ball off your left side.'

After that I came back in and I think he kind of took me under his
wing because I was still playing a lot of junior hurling, maybe holding
onto the ball too long, and maybe a big wide swing, and I would credit

him with getting a lot of that out of me. I would do anything I was asked to.

Throughout 1980, on Saturday mornings Carroll practised at the ball alleys at St Munchin's along with Liam O'Donoghue, Éamonn Cregan and Joe McKenna. He believes that it made a difference to his game:

There was an open back on the ball alley. I found this amazing, a full twenty-one game, hop the ball and toss it with the hurley full blast. And then we'd finish up with the alley cracker, and it would be coming at you at maybe 100 miles an hour, and you would whip on it and send it back and the next thing it would fly back out 50 or 100 yards into open yard. McKenna and Cregan used to play together – they were very clever – and O'Donoghue and myself spent a couple of months trying to beat them. Eventually it happened. That brought on my hurling unbelievably.

Before long, Limerick had overcome their patchy League form and reached the final against Cork. The Leesiders won it after a replay, but there were signs that Limerick were improving. After an impressive debut season in 1979, Brian 'Bomber' Carroll suffered from 'second season syndrome'. 'I didn't play well in the League final, and was dropped for the Munster championship,' he recalls.

The League final replay was fixed for Cork, even though the drawn game had also taken place there. This caused some controversy, as Éamonn Cregan recalls:

We thought the replay should have been in Limerick, but Cork got their way again and they beat us by 4-15 to 4-6. When we met them in the Munster final it took place in Thurles. Cork were looking for a home and away agreement but Limerick county board, to their credit, said no and we met them at the neutral venue. The replay of the National League final had rankled with the players. I knew the lads were saying, 'Jesus, they are not going to beat us again.'

Jimmy Carroll remembers the game:

They brought on Jimmy Barry-Murphy in the middle of the second half, and he won the game for them. We went into the dressing room afterwards and were a bit devastated, but not too much because we knew we had a good enough team. We knew we were going to meet Cork in the Munster final; we were confident of beating Clare in the semi-final.

Although Cork were League champions, Jimmy Barry-Murphy says they remained wary of Limerick. 'There was very little between the teams in the League final, and we were very conscious that Limerick were a very good team.'

John Flanagan recalls his championship debut in the first round game against Clare:

It wasn't an easy game but we got a result and it was on to the Munster final. I remember around that time Tim Crowe segregating some of us for extra training at the Na Piarsaigh grounds, and there was a deadly push to get Seán Foley, Mossie Carroll, myself and a few others fit. Seán Foley wouldn't grub after training. He might carry extra weight in the winter but when it mattered most he would shed it all.

The game, played at the Gaelic Grounds, saw Clare easily despatched, despite an early second half rally that brought them to within three points.

Sunday 20 July is one of those red-letter days in the history of Limerick hurling. From a gritty, tense encounter, Limerick emerged as Munster champions, ending years of heartbreak at the hands of Cork. It took two late pressure frees from the steel-nerved Éamonn Cregan to seal the game. Cregan gives great credit to the swashbuckling John Flanagan from Feoghanagh:

He was one of these wholehearted players, and when you spoke to him he listened. I had a few words with him before the match and as a centre-forward his objective was to break the ball, keep the ball going through.

Flanagan nearly missed the game following a late scare, as Jimmy Carroll recalls:

We were going into the dressing room, and he said to me in his west Limerick accent, 'Tell me Jimmy, have you anything for a headache?' 'Jesus, Johnny, what's wrong?' I replied. 'I can hardly see, I have an awful headache,' he said. Dr Richard Flaherty was our doctor and while the minor match was on, Johnny was put lying down on the seat with a towel over his face and he gave him a couple of Anadins or something; sure, they mightn't have been anything but they were something. And I remember Johnny got up anyway and says, 'I am right, I never felt this good.'

Flanagan has his own view:

I had a terrible headache before the final but I would say it was from tension and pressure more than anything else. Cork had beaten us in the League final and there was great pressure on the team. The other players would be used to that.

According to Cregan, Flanagan hit the ground running:

The first dropping ball that came he pulled on. He was as strong as a horse and he drove man, ball and all through the middle. He then crashed into Diarmuid McCurtain, then it was John Horgan, and also Martin Doherty. He totally unsettled them.

Flanagan remembers the collision with Doherty:

It would be in my nature to stop him even though he was twice the size of me. When we collided, I felt every bone in my face shaking. I had to get up and play away again; there was no such thing as lying down.

Jimmy Carroll recalls another incident:

Flanagan and McCurtain went for a breaking ball and collided, but Johnny got up and Dermot didn't. It was an unbelievable collision, but the two of them met fairly shoulder to shoulder. Johnny was a terribly strong man, and had a pair of shoulders on him that were unreal, yet there wasn't a bad blow in him, it was just pure toughness. Dermot McCurtain just folded and that was one of the main reasons we won that Munster final.

Cregan agrees:

You always need leaders in a match and Johnny was the leader that particular day because his sheer strength alone was enough to disrupt the entire Cork half-back line. I always remember the first goal; the ball came in and was hopping in along, and Timmy Murphy put his hurley down to block it. I was coming in from the left and next thing I could hear this pounding on the ground from Johnny Flanagan who was running in. I think the ball deflected off Timmy Murphy's hurley and it broke to me and all I did was tap it in. But it was the sound of the pounding feet of John Flanagan that caused it because in those days you could hit the goalkeeper.

Limerick did have an element of luck in the game, including a point by David Punch when the referee overruled an umpire:

Galway's Joe Connolly scores a crucial second-half point in the 1980 All-Ireland final. (L–r): Finbarr Gantley (Galway, No. 18), Joe Connolly, Leonard Enright (Limerick, No. 3), Bernie Forde (Galway, No. 13), Seán Foley (Limerick), Donal Murray (Limerick), P. J. Molloy (Galway) and Pat Herbert (Limerick, No. 17). The goalie is Tommy Quaid (Limerick) and the referee is Noel O'Donoghue (Dublin). Picture taken from Hill 16.

I think the reason we got that score was due to Joe McKenna going in disputing it with the umpire. I was credited with a score but I can truthfully say that the ball was about a foot wide.

Jimmy Carroll remembers running on empty near the end of the game:

One of their players was going through with the ball, and I thought I was going to die trying to catch him but eventually I hooked him. The ball was cleared but didn't Seánie Leary get it, and he pulled on the ball and it hit the butt of the post and rebounded out. I remember after the game Tommy Quaid went over and showed me where it hit the post and all I could say was, 'I should bless that.'

Seán Foley, captain that day, remembers the 'great desire to beat Cork' within the squad, while Mossie Carroll recalls the confidence in the side and the significance of the win:

That was a huge win because they had won three All-Ireland finals in a row, and we had lost the previous year's final to them. We had suffered at their hands a lot during the '70s. They would have been seen as an exceptional team. Naturally, going into a Munster final, you are going to be confident, but there was an acceptance that we had a nucleus of a good team capable of taking them on. We were closing the gap.

Jimmy Carroll concurs:

The attitude going down to Thurles that morning, the atmosphere in Hayes' hotel, for probably one of the only times I played with Limerick, was one of absolute confidence. Throughout every single player, there was no worry on anyone, we just went out with unbelievable confidence. We knew we were going to beat them, but that it was going to be a struggle at the same time.

Beating Cork in the final was particularly pleasing for Limerick, as Leonard Enright explains:

I suppose winning Munster in 1980 was the greatest highlight of all. It meant an awful lot to supporters. All I was ever doing was losing to Cork. We were beating Clare, we were beating Tipperary, they were beating us the odd time as well, on and off, but Cork were always beating us. And it was a Munster final and it meant so much to win a Munster final, but beating Cork before a full house was brilliant.

Liam O'Donoghue agrees:

We were trying to make a breakthrough in 1980 and hadn't won anything since '74. A lot of the public and the media had given us no hope, but we felt differently. There was wicked determination to win that game to get back on the map. Ollie O'Connor, who was a big find, scored that famous goal when John Horgan's hurley was thrown at him. I remember the celebrations on the local radio with Seán Murphy. The hype was unbelievable.

John Fenton, who had a first-half penalty saved, believes the game was a watershed for Cork:

It possibly signalled the end of a lot of the players that had won the three-in-a-row and probably meant that the selectors had to go back to the drawing board. The League final illustrated the difference between League and championship, and even though we won the League, Limerick still got a decent score against us. They probably learned more from defeat than we did from victory.

Jimmy Barry-Murphy believes Cork's League final success was instrumental in their missing out on a record sixth consecutive Munster championship:

Winning the League maybe took more out of us than we thought at the time. We had been there since 1975 and that was Limerick's chance to turn the tables. We still thought we would win, to be honest. When Ollie O'Connor got the goal, and two of our defenders collided, that was the turning point. It was a tremendous final and, in fairness, Limerick's time had come, they were due a win against us.

The seven-week break before the All-Ireland final on 7 September had a major impact, according to Joe McKenna. 'A four-week break is a long time, but having seven weeks is crazy.' However, the structure of the championship meant there was no alternative but to wait for the winners of the Galway and Offaly clash.

Dave Punch says the long wait particularly affected the younger players:

If you look at the guys who had played in 1973 and 1974, they knew what it was about. There were some of us and it was our first occasion and without a doubt it got to a lot of us.

One of those newcomers was Jimmy Carroll:

There were a few players on the team who never performed on the day and it was purely down to nerves. Why that happened, I will never know. We were well prepared and we were very relaxed going up. We stayed in the Green Isle hotel that night. I remember Noel Drumgoole took myself and Leonard Enright down to a local pub he knew up there, and we had a pint of Guinness each. Noel Drumgoole bought it, and we came back in the car with him, and were in bed by a quarter to eleven. We slept like logs and got up that morning and went to Mass and went out into the Phoenix Park and did all the right things. Yet the nerves probably even got to me a little.

Seán Foley feels they lacked a cutting edge against a very good side:

There was good belief in that team, but there was still an unsettled nature over that half-forward line and as a player you want things to be more settled. We were hungry but we didn't realise that there was massive hunger coming from the west of Ireland. They had fantastic hurlers too. We have to admit they were very strong on the day, on the ball, hard and fair. We didn't have the killer instinct to put anyone away in 1980. Galway were an exceptionally strong team. It was disappointing as captain to lose. At that stage I was there a good number of years and I would have always thought that there was another All-Ireland in us. We just don't seem to have that element of luck. Mind you, Mick Mackey seems to have had it when he was up there.

Leonard Enright feels the players simply failed to perform on the day:

Losing the All-Ireland was down to ourselves on the field. We were picked to play a game, played it, didn't win, no cribs, I don't blame anyone at all who was over us. We were out there to do a job and we didn't do it on the day.

A lack of scores from the half-forwards was a concern coming into the final. Willie Fitzmaurice had 0-3 to his name but John Flanagan had failed to score and Paudie Fitzmaurice started both of the earlier games in defence.

Flanagan acknowledges that Galway were the better team on the day:

They had lost two finals and were up for this one. A lot of our team didn't play to their Munster form, myself included. You need that bit of luck as well to win those types of matches.

Éamonn Grimes had seen it all before:

I suffered a severe groin injury in early 1980 and never really came back right. I was at the end of my tether anyway. We had two players on the team who had never been in Dublin, let alone Croke Park. As I walked out the tunnel, I was behind one of them, and he was shaking so much that he hit the two sides of the tunnel as a result of the roar of the crowd. That's my main memory from that game. The 1973 final was a completely hair raising experience. In 1980 it was different. There's no comparison between playing and going for the first All-Ireland title, and being a substitute, anticipating if you were going to be called or not. It was great to get on in the final, but it was just different. It's strange, having been central throughout my career, to being on the periphery, but if you have the love for it you are only too delighted to be involved.

Éamonn Cregan says poor organisation once more was to blame:

It was a match that again involved bad planning. The management had been asked to bring the team up to Croke Park the week before to show the players around. Some of the players had never been to Croke Park and it would have been in their best interests to go just to walk around. But it was decided there was no need. The team ran out onto the field in 1980 and the legs went weak on a number of players and they didn't hurl. I don't even look at the final of 1980 because the hurling was terrible. We were going reasonably well near the end and I tried to get a handpass in to Joe McKenna who was inside me and I only got it with the tops of my fingers and it was intercepted. If Joe got that ball inside we would have won, but that's a case of 'ifs, buts and maybes'.

Dominic Punch agrees that the lack of experience of playing at Croke Park unsettled Limerick:

The disadvantage of being favourites and the fact that most of the team had never walked Croke Park, let alone played there, was a hindrance. It's quite daunting going out onto Croke Park for your very first time, let alone playing in an All-Ireland final. For the second goal, P. J. Molloy got the ball and everyone stood up thinking it was going to be a free. It was a split-second thing; we stood, still expecting the whistle and suddenly it was in the net.

Jimmy Carroll has regrets surrounding a change made in the game:

The one thing I remember about that match is that it went so fast. One of the most frightening experiences I ever had was when the whistle was blown for half-time; I just couldn't believe that there were thirty-five minutes gone.

Then we made a change that I was never happy about, taking off Mossie Carroll. It was a serious mistake. It was known that time, by the pundits and by all of us, that Mossie wasn't finishing games that well. Mossie did find it difficult enough to get to full fitness, but he always got there. It was a bad decision, because he probably had one of his finest games. The decision to take him off was a reflection on other games he had played during the year rather than that one. We discussed it afterwards and there were a few of us who were very annoyed. OK if he did go on and get tired, which I don't think he was going to, well then, the move could have been made, but sure, he was absolutely flying it when he was taken off. He was hurling the best of the six backs as far as I was concerned.

Mossie himself reflects on the overall outcome:

It was a huge disappointment, we didn't really perform on the day and it was a game that was there for the taking. It was disappointing from everyone's point of view, it was a title that everyone felt was left behind us. Not taking anything from Galway, but it was a huge opportunity to make a breakthrough as far as we were concerned.

Richie Bennis throws some light on the issue:

Mossie Carroll was known as a half hour man at the time. They had decided going up to that final that, irrespective of how Mossie was playing, they were going to take him off. Tony O'Brien himself told me that. Mossie was giving an exhibition, and they did take him off and Galway came into the game then. Would he have lasted the pace if he stayed on? As Charlie Haughey would say, 'That's hypothetical now.' But there was no logic to replacing him, you cannot pre-empt anything. If a player is on his game, you can't take him off.

Éamonn Cregan feels Carroll may have had his best hurling done:

Mossie was a tremendous hurler, very skilful, but he was notorious for hurling for only thirty minutes. That was his form at the time; he would play tremendous stuff, left, right, he would drive ball all over the field. When you are playing centre-back you can't afford to allow the ball go through the middle. For thirty minutes Mossie played tremendous hurling and then suddenly he disappeared out of the game. I suppose the selectors felt at this stage he had played his All-Ireland.

It's an awful thing to be taken off in an All-Ireland final. Bernie Hartigan was taken off twice, in my view unfairly. Today it's different because you have a panel and you have what are called impact subs who come on at various stages and that's understood. That time you were taken off because you were playing badly, and that the selectors felt you were playing badly.

According to Ned Rea, one of the 1973 heroes should have been on the panel:

They should have definitely won in 1980. Paudie Fitzmaurice became a great defender after and won an All-Star but you had three of a kind in the half-forward line, there was a need for more balance in that line. A player of the experience and ability of Frankie Nolan should have been there. If Frankie was playing that day we would have won. He was still playing in 1983, yet wasn't playing in 1980. It was crazy; there was a lot of that stuff going on. Every selector had their own ideas on their own player, and opinions differ. It's definitely accurate to say that some unusual team selections have cost Limerick games down through the years. I also think in the early '80s the All-Stars became a big factor and if players got sent off they didn't receive All-Stars. I think it may have stopped players from being as physical as they could be. I personally would prefer an All-Ireland medal.

Frankie Nolan was in the stand that day and found it 'very sad looking down on the field', while Stephen McDonagh reckons Éamonn Cregan gave 'the best individual performance I have ever seen in an All-Ireland final'.
Jimmy Carroll recounts the pain of defeat:

I remember coming out of the dressing room in 1980. Not a nice place to be, a losing All-Ireland dressing room. There aren't too many places you can hide after that. But when we were inside Noel Drumgoole said, 'Lads, I told ye last year that I'd get ye to Croke Park and didn't we achieve it? I am telling ye now I will get ye to Croke Park again next year but ye will win it.' And that lifted us all. OK, we all went away for a few drinks and a bit to eat and stuff, but we actually felt that we never got the heads down because we were so confident that the team was going to come back and win another one.

Con O'Connell of the 1958 All-Ireland minor winning team was probably the only Limerick man who could draw consolation from the result in 1980:

Johnny Butler in Doon was selling lines for a draw for a car, you had to guess the correct score for the All-Ireland final between Limerick and Galway. I had predicted the correct score and won £100.

In 1981 Limerick lost Mossie Carroll, who had transferred to Tipperary:

At that stage I had moved to work in Chadwicks and I had bought a house in Clonmel. Like any young fella in his early twenties, I wanted to move out of home and the job offered me an opportunity to do that. I was living in the town, and St Mary's were a club I had done a bit of training with at the time. The burden of travel and the fact that I had a house bought there was the main reason. It had no bearing on being taken off in the All-Ireland final. It was a big move from my own point of view.

Jimmy Carroll feels Mossie was a huge loss:

Mossie would have made a serious difference. He was a strong physical man, had a great delivery, and great hands. He was your perfect centre-back; he might not have been as pacy as others but he was always able to do the job. He was a major loss. Mossie brought discipline and honour into the dressing room and people looked up to him. Even though I went to school with Mossie and we were the same age, I would always have had massive respect for Mossie and he commanded that respect.

I'd say there was very little done to stop him. I can't figure this out. A man we all had so much respect for was 'the Jap' Ryan. He was a tremendous man around a dressing room because of his attitude. He was very confident and he was very funny about incidents that would happen, and he took away a lot of the pressure. Plus he was a big influence in the running of that team and he was a big influence on the county board and he always asked the questions that people didn't want to hear. He was a very good friend of Mossie. I was surprised that 'the Jap' couldn't do more. Maybe he did more and I didn't know anything about it.

I think Mossie probably got very upset and he was such a deep individual I think he probably took it personally. Plus he was working in Tipperary at the time, and I'd say they were on to him and putting pressure on him the whole time. If he hadn't been working in Tipperary it might have been a different story. The transfer was done and dusted very quickly. I know I went to him on numerous occasions, and any time I went to him I could get a sense of hurt. He wasn't the same after that. Tommy Quaid and myself went to him and I kind of knew the writing was on the wall. Even though he didn't say anything bad, because he didn't have a bad word in his mouth, you got the feeling that he had enough.

He was getting on well with management through the year. You had to get on well with Mossie because he was a gentleman; he would never say anything out of context and he would be very loyal. I think

The Limerick team that beat Clare 3-12 to 2-9 at Thurles to retain the Munster title in 1981. *Back row (l–r):* Joe McKenna (South Liberties), Paddy Kelly (Kilmallock), Dominic Punch (Patrickswell), Leonard Enright (Patrickswell), Éamonn Cregan (Claughaun), Tommy Quaid (Feoghanagh), John Flanagan (Feoghanagh). *Front row (l–r):* Liam O'Donoghue (Mungret), Seán Foley (Patrickswell), Jimmy Carroll (Hospital/Herbertstown), Mikey Grimes (South Liberties), Paudie Fitzmaurice (Capt.) (Killeedy), Brian 'Bomber' Carroll (Garryspillane), Pat Herbert (Ahane), Vincent 'Ollie' O'Connor (Ballybrown).

he did feel that some people had this thing that he wasn't finishing games strong; once that perception gets into fellas' heads, it's hard to stop it. That's why he was taken off in the final and I think once that stigma gets out and sticks, it's like tarnishing someone's name.

Leonard Enright has his own take on it:

Mossie was and is a great friend of mine but sometimes you have to deal with being taken off. I was taken off myself enough of times. If Mossie felt he needed to do what he did, then he was right, and I will never condemn him for it. Mossie was A1, and him going to Tipperary didn't lift me in any way when we were playing Tipperary afterwards. We were playing Tipperary, not Mossie Carroll. It happened very fast; nobody had a chance of stopping him from transferring. If there was a proper chance we would have tried. Regardless of who he played for, Mossie Carroll is still a Limerick man and a Garryspillane man and always will be.

Éamonn Cregan recalls a niggling encounter:

My memory of Mossie was in 1981 when we played them [Tipperary] in the drawn game in the championship. They were fourteen points up, I remember a ball coming in, and trying to block it and the ball went wide. I was just turning to come out and I got a butt of a hurley into the back. 'Twas Mossie had hit me. In those days you sorted out problems yourself so that was an obvious little bit of needle from the previous year. There was needle all right because Mossie had gone to Tipperary. I could understand that. As regards him making a difference in 1981 with Limerick, again, would he have hurled for more than the thirty minutes?

In the Tipperary game, brothers Mossie and Brian 'Bomber' Carroll found themselves on opposite sides:

We stayed at home in Knocklong the night before the game and he went off in a white Escort and I went with 'the Jap'. We were in the same hotel in Thurles before the match, but he was upstairs and I was downstairs. When the match started I remember shaking hands with him. I suppose there was a lot of animosity at the time; it wasn't a popular decision to transfer. Mossie, who would be twice the size of me . . . and when the first ball broke around centre field, he knocked me on my arse. I just had to get up and dust myself down and get on with it. It just happened that I had a good game, and we beat them handy the second day. That was the one clash. I only remember shaking hands and wishing him the best, because no matter what, blood is thicker than water, but it was an unusual thing all right.

Mossie himself says it was 'an interesting experience' playing against Brian, while Seán Foley describes playing against his former teammate as 'a little tense'. Jimmy Carroll explains what happened at half-time:

Thurles is definitely the best pitch of all but I'd say that day there was 3 inches of muck on it. Whatever kind of weather we were after getting, conditions were atrocious. It was raining and it was cold. We were thirteen points down and we had the wind in the second half but they got the first score. And I said to myself, 'This is all over.'

Joe McKenna didn't ever say too much in a dressing room, but that day at half-time he really lost it. We were all kind of looking at each other and the heads were down and we were just about to walk out onto the field and McKenna just stopped, closed the door a bit and he tore into us, and he particularly tore into me, and looked at me and he said, 'You didn't hit a ball all day. If you can get a ball, give it into me and I will score a goal, do it a few times and I will get a few goals.' He was putting pressure on himself now, and to be fair he did it. He scored three goals and we drew with them. Talk about confidence; we knew the replay was in Limerick and we were so confident after the game that we would beat them.

McKenna remains modest:

When you are down fourteen points you go for broke, and you get one goal and then get another. You go on a run and momentum goes with you. The main thing is to get the ball in; when you are full-forward you are depending on getting the ball in, and that doesn't always happen with Limerick. We got the momentum and luckily enough we got the scores.

Seán Foley, amusingly, takes some of the credit for McKenna's performance:

I was throwing the ball into Joe that day. I made an All-Star out of him. On a more serious note, though, he was a fantastic full-forward, could catch the ball, and turn on the spot and strike it.

Ger McMahon of St Patrick's, who landed an important long-range point at the Killinan end, has never forgotten his moment. 'I tell everyone it was like a cannonball but to be honest it was more like Fionn McCumhaill. It was a one-day wonder.'

Jimmy Carroll did not feature in the replay, which Limerick won easily:

At the very end of the drawn match, the tension was unbelievable. I had actually been on Mossie Carroll for some of the first half; he came out midfield and they took him off at half-time. I couldn't believe it. He wasn't playing badly and they were totally on top.

With a few minutes to go, a ball broke and the name of the game that time, like rugby, was to get possession and hold onto it. Just keep the ball, don't let anyone else take it away. I remember going down over the ball and Dinny Cahill, a tough guy, was running in as I was getting up and I remember his knee collided with my shoulder. I knew I was in trouble. I couldn't move, but there was no point putting your hand up to go off. There was only about two minutes left, and a fella coming on wouldn't be as good because you were so fired up at that stage of the game. We finished the match anyway and I went to Noel Drumgoole and Richard Flaherty and I said, 'I am in serious trouble with my shoulder' and they were trying to move it around and the whole lot and they put it in a bit of a sling anyway, and lucky enough I had reported it to them. I was to go to Limerick and get it x-rayed the following morning.

We were coming home though Tipperary, myself and Paddy Sullivan from Kilfrush and a few more who always socialised together after games. We had to celebrate a bit. Even though it was only a draw, it was as good as a win. When we went to move our car it was locked inside another car. I asked this fella to move his car and he said to me, 'What do you want to move the car for?' or something like that. I probably had some kind of a Limerick shirt on me. I asked him to move it again, and he refused to move it, and next thing I made an effort myself to move our car. He didn't like that, so I went up and said, 'I will move your car so,' and he got out and there was a little bit of a row, I have to admit, but it was all over in a few minutes.

The word was out then that I was after being in a big row, but sure I went in and got it x-rayed. It wasn't dislocated but the ligaments were pulled. I tried to get it ready for the replay through injections, but no way could I get it right. My pal, Surgeon Meaney in Croom, was a huge help to me at the time. The official line is it was the shoulder rather than the row that kept me out of the replay. The row didn't help, admittedly, but one must be politically correct and state that the shoulder was the real reason.

After beating Tipperary, Limerick defeated Clare in the Munster final. Joe McKenna acknowledges that they were going well:

We were very sharp in the Munster final, we played very well. You know how Limerick are going in games by the amount of ball you are getting at full-forward. It's one thing to get it and not make use of it, but the full-forward line needs ball all the time. It's like goalscorers in soccer; if the ball is not coming they find it harder when they do get the ball, but if they have a constant supply of ball, they find it easier to score.

There is an acceptance among the players that Limerick were better equipped for All-Ireland success in 1981 than they were the previous year. Paddy Kelly, Brian Carroll, Mikey Grimes and Pat Herbert had come in, Paudie Fitzmaurice had dropped back to strengthen the full-back line, and Dominic Punch was in the half-backs. Many believe that had everyone remained fit, Limerick would have beaten Galway in the semi-final and gone on to claim the title.

However, they were without Mossie Carroll and also David Punch, who had departed temporarily:

I took a sabbatical and I went touring Europe for six months, and you didn't have the internet or mobile phones then to keep in touch. You had to find a telephone box and ring home; that was the only way of communicating back then.

Limerick lost to Galway after a replay. By the end of the second game Limerick were without Dominic Punch and Pat Herbert (who did not start due to injury), Leonard Enright and Mikey Grimes (who were taken off injured during the game), and Seán Foley, probably the greatest loss, absent through suspension. Very few teams could hope to close out a game without four first-choice defenders.

In the drawn game, Seán Foley was sent off following an incident with P. J. Molloy. Molloy, who had scored a goal in the 1980 All-Ireland final, was in motion as Foley's hurley came down, suggesting that his momentum carried him into the impact. However, having the greater physical strength, perhaps Foley should have used his body rather than his hurley to challenge Molloy, which would have lessened the risk of a sending off. It should be remembered too that, although Molloy received a nasty wound, he was fit to play in the replay two weeks later.

Éamonn Cregan feels the sending off was harsh:

Seán was unlucky in the sense that P. J. Molloy was a small player and when he ran through with the ball he would duck down. Seán's hurley was only about waist high when he hit Molloy. Molloy was about 5 foot 6 or 5 foot 7 so when he crouched down lower he was about 5 foot 2.

Frank Burke was part of the Galway setup:

It was an unfortunate incident. Molloy's style of crouching down over the hurley meant that his head was close to the ball on the hurley. That meant that his head was in the way when anyone used their hurley to dispossess him. Today, with helmets, it wouldn't be an issue.

Jimmy Carroll went to centre-back on Joe Connolly after Foley's dismissal:

Connolly was very physical and very vocal. He would do everything to get you to do something stupid. I remember Éamonn Cregan coming out and saying to me, 'You are going back centre-back now and close your ears, because that fellow can't stop talking.' And then with about three or four minutes to go, Connolly came out and the two of us basically caught onto each other and pulled each other onto the ground. I think they described it the following day on the paper as chickens in the dust or something. It was nothing major, there was no thump or no nothing. It was the umpire that called the referee. I saw the umpire and I said to Joe, 'We could be in trouble here,' and he says, 'No. Say nothing, say nothing.' We started patting each other on the back and having a bit of a laugh, and the next thing O'Donoghue, the ref from Dublin, went all the way back and he had a quick word with the umpire and sent the two of us off. And the two of us just looked at each other and we held and clapped each other on the back because we were devastated. The very minute I got sent off they got a free to make a draw of it. That didn't help.

Liam O'Donoghue feels that free was harsh:

The referee did us out of it that day. He penalised Pat Herbert who was coming out with the ball and Bernie Forde was hanging off him. He gave a free in when time was up. It should have been a free out.

Joe McKenna is of a similar view. 'To this day I hold the strong view that it was no free, and that it was a free out if anything.'
Seán Foley believes the sendings off were harsh:

I am sure the referee made a mistake sending off Jimmy like he did on the earlier sending off. There will have to be a book written on that incident alone – from my point of view!

Jimmy Carroll recalls the hearing in Dublin:

I remember Noel Drumgoole, 'the Jap', myself and Seán Foley had to go up to a Central Council meeting at Croke Park. We had to write out our own statements about the event. Joe Connolly was there as well. I met with Joe Connolly before we went into the meeting. I remember there were about twelve fellas inside sitting down and they all had caps on them. One of them was 'The Pudding' – P. S. Ó Riain. I remember I got a bit of a smile off him when I went in. Joe and I had a quick look at what one another had said and we both went in and said the same thing. I waited outside the door for Joe to come out and he said, 'We are fine, two weeks.' That was grand, we were back for the replay.

Seán Foley was next in with P. J. Molloy. Foley went in and gave his statement and next thing there's no sign of P. J. Molloy, who was represented by the doctor instead. The doctor came up with a vicious report stating that P. J. Molloy was in danger of losing his eyesight and probably would never play again. And that was it; and we sat into our cars and drove home. Seán Foley got three months and P. J. Molloy played in the replay.

I remember coming down in the car; we couldn't talk and Seán Foley was like an antichrist. We all assumed that if the reports were kind of matching that we would be all back, the same thing that happened between myself and Joe would happen between Seán and P. J. Molloy. But half way through it Galway changed their minds. Once Galway got Joe back they didn't care, they knew they would be getting me back with Joe, but they didn't want Seán back. That was it and they got their way. We stopped coming down for a meal and Seán wouldn't eat the meal, he went straight to the bar for a few drinks for himself, trying to calm himself down. We had a bit of a laugh after that on the way home, but we knew he was gone and that was it.

I started centre-back in the replay and was playing fairly well at the time. You can get a kind of a boost then when you feel you are being done, and every fella was up for it big time, and I always felt that we were going to win. And I think we were good enough, there wasn't a whole lot in it but we were missing too many players at the end of the game. Galway were probably a better team in 1981 than they were in 1980. I am convinced that we were a better team in 1981, we were up for them and I was sure we would beat them. Don't forget it was Offaly waiting in the final. While it's always difficult to beat Offaly, Galway had them in all sorts of trouble at half-time. They were so far ahead that they were taking pot shots at goal. Next thing, Offaly came back into the game and Johnny Flaherty scored the famous hand passed goal. I think myself that '81 was the one that got away.

And so the heartbreak continued for Limerick. Those years – 1980 and 1981 – presented great opportunities for silverware, with the 'big three' at a low ebb. But the chances were not taken, and almost thirty years later the regret remains.

☙

SIX

1982–1985: HOPE EVAPORATES

*I*n *1982 Limerick were beaten by Waterford in the Munster championship and Noel Drumgoole departed as manager. Although the talent was still evident, there was a lack of inspiration among the team.*

Jimmy Carroll remembers the defeat:

Joe McKenna has always been our hero and was again that day but he got a ball and turned to stick it over the bar, which he normally would. That would have made a draw out of it but it went wide. If we had got a second go at Waterford we would have beaten them.

McKenna agrees:

I had the chance and I drove it about 50 yards wide! Waterford caught us in the first round, and if we got over them, we might have gone a long way again. That Limerick team had been coming since '78 and '79 and outside of winning an All-Ireland final we got the most out of that team. We had some quality players, but I would have considered the 1973 team to be a better team.

The search for new players continued and Michael John Coffey of Glenroe received a late call-up to the championship panel:

I was in the subs in 1982 against Waterford. If we had got a draw against Waterford I might have been on for the replay. I was called onto the panel only five or six weeks before that and my fitness was improving, but I needed more time. I would have been hoping to have had a role to play if we went on in the championship.

Pa Foley recalls the disappointment:

That game was a nightmare, At that time if you were playing Waterford in the championship, you were thinking it was only a case of playing the game and getting it over with.

John Flanagan rues a lapse in concentration:

Éamonn Cregan used always say never turn your back on the ball. The Waterford goalie took an exceptionally quick puck-out and they scored from it. The game could have gone either way but it was an awful disappointment and the expectation was there that we would win it.

Leonard Enright feels Limerick left the game behind them:

To me we threw that away. I think we were better that day than Waterford, but a small lapse in concentration cost us. Jim Greene set up a goal for Stephen Breen that finished that game.

Jimmy Carroll believes the ghosts of the previous two years did not help:

Cork gave Waterford an awful beating in the Munster final. I think the 1980 and 1981 defeats took a bit out of our team. We took a fairly long break that winter and went back into training and got the thing going but I have a feeling there was a bit of jizz missing from the team. But if we got over Waterford, you would never know. But then in hindsight we all got a break and I think we needed it to go back and play with the club and we all had good club championships that year.

'Bomber' Carroll joined his brother Mossie in Tipperary that year:

I had won two Munster medals at twenty-one years of age, which was brilliant. It just happened that I was after crashing the car in 1981, and I decided to go with Tipperary because I didn't have the transport to get home for training. I didn't enjoy it, to be honest.

I said to Mossie in the winter of 1982 that I was going back. I played with St Mary's and they were a very nice club, but when you walk into Kilmallock or Bruff, you know the gatemen, you know everyone, and you are after growing up with the players. Home is where the heart lies. Brother O'Grady rang us and asked us would we come back, and I said it to Mossie, and that was it.

O'Grady had taken over from Noel Drumgoole as manager, but his election was put on hold due to the death of a Limerick legend:

The appointment of the manager was based on a PR system. I was nominated by quite a few clubs in 1982 having been over the under-21 team in 1981. The voting for the position was due to take place in September because Mick Mackey had died, so they actually postponed the voting until the following month and it was actually October before I was appointed.

Limerick lost the 1983 League final to Kilkenny, having come from Division 2 that year. Jimmy Carroll believes the introduction of new players gave the team a lift:

In 1980 and 1981 we had got to the All-Ireland final and the All-Ireland semi-final. In 1982 we fell off the rails. That was a year off and a chance to regroup. The nucleus of the team was still there in '83 but we were after getting three or four other players coming onto the team in '83 who were able to hurl. The likes of Pa Foley, Danny Fitzgerald and Matt Rea had come in. We were full of running, we were rejuvenated and we felt that we were back as good and young as we were in 1980. We should have won another Munster, if not an All-Ireland.

Leonard Enright had high regard for one of the newcomers:

I thought one of the greatest players we ever had in Patrickswell and Limerick was Pa Foley, and he never got recognition for it. Pa would mark his own man but he would mark yours as well if you were caught. When he saw someone else going through he was gone. He'd lift and strike like his brother Seán, but this fellow had something that I haven't seen a half-back having since, and played for Limerick and Patrickswell and not for himself. An absolutely gifted hurler. He didn't use weight because he didn't have any to begin with but it was pure skill.

Éamonn Cregan suggests one of those introduced should have been involved earlier. 'Danny Fitzgerald was on the Munster team before he got on the Limerick team.'

Matt Rea was rejuvenated under the O'Grady regime:

My first League game was against Mick Jacob in Wexford, and I was centre-forward in late 1980. I played more or less all the way through the League but I was dropped for the championship. I came back under Brother O'Grady in 1983, who was a great manager and was just very unlucky. Skehan made great saves in that final.

Michael John Coffey was one of the stars of the League final:

We were very unlucky against Kilkenny. It would have been nice to win it but we had a lot of young players and they were a great team, they were All-Ireland champions. We had come from Division 2 in the League that year, so to come so close would have given us massive confidence. I got injured about six weeks before the championship. I did my cruciate ligament. I got back for 1984 but I was never the same player.

Micheál O'Grady recalls gaining confidence from that League final:

Kilkenny were really hot at the time but I was very pleased at the way we played. I thought we played well and would have beaten most teams on that day. It meant we were approaching the championship with confidence. One of the problems that time was that the board were committed to playing a tournament game between the League and the championship. I always felt we didn't have enough time to prepare for the championship.

Regular free taker Paddy Kelly, in top form at the time, missed the 1983 championship through injury:

It's no coincidence that my best spell with Limerick was when O'Grady was in charge. It was my most permanent spell on the team and I had a run of games. I wasn't looking over my shoulder to see if I was going to be taken off. It was a very unlucky period for Limerick, and we probably hit as good a Cork team as was ever around. I broke the finger two weeks before the championship in a challenge against Offaly. We actually ran riot against Offaly in that challenge game. I remember in the Cork game we had the 21-yard free at the end, and I was screaming to go for goal, because we knew the replay was going to be in Cork, but they tapped it over the bar and Cork won the replay.

O'Grady sums up the drawn game at the Gaelic Grounds:

We played very well, even though we were down well at one stage. We missed about eight frees that Paddy would have tapped over the bar.

Ollie O'Connor, Jimmy Carroll, Joe McKenna, Pa Foley and Danny Fitzgerald all took turns to take the frees. Pa Foley recalls the equalising point in injury time to secure a replay:

It was a bit crazy, you should have only one appointed free taker. Myself and Danny were taking them at random between us. For the last free, Éamonn Cregan told me there were five or six minutes left,

Jimmy Barry-Murphy celebrates his crucial goal in the 1983 Munster Championship replay with Limerick as Leonard Enright looks on in dismay.

to pop it over the bar. That was purely to take the pressure off and it worked.

Cork secured a narrow victory in the replay, the day Éamonn Cregan resigned as selector, came out of retirement and on as substitute:

I felt I should have started the replay given the difficulties with the frees but I didn't have the training done. The previous year I had taken the frees, and that alone would have been enough reason to start. I suppose you make mistakes and I shouldn't have gone in as a selector. I should have stepped back, but you are so enthusiastic that you want to think you have something to offer and you go and you do it.

O'Grady feels Limerick's luck was out that day:

We played very well. The game was touch and go and we lost by two points, but we were very unlucky. Leonard Enright held Jimmy Barry-Murphy for most of the match and then Jimmy Barry-Murphy got one break and it was in the back of the net: it was a crucial goal.

Barry-Murphy had huge admiration for Enright:

Leonard was a fantastic full-back. I couldn't ever get the better of him for speed; I hated being marked by him because he was so fast.

John Flanagan could not but admire the goal:

Jimmy whipped on a ground ball, he got out just ahead of Enright. A fantastic goal, an unbelievable ground stroke, so fast and so furious.

O'Grady remembers a late chance for Limerick:

There was a 70, and Éamonn Cregan decided not to take it, which at the time I wasn't impressed by. I felt he was the obvious choice, but he decided to stay inside on the edge of the square. Ironically, as it happened, the 70 was lobbed into the square and Éamonn almost won the game for us by pulling on it, leading to a great save by Cunningham. That won the game for Cork. Freetaking is always a specialist job and Éamonn hadn't taken frees for a while for Limerick but he would have still had it.

Éamonn hadn't been training with the team and had been away on holidays. He wasn't fit; the legs were going, if not gone. I do remember he trained the week before the match and some of the players insisted that he trained because they reckoned he needed to be fit to play and I remember he struggled at the back of the group in some of the training.

Jimmy Carroll is adamant that Cregan made the correct decision to return:

Éamonn Cregan returned as a selector and there was stupid talk that he shouldn't have played. Cregan was a tremendous player and also a very good manager, and a necessity arose where he had to come on. We were in trouble and we needed to get scores.

Liam O'Donoghue disagrees, however:

I think Éamonn made a wrong decision. When you are gone, you are gone. Cregan was one of the greatest hurlers Limerick ever had and with the career he had he wasn't going to do himself any favours.

The Limerick minor team are paraded through Bruff after the Munster final of 1984.

I thought myself that Brian Murphy cleaned him out on the day, and in his day that wouldn't have happened. He was away a while and when he was playing full-time he minded himself and he looked after his body, but when you get to that age and you are gone for a few months, you never get it back.

Richie Bennis has his own view:

Cregan was a great hurler and not many would ever get the better of him. But when Cregan was playing to his very best, Brian Murphy could always beat him. There is always someone who will beat you, and in Cregan's case it was Brian Murphy. I think it was silly to be in a situation where you pick yourself at corner-forward because he wasn't officially a selector but he was a selector at the same time. You can't be a selector and a player. Cregan was always a selector anyway [laughs] even back when he was playing with me.

Many believe the most heartbreaking defeat ever was against Cork in 1984. Limerick had defeated Wexford comfortably in the League final, and George Ryan, one of the top referees at the time, believed they were on the verge of a breakthrough:

I left Thurles that day of the League final, and felt that Limerick had a great chance of winning the All-Ireland. Leonard Enright, a player I had huge admiration for, was at the top of his game, and they were without doubt major contenders. Paddy Kelly and Joe McKenna were in excellent form as well. Limerick had the talent to win an All-Ireland in those years.

Limerick were well in control against Cork but conceded two bizarre own goals in the second half, as 'Bomber' Carroll recalls:

We were at the top for four or five years and that was the one day we really thought we could beat Cork. It was a disaster. There was a schemozzle around the square in the first half; Mossie, Tommy Quaid and Pat Herbert were in it and the ball broke loose. The ball was coming out towards me and I said I would go down and smother it. Kevin Hennessy got to it before me and they got a goal from it. If I flicked it away rather than going down on it we would have been better off. It was the wrong decision.

In the second half, Leonard Enright's own goal killed us. It was just a freak thing. I went in centre-forward as I often did. I started marking Johnny Crowley and Joe McKenna got a goal that brought us back into the game again. But they got the goal from John Fenton's line ball, and won the game. That killed us and we were never the same team after, and I don't think I was ever the same player after. It knocked the heart out of me anyway. I was there since 1979 and that was 1984 and you would say at that point that you were never going to win an All-Ireland.

Leonard Enright was captain on the day:

Being captain to me didn't mean anything compared to just seeing the supporters being so happy. The League meant a lot in 1984 because we still weren't winning much. And when you see the crowd turning up afterwards and the excitement, it meant an awful lot. For the own goal, I was trying to hit the ball and get it out of the way and I slipped and it ricocheted off my leg and went in. I will never forget the way Tommy Quaid was looking at me after it and all I could say

Gerry Rea (London) *(right)* marked his brother Ned in the 1973 All-Ireland semi-final. He is pictured here with another brother – Matt *(left)* – during a Limerick trip to London after they won the centenary league title in 1984.

was, 'Look, these things happen, we have to try and forget about it and move on.' It was disappointing to lose that match.

Richie Bennis identifies two key moments:

We had Cork on the ropes in the first half and Joe McKenna got a ball going in. Paddy Kelly was roaring for it but Joe wouldn't pass in a month of Sundays, that wasn't his style of play. His style was grab and strike, and you can't argue with that, it was successful for him. Paddy was roaring but never got it and Joe ended up getting injured and taken off. Danny Fitzgerald came through before half-time and went for goal from about 30 yards. Cunningham saved it and they went down and scored a goal at the other end. The small little things like that make such a huge difference.

Joe McKenna punctured a lung in that game, yet still managed to score a second-half goal:

I was bearing down on goal and got a small tip of the hurley into the side. I was outstretched, trying to palm the ball into the net and someone just came in and it cracked my rib and I got a collapsed lung. I felt very good that day prior to the injury and I might have scored more if I hadn't been restricted by the injury. I spent ten days in hospital after that.

We could have had a greater half-time lead if I didn't get the injury. It would have suited us better to be playing an All-Ireland final in Thurles. I felt at the time that if we got there we would have had a better chance of winning it than in Croke Park.

Seán Foley had retired the previous year:

Like Tony O'Brien felt in 1972, there were a lot of young players coming through. Looking back I should have held on for the centenary year. I had a very good year for the club, we won the championship; that's history, you make those decisions. The only thing that bothered me about not being there in 1984 was that [Cork's] Tim Crowley threw his weight around in the half-forward line and there was nobody to match him physically. We had nobody to stand up to him and I would have loved the challenge. He was waltzing through the boys. They just didn't have the physical strength, I suppose.

John Fenton took the line ball that led to the first own goal:

We were up against it because Limerick had won the League and we were relieved to get through that game. I don't know if my line ball decided the game, perhaps it did. I would say that what probably happened was that Tommy Quaid had too much time to see the ball, as it was a good distance out, and it hung in the air. My own opinion was that he was making up his mind where he was going to put the clearance. That happens when someone has too much time to think about it.

We didn't win by a lot. We were struggling for long spells. I think the previous year they were possibly not good enough, but in 1984 they were definitely good enough. Limerick had top class players throughout the field and would have troubled anyone at that time. I had played with them on the Munster team that had won the Railway Cup that year. I would have known from talking to the players on the Railway Cup team and seeing how they approached it that Limerick were up for a big year in 1984.

Jimmy Barry-Murphy reveals that Cork were extra motivated for the game:

I had been captain in 1982 and 1983 and we had lost both All-Ireland finals, which was devastating for us. We had a new regime in 1984 with Justin McCarthy and Fr Michael O'Brien at the helm and there was a huge focus because every team wanted to win the centenary All-Ireland. We realised that it was a big one away from home and it was never going to be easy. However, we were well geared towards it, and once we won that game we were on our way.

In 1984 the Limerick minors defeated Kilkenny after a replay to win the All-Ireland for the first time since 1958. Phil Bennis was the manager:

We should have beaten Kilkenny well in the drawn game. We nearly slipped up. The referee Frank Murphy brought Kilkenny back into it because we had been beating them by so much but he gave us a break in the end. The hardest decision I ever made in my life was not to pick Don Flynn for the replay.

Anthony Carmody set up the equalising score in the drawn game:

I remember the puck-out from Val Murnane and remember thinking, 'Whatever happens we have to secure possession'. Luckily enough, I caught it and sent it straight in towards the goals where Brian Stapleton grabbed it and put it over the bar for the equaliser. It was a game we had dominated and should have won by five or six points. It was very nearly another case of heartbreak. The replay was a dour, boring battle and I would say that Kilkenny were concentrating more on trying to stop us.

A source close to the camp at that time recalls an amusing tale surrounding a player being taken off in the All-Ireland semi-final against Down:

Phil [Bennis] was fierce friendly with that player's father for years, and after the game he was on to Phil the whole time about the selectors taking off his son. We travelled down by train, and that player's father drove down by car. When we arrived down we all went to a pub in Patrickswell, and the next thing who came in the door only the same player's father. Phil ran to hide in the toilet!

Ger Hegarty believes the Limerick CBS Harty Cup team played an influential role:

We had eleven players that were involved and went on and won an All-Ireland minor, but couldn't win a Harty, which was incredible. During the first part of that year, the focus was firmly on retaining the Harty, and once that was out of the way the focus switched to the Limerick minor team.

A source close to the inter-county setup recalls life on the sideline with the minors with amusement:

Mike Weekes and Seán O'Connor would be over the forwards during a match, and Tom Bulfin and Gerry Molyneaux would be with the backs; Phil, as the manager, would have a free role. The selectors would consult as a group every couple of minutes, but Seán O'Connor would often be beside his son Leo who was playing. The selectors were looking for Seán O'Connor to make an important switch one day and he was above talking to Leo and they had to make the switch without him.

Mike Weekes took his mentoring seriously:

I did an intensive one-week coaching course in Gormanstown, County Meath, in 1983 where I became a qualified senior inter-county coach. It was unbelievable what we went through to complete the course. However, it was beneficial in that the knowledge I brought back helped Limerick hurling and the proof of it was in winning the All-Ireland minor title in 1984. We had great players, though. Ger Hegarty was a great bit of stuff. Gary Kirby would never go for a

The Limerick team that beat Down in the 1984 All-Ireland minor semi-final at Croke Park. *Back row (l–r):* Pat Davoren (Ballybrown), Anthony Carmody (Patrickswell), Gary Kirby (Patrickswell), Brian Stapleton (Garryspillane), Tony Byrnes (Old Christians), Ger Hegarty (Old Christians), Mike Reale (Bruff), Pa Carey (Patrickswell). *Front row (l–r):* Don Flynn (Killeedy), Andy Cuneen (Claughaun), Anthony O'Riordan (Capt.) (Bruff), Val Murnane (Caherline), Gussie Ryan (Claughaun), John O'Neill (Blackrock), Anthony Madden (Bruff).

score unless he was sure of getting it. He always worked his way in towards goals rather than shooting from the sideline.

Gary Kirby has his own memories:

We beat Cork minors in Bruff in a cracker in 1984. Anthony Carmody, my own clubman, was the free taker, but during the game that task was handed to me and I have been stuck with them ever since. I took three tough ones from the sideline and luckily all of them went over.

My only memory of the Munster final was the buzz after winning it. It had been so long since Limerick won a Munster minor title. We played super hurling, good flowing hurling against Kilkenny in the first half and we were well ahead. We were moving very well. Next thing, all of a sudden, they got three goals. Val Murnane, the goalie, got a knock on the head; he got stitches and a bandage on the head. They were going to take him off but left him on. Kilkenny didn't get soft goals, so you couldn't blame the injury to Val for the goals. You were thinking that was it, that you were goosed and the next thing Anthony Carmody caught a great ball from the puck-out and on the turn he hit it in and Brian Stapleton caught another great one and he put it over.

We were very unlucky not to retain our title the following year. In 1985 Mark Foley scored a late goal for Cork to beat us. Pa Carey thought he had the goal covered. He had Foley covered for catching it, but all of a sudden Foley turned and doubled on it instead and got the goal.

When Brother O'Grady was transferred to a Wexford school, Noel Drumgoole returned as senior team manager in 1985 and 1986. In 1985 Limerick defeated an Éamonn Cregan-managed Clare in the League final – but then disaster struck when the inspirational Jimmy Carroll was injured in a challenge game against Tipperary:

You will always get belts, that's what hurling is all about. We were opening the pitch over in Holycross and were playing Tipperary. We were supposed to put out our strongest teams, but for some reason on the night we didn't play full teams. Anyway, they decided to play me and for some reason they put me wing-back where I never played. Tipperary were on top at midfield, so I was told to go out midfield for fifteen minutes to steady things up. I went out anyway and I got a bang in the head in through the helmet. The first thing that hit the ground

(*L–r*) Mike Reale, Anthony O'Riordan (Capt.) and Anthony Madden pose prior to the All-Ireland Minor semi-final against Down at Croke Park in 1984 as Mike Weekes (*far left*) looks on.

was my head and I don't remember another thing, I woke up in Cashel hospital. For months after that I used to get blackouts if I was sitting or lying down. If I turned quickly, I would lose everything for a second. Obviously it was a lingering concussion.

Selector P. J. O'Grady could see Limerick's championship aspirations evaporating:

Jimmy took an awful long time to recover from that. He played against Cork but he wasn't himself. He wasn't the Jimmy Carroll we knew. It definitely finished him as a hurler. He was a lucky man. I drove him to Cashel hospital that night. I was frightened because he got an awful belt.

Joe McKenna had been injured leading up to the League final and we persisted with a new full-forward, Pat McCarthy, for the League.

We brought Joe McKenna in for the championship. It mightn't have been the right decision, but Joe McKenna was Joe McKenna, there weren't that many like him. The other setback was that Pat Herbert got knocked out early in the game, which was a huge blow to us because we had to move 'Bomber' back to corner-back. That took the sting out of us. Maybe it was our own fault that we hadn't someone to go in corner-back at the time, but you wouldn't be expecting that to happen.

John Fenton says Cork took nothing for granted:

Coming into 1985 we had gotten a serious monkey off our backs in that we had won the All-Ireland in 1984. No Cork team had lost three All-Irelands in a row and it took pressure off us. We knew from 1984 that we were going to be up against it. There was never going to be any complacency and once we got on top, we stayed on top.

Shane Fitzgibbon was the new kid on the block in 1985:

The wheels came off after the League final, and there was an element of complacency for the Waterford game in the championship but we pulled through. I remember playing a couple of challenge games at that time and thinking we were very flat. Cork were sharper and hungrier than us in the next round. I think the League took a lot out of us. While we trained very well for the League, post winning the League our training was terrible. The numbers dwindled because the bigger clubs were pulling on their players to prepare for the club championship.

It was the last hurrah for Joe McKenna:

When I got injured in 1984 I was out of hurling for six months, on medical advice. I hadn't really intended coming back, but I did, and 1985 was really the end of that Limerick team. They were great years, very enjoyable. I was lucky to be involved with a Limerick team that were there or thereabouts almost every year. I won four Munster championships, two Leagues and one All-Ireland.

Paddy Kelly believes that Limerick were a force at the time:

We were the third best team in the country in the early to mid '80s. I often remember beating Kilkenny at Nowlan Park in League games, but we never got a chance to take them on in the championship because we couldn't beat Cork. We just never seemed to get the break against them. I don't know if it was psychological or not. It's a pity the present qualifier system wasn't there because I think we would have revelled in it.

Séamus O'Sullivan outlines the realities of wearing the number 16 jersey:

In 1985 I played the full League campaign. Tommy Quaid was outfield and I went into goals. I remember having a fantastic record that year, I played seven League games and conceded six goals. I remember seeing an article from Jim O'Sullivan in the *Cork Examiner* at the time. Ger Cunningham, the All-Star goalie, had conceded eighteen League goals, yet heartbreakingly for myself when it came to the knockout stages they brought back Tommy and put him into goals, which was hard for me to take. Tommy always seemed to be playing out the field with Limerick when it was his second game that day. His club Feoghanagh were going well at the end of 1984 and he would play for his club in the morning and then play outfield in the League. I felt that there was more in him outfield but that he couldn't give it because he was drained from playing already that day.

And so the heartbreak continued for Limerick. Kilkenny won League titles in 1982 and 1983 en route to All-Ireland success, which proved that winning a League title in that era was not detrimental to championship hopes. However, the injuries suffered by Paddy Kelly in 1983, Joe McKenna in 1984 and Jimmy Carroll and Pat Herbert in 1985 made Limerick's championship hopes evaporate. To lose one key player in one year can be devastating for a team, but to lose key players in successive years is simply tragic. Perhaps it was not meant to be.

 view

1986–1993: VALLEY YEARS

*B*y *1986, Limerick were in decline, with many of the heroes of earlier years slipping into retirement. Of those that started against Clare in Ennis, only Tommy Quaid, Paudie Fitzmaurice and Jimmy Carroll had begun the 1980 All-Ireland final.*

Pa Creamer made his championship debut in Ennis:

It was a funny match; we were well on top up to half-time. Danny Fitzgerald was playing and turned to the crowd and put his fist up into the air after scoring a great point.

Liam O'Donoghue, who was nearing retirement, came on as a substitute:

We were very flat against Clare in 1986 and I'd say Clare were up for it. We probably had prepared well, but in 1983 and 1984 we put an awful lot of effort in and got nothing out of it and you had players coming and going and it was a transition period. You would always meet a situation that time where Clare would come good against you and that was it, and the crowd got behind them. They should have beaten Cork in the Munster final that year.

It was the final championship appearance for 'Bomber' Carroll:

Going down to Ennis they picked a new inexperienced half-back line of Brian Finn, Ger Hegarty and Pa Creamer and dropped Mossie and Liam O'Donoghue. Clare devoured us. When you go down to Ennis you need experienced players.

Mossie was on the bench:

There was a new team coming in 1986. It was a game we should have won; we got off to a good start and seemed to lose our way, and Clare took advantage.

Paddy Kelly is in no doubt why Limerick lost their way:

We completely and utterly controlled the first half in 1986. We were well ahead and I think the whole game turned with a switch of 'Bomber' Carroll. 'Bomber' was breaking ball and myself and Danny Fitzgerald had something like 0-7 from play between us. Then 'Bomber' was switched back into the half-back line and the ball was no longer breaking for us, and the Clare half-back line came into the game. I felt that when 'Bomber' was moved out of centre-forward that day the whole pendulum of the game switched. He had been the catalyst for all the scores even though he wasn't scoring himself. It was the likes of 'Bomber' who made life easy for the fancy dans.

Ger Hegarty remembers his championship debut:

I was physically bigger than the other 1984 minors at the time, and that's probably why I got in first. Noel Drumgoole was the manager and I joined the panel in late 1985 and made my full debut in Ennis in 1986. It was a tough venue to make your debut. It would probably have been much easier if that match was in the Gaelic Grounds.

The successful minors of 1984 were blossoming and in 1986 they beat Clare after a replay in the Munster under-21 final. Minor captain in 1984, Anthony O'Riordan became the first Limerick player to raise the Munster under-21 trophy.

Gary Kirby remembers the occasion:

We had a close encounter with Clare in the under-21 final. We were four points down with a few minutes to go but I got a goal and Pat Reale got a point with nearly the last puck of the game. We were both going for our first ever Munster title at under-21 level. We went up to Ennis for the replay and beat them well.

The All-Ireland semi-final was lost to Galway, as Anthony Carmody recalls:

My biggest memory of 1986 was that we were going well and Joe Cooney was corner-forward. He wasn't doing an awful lot and they moved him out around the middle of the field in a free role and it turned the game for them.

Phil Bennis regrets not making a switch to counteract Cooney. 'We left him loose and should probably have sent his marker out the field after him.'

The following year, the under-21s achieved All-Ireland success, defeating Galway in the final. Ger Hegarty remembers the confidence within the team:

Winning the under-21 was superb. We lost the semi in 1986, and the guts of the 1986 team were from the 1984 minors. Phil did a tremendous job with us, and we kind of breezed through Munster in 1987. Even though Galway ran us close in the final, I always felt we wouldn't be beaten at under-21 level in 1987.

Michael 'Haulie' O'Brien missed out through injury:

We were playing against Blackrock of Cork in a challenge game with the Limerick juniors in 1986. I got a bare touch of a shoulder when I was running at speed with the ball, and my knee collapsed from underneath me.

A ruptured cruciate ligament required four operations, but he was never the same player afterwards. Gary Kirby recognised his potential:

Haulie could have made a Limerick senior hurler. He was promising, he was lively and he knew how to get to the ball. His touch was good and he was an aggressive hurler. You don't ever know how things would have worked out for him, but he looked to have it.

P.J. O'Grady managed the Limerick minors in 1986 and 1987:

Clare beat us in 1986 and Tipperary hammered them afterwards. We had the makings of a good team in 1986 but a lot of them were underage the following year and we viewed it as a development year. We had five from Flannan's on that team and it cost us the match. They were after winning the All-Ireland and were on a bit of a high. Pat Heffernan was playing centre-back for the colleges, and I didn't want to play him at centre-back on the Limerick minor team, particularly against Tipperary; I wanted to play him at centre-forward. He was due to mark Justin Quinlan from Tipperary Town, a schoolmate of his from St Flannan's.

We had beaten Clare in the minor League final in late '86 and Anthony Daly, also of Flannan's, was playing for Clare, and himself and Heffernan were niggling and acting the maggot all day. I was determined that the same thing wouldn't happen in the Tipperary game and I wanted to pick Anthony Kirby with Heffernan at centre-forward. If we had put Kirby at centre-back we would have beaten Tipperary. But because Heffernan was starring centre-back for Flannan's there was massive pressure to play him there with Limerick. I got beaten on the vote. Colleges hurling is a different hurling and people don't realise it. He never really got going in the game that night.

The Limerick team that beat Galway in the 1987 All-Ireland Under-21 final at Ennis. *Back row (l–r):* Mike Reale (Bruff), Anthony Carmody (Patrickswell), Pa Carey (Patrickswell), Val Murnane (Caherline), Gary Kirby (Patrickswell), Ger Hegarty (Old Christians), Anthony O'Riordan (Bruff), John O'Neill (Blackrock). *Front row (l–r):* Joe O'Connor (Ballybrown), Anthony Madden (Bruff), Gussie Ryan (Capt.) (Claughaun), Leo O'Connor (Claughaun), Declan Nash (South Liberties), Pat Barrett (Bruff), Don Flynn (Killeedy).

Surprisingly, considering his senior career, Stephen McDonagh was never a Limerick minor:

In those times a lot of those Harty Cup lads were looked up to. The big thing when I was minor was to have played in the Harty Cup. I was in school in Pallaskenry and and wasn't asked in for a trial. There were a couple of factors; in the Salesian College in Pallaskenry there wasn't a massive hurling team, and perhaps my development was a bit slow.

Turlough Herbert, a son of Mick Herbert, was also one of the St Flannan's stars:

In 1987 we had quite a good team and had five of the Flannan's Harty Cup team and were expected to go up and beat Tipperary. We had played a lot of challenges and thought we were quite hot. We were fairly sure we knew every decent player on the scene from other counties, through the Harty Cup scene, but nobody told us about the great John Leahy. He was amazing. Nobody had ever heard of this guy. I think they beat us by five or six points on the night and that was a big disappointment. In 1988 I played at centre-back, with my neighbour, Adrian O'Sullivan, beside me at wing-back, God rest his soul.

O'Sullivan, a hugely promising underage player, drowned in a freak accident on the Shannon. John Kiely recalls marking him in a trial game for the Limerick minors at Knockainey in 1989:

We were chatting away, as you do, and he was asking me where I was from. I pointed towards the Galtee Mountains and said that I was from there. Being from Castleconnell, near the city, he was fascinated at the idea of me being from the mountains. So he said to me, 'I have been on this panel since last year, and will make it again this year no matter what, so what we will do is we will go for every second ball.' So that's what happened, and we both hit loads of ball, and I ended up making the panel. I'll never forget him for that. It devastated me when I learned about his death in 1990.

A youthful Limerick side approached the 1987 senior championship with confidence, having narrowly lost a League quarter-final against Tipperary after extra time. Owen O'Neill Snr was one of the selectors:

In the 1987 League quarter-final in Thurles, Pat McCarthy wasn't on the team list submitted to the referee. I wanted to bring in McCarthy, and we discussed it with a couple of the officials who were on duty at the game. If we had brought on McCarthy I believe we would have won. We discovered subsequently that McCarthy would have been eligible and it's a huge regret of mine that we didn't put him in.

Éamonn Cregan was the man in charge:

In 1987, I wasn't manager as such, it was chairman of selectors. I suppose the title 'manager' was coming through at that stage. The team was ending age-wise, its natural cycle had come and there were players coming through like Gary Kirby and Ger Hegarty.

Gary Kirby was not picked initially for the game against Waterford in the 1987 senior championship:

Leonard Enright pulled out so Pa Carey who had been named in the forwards went back to full-back where he was the man of the match, and I came in at corner-forward. The difference was that Tommy Quaid made a great save with about five minutes to go. We were only two or three points up at that stage.

All-Ireland champions Cork were Limerick's opponents in the Munster semi-final. Limerick dominated the early exchanges, but trailed as the final whistle approached. However, Gary Kirby and Shane Fitzgibbon scored goals to put Limerick ahead, only for Cork to conjure an equaliser.

Ger Hegarty considers it a game of huge importance:

For me the defining match in my career was the game against Cork in 1987. That was a huge game when I look back. I remember going up catching a ball near the end and coming down and being fouled. Dr Richard Flaherty came over to me and said, 'Stay down, stay down, we are in the Munster final.' I thought the crowd were booing me for lying on the ground, but when I got up I realised the crowd were booing the referee for giving a free against me, which mystifies me to this day, having being fouled on the way down. If we had held on and won that match, we were playing Tipperary in the Gaelic Grounds in the Munster final where both teams were trying to make a breakthrough. Anything could have happened.

Pa Creamer takes responsibility for Cork's equaliser, but queries the referee's timekeeping:

I was marking Kieran Kingston, I backed into the two boys behind me and batted it down to him and it was straight over the bar to draw the match. There was a good bit of injury time. I had actually played well but was caught with the wrong incident at the wrong time and was the cause of the equaliser. Coming near the end of the match the referee told Ger Hegarty that there was a minute or two of injury time left, and the game kept going on and on. It was like as if the referee held out for a draw, but it's easy say that when you don't win.

At least one daily newspaper concurred on the injury time issue, although. Hegarty's recollection is clouded by time:

I can't remember exactly what he [the referee] said, but I think he may have said to me that there were two minutes left at some stage near the end. Based on that I would have thought the game was over once John Fenton struck the free and missed. But he still allowed play to develop after the missed free and again after the puck-out. That match seemed to go on forever, we got late goals, and seemed to have the match won. When you are trying to make a breakthrough, and trying to run down the clock, every second is like a year.

Terence Kenny regrets not being more ruthless when attempting to close out the game:

We let Denis Mulcahy clear a ball down the field near the end, and in hindsight it might have been better to pull him down. I thought the ref gave a lot of handy frees to Cork. I was disappointed with the free against Hegarty. The referee gave them a chance to equalise, and they missed. Eventually they got an equaliser. It was typical Cork, you only got one chance against them.

Anthony Carmody feels the officials did Limerick no favours:

During a game you aren't going to be thinking about the time being played, but I think the referee seemed to play it on and on until Cork got the point. The big counties Cork and Tipp will always get those breaks. Then there was the pool ball incident.

Liam O'Donoghue takes up the story:

We hurled Cork off the field in '87 but one of the Cork supporters threw in a black pool ball and Cregan came down onto the sideline and picked up the ball and went out onto the field to the referee and the game was stopped. Cregan himself was at fault for that game going on a little bit longer, because he got involved with the referee and he got involved with the supporters. And only for that delay of time we would have had Cork beaten. We rocked them completely on the day, they didn't know what hit them. Pat McCarthy was still there, we had a good outfit there. We went into that feeling we had a great chance. Again, like in 1980, the public mightn't have given us a chance because of the previous two years but we had a great chance that day. If we won we were in a Munster final and it might have given us the lift that we needed, but we put so much effort into the drawn match that when we met them in the replay it wasn't there.

Joe O'Connor raises the League trophy after beating reigning
All-Ireland champions Tipperary in the 1992 League final.

Leonard Enright came on in the drawn game despite suffering a health scare:

I had a threatened heart attack around that time which thankfully didn't happen. I didn't have any chest pains or anything but there was something that didn't feel right and I was sent into hospital to get a check-up and ended up being kept on for just short of three weeks coming up to the championship. Pa Carey went to full-back. In the second half I was put on. I wasn't right and I probably should have said 'no' to going on. You must call your own shots at times.

Jimmy Carroll feels Limerick lacked a certain nous:

We felt unlucky in 1987 but we weren't able to close out a game. I feel that when Cork were coming back at us, we used to panic rather than toughen and close it out. I think we did a bit of that in 1987 but we felt the team was good enough. We had gone from 1981 to 1987 without a Munster. We won the Leagues which woke us up a bit, but the further away you get from winning a Munster final, your expectations lessen, which is not a good thing.

John Fenton scored a wonder goal in the replay:

There were five or six of us coming to the end of our careers in 1987 and we needed to be going really well to put teams away, and we gave Limerick a chance the first day and they nearly took it. Kieran Kingston tells me that only for his point in the drawn game that my goal would never have been scored!

We were ready for Limerick in the replay, whereas, having beaten them easily in 1985, we mightn't have been as tuned in the first day. On the second day we got a couple of goals. Once we got them we drove on. My goal was the third goal and Limerick got a point immediately before it.

I was running back out to midfield, and remember saying to myself that we needed to get another score before half-time. Ger [Cunningham] pucked out the ball, and what Tomás Mulcahy and Leonard Enright were doing out there I don't know, and they probably don't know themselves either. The ball seemed to break away from a crowd rather than being laid off to me. I just pushed it ahead of the crowd, and I didn't want to pick it up in case I would get hooked. I could see a Cork jersey in front of the goals and that's what I was aiming for. I didn't know who it was and, as it turned out afterwards, it was John Fitzgibbon. I suppose it was one of those things. I connected perfectly, dry sod, dry ball. It had everything going with it, the momentum and the whole lot and it hit the net.

Leonard Enright missed the goal:

All I remember was I went out and was knocked by one of my own players and didn't even see the goal. When I got up and walked back I knew from the roar of the crowd that something had happened, so I went back and I asked Tommy Quaid what was after happening and he said nothing. When I looked at the scoreboard I saw that a goal had been scored.

It was Pa Creamer who collided with Enright:

I was marking Teddy McCarthy, but just as the John Fenton goal was scored, I had been switched to midfield and was making my way out to pick him up when Leonard Enright and myself had a collision. Tomás Mulcahy and Leonard were running out to the ball and Mulcahy pushed Leonard into me, and the two of us collided and fell over. It left John Fenton free. It mightn't have been blocked anyway; it was just one of those great goals.

Gary Kirby feels Limerick had missed their chance:

We were confident coming into the replay. Cork upped their game, and we probably weren't able. It was always a known fact that if you wanted to beat the top teams back then, you had to catch them in the first game. Once Cork got a game under their belts maybe they improved, where we might have gone back from the first day. We won the under-21 final between the draw and the replay. We were after winning the All-Ireland final and we played the following week with the seniors. I think we would have been better off if Pa was left at full-back. Leonard probably wasn't right. I remember Tommy Quaid saying that he had the ball covered from Fenton's shot, he was lined up to stop it, and as the ball came in, it swerved, and with that change of direction it was gone in. There was nothing he could do about it.

Jimmy Carroll believes the goal was not unstoppable:

The '87 ground ball was a tremendous goal. I remember talking to Tommy Quaid at the time. He was devastated and said the ball was in his vision at all times, and hadn't taken any deflection but when he went to save it the ball dropped, lost its momentum and swerved. They said at the time that it rocketed to the net, but I don't believe it did.

Between 1988 and 1991 Limerick were defeated by Tipperary each year in Munster and could scarcely afford to lose any player. Seán Herbert, now involved in schools coaching in Limerick, was on the League-winning panel of 1984. A younger brother of Pat from the famed Ahane dynasty, in 1988 he played senior inter-county hurling for Dublin:

I played club hurling with Ballyboden. My brother Pat was with Ballyboden, but he was already established with Limerick. I would have needed to be Limerick based to make it.'

Another League winner, Ray Sampson, had also drifted from the scene and played for the New York senior hurling team for a while.

Éamonn Cregan was still in charge for the 1988 championship but departed after that:

I couldn't get it across to the players in 1988 and get them to understand that Tipperary had never beaten us in the championship for sixteen years. I pulled out after two years, it was time to go, my two years were up.

The final link to the 1973 team, Liam O'Donoghue, also called it a day:

I got sick at the end of 1987, I got the ME virus and it knocked the stuffing out of me. I went back for 1988 to prove I could come back. I played as a sub against Tipperary in Cork for the last fifteen minutes and I retired after that. Preparations weren't great that year. A lot of our training for that match was in Kilmallock. We weren't firing on all cylinders at all and that was probably down to being beaten the previous year.

Almost immediately, O'Donoghue became part of a three-man selection committee with Donie Flynn and Tony Hickey:

When I finished up in 1988, Jim Hickey, the chairman, got on to me to get involved. A lot of people said to go for it. There was no voting, it was just ratification. I think Jim Hickey didn't want to lose me to the game straight away. I enjoyed my time when I was there. We certainly contributed a certain amount to what came afterwards. We brought in the best talent that was there, and we weeded out a lot of the guys that weren't going to make it. We had a lot of trials and gave

Phil Bennis polices the sideline during a national league game played at the
Gaelic Grounds in 1992.

everyone a chance. I think anyone good enough at the time was brought in and looked at. I don't think anyone was ignored. We also took recommendations from others at the time as well regarding players who were going well.

Phil Bennis was also involved:

Donie Flynn took over the senior team and I came in as a coach. It didn't suit me. I had never worked as that. I wasn't in charge, and when you are not in charge you aren't comfortable. In fairness, the three selectors gave me everything I wanted, but still I felt I wasn't in charge. It's not bigness but I prefer to have the full input. If you are the boss you take full control, and if it all goes wrong you are the one to blame, not anyone else. I could be wrong too because there are other people who can work like that but I can't. That was a time when you needed great fitness; I think Seán Hickey, an army man, was training them that time. I felt I hadn't much to offer in the setup and I felt I was going to only do harm to myself and to them so I left it be after the first year.

The nadir of Limerick hurling came in 1989 against Tipperary in Páirc Uí Chaoimh. Nicky English recalls the game:

We had been in the All-Ireland final in 1988, and 1989 was a big year for us. We were expecting big things, and Limerick weren't bad at the time. The Limerick games would carry extra spice for the likes of Pat Fox and myself in west Tipperary who weren't far from the border. Some players would be bordering different counties, so the natural rivalry depends on where a player is from. There was an unusually high number of players from west Tipperary. There was a heightened atmosphere around Cullen, Oola, Cappawhite, Annacarthy and Doon. It was a neighbourhood rivalry. I remember Tipperary being very worried at half-time and Declan Ryan having to be switched to midfield on Ger Hegarty who was playing well. We brought on Cormac Bonnar who went to full-forward and I went corner-forward and that was the birth of the Fox/Bonnar/English full-forward line. That was the key switch in that match; it really released myself and Fox and there was a lot of damage done that day in the second half and we ran out easy winners.

Babs Keating, the Tipperary manager that day, focused on his side's scoring potential:

We had a serious full-forward line. When I took over Tipperary, I analysed every Munster final and All-Ireland that was played and I discovered that 73 per cent of scores from play came from the full-forward line of the winning teams. Nicky English was playing in the half-forward line when I took over and I moved him into the full-forward line. I was determined to put together a full-forward line that had the strength to achieve those kind of scores. And Fox, Bonnar and English were able to do that and they did it against Limerick that day. They were lucky enough to have John Leahy and Declan Ryan outside them.

For Limerick, Terence Kenny recalls his telepathic relationship with Shane Fitzgibbon:

Fitzgibbon was one of the best corner-forwards I played with, and he was great to read the breaks. Tipp were strong that year, and went on to win the All-Ireland. It would have been my style of play to win it and lay it off, and Shane was exceptionally fast and able to read it. We profited from that early in the game.

Phil Bennis says they had worked on developing the partnership:

We had trained Kenny and Fitzgibbon before the match to work off one another. Fitzgibbon's role was to run off the ball and Kenny had to lay it off. Ger Hegarty had a fierce game in the first half but the team all stopped in the second half, whatever happened.

Dave Punch recalls Tipperary's second half onslaught:

We were level at half-time but Tipperary got two goals early in the second half and within the fifteen minutes we were down about twelve points. The game was over then. Once we had succumbed to that sort of scoring there was no hope of getting it back.

From 1988 to 1991, Limerick lost four Munster under-21 finals in a row. Phil Bennis recalls the 1988 decider:

Cork beat us in 1988 in Midleton, we were in the game until the last ten minutes. We got a goal. It hit the stanchion and it wasn't awarded to us, and Cork went down and got a goal immediately. We had a good enough team but not as good as the year before. Mike Houlihan was away in the States and was being flown home. We should have started Ciarán Carey. He came in and scored a goal that night. He was only a minor but I believe if a player is forty or ten, if he is good enough he should be played.

Stephen McDonagh says the 1990 defeat was a learning experience:

I was a sub in 1989 in Thurles for the under-21s. We were hammered by Tipperary with the likes of Declan Ryan, John Leahy, Conal Bonnar and Liam Sheedy on their team. The following year I was playing corner-back and conceded two goals in the first twenty minutes and was taken off at half-time. I was marking Anthony Wall and I never forgot him. The one thing I took from that was that I never forgot those beatings, especially the night in the Gaelic Grounds in 1990. You are playing for Limerick. It's a big thing for your family and next thing you are gone after half an hour. It was either row in or row out then. I felt that unless I trained like blazes that I had no chance. I made up my mind that it would be the last time it happened if I got the chance again. I suppose I met a few humps and hollows along the way.

In 1991 Limerick finally beat Tipperary after a trilogy of games before losing the Munster final to Cork. Joe Quaid recalls the semi-final encounters:

We were being well beaten by Tipperary in the first game in 1991. Michael Ryan was corner-back on the Tipperary senior team but was full-forward on their under-21 team and had scored two goals. With about fifteen minutes to go, Pat Heffernan told me to look after Ryan, that he was going up the field. He went up and turned the game and we got a draw.

I will never forget the second game. It was a dreary night in Kilmallock, and Ken Ralph pulled on a ball and instinctively I put my hand up. I looked up and there was the ball stuck to my hand, and I cleared it over the sideline. The crowd cheered and the umpire went for the flag but hesitated. The ref went in and said to the umpire, 'That was a goal, wasn't it?' and the umpire said, 'I don't know what happened but it didn't go into the back of the net anyway.'

Frankie Carroll says the underage performances represented hope for the future:

At the time in 1991, the Limerick seniors weren't going well, and that under-21 team seemed to catch the imagination of the supporters more so than the under-21 teams of the previous three years. There

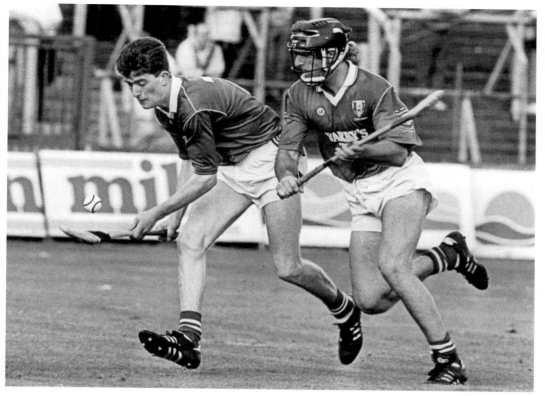

John Kiely (*left*) tries to evade a challenge from Cork's Brian Corcoran (*right*) in the 1993 Munster under-21 final at Páirc Uí Chaoimh.

was massive support for that team; for an underage team, the crowds were unprecedented. We turned over a Tipperary team that had beaten us well at minor so we were making progress. We could have won the Munster final against Cork. The scoreline didn't reflect the performance. I kicked a ball for a goal and it hit the crossbar.

The senior team started the 1990 championship in fine form, defeating Clare convincingly in Ennis. However, the semi-final defeat to Tipperary is remembered for the controversial sending off of Mike Barron following an incident with Cormac Bonnar. Barron was sent off for retaliation, while Bonnar stayed on the field. Many felt that if one was being dismissed, the other should have gone too.

Nevertheless, Donie Flynn feels progress was being made:

The 1989 game was a disappointment but we still felt we had the nucleus of a good team who could go on to be successful. In 1990 we went to Ennis and won by 2-16 to 1-5. We felt that Dave Mahedy had the team in peak condition and played the first half against Tipperary in a manner that endorsed our belief. Luck deserted us with the sending off, as we felt both players should have been sent off rather than just one. We had Mick Doyle lined up to assist us in motivating the team in 1990, but before everything was finalised with the county board, he mentioned it in his Sunday newspaper column on the weekend of national congress in Dublin. The Limerick delegates were probably frowned upon there when it appeared in the paper and we never got the go ahead to bring him in.

Dave Mahedy feels the old championship system was a hindrance:

Maybe there was a bit of naivety on my part: it was my first time involved. The team seemed to click but the sending off took its toll. In those days there was no back door, you worked your socks off for nine months in training and then you were gone. The Clare game gave us confidence going into it. It wasn't a bad team, it was a good mix of core players; they weren't a million miles away. In the championship you need to get on a run like 1994 or 2007. In 1990 the team never got momentum so we never really got to see the potential of that team.

Shane Fitzgibbon feels the skill level needed improvement:

The big lesson from 1989 was that while we had performed well in the first half, Tipperary steamrolled us in the second half. Dave Mahedy came in 1990 and there was a huge step up in terms of how the team was being prepared physically. Even then, though we were close to the mark from a physical perspective, our hurling was still a long way off the mark in 1990. Despite the difference in hurling levels, I believe to this day we would have beaten Tipperary in the Gaelic Grounds in 1990 but for the sending off of Mike Barron. We were physically fit enough that year, and if we had played fifteen versus fifteen for the full game, I think we would have pulled through.

In January 1991 Gerry Bennis became chairman and Mike Fitzgerald, treasurer of the county board. Fitzgerald recalls being in the midst of controversy almost immediately:

Soon after we were elected, the senior hurling selectors weren't getting along with each other and they actually resigned. For one League game it looked like the county board officers would have to put out the team. They came back eventually and agreed to pull together again for the championship.

As in 1990, Limerick defeated Clare, this time at the Gaelic Grounds, with the half-forward line of Ciarán Carey, Gary Kirby and Mike Galligan contributing 0-19 out of 0-21. Kirby ended the year with an All-Star. Next up were Tipperary in Thurles. In the run-up to the game Ciarán Carey was involved in a horrific accident:

I was after buying a boxer dog, and on a Friday afternoon, I was driving a few posts to build a run for him. I broke the handle of the sledgehammer and there was a lump of timber stuck in it that I was trying to get out to replace the handle. I was tapping it out and eventually I tried to burn it out using petrol. It was a beautiful day and I was only wearing a pair of togs and runners. It was still lighting and some of the residue fell on the can of petrol. I pulled back the can and the petrol fell all over my chest and my right leg. I was blessed! I remember racing out the garage door and jumping over a heap of cement blocks to throw myself on the lawn to quench my chest and my leg. My mother phoned Dr Hurley, RIP, straight away. He said to pour constant buckets of water over me and then wrap me in a white sheet. P. J. O'Grady brought me to the hospital and the first thought in my head was, 'That f***s Sunday week.' I came back for the under-21s. Once I was back, I was back. The marks were there because the wounds were fresh but the healing process was under way.

Carey's loss in the Tipperary game was incalculable, and the team suffered another blow when Shane Fitzgibbon failed a fitness test. Mike Galligan says Semple Stadium was not a place for the faint-hearted that day:

That was a dirty game. I was blamed a lot in the media for injuring John Kennedy and damaging his cruciate, but it wasn't a dirty belt. He stood over a ball and I pulled. Everyone on the pitch knew the next person to pull on someone would go and Anthony Carmody got the line for a loose pull on Michael Cleary.

Carmody concurs:

It was a wet day and a lot of things flared up. I think there was an incident in the square that Terence Kenny and Bobby Ryan were involved in and there was a boot drawn on the ground. Some things were let go and in the next incident Cleary got the ball and I was probably trying to reach to knock the ball off his hurley. Whatever way he turned as I was pulling, he got it across the side and of course he dropped like a bag of potatoes. It wasn't malicious or vicious. The referee had already his mind made up that there was someone going to walk for the next incident and unfortunately I got caught up in that. I suppose that was probably the end of our hopes of winning.

Preparation most years was universal and there was no year you could say that we weren't well prepared. It's trying to put your finger on what went wrong in the game itself is the thing.

Terence Kenny believes the heads dropped in the second half. 'Things weren't going our way and we threw in the towel.'

Dave Mahedy says the mindframe was not right:

In 1991 it was one thing after another. Ciarán Carey's accident was a freak; I think something similar happened Peter Clohessy prior to a Munster [rugby] game. How do you plan for those things? Discipline is key and you need to have that experience and that winning feeling to get through games but it was a case of 'here we go again'. The psychology of that in your head is that you accept that you are not going to win. That's how important psychology is in sport. We lost to a Wexford team that lost a man in 1996 and they won, and sometimes it can go in your favour. Because we didn't have the confidence built up from winning in previous years, it was a case of 'here we go again' and it will be another Limerick sad story of so close and yet so far.

Following the championship exit, there were changes to the management structure, as Gerry Bennis explains:

The management began to disagree with one another, and we replaced them. Donie Flynn pulled out and we went for a new management. We felt that Donie Flynn was the stronger of the three at the time, and we wanted Liam O'Donoghue to go in as a selector as part of a new management but he wouldn't. He wanted to stay with Tony Hickey, he was probably right not to part from him. At the time we thought that he might go in as part of a new package with a new manager, whoever it may be, as Phil hadn't come into the equation at that stage yet.

The appointment of Phil Bennis as manager did not please O'Donoghue:

We were supposed to have another year, and Donie Flynn left the three-man setup and Gerry Bennis then said, 'If there's one gone, ye all have to go.' At that stage I said, 'If that's the way the chairman was talking it's a disgrace.' Gerry was lining up his brother Phil for the job, and I knew that and I lashed out in the media. At the time, people had said to me that I should fight him on that issue but I left it go. I didn't contest the position. We felt that the talent was there, that we had unfinished business and weren't allowed to finish it. Tony and myself were prepared to plough on. Donie had enough, but there were plenty people there willing to replace him. To this day I think we should have been left to see out our term.

Phil Bennis has regrets:

The previous selectors shouldn't have been shafted, they had a year to run. Liam O'Donoghue was a good man on the sideline. I felt a bit sorry for them to be honest. I slipped up and should have left it be. I would have waited for the job. There was a bit of sourness there but they were right and the county board shouldn't have done it. They were good, passionate men. They were unlucky; when you lose a match you should get a chance. I was disappointed for them. When I was asked to do the job, they were already gone. I was hoping I wouldn't be asked given the circumstances and I didn't expect it, but when the call came it was hard to turn it down.

Ciarán Carey is full of praise for O'Donoghue. 'Liam was a good manager. I had great time for Liam O'Donoghue as a person and he was good to address the team and he had a nice way about him.'

Limerick won the 1992 League final against Tipperary 0-14 to 0-13 having been 0-11 to 0-3 down at half-time. Ciarán Carey was a revelation. He recalls being converted into a centre-back a couple of months earlier:

One Thursday night we were in Punch's in Patrickswell having a meeting about the club history being produced at the time, *Up The Well*. The Limerick selectors happened to be having a meeting in another part of the pub. I went into the toilet and no sooner was I in there when Phil arrived in and he told me straight up, 'You are playing centre-back on Sunday against Kilkenny and you are marking John Power. There's no fear of you, you will manage him.' I would have been hurling senior with Patrickswell under Phil for six years prior to that, so anything he would have said, I would have treated as gospel.

When I look back on my inter-county career I would have a special place in my heart for 1992. It was the first time I started playing centre-back and we won the League, beating Kilkenny, Cork and Tipperary along the way. They were three serious scalps. And in the final itself, aside from being down at half-time, Tipperary were after hammering us four years in a row in the championship and I had my own misery against them at underage level so it was payback time. The manner in which we did it was unbelievable.

Frankie Carroll was excited at the prospect of working with Bennis:

Players had a spring in their step when they heard Phil was appointed, because he had a proven track record of being successful at club level and underage level with Limerick. Everyone was hoping he would bring that to the table. He got the team at a low ebb, and won a League, which was a massive boost considering the team were in the doldrums in the late 1980s and early 1990s. It lifted the team and the supporters. Ray Sampson got the winner in the League, a superb overhead strike. I had never seen a score like it before and it hasn't been repeated since.

In the championship a confident Limerick just scraped past Waterford in the Munster semi-final thanks to a superb Tommy Quaid save late in the game. Terence Kenny was an unexpected choice at wing-forward that day:

We had a challenge against Cork in Cork on the Saturday before the Waterford game and I was on a young, inexperienced player. I caught every ball in the air and was able to do what I liked. The following day was the official opening of the pitch against Monagea and I was playing wing-forward again. Offaly were a bit mixed up and were late arriving. I got the man of the match award. After two good matches, he [Bennis] kind of had to give me the run in the championship and I started at wing-forward. When things weren't working on the wing I thought he could have put me in at full-forward on Damien Byrne but he moved me in corner-forward and then he took me off before half-time.

The story goes that Offaly had only fourteen players that night in Monagea and that Kenny was, in fact, marking the Offaly bus driver. Due to lack of video evidence, the tale is best catalogued as an urban legend!

Limerick lost the Munster final to Cork by 1-22 to 3-11 in extreme heat at Páirc Uí Chaoimh. Phil Bennis sees it as one that got away:

We brought Declan Nash to midfield and the forwards. He was going well at wing-forward in training, but it didn't work out in the Munster final. We should have brought Frankie Carroll in. He ended up proving us wrong afterwards.

Tomás Mulcahy got the goal that cost us the game; he ran about ten yards and threw it from one hand to the other. It would be a free fifty years ago not to mind in 1992. We should have been five or six points up at half-time. Kirby, Carmody and Fitzgibbon missed goals before half-time. We should have won that match.

Anthony Carmody remembers his miss:

The ball broke in to me behind Jim Cashman and I had a straight run in. They closed me down and you couldn't handpass a goal by then, so I was caught in two minds: do I flick it with the hurley or do I kick it? I made up my mind to use the hurley and Cunningham saved it. It should have been a goal, but I was never renowned for scoring goals and I suppose I got a nosebleed!

Frankie Carroll acknowledges that the better team won. 'Cork beat us well in that final. We took a big hiding; we got late goals to camouflage the scoreline.' Shane Fitzgibbon feels the tank was empty:

We had left everything in the League and on the training field and were a spent force by the time we got to the Munster final. We were primed to win the League and we didn't make the step up for the championship.

Mike Houlihan recalls the controversial Mulcahy goal:

We were approaching the Cork game with confidence. We would have seen them in 1990 winning the double but we hadn't played them in the championship for a few years. We met them in the League semi-final in 1992 and beat them easily enough. Mulcahy caught the ball over me and I fell down on the ground with his hurley in my hand and felt, 'He isn't going to do much here.' He juggled the ball in his hands and Pa Carey had hit him a flog of a hurley going through. He had travelled ten or twelve steps but the referee let him through and he kicked the ball to the net. We protested anyway but he didn't see any of it. At that time referees didn't consult the umpires like they do nowadays. It was an extraordinary decision. I have heard Tomás Mulcahy joke about it on *The Sunday Game*. That's all right for him, having a Munster medal in his pocket and working in the bank. It was a big thing for us to get us off the ground. Business-wise that time, if you won a Munster title with Limerick, the world could be your oyster as things did open up for people that time. If you won a Munster medal, it would be a serious thing, and I am not saying we would have won the All-Ireland but we were there with a chance anyway. You would prefer to have the chance of doing it than not have the chance of doing it.

We made mistakes, Cork made a lot of switches that day. I had marked Tony Sullivan several times and whatever way it worked out for me, I used to enjoy O'Sullivan. I was able to wrap him up. He was brilliant to get the ball but he used to be one sided. I was a right-handed hurler, and whereas Ciarán used to try to block him, I used to try to hook and go out over him and push him and shove him around the place. I marked him a few times and nearly always held him scoreless, even in the League semi-final that year. I always felt I had the measure of him and I wouldn't ever say that about too many players, to be honest. Mulcahy wasn't any different but he was a breaking player who would run at you. Maybe I hadn't the same pace as Ciarán and he would have suited Mulcahy better. Cork made a lot of cute switches, they moved Barry Egan in on Anthony Riordan and they moved Ger Fitzgerald out on Andy Garvey. And once that went against us, everything was against us and the goal went in.

Declan Nash was a naturally fast player and Phil wanted to see if he could introduce pace into the forwards. He was forfeiting Ciarán Carey from wing-forward to go centre-back, so he needed to add pace to the forwards.

Willie Barrett does not have fond memories of the decision to allow the goal:

There were two Cork forwards there, one was Hennessy and the other was Tomás Mulcahy. What I thought I saw was that Hennessy caught the ball – he was the taller of the two – and he moved to the left while the other players moved to the right. I was a good bit back from the play as the ball had been cleared quickly out of defence, and as I was making up ground, I followed Hennessy. When Hennessy turned around I saw that he no longer had the ball, so I switched to

Mulcahy and what I saw was Mulcahy kicking the ball to the net, and the flag went up. The goal was given, the umpire put up the flag, I didn't make any more of it at the time. We went in at half-time and at that stage I still wasn't aware that the ball was fouled. When we came in after the match at full-time, I asked them what they thought, and one of the umpires said that he didn't think I would be happy about one of the goals. I asked which goal, and he said, 'Mulcahy's goal, I think he fouled it.' And I said, 'Why didn't you tell me that at half-time?' They said that the goal had been given and they didn't want me refereeing the second half thinking about a mistake.

I will always remember walking into the Galtee Inn in Cahir that night and just as I came in the goal was being shown on *The Sunday Game*. I looked in absolute horror when I saw the goal on the television. One person in the bar said to me, 'Did you allow that goal today?' They showed it about seven or eight times and I wasn't able to eat my dinner. I remember reading the paper the next day and, to be honest, it destroyed the day for me. The margin by which a team wins in the end is irrelevant; nothing can take away from what was a bad error on my part by allowing a goal of that nature.

A source close to the inter-county setup at that time believes Tommy Quaid should have made a stronger protest:

He should have refused to puck out the ball in 1992. If I was in goals I would have caused trouble, I would have gone out the field after the referee with the flag, even if it meant getting myself sent off for the sake of the team.

In 1993 Limerick were beaten 3-14 to 1-11 by Wexford in the League semi-final. Rumours about discipline were rife, with some players regularly seen out and about on Saturday nights before big games. When Limerick were knocked out of the championship by Clare in Ennis, Phil Bennis was removed as manager. He believes the signs for Limerick were ominous:

There was a storm of a wind that day and we should have played with it instead of going against it. They came out all guns blazing, and we probably came out not hyped up enough. I am a believer in not hyping a team up too much. We were well down at half-time and we came back and Houlihan was sent off but shouldn't have been. The team was slipping a bit and I knew things weren't right but I was trying to put it right. Before we played Clare in the championship, we brought a few players into the panel. I knew that there wasn't an All-Ireland in them but I thought we would have got over Clare. There was something wrong with the team. I knew there was something wrong two months earlier and I should have stepped in and taken action but I didn't. If we had got over the Clare match, I would have shook that team up a bit. A lot of it was that I wasn't happy with certain players but I was the manager and I must take the stick.

After the Wexford game I should have been honest with the media. I went into the dressing room that day and was raging; they pushed us around a bit. We were missing Pa Carey and Ger Hegarty in Ennis. Anthony Carmody and myself had a few words earlier in the year because he wasn't getting games. We are closer to one another since, because he played for Patrickswell. He would have been honest for us below in Ennis and we would have got through if he was there. I wasn't there the following year to rectify it. In 1994 we would have won the All-Ireland. I knew the problems that were there, and knew the mistakes that were made. I didn't have the team as right as it should have been but I knew where it went wrong. But I was very disappointed with the decision to go down to Ennis after asking the county board not to. We wanted that game in Thurles.

The decision to play in Ennis was not endorsed by management, as Mike Weekes explains:

I could write a book about that and the county board fixing the game for Ennis in 1993. Donie Nealon had wanted to arrange the fixture for Limerick and Clare months beforehand so we met the players in Mary Immaculate College and we all agreed on Thurles. The team management then met the county board – Mike Fitzgerald, Gerry Bennis and Jimmy Hartigan. We all agreed on Thurles but Mike Fitzgerald hesitated and said, 'Would ye not think of a toss because we are trying to get home fixtures to bring money in for the Gaelic Grounds?' I will never forget – we were coming down the stairs afterwards – Phil said to them, 'Make sure ye don't change your minds, it's Thurles and nowhere else.'

A few nights later the county board met Clare and the Munster Council and they tossed without us knowing and lost it. Phil rang me the following day and told me they were after tossing, and we had to go to Ennis. I arrived for training that night and it was like a morgue, the players were inside. Mike Houlihan was the captain and thought we were responsible and wasn't impressed. Once they knew they were going to Ennis, the effort wasn't the same. Their attitude was all wrong. I think we would have beaten Offaly the following year if we were still in charge.

Stephen McDonagh was superb in the League quarter-final against Galway earlier in the year and, given that 'Sparrow' O'Loughlin ran amok, many believed he should have been playing in Ennis:

There was probably a theory out there that I should have been playing, but that was hindsight. I was coming from a low base and it probably was a big risk to play me. The unfortunate thing about that game for Phil Bennis was that it cost him his job. Good Limerick teams found it hard to win in Ennis, but the knives were out for him.

That evening in Ennis we went up to the Old Ground for a bit of grub and the Limerick crowd were baying for blood. I remember talking to Vincent Foley in the lounge that night and they knew they were in trouble. I was young and keeping my powder dry. It would have been nice to be on the team but I would never have held it against Phil. If I was twenty-six or twenty-seven you would say something, but for a young fella to go out in Ennis . . . if he played me, it could have ruined me. They would be saying, 'What did he go out with a young fella for?' It's such a fine line.

Jim McInerney gives an interesting Clare perspective:

We were at a very low ebb coming into the game, having been beaten badly in the League quarter-final. John Russell carried an injury into the game, and hadn't trained for three weeks, but he had a tremendous game at centre-back. Things weren't going well training-wise. 'Sparrow' was dropped off the panel, and the week prior to that game they brought him back again, and he trained once or twice. Alan Neville got injured, and 'Sparrow' came in and scored 1-5. Another guy might never have made it again.

Gerry Bennis regrets the decision of the county board to go against the wishes of the management, a decision which cost his brother his job:

Ennis was a graveyard for Limerick hurling and they barely came out of it against London in 1973. I felt at the time that if they were good enough to win it, the venue wouldn't matter. Jimmy Hartigan and myself agreed to toss with Brendan Vaughan, the chairman of

Clare county board at the time. We lost the toss. I will never forget when I told the selectors, they nearly killed me. Phil said if it was anyone else only me as chairman that he wouldn't go down to Ennis. I think people get paranoid. I think if they went down with a positive approach and said, 'That's the right place for us,' they would have won it. I think they may have been a beaten team before they went down there. It was a stumbling block for them. Jimmy Hartigan and myself have to take the blame for tossing. I think we should have given Phil and his selectors another year. I think he would have won an All-Ireland with them. The big problem after Ennis was that the county board meeting was held on the following Tuesday night, and the defeat was too fresh in people's minds on that night.

Mike Fitzgerald also feels the timing of the meeting cost Bennis his job:

When Phil's team got caught in Ennis, there was uproar. He was very unlucky that the county board meeting was very soon afterwards. There was a feeling that the team was badly managed. There was probably an anti-Bennis thing as well – Phil as manager, Gerry as chairman and the team not going well. Phil was removed.

Bennis had reigned for just eighteen months. A positive note was that, in 1993, the under-21s reached the Munster final against Cork, having defeated Waterford and Clare en route. Joe Quaid was in goals:

We beat Waterford in the first round and I think I conceded four goals that night. They were very fancied. I crashed my car going to the Clare game. I had been in college in Carlow and I picked up David O'Shaughnessey, who was in the army. I was passing out a car and another car came up outside me and side swiped me. It was my fault because I was rushing. I pulled in and said, 'Here are my details, I have to go,' and he left me off. I was fine and played the match and we beat them.

We should have beaten Cork in the final. John Anthony Moran got a ball and I think he hit the post. Billy McCarthy of Cork came through in the second half and it hit me on the forehead and went out wide and the ref gave a wide ball. It was an exact replica of what happened with Ger Cunningham and Martin Naughton in 1990. Afterwards Tommy Quaid said to someone, 'I can retire now, it's in good hands.'

Although three Limerick clubs – Ballybrown, Patrickswell and Kilmallock – lost All-Ireland club finals in the early 1990s, it proved there was talent in the county. Ciarán Carey was on the Patrickswell team beaten by Glenmore in 1991:

We thought we would get another chance after losing in 1991 but we didn't. It's a very difficult thing to win an All-Ireland club final in Croke Park unless you have an exceptional squad and have top class managers all the time. I knew going up that we made a mistake in that we stuck to our normal team. Glenmore had a few county players – the Heffernans, Michael Phelan, the O'Connors and Liam Walsh. We didn't have that, and I don't think we had it covered. They should have been handpicked out and we should have put lads on them to babysit them for the day. I don't think we reached our potential as a team on the day. I don't mind losing as long as we perform.

Mike Houlihan feels a lack of organisation cost Kilmallock in 1993:

Sarsfields won it back to back and were a good established club side. I cut my hand three days before the final and got eleven stitches in it. I slit my hand on a latch of an outhouse door. It was a bit of a hindrance on the day. The club made a massive effort but the biggest problem I would have was about being organised.

We got the 8 a.m. train to Dublin, and we were playing in the second game. The biggest problem was that one player was up at 5.30 a.m. getting kids ready and stuff. That's not the best preparation for the All-Ireland. I will never forget it . . . in the dressing room we were all yawning. We should have gone up the night before; Sarsfields were up the night before. I can't say it would have won us an All-Ireland but it certainly would have helped us.

Tom Ryan believes Ballybrown were unlucky in the 1990 final:

We played Loughiel in the semi-final and they had half of Antrim picked when we went up to play them. That was unbelievable altogether because it was played in the Glens of Antrim and every trick in the book was pulled to try and sidetrack us – drink and pubs, you name it. They were giving us free drink the night before and everything! We won in the North by a point and there was a battle royale after the match, the referee even got clocked. It was unbelievable altogether. That match in the glens was played like it was an arena. The place was mobbed. There was a huge crowd there from Limerick as well.

The All-Ireland final went well for us; the team played well and we kind of had it in our grasp and it slipped on us anyway. They got a fluky goal, a deflected goal. A few refereeing decisions went against us and we lost it by a few points. When you go that far, you have to win it to prove yourself. In Limerick, every day you go out you have to prove yourself, which is another mountain to climb, which shouldn't be the case.

The following year Ballybrown met Clarecastle in a tempestuous affair, as Tom Ryan recalls:

We won the county title in 1991 and made the Munster club but we walked into an ambush in Ennis. There were men sent off and the match against Clarecastle was abandoned with a few minutes to go. They actually took over the field, and there were Clarecastle people going around the field with hurleys that I hadn't seen for twenty years previously. We didn't play well, and were well beaten, but we were thrown out of it then and that finished our team. For the first time ever their officials came into the dressing room afterwards to make the speech and they came in with hurleys. A big row broke out in the game about nothing, became a row, and ended up as nothing again and the referee decided to abandon the game. He decided he would pull the plug, and we came out of that badly, both as losers and because the Munster Council had an investigation into it.

The Limerick clubs' success proved that there were hurlers of a decent standard in the county. It must be noted, however, that those All-Ireland club final appearances did not benefit Limerick in the championships of 1990, 1991 or 1993. Ironically, the one year that the county did not have a representative in the All-Ireland club final – 1992 – Limerick won the League and appeared in a Munster final.

❧

EIGHT

1994 (1): GREEN REVOLUTION

Following Phil Bennis' departure, the mantle was handed to Tom Ryan after an interesting selection process:

I think they got seventeen or eighteen nominations, there were a lot of nominations anyway. Ballybrown put in my name and reluctantly I left it in. I had no interest in the job. I didn't think I'd get it. I had no aspirations for it. I didn't canvass and while certain people, who are still in the county board, wore the tyres off their cars going around looking for votes to be elected, I didn't even go to the convention. Liam Lenihan and Rory Kiely were mad to become selectors. I didn't look for a vote. I didn't care whether I got a vote, and I didn't want the job at all. I was one of three candidates who was elected on votes after a PR system of voting, a great system which, in fairness, lasted a long time. It was by pure chance I got elected. A fortnight before the election my name had been withdrawn from the race. It wasn't withdrawn by me, or by my club, but by mysterious people. I was elected and straight away I was walking into a hostile county board. Gerry Bennis was chairman. He had originally agreed that Phil would have to go, and then he changed his mind at the end of the week. They were fighting a rearguard action to get Phil back in. But I had nothing against Phil Bennis, he was nothing to do with me. That management team had their chance.

Gerry Bennis says he was in an awkward position:

Tom Ryan came in as manager under the PR system. It was awkward for me, and if I wasn't there, if there was a chairman who could speak up for Phil, it would have helped him. Having a brother as chairman weakened his position. I acted as chairman, but I couldn't take sides, with the situation that was there. We should have waited a month before coming to any decision.

Ryan says relations were fraught from the outset:

The county board meeting was on a Tuesday night, and I was notified on the Wednesday. Gerry Bennis called into me at work and told me that I was elected as a selector. It was some time in mid-July. What happened then is important now, because it showed the hostility that we started with. My issues with the county board didn't develop overnight. I had known since the night before that I was elected because someone had contacted me. I didn't know what I was going into. I was involved with the club, I was involved in hurling, and I had no interest with any of them in the county board whatsoever. None. Gerry Bennis said he was going on holidays and that I wasn't to do anything until he came back at the end of August. The end of August was six weeks away. There was a League starting in early October. Limerick had no team.

I immediately reacted when he said that to me, and serious hostility developed. I don't know what he said to Rory Kiely and Liam Lenihan, because they were with him. They were his own people and he probably spoke to them the night before. I wasn't privy to what he said to them, and it didn't worry me. We had communicated during the day, we had arranged that, and they were very anxious for a meeting, and very anxious to dump the manager's job on me. They wanted to be on the bandwagon as selectors, had no interest in being manager . . . As far as they were concerned, it didn't matter if it was myself, Bock the Robber or anyone because he was going to be the manager anyway. You can quote me on that, because they are the facts. So anyway I said to him, 'Gerry, we [Ryan and the two selectors] are having a meeting on Friday night in the Woodlands at 7.30 p.m. We want to meet with the county board. If, as it looks like, you can't be there, have somebody in your place that can make decisions.' Those were the words I used. It was nearly solicitors' words at that stage, and this was our first encounter. Gerry Bennis didn't want me as manager. He still wanted Phil. He didn't want me anyway. I can guarantee you that.

Gerry Bennis vehemently denies any ill-feeling towards Ryan on his appointment:

It's not true to say anything other than that Tom was very well accepted from the start. He may have felt that because Phil was my brother that he wasn't accepted. I harboured no issues over Phil. Tom was elected fair and square and he had nothing to do with getting rid of Phil. What I felt about Tom was that I didn't know much about him, and I will be honest, I didn't think he would be as good as he was. The first thing I said to Tom was that if we had a problem, we would talk about it. And that's what we did, that was the system we had. If Tom had a problem we sat across the table, and we sorted it without going any further. I thought that it was a very happy year, until the holiday after the All-Ireland final in 1994. I found it very easy to work with Tom Ryan.

He does feel, however, that his brother would have gone one better:

Tom did well getting to two finals, but I think Phil would have gone one better. He had enough done with those lads at underage level to cross the finishing line in 1994. I thought at the time Phil was ousted too quickly, after only about a year and a half. He got two seasons; he was in the autumn of 1991 and he was gone in May 1993.

Ryan says the negative feeling goes back to when he was a contender for the under-21 manager's job some time earlier:

I'm not looking for conspiracy theories or anything, but I wouldn't be a fool. Jimmy Hartigan had asked me would I take over the Limerick under-21 team in 1993. I think it might have been the spring of that year. I said that I would come back to him. After asking me to become under-21 manager, they never actually contacted me any more from that point. They hadn't the courtesy to say you are not getting it, we are after giving it to someone else. Goodbye, good luck and f*** off.

I know that when Hartigan went back to Gerry Bennis . . . bang, that was the end of me. And they gave it to Canon Willie Fitzmaurice instead. I don't know what he had against me. He didn't want me anyway. I don't know why. I doubt if it was club rivalry. But why are we winning f*** all? There was a paper trail here. And then he came to me that day inside at work and said you are a selector, and don't do anything for six weeks until I come back from my holidays. Hadn't he fine holidays from the middle of July to the end of August.

Gerry Bennis has no recollection of the meeting with Tom at his place of work, but acknowledges that it may have taken place:

If I said anything like that it definitely had nothing to do with picking a panel. You can't interfere with selectors in those things, the only input I might have had could have had something to do with the appointment of the trainer.

He has no recollection, however, of the planned six-week holiday:

I don't go on too many holidays so I don't remember that. Tom was sticking out as the obvious choice for manager. I'd say Rory would have liked to have been manager, but they agreed on Tom.

Ryan recalls the first meeting with the county board on becoming manager of the senior team:

At 8 p.m. the contingent arrived from the county board. Mike Fitzgerald as treasurer, Jimmy Hartigan the secretary, and the man who couldn't be there until the end of August, Gerry Bennis, was the first man in the door. We sat down at the table. There were three of us at one side, and the three of them were sitting across from us. Gerry said he had something to say, and I said, 'That's what you are here for.' There was no cordiality; it was very formal. He said that Limerick hurling was in the doldrums and that we, the new management, were a disgrace in the eyes of the public. And bear in mind, we had two members of the county board on our side of the table; Lenihan was chairman of the west board and a member of the county board, Kiely was on the county board since the f***ing 1960s. He was the main man, Munster Council delegate and whatever else. I said to Gerry then, 'Sorry Gerry, I don't mean to interrupt you at all and I understand your position, but hold it a minute, don't be bringing any legacies onto us about the past (I'd be a bold bastard like, I wouldn't be for listening to someone like Gerry Bennis telling me what the story was). I don't disagree with you in your analysis of Limerick hurling, but remember that it was your brother Phil who was in charge of them. Don't be bringing any legacies onto us here, or onto me. I am not responsible for Limerick hurling the way it is up to this point.'

That was what you were dealing with from the word go. Those were facts. They were trying to force us out, trying to intimidate us, and hope that we would bow under the pressure. The intimidation that I, in particular, was subjected to, the other two fellows were oblivious to it, and they were in the sidelines anyway. I wasn't there with them. So that was how my reign as manager started and that wasn't conducive to success.

As well as opposition from the county board, Ryan says he also faced a revolt by some of the more senior players:

Between July and September we had an intensive trawl of the county for players. I decided then that I would make the call for divisional trials. We would set up a tournament and play for it. We had a lot of reaction to that, in the form of a boycott by several senior players. So it was intimidatory as well. You had factions again that didn't accept the management, a bit like what has happened in Cork in recent years. We were elected democratically in a vote, though. There was an orchestrated campaign at that time, and there were some key players who decided that they wouldn't turn up for the trials. There were more of them who decided to turn up at the last minute, reluctantly, but some members of the existing team felt they were above trials, that they weren't going presenting themselves for the trials, and they didn't. We were there, feeling our way, and that's all we were doing, feeling our way.

Rory Kiely recalls a trial game arranged for Bruff:

I was going out towards the entrance gate and a fellow said to me, 'It looks bad when you are going out to the gate to see if they are coming in,' and we actually were going out to see if they were coming. It was very hard to pick it up that time, to be honest. The interest wasn't there.

But it did not deter management from the job in hand, as Ryan recalls:

We kept at it, and we took on the brickbats that were being thrown at us and I decided myself that anyone who didn't turn up at a trial was gone from the panel. And that's what happened. A huge amount of work went in. We played Kerry twice behind in long grass outside Tralee, to try and get an auld team together. We went back on a bus of a weekend evening. It built up from there. The hostility of the county board was all the time ringing through. They did everything in their power to f*** me up. They blackguarded me. They blackguarded the team. There were incidents that took place over my four years and what happened was unbelievable.

Gary Kirby, a nephew of Gerry and Phil Bennis, was a well-established player at the time:

Phil was not reappointed and he was removed within a week of the Ennis game. I was disappointed because I felt we had something going for us. But at the end of the day a player has to go with whoever is put in front of him. If I had gone in with the attitude, 'F*** them, what they done to Phil, I won't bother any more,' who else is going to lose out only me. There's nobody else going to lose out. I wanted to play for Limerick and that was it and I was going to be fully behind whoever was there. Once Tom was in, I was behind him. I was made captain for the year, the club [Patrickswell] left it to Tom to pick it. They didn't want to pick between Ciarán and myself. And I remember I went home and I said it to my mother, and she said, 'Of all years you get picked as captain,' as if we were going nowhere.

Limerick finished the League around mid-table and Tom Ryan was determined to impose a strict regime in an effort to improve things:

I dropped Mike Houlihan for disciplinary matters in early 1994. It showed the players that we weren't going to put up with what was going on before. It's hard to say that there was a lack of discipline under Phil Bennis but there were certainly players trying to push out the boat at the start of my regime. I was tested from the word go. We weren't afraid to use the disciplinary procedure when it was needed, and I got severe criticism from all and sundry for that, including the county board, and got phone calls from the county secretary about it. Those things didn't worry me. We were all aware of the rules and regulations and there were no exceptions. The rules applied to everyone.

I'm a firm believer that county standard is three times above club level. The upgrading and the coaching of players, that I never got myself as a player, was foremost in our preparation, in our programme. We trained during the week and rarely trained on a Saturday or Sunday; they were rest days. We trained in the Gaelic Grounds. They are talking now about Brian Cody's methods. They were our methods, we were doing the very same things fifteen years ago. There were no weekends away in any hotel, in Breaffy or out in the Algarve or anywhere like that, and we got on fine without them.

We had a very strict regime. Dave Mahedy took charge of training, and he was the main man in the setup. He had a huge influence on the team preparation, team tactics, in so far as the physical aspect of the tactics. He had no restrictions put on him at all. He had a free hand to do whatever he wanted and he was under constant pressure from me to achieve higher.

Mahedy recalls Ryan's inspirational methods:

Because we had worked so well in Ballybrown and had success there made it that little bit easier, and we had a very good working relationship. I often meet Tom nowadays and he is always saying to me, 'I made you, Dave.' I don't argue with that. I was involved in soccer and rugby but Ballybrown was my introduction to hurling. Some of Tom's team talks were fantastic, lots of colourful language. Talk about a culture shock for me coming from the relative quiet of a soccer dressing room into the Limerick hurling dressing room with Tom Ryan giving a team talk. It wasn't just shouting and roaring though, he had a point to make.

I remember one day he brought in a heavy-duty chain of which one of the links was well worn and partially filed down almost to nothing. Every other link was perfect. I remember Tom bringing in the chain, putting it on the table and asking, 'Would you pull a vehicle with that? You are only ever as strong as your weakest link.' Anyone can speak about the weakest link but it was the visual aspect that he brought: it doesn't matter how strong the rest of the chain is, it's how strong the individual links are.

Tom could get the best out of players. His speeches couldn't have come off the top of his head, even if he never spoke from notes. There was order and method to what he was saying, and he would put a lot of thought into it. He was also very good at calling a spade a spade, and people knew exactly where they stood with him.

Ryan agrees that his methods were not for the faint hearted:

It was a very tough regime, very severe, but it was very fair. It was fair because there were no favourites. One of the most important aspects was that everyone knew what the position was. The first time we got together and trained as a team, the panel was picked to start the League in 1993. The rule was nobody would be told beforehand whether they would be playing or not. Charlie Hanley called out the team. There was very little contact with players on a one-to-one basis, except on a coaching basis only. If we were going down to Kerry to play a challenge game, Charlie Hanley called out the team, and if we were going up to an All-Ireland, Charlie Hanley called out the team. No one knew what the team was. There was never going to be a case of me going to a player and saying you aren't starting, but you will be on after ten minutes. Every time a player was dropped the first person that knew was himself, because we played the game on form. Form decided who played, form in training, form in the previous game.

On the Tuesday night after every game we played, we sat down for fifteen to twenty minutes in the dressing room and discussed the game. We closed the door and discussed the game. Every aspect was spoken out. I'm talking about the game as I wanted it to be played, not everyone else. We played to a pattern, we played to a style, our tactics were known, everyone knew. It was so intensive as regards the tactics of the match.

I look at rugby now and the intricacies of it and we were nearly the same. We rarely gave away frees. Look at the records – six or seven frees against us. I have never heard anyone comment on that. No man put off for four years in championship hurling. They don't count when you don't win, and even when you win they don't count for much either. All the bolloxes and experts outside in the public, and writing on the papers, they don't see these things. I wasn't going to spend Tuesday night telling someone that he wasn't playing for this reason or that reason or whatever. Nobody f***ing knew whether they were playing or not. And when the team was called out then everyone knew. And whether they liked it or not didn't matter to me. It was the same in the game – persistent fouling, pulling fellas down, all that kind of stuff was not allowed. And all that work in the background played a vital part.

A vital interception in the Munster club final between Ballybrown and Sixmilebridge in 1989 really brought home to Ryan the importance of a team holding its shape:

One of the Sixmilebridge midfield players broke through with the ball. Our policy was that when a player broke through with the ball from centre field, nobody would come to meet him. Nobody. Everyone has his own man, and the instruction was always to back off. He is the f***ing responsibility of his own f***ing man, and even with the situation of giving away a major [goal]. Because if a defender leaves his man to meet the player coming through, it's a simple handpass to the man he should be marking and bang – it's in the net. In that club final the boys were all in their positions marking their own men, and backed off. As the Sixmilebridge player was throwing up the ball to plant it in the net, and I mean plant it, Joe O'Connor, at the very last second, stepped in, intercepted and drove it 90 yards down the field. That's what we were at. Sit back. Teams like Kilkenny in every era would always try to draw you, and give out the ball to D. J. or Keher or whoever was loose. We were working to a game plan, and that wasn't just for finals, it was for every day. That was inside in training. That's why always I said in training, 'We are not here now for passing away time, we are here for a purpose.'

I don't want any credit for tactics, but these things were never noticed. I don't give one bollox about the public, don't give a f*** about supporters or anything, because they will blow with every f***ing wind that's blowing anyway. F*** them. That's what we did about tactics. The tactics consisted of about twenty minutes or half an hour of hurling and forty minutes of physical training, which was Mahedy's area, and I was watching it. After that we had forty minutes of hurling with a referee and four umpires. Mike Quaid of Feoghanagh was the referee most of the time. When we played matches, we sat into our cars and went to the hotel, had the meal. Everyone had the meal and then home. I was at home milking cows at 6 p.m. whether we won a Munster final below in Cork or not. The cows had to be milked and that was it.

All through winter and spring, the search for players continued. Frankie Carroll had been there under the previous regime and says the change in approach was clear:

Tom definitely brought discipline to the table in a major way. Tom was in charge and that was it, you knew who was boss. It's the big thing he brought to the party, he had an air of authority about him – 'Don't f*** with me' kind of a thing. There was probably a bit of indiscipline in previous years but he came in with a deliberate intention to have discipline. He was getting a team that had won a League and were getting to a Munster final, he was getting a nice team.

Joe O'Connor, who was dropped by Ryan, says the manager was 'definitely less tolerant' than those previously in charge.

Ger Hegarty was recovering from injury and feels the incessant gym work made him a better player:

I actually came back in the autumn of 1993 even though I didn't get back hurling seriously until March 1994. I came back a stronger player because you are physically stronger from all the training you are doing trying to get yourself right. You are also mentally stronger, because you have seen the other side of the fence and what injury can do. I was mentally stronger in 1994 than I had been in previous years.

Damien Quigley, who would finish the year as an All-Star, was slow to grasp the inter-county opportunity:

John Kiely was on the Limerick panel and I was living with him in Cork at the time. He was going up and down to Limerick the whole time for training and I was laughing at him. I thought he was f***ing mad, up and down training all the time with both Limerick and UCC and he loved it. I was captain of UCC and training so much with the college that I couldn't even get my head around it. When the Limerick selectors asked me, I didn't even join them straight away, I told them I would wait until the Fitzgibbon Cup was over. We were training so hard for that, combining it would have been madness anyway. I don't know how Kiely managed to combine them, he was mad anyway, but he loved it in fairness, loved going up and down. I couldn't have done what he did anyway. I really couldn't.

Quigley admits that he did not see himself as an inter-county contender:

I remember playing challenge games against Cork for UCC, being marked by lads that were nowhere near the Cork senior team, and getting nothing off them. I remember thinking if I can't get anything off those, there's no way I would ever make it as an inter-county hurler. There was no rocket science to it. Because of that I was very relaxed about the whole inter-county scene and I just didn't think I was good enough anyway.

In 1994 UCC defeated Brian Corcoran's Cork RTC in the Fitzgibbon Cup following a replay, a victory that Quigley believes won him his call up:

Cork RTC had a serious team. Actually I don't think we would have beaten them had they been wearing any other jersey, but for tradition sake alone, UCC couldn't be seen to be beaten by Cork RTC. Funny enough, the drawn game was on a Wednesday before a huge crowd at the Mardyke and I didn't puck a ball. The replay was on the following Saturday four days later and we scored 2-6; I banged in 2-2 of it. I started on Corcoran and he was moved off me. I'd say the Limerick selectors were at that game. If they had been to the Wednesday game it would have been a different matter. It wasn't that they were watching me in particular; it's just that they would have gone to the matches anyway to see all the Limerick players. If you can play Fitzgibbon you have a fighting chance of playing inter-county.

Quigley's inter-county career was nearly over before it began:

I never even started a National League match; all I played was ten minutes of the final game in Waterford. We played a few challenge matches with Limerick prior to the championship and in the last challenge game against Laois I very nearly didn't make it onto the pitch. As was the done thing for students at the time, I thumbed up from Cork to Limerick on Sunday evening. The match was in Doon at 7 p.m. and I was still in Charleville at 5.10 p.m. I was due to be picked up at my house in Limerick at 5.45 p.m. There were no mobile phones in those days. I was f***ed. There was the career gone before I started. That's the truth. Would you believe the father of one of the lads who I played with from Na Piarsaigh coincidentally happened to pass me on the road and picked me up in Charleville. I said, 'Jesus, Pat, am I lucky to see you,' told him the story, he put down the boot, barely made it in the door of my house at 5.45 p.m., got the gear in a bag, and gone out the road then to Doon.

Looking back now, the Charleville thing was a bit of a laugh. I mean, it wasn't as if I didn't allow enough time or was flippant about it. I always thumbed; you would always get a lift with the hurley in your hand. Times were different then, loads of people thumbed, it was the way to travel. Inter-county hurling is really all about small margins, tiny stuff. I actually hurt my ankle in that Laois match, and Tom said to get it right for the Cork game on 31 May. I gave an exhibition in that match, I didn't score very heavily but I was winning ball in the corner, it was one of those days where things happen, and I was very relaxed about it. In an earlier game against Offaly I scored a goal. Pat Heffernan put it on a plate for me. That ball barely scraped in under the crossbar, and it looked great but it could have hit the crossbar. In another challenge game, I scored a goal against Galway, and my marker's hand was there with mine, and he could have caught it just as easily. At that level it really is that close all the time.

Mike Nash, who had represented Limerick previously at senior level in 1989, became the new full-back on the senior team. Due to injury, however, he almost missed the first round of the championship in 1994:

I was playing against Doon in the county championship in Caherconlish and was chasing John Stokes when my boot got caught up in his and I did all the ligaments in my ankle. That was six weeks before the Cork game. I strapped up the ankle and barely got through the Cork match but I did the ankle again and missed the Waterford game. Playing that match destroyed it completely and put me out of the next match. It came right then for the Munster final.

My first real year was 1994, and I thought it was all over when I got injured before the Cork match. I thought, 'That's it, game up.' I was twenty-eight years of age. I went away and got my ankle strapped up to the last and I got to play anyway and I could hardly feel it under me. I thought my first match against Cork would be my first and only match for Limerick. We weren't too used to beating Cork – or anyone that time – and I said I would do the whole hog and take a chance on the ankle for that match as it could be the only one.

Joe Quaid, the star of that Cork game, might not have made it either:

I got injured that year, I had trouble with my groins and I was booked in for an operation with Gerry McEntee, but Dave Boylan [team doctor] said to me not to get them done, as the operation is not a guaranteed success. So I didn't bother. I remember coming out of training in the Gaelic Grounds some nights and going home on my tiptoes, barely able to walk, and getting two bags of garden peas out of the freezer to ice the injury. That was all through the League and on the lead in to the championship. That year we went up and played Meath in Trim and I had a bad game; I got dropped after that and Tom Hennessy was in goals for a while. I can't remember how they eventually decided which of us was going to be there, but I got the nod.

The Cork game was a watershed in the development of Tom Ryan's team – despite a wobbly start, as Declan Nash recalls:

We were in trouble. I'm sure Tom Ryan was having palpitations having put out his fresh new team and it was all falling apart before his eyes. It was the confidence booster we needed and we got it, and Tom was able to build on that, along with Dave Mahedy. Dave had a huge influence but it was Tom who put it together. Tom did a lot of the talking, Rory and Liam were really stepped back from it and Tom seemed to be, from our viewpoint, the driving force and seemed to be doing the lot.

Dave Mahedy also remembers the less than impressive opening:

In the Cork game we were two goals down and suddenly the whole thing took off. It should have been, 'Here we go again, another s**tty day against Cork on the Ennis road,' but we said to ourselves, 'We have nothing to lose, let's have a go here.' And we were waking up on the Monday morning and thinking, 'Hey, we are still in this.'

Gary Kirby recalls the turnaround before half-time:

I got a 21-yard free out a bit, at an angle. And I meant to tap it over but I mishit it, and it was deflected out for a 65. So [Mike] Houlihan took the 65 and I doubled on it and got a goal from it. And then nearly from the puck-out Pat Heffernan got a goal from it. And then I got another goal. It was totally turned around and the standing ovation we got at half-time going in lifted us big time. We just needed that bit of luck, which we got that day. Heffernan got the overhead flick near the end, which was a great goal. We scored 4-14 that day. It all took off from there.

Tom Ryan concedes that Limerick were extremely lucky:

Once Cork were beaten they were gone, you hadn't to meet them again that year. There was no such thing as saying, 'We would be better off in the qualifiers.' I'm a firm believer in championship hurling. One chance and you are gone, the knockout element. It improved hurling immensely for us. That win over Cork was lucky enough, but, sure, we were often without luck too down the years but we had it that day in the Gaelic Grounds.

Kirby recalls a humorous moment prior to the Cork game:

Tom Ryan brought in all the forwards to have a general chat before the start of the 1994 championship. I made the point that all the forwards shouldn't be afraid to shoot, to at least have a go. Frankie [Carroll] turned around and said, 'It's OK for you, you know if you miss it, you won't be taken off, but we have to look over our shoulders.' But that was the way they were thinking at the time. They weren't playing with confidence.

Joe Quaid remembers the turnaround in fortunes, and the effect it had on the whole team:

I will never forget getting up the morning of the Cork match. If there is one thing a goalie hates, it's a wet day. Fifteen minutes into the match there were two goals scored on me and I remember looking out towards the stand and thinking, 'What the f*** am I doing here?' My father was sitting in the stand, and although none of the goals were my fault, a fella behind him in the stand shouted out, 'For f***'s sake bring back Tommy Quaid.' By the end of the match he found out it was my father, and he was telling him I was the best thing since the sliced pan. I know we didn't win an All-Ireland but it was the first time Limerick had beaten Cork in fourteen years and the atmosphere in the dressing room after was just unreal. I couldn't imagine if we won an All-Ireland that it would be any better. It was probably my best game for Limerick, although nearly every save I made afterwards resulted in a goal.

Damien Quigley remembers some fickle supporters that day:

There was fierce abuse coming from the terraces. Some players just seem to draw abuse. It was a miserable day and the terrace was only half full, everyone else was all down at the other end of the field and Pat Heffernan and myself were inside in the full-forward line. And we may as well have been sitting at home having a cup of tea. Here were these two geezers roaring abuse at Beefy [Heffernan]. And Seán O'Gorman was at full-back and he hadn't pucked a ball either. It was only because it was so quiet at our end of the field that you would hear the noise. We were being destroyed as well so it was exceptionally quiet. When Beefy knocked in a goal and set up one for Kirby I heard the very same voices, 'Go on, Heffernan boy.' That's the GAA, isn't it?

Ironically, Heffernan finished the game as hero, following an audacious flick that deceived Ger Cunningham to seal the game.

Mike Houlihan says Cork expected to win – and with good reason:

I used to feed a lot of cattle that time and I remember the day of the game. Dave Clarke and myself were back at Rourke's Cross feeding the cattle and saw the Cork flags passing on the cars. We hadn't even left to go in at that stage. They would have been expecting to win. We didn't meet Cork that often, but they had the hoodoo over us. They beat us whenever we played them and expectations were the same again before this one in 1994. It just seemed to steamroll from there.

Mike Galligan remembers the commitment of the team and the satisfaction at winning:

We kept plugging away. Cork were an ageing team maybe . . . I was on Timmy Kelleher. It was great to finally beat Cork; you realised waking up the following morning. There was great satisfaction beating great players that you had watched winning All-Irelands.

Frankie Carroll agrees:

To win it in the fashion we did, having been down so much at the start, was excellent. Limerick teams in the past might have stayed down, whereas that team kicked on and won the game.

Next up was Waterford. Stephen McDonagh is grateful for the faith the manager showed in him despite a poor performance against Cork:

I got caught for two goals again, just like in the under-21 game against Tipperary. I suppose I will always be indebted to Tom Ryan for sticking with me after that. Putting me on Paul Flynn for the Waterford game was a huge vote of confidence because I was so disappointed after the Cork game. My confidence picked up then. It's amazing what the bit of faith can do, and I have never forgotten that. Even trying to deal with people you have to show faith in lads. Once it's shown in you it kind of rubs off and gives you great confidence.

After a one-sided first half Limerick went to sleep against Waterford, and it took a masterful performance from Ger Hegarty to pull them through. John Roche from Croagh/Kilfinny scored a crucial point that day, as Quigley recalls:

As in the Cork game, I was taken off in the second half again and he [Roche] came in for me. To be fair I shouldn't have been taken off as the ball hadn't come in. That shouldn't happen. The guys over the team should know that if I am not hitting the ball and the corner-back isn't hitting the ball either, then it's not coming in. John came in and got a great point, in fairness. He was an honest, tough guy with fierce raw potential if he got more coaching. I loved playing beside him because the ball would break all day. That was typical of Tom [Ryan]; he had the ability to recognise things in certain players and he would bring them into the panel. People would be seeing them in club games and saying, 'Jaysus, what's that guy doing in there?' but Roche had certain qualities.

Limerick defeated Clare to win their first Munster title since 1981. Gary Kirby had the honour of lifting the cup:

We had a mighty game with Clare, a very warm day. I used to love that, the hotter the better. We were on fire in the half-forward line; I ended up with 0-9 and Galligan got 0-7. It was a great honour for myself being the captain. We celebrated for a day or two afterwards, but we wanted to push on from there once we had it won.

Frankie Carroll became the third member of his family to win a Munster championship medal, following in the footsteps of his brothers Mossie and Brian. The Herberts were another great hurling family from many years earlier, but were not as fortunate in terms of silverware. Carroll was delighted with the success:

Both teams were looking at the Munster final as an opportunity. It was the first time in years that neither Tipperary nor Cork were there. We were on fire in Thurles. There were scores coming from everywhere and I have to say it was quite nice winning a Munster medal. It didn't match the euphoria of the Cork game, but it was lovely to win it. That's not belittling Clare, as they proved themselves a great team afterwards, but it was just that Limerick were so used to Cork shoving it down their throats for years that beating them was incredible.

Coming home from the Munster final, it didn't feel as good as the Cork game; perhaps it was due to the one-sidedness of that game.

Mike Houlihan concurs that Limerick were confident facing Clare:

We wouldn't have been frightened by Clare, but they were probably feeling the same about us. We were going well at the time, and the scoreline would reflect that.

Galligan feels Clare were tactically naive but that Limerick had a sureness about them:

Gary Kirby ends a fourteen-year famine as he raises the cup after
winning the 1994 Munster final.

I was marking a work colleague in John O'Connell. Clare made switches that made things worse. All they had to do was move both corner-backs, Anthony Daly and Liam Doyle, out to the two wings. We had a confidence about us in 1994; I suppose when you have the work put in you are confident enough. It was brilliant to win a Munster medal. They are occasions that don't happen every day. It's only now looking back that you appreciate that. I ended up back in Dromcollogher with my uncle and went up to my grandfather in Charleville. It was more pride than mad celebrating.

Anthony Daly captained Clare that day and harbours regrets about those switches:

We would have had fierce expectation in 1994; we were after beating Tipperary. There was a real buzz and we were after being hammered in the final the previous year. We were ready for this one, I thought. But it wasn't as bad as the previous year's game against Tipp, because I felt we were in the game at half-time. They made a few crazy decisions on our bench – unbelievable decisions. They took off John O'Connell who wasn't going that badly and he was the kind of player that was always going to come into the game. They brought on a rookie from Éire Óg, Francis Corey, at centre-back. At the same time Kirby was on a roll and Galligan had a great game in the first half. Ciarán was flying it. Our full-back line probably got the better of their full-forward line, but every other line was beaten by Limerick.

Jim McInerney says the Clare management showed a lack of faith in their centre-back:

It was Seán McMahon's first final and Gary Kirby had a big reputation. Our selectors had pre-empted that McMahon wouldn't be able for Kirby when, in actual fact, McMahon finished the first half of that Munster final fairly well. Then they made a cardinal mistake of putting him out to wing-back on Mike Galligan. Seánie McMahon was the greatest centre-back I ever saw but he definitely wasn't a wing-back and Galligan went to town.

For the All-Ireland semi-final against Antrim the injured Pat Heffernan was replaced by Leo O'Connor:

Rory Kiely had told me after the Munster final not to be disheartened at not getting a game that day. We played Cork in

Newtownshandrum in a challenge game after the Munster final and I came on and did well. We were training in Croke Park the week before the game and Tom [Ryan] came over and told me I was starting against Antrim. I actually thought Mike Wallace would start the Antrim game.

Frankie Carroll is modest about his exceptional performance:

The Antrim game was my first game in Croke Park and while there were no prizes on offer, it was nice to go up to Croke Park as a young player and score 0-7 and get the man of the match award.

Mike Galligan suffered an injury in the Antrim game, however:

Antrim weren't a bad team at the time. You could easily find yourself losing a semi-final to them, as Offaly found out in 1989. We were coasting. I remember Gary got a few bad belts. Then I broke my knuckle. It was half way through the second half, and I knew straight away. I remember getting the ball a few minutes later and I couldn't strike it. It's not the nicest thing in the world four weeks from an All-Ireland final.

Frankie Carroll recalls the build-up to the final:

It was like the Munster rugby team reaching a Heineken Cup final. When we got to the final in 1994, it was the only show in town. There was major hype before it. Tickets were the big hassle before it and it really caught the imagination. That Limerick team was a team worth following, a team that was going to perform, and perform we did – for sixty-five minutes.

Brian Whelahan says Offaly were very aware of Limerick's strengths:

The over-riding memory of it was that it was a fabulous occasion to have two teams outside of the big three that had a lot of success in the mid- to late '80s at underage level coming to the fore and fulfilling their promise by reaching an All-Ireland final. It was a huge occasion. There was great colour. There was huge expectation from both sides going in. We had a healthy respect for Limerick. We wouldn't have feared them in any way but at the same time knew there was huge capability within the team, if they were allowed to function, with the likes of Ciarán Carey, Gary Kirby and Declan Nash. Ger Hegarty was back with them that year after a long-term injury and things looked to be falling into place. We played against Limerick a lot that year between practice games and League and squared off against one another very evenly.

For Mike Galligan, it was a race against time:

The Wednesday three days after the Antrim match, I went to Paul O'Byrne in Barrington's clinic and he said to have any chance of playing in the final I needed to start bending the fingers immediately, that if I left my hand in the cast I wouldn't have the use of it. Annette Shanahan was the team physio, and I worked intensively with her to strengthen my hand.

However, I had no physical training done and it wasn't the best way to go into a final. I had back trouble at the time as well, and I got married the week before the final. I had been in top form that summer prior to the injury. Going in on Brian Whelahan in an All-Ireland final, I needed to be on top of my game but everything came all at once. I remember Anthony Daly in a preview saying, 'It's going to be very hard for Galligan to be up to speed with no training done.' He was right.

Brian Whelahan remembers Éamonn Cregan's predicament:

Going into that game all the hype was about Cregan training Offaly and being such a staunch hurler and Limerick man his whole life, and here he was managing a team trying to take down his own county. It was a job we had to do but it obviously didn't lie too well for him in the sense that, as he said himself, he got up that morning to come from Limerick; his son was in the Limerick colours.

From our point of view we had a job to do and didn't dwell too much on that. Well, I certainly didn't anyway. We started well and Limerick took over then for a lot of the game up until half-time. At the start of the second half we scored four unanswered points and Limerick kicked on again as if they were going to win it.

Cregan never foresaw such a situation arising when he accepted the Offaly job:

I was approached in 1993 by Offaly and I took it for the simple reason I didn't expect that they would ever meet Limerick in a championship match. Kilkenny beat us by three points in the first round of the championship that year, with us having a player sent off.

But that Offaly team always had the ability to beat Kilkenny. They played a beautiful brand of hurling, what I would call a Munster ground hurling plus Leinster Kilkenny style of flicking, plus their ability to score points from outside on the sideline was uncanny.

Cregan feels that first-half wides and a crucial switch were Limerick's undoing:

I can't understand why, to this day, Tom Ryan took Ger Hegarty out of centre-back and put Ciarán Carey back instead. Ger caught everything that came out of the sky in 1994 and drove it back up field. The moment that switch was made, the game started to go from Limerick.

Hegarty disagrees, however:

An awful lot of people mention the switching of myself and Ciarán as a turning point, but I don't agree. I was always just as comfortable at midfield as I was at centre-back and Ciarán was the same; he was equally comfortable at centre-back as he was at midfield.

Joe Quaid believes the switch definitely had an impact:

I think the big turning point came earlier than Johnny Dooley's goal, and that was moving Hegarty out of centre-back, because he was lording it there. At one stage, two balls in a row came and Hegarty dropped both of them and they got points from them. The boys switched Carey back to centre-back then. Jim Troy had been sending the puck-outs down on top of his brother John all day, and Hegarty had caught most of them cleanly. But when Ciarán went back centre-back, Ciarán was pulling rather than catching, and their forwards started to get more breaking ball.

Tom Ryan explains the switch:

Hegarty was after giving a great performance, but he was gone. He was no longer able to follow John Troy, and was beginning to fade at centre-back, so we brought him away out of it, we brought him up midfield.

Damien Quigley has a unique memory of the final:

You often hear about players being in the zone with regard to professionalism and mentally being in the zone. I actually got into the zone for that All-Ireland final. I actually got no kick out of that final at all. Not a dickey bird. There was no emotion anywhere, there was no joy, there was zero. The job was the job and that was it, which was a pity, because it would have been nice to get a kick out of it. Obviously there was desolation afterwards.

Everything I saw during that game happened in slow motion. I remember the point I got in the second half, which could have been a goal. I remember we hadn't scored for a while and I angled the hurley slightly when I was pulling on it; I felt that at least then if it didn't go into the roof of the net it would go over the bar and we would have a score. It all happened in a split second in real time, but it happened in slow motion for me. I felt no emotion until a couple of minutes before the final whistle when I thought, 'F***, we are gone here.'

And gone they were, in what remains one of the most inexplicable conclusions to an All-Ireland final – ever.

NINE

❧

1994 (2): HOLOCAUST

With six minutes left Limerick led by 2-13 to 1-11. Buoyant supporters who remembered the final defeats of 1974 and 1980 and the semi-final loss of 1981 began making their way down the steps of the incomplete Cusack stand.

As the game proceeded, a Johnny Dooley delivery found his brother Billy. Joe O'Connor was his marker:

Dooley got the ball and I had a decision to make: do I take him down or do I take my chances? Out of the corner of my eye, I saw an unmarked Offaly player inside. I decided to take him down.

Twenty-nine minutes and forty-three seconds of the second half had elapsed as Johnny Dooley stood over the ball. Going for goal, surely, was out of the question, and Éamonn Cregan urged him to go for a point. The angle was unfavourable, and he would find it difficult to break the defensive line. The rest, as they say, is history.

Dooley scored a goal from the free, and almost instantly Pat O'Connor added another. Indeed, in those fateful last five minutes of the game Offaly scored 2-5 without reply to take the title.

Mike Galligan recalls being substituted minutes earlier:

I came off near the end and was convinced I had my All-Ireland medal in my back pocket. I still slag a few of the lads that we were so far ahead that they took me off and gave other fellas a run.

Leo O'Connor replaced Galligan on fifty-five minutes and almost immediately scored a point. A Gary Kirby free made it 2-13 to 1-11. O'Connor recalls a conversation with Joe Erritty:

After Gary Kirby took the free, I asked the umpire what was left and he said that after the puck-out there would be five minutes remaining. I was being marked by Joe Errity and he turned to me and said, 'It will be the shortest five minutes of my life,' and I said it would probably be the longest five of mine.

Joe Quaid recalls an arrangement he had made with the hurley carrier prior to the game – and a strange premonition:

I had him told before the match that if we were ahead with five minutes remaining, to come over behind the goals and I would give him my spare hurleys. I didn't want to lose them. I wasn't that worried about the one I had in my hand but I didn't want the rest of them taken on me. With five minutes to go, he came over and asked for the hurleys. I said, 'No, this match isn't over yet.'

Éamonn Cregan recalls Dooley's free:

Limerick became totally disorganised; there was a photo in the newspaper of how the Limerick defence lined up for the free, with Joe Quaid on the line but Ciarán Carey in front and Mike Nash beside him, so the panic had set in.

Quaid takes responsibility for the poor organisation on the line, but has strong views on the severe criticism he received over the Pat O'Connor goal:

I will accept the blame, no problem, for one thing that day, and that was Dooley's goal, because I would normally leave two men either side of me on the goal line. Mike Nash came in beside me and said to move over, so I took half a step to the left. When Dooley hit the ball it was a weak enough shot, but I couldn't get to it. But I thought, 'No bother, the boys have that.' But it went in between Ciarán and Dave Clarke. I took a fair bit of stick over the two goals and the so-called fast puck-out. I don't think I ever hit a puck-out as accurately.

The puck-out immediately after Dooley's goal continues to provoke debate. But due to a replay of Johnny Dooley's goal being shown, many viewers never saw the puck-out and its immediate aftermath. Quaid is keen to set the record straight:

I didn't rush back to the goals. I went back and picked up the ball, walked behind the goals like I normally would. Hegarty was out in the middle of the field on his own. I dropped the ball into his hand 70 yards out from goal. He caught the ball and in contact the ball squirted out of his hand.

Hegarty agrees:

I still can see the ball being pucked out in my direction and me spilling the ball. It was like a blur, it happened so quickly. A ball that I

Before (above) and after (below): the Limerick backs in a disorganised state when defending Johnny Dooley's free.

would have dealt with normally ninety-nine times out of a hundred, it was just one of those things . . . the ball was spilled and instantly it was in the back of the net.

Dave Mahedy has sympathy for Quaid:

A lot of people blame Joe Quaid, but the ball landed in Hegarty's hand and we had possession. A stats man would consider that to be clean possession won from the puck-out.

And while Gary Kirby agrees and says if Hegarty had scored a point people would say it was a great puck-out, Damien Quigley still has reservations:

Everyone talks about Joe pucking the ball out too fast, and in hindsight he probably did, even allowing for Hegarty catching the ball. Would, say, Ger Cunningham have pucked it out as fast? Probably not. You can't put an old head on young shoulders.

Mike Nash had gone out towards the 21 as per usual for the puck-out and was in the process of turning back in:

It happened so quickly . . . the ball landed into Hegarty's paw, and you would expect it to have gone over the bar at the other end, and in a split second it was back in over my head and in the back of the net. But look, these things happen. Another day it would have been driven wide or Quaid would have stopped it.

Cregan sensed a second goal was coming:

When the ball went in I said to myself, 'If this hops up well, it will be stuck into the back of the net,' because Pat O'Connor had done it many a time in training with the ball coming in over his shoulder like that.

Stephen McDonagh feels the O'Connor goal was the sucker punch:

The killer was the second goal. If we had weathered it for two or three minutes we might have survived, but Pat O'Connor's goal came so quickly after Dooley's goal that it really finished things. After that it was like the parting of the Red Sea, it was all over.

Frankie Carroll agrees:

The first goal was bad, but the second was like being shot. We were leading for most of the game, and just coming into the final furlong we

A dejected Mike Galligan leaves the dugout following the
capitulation to Offaly in 1994.

were behind and chasing the game. The wheels came off the cart
then. Looking up at the scoreboard, we were five points ahead in an
All-Ireland final and thirty seconds later we were a point down, and
another minute later we were three or four points down. It happened
so quickly. It was like blitzkrieg. Did the team stop and think they had
it won, or did Offaly just find another gear? Who knows?

*Leo O'Connor recalls a conversation with Billy Dooley at the Burlington
hotel:*

I always remember meeting him the following day at the function,
and he mentioned that he suffers from asthma and he was on his way
out to the sideline to ask Derry O'Donovan to get Éamonn Cregan to
take him off. And on three occasions the ball landed at his feet and he
just hit it to get rid of it and the three times they went over. When I
heard that story I began to think that we were never going to win. The
three balls could have gone out over the Hill or out into the Nally
stand but instead they all went over the bar.

Nicky English says it was simply a freak series of events:

I would say it was downright bad luck in 1994; I think that match is unexplainable. Billy Dooley wasn't able to walk, he was standing by the sideline catching his breath and the ball came to him three times. I thought Limerick had enough done.

Brian Whelahan gives an Offaly perspective:

The last six minutes we had one of those unbelievable purple patches that will never again be seen in an All-Ireland final. There was euphoria around the place in that nobody could believe what was going on. Limerick were shell-shocked, supporters and team alike. It was just something that took a long time afterwards to register with people that Offaly had come out champions, and not Limerick, because people had left the ground to get a head start with traffic, believing that Limerick were champions.

Gary Kirby, Limerick's captain that day, feels the team played well overall, despite any criticism:

Everyone focuses on the last five minutes but when you look at the final as a whole, we didn't do what we did getting to the final. In getting to the final we played more as a team. In the final itself we played more individually. Look at the amount of wides we had, including myself. We took shots from crazy angles that we probably shouldn't have taken them from. Possibly the pressure being exerted from the Offaly backs had something to do with that but I feel we should have been more controlled within ourselves. It's a big occasion, like. We hurled well. We actually hurled well that day, no matter what anyone says. It was just that freak thing at the end. I don't give a s**t what anyone says about Tom Ryan, that he should have been on the line motivating guys. They didn't say that about the previous games that had got us there.

Tom Ryan was concerned about the number of wides:

I remember being interviewed at half-time coming onto the field and I said that we had far too many wides, that we couldn't let it continue. Wides don't count; you can't cash them anywhere.

Richie Bennis, never shy about leaving the dugout when he was Limerick manager, feels Ryan should have done likewise:

A horror-striken Éamonn Cregan (*centre*) comes to terms with the reality that he has just denied his native county an All-Ireland title in 1994.

That was the day when you got up off your arse whether you like it or not and you became the extra man, and get suspended if you have to. Loughnane was never worried about the Clare county board being fined that time for him going onto the field.

Ryan, however, rejects any such criticism:

We f***ed away that All-Ireland ourselves. I know what they are saying about Croke Park that day: they are saying I didn't get up out of the dugout and all that. I have no comment on that talk, it isn't even worthy of comment. It shows the thinking of supporters and it shows the showmanship that goes on among other managers on the sidelines. People can think you can affect a game by roaring and shouting at players from the sideline, but what people don't realise is that I never went up and down the sideline. It wasn't just that day, what about the days we won all year?

Ryan identifies a number of turning points in the game and says the lack of discipline proved crucial:

There was the freak effort by Quigley, who was a great player, where the ball went over the bar from nearly inside the square and it couldn't happen again if you tried. He scored two goals and he could have scored four, and should have scored four. The way the game ended was a bit of a freak; everything went wrong that could have gone wrong and it was just an unbelievable scenario. Also Leo O'Connor lost the ball in possession, after already scoring a brilliant point.

Our game plan earlier was very much part of what we were at all year. We worked on that every night in the field, we worked on it in training, we worked on it in all our games, that's how they were contested. We lost that final because we changed from our game plan. A player got pulled down. The players on the field were aware it was a cardinal sin to pull somebody down, that nobody gets pulled down. I was very focused on the non-concession of frees and had drilled it into them all year. And the players started goul acting around the field. The goals Offaly got were absolutely criminal.

Stephen McDonagh believes it was just one of those days:

I suppose there has been a lot written and an awful lot spoken about it and what I will add to it is that it hasn't been seen since, and hadn't been seen for a long time before that and it was just something that happened. Unexplainable really, momentum and the tide turning . . . I remember with about ten minutes to go, a flash came into my head that we could win this and that 1973 was nearly gone, and suddenly the whole thing falls down around you.

Mike Houlihan gives his view:

I remember hitting a shot that went about three inches wide. I struck it well and it was going over and the next thing it died and took a tail and dropped wide of the post. There were several chances and there was no greater certainty but that we were the more dominant team. We all know it went wrong, but how do you define it down to what exactly went wrong? There were so many things. I don't think there's much point in pointing the finger at anyone now. You couldn't stop it once it happened. Typical Offaly, they kept in the game, you have to give them credit for that, but they definitely got an All-Ireland from us. Not soft, they earned it, fellas were out on their feet. Things really avalanched.

Declan Nash agrees that Offaly earned their win, and that Limerick could not handle the speed of events towards the end:

We had Offaly beaten so well; it was unbelievable to see it going that well. There were crowds jumping over the wall and in one way we were sure we had it, but in another way we weren't so sure of ourselves because we were under pressure in the backs. The wind was against us and we were working hard, and the forwards were putting us under pressure. We were at the pin of our collar. When Dooley scored that goal it happened so quickly that none of us had the mentality to go down on the ground and stall it, and the game went so fast it was frightening. In defence, our tongues were out having been under so much pressure from Offaly. In hindsight you could do a lot of things, you could go down, you could bring back three of the forwards to pack the defence, and it's fine to think those things but it just happened so quickly.

Leo O'Connor concurs about Offaly's determination throughout the game:

I was sure I had a second point and Brian Whelahan came out of nowhere and blocked down the ball. On another occasion I turned Joe Errity twice and on each occasion he flicked the ball off my hurley. It was just down to pressure. And they were at that for the whole game.

Dave Mahedy feels criticism of the management was unjust:

Lots of people blame the fast puck-out. There was no way you could slow it down from the bench. Lots of people gave Tom criticism for that. The stadium was full and there were about five seconds, and realistically even if you were to be standing in Claughaun field shouting at a goalie, it would be difficult to be heard. He would have had to be faster than a bolt of lightning to get down to the goals. It's back to momentum; once someone gets momentum like that it's very hard to stop it. It was an eleven-point turnaround and the game never suggested that. Often people ask me my favourite sporting memory, and I say I have lots of favourites but I can tell you the one bad memory that will stick in my head and never leave me and that's the Offaly game. I had started a master's degree the week of the final that was to take me two years to complete and the idea was hopefully win the game, objective achieved, and go off and study and let someone else come in as trainer. But I couldn't leave; we all agreed to stay together. Trying to balance a master's with doing my job and training the team was tough.

However, Rory Kiely, a member of the management team, feels things should have been slowed down:

You don't rush things, especially when you are in front. We were five points in front, and when Dooley got the goal it was back to two points. Davy Fitzgerald did it two years later against Limerick at the Gaelic Grounds. When we drew level he caught the ball and pucked it out fast and Ciarán caught it. Willie Barrett was going to blow it, and when he looked around he saw Ciarán soloing in and he couldn't blow it then. Ciarán put it over the bar. Davy Fitzgerald made the mistake that day by pucking it out too fast. He should have pucked it out into the Mackey stand, which wouldn't be sportsmanlike.

Éamonn Grimes draws comparisons to the 1973 final:

The one thing I would say is that when Declan Moylan was with us he was the one man who would go behind the goals. In the 1973 All-Ireland final he was instrumental in slowing the game down, running down the clock.

Again Quaid stresses that his conscience is clear:

I regret the 21-metre free, and accept full responsibility for that – but that only. If Hegarty went on and put that ball over the bar, there would be a statue of both of us erected in Limerick city, the two greatest heroes that ever came out of Limerick. There wasn't a word about the puck-out until someone rang *The Sunday Game* that night. One fellow said I should have pucked it out over the Hogan stand. There's a fellow who thinks there's only one sliotar in Croke Park. If I pucked the ball out over the stand and they got a goal from the resulting line ball, they would be saying why didn't they puck it out to Hegarty, he was standing on his own.

Ciarán Carey is clear in his assessment:

1994 was an All-Ireland we left after us, that's the bottom line. It's very easy to pinpoint things, but all that is total bull. We had enough chances on the day to put them away. We lost it ourselves.

The faces say it all: Tom Ryan and the Limerick mentors leave the field after the 1994 final. *Back row (l–r):* Gerry Bennis (Chairman), Dave Mahedy (Trainer). *Front row (l–r):* Mike Fitzgerald (Treasurer), Tom Ryan (Manager), Liam Lenihan (Selector).

Frankie Carroll says he prefers not to revisit the day's events:

We hadn't been getting to finals, maybe it was inexperience, it was just a freak thing. Even fifteen years later, I don't know and wouldn't be inclined to watch it. Even when it comes on TG4 now, I switch channels. The 1994 final is one of those finals that will be remembered forever, even outside of Limerick.

Mike Galligan cannot bear thinking about it:

It was devastating. I try not to think of it too much. To this day if I meet an Offaly person I can't say anything to them without it being brought up.

On a positive note, Turlough Herbert says Limerick hurling at the time got a massive boost:

I recall it was a novelty getting to the final and it was very disappointing losing it, but still there was a sense we had achieved something but that there was something more to be achieved. I remember hurling got a serious lift over that, and the drawn and replayed county final between Kilmallock and Bruree were superb games and Limerick hurling was on the way up.

Damien Quigley summarises the All-Ireland winners in the decade overall:

My view on the 1990s would be that Limerick were worth probably one or two All-Irelands, certainly one. I think Clare were worth two, but not the two they won, funny enough. They shouldn't have won 1995; Offaly should have won in 1995 and Clare should have won in 1997 and 1998. Clare were a super side in 1998, way better than in 1995. That Clare team were super, they were worth their two All-Irelands but they were lucky in 1995 and Offaly by virtue of their skill levels were full value.

My take on it would be Limerick 1994, Offaly 1995, Wexford 1996, Clare 1997 and 1998. Offaly having two All-Irelands wouldn't flatter their skill levels; as a team they were worth two All-Irelands on skill alone. They had unbelievable skill, but their application might have been at the same level. It's a nice way, I suppose, of saying that a team got their two All-Irelands based on perverse skill. Those lads were just gifted beyond all.

As autumn became winter, the horrors of that final embedded themselves in the psyche. Damien Quigley says it should have been exorcised:

I still get nightmares about it, not as frequently as I used to. I don't think we ever addressed 1994 properly and it cost us 1996. We didn't hurl at all in 1996. The 1994 final was living hell, the game was wrapped up and it got away from us. And we never talked about 1994 at all ever. That was traumatic stuff. As a group we never watched the game together and learned from it or whatever. You hear Declan Kidney saying the whole time that you learn more from defeat than victory. That was probably the only game we were beaten in all year and we never spoke about it and that was a mistake in my opinion.

For Stephen McDonagh, the reality of farming helped put things in perspective:

There wasn't really a psychological impact as far as I was concerned. I came back, did a bit of farming and got going again and moved on. A lot of people made an awful lot more out of the disappointment of it. If I was to look back on my time hurling with Limerick, even though a lot of people would say the All-Ireland defeats were the kernel of it, I wouldn't; I would look back at happier times.

I moved on quickly. I remember coming home and there was a mountain of work waiting for me. I got up the following morning and milked the cows. That's what I would have said about farming, it's a great discipline.

His father John recalls a conversation with his son:

On the Tuesday morning after the Offaly All-Ireland while we were milking, Stephen said to me, 'Dad, I will never again be as near to winning an All-Ireland.'

Éamonn Cregan was bitterly affected. 'The 1994 final killed me. The wides in the first half were what cost Limerick the game.'
Brian Whelahan summarises the effect on the former Limerick great:

When Cregan went back home after the All-Ireland on the run up to Christmas, it would have taken a lot out of him, because Éamonn would have coached a lot of those players in earlier years and would have been bumping into them. He was a Limerick man and wore the jersey with great pride and naturally it knocked him because you never know if a team was ever going to get back there again. There was such a long gap to Limerick's last success, at that time it was twenty-one years and now it's facing down forty years. He would give anything to see Limerick win the All-Ireland. Training a team to win an All-Ireland is on his CV, but the only problem was that it was against his own county.

Jimmy Barry-Murphy was manager of the Cork team that lost the minor final that day:

I couldn't believe what was unfolding before my eyes. Limerick should have been out of sight, they should have been further ahead. It was one of the most extraordinary finishes to a final that I ever saw. I think the finishing line seemed so close that the players lost their focus and didn't close out the game as they should have. It was a cruel way for it to happen.

Only days after the final, Tom Ryan resigned over a dispute surrounding a holiday for the players. Gerry Bennis explains the background:

For the first year I thought Tom Ryan was the easiest manager I ever worked with. We were great friends. He fell out with me at the end of the year over a very simple situation. We met about a holiday, and Tom wouldn't allow the holiday. I ended up taking the belt as chairman for the holiday not going ahead. The county board wanted the holiday but Tom didn't. Myself, Jimmy Hartigan and Mike Fitzgerald were at the meeting. We went back to Adare to see how many people were going on the trip. Tom wouldn't allow them to go as they had won nothing, which was a good point. There was a lucrative fund set up for the All-Ireland through sponsorship etc. I don't know what Tom thought of me, but I thought that Tom was very easy to work with until then. Rory Kiely sided with Tom but Liam Lenihan wanted the holiday. They wrote a letter of resignation.

At that time there was also hassle over John Roche, because many believed he wasn't worth his place on the panel, that he was a pal of Tom's. A key player was involved in that. We had a meeting and it was a bit hot. I tried to persuade them to stay but they wouldn't stay. Eventually when we were just about to accept their resignation, Jim O'Grady of Patrickswell proposed that we go and meet them. We met them and they went back.

Tom Ryan gives his side of the story:

We had a problem after the 1994 All-Ireland. We had a situation that developed in that there was a holiday mooted for the team. I had a problem with the holiday for the team because it was going to be paid for from the training fund. I had no problem with it, if the county board were going to fund the holiday out of their own coffers. There was a kind of a meeting between the county board and the players and there were promises made, but I stuck to my guns. I said there would be no training fund used for a holiday. First of all, a meeting took place between the players and the county board, but it was never discussed fully with me. The players went to the county board, and Gary Kirby was there with his uncle Gerry and the whole lot was grand. When it came to funding the holiday, the idea was that it would be funded from the training fund.

Whether I was right or wrong, my stance was my stance: 'If ye want a holiday the county board can pay for it out of their own funds.' Then you had a reaction to that. I stepped down. That was a time which was prior to the GPA being formed. It was the county board and a combination of key players testing the water. I wasn't denying any player's right to have a holiday. If what happened to them happened to me above in Croke Park against Offaly there would be no holiday. I'd be at home grieving. Walk away, get ready for next year, look at what you are after doing. I would be really a traditionalist in that regard. I might be the wrong man for the current era of thinking; it's all holidays now and training camps and all that kind of s**t. I don't see how that would improve any hurling.

The situation was sorted out by straight talking. You had a few battles going on all the time. On the field, which was no problem, but you had a political battle which was always going on in the background with county board. I always had a hostile board. I had no support. They were actually hoping we would be beaten, to see if they could get rid of me.

Then a dispute arose at that particular time when we played a match in Cork. There was a semi-strike over the holiday. John Roche played in Cork that day and was subjected to what you would call intimidating comments and remarks. There was a kind of a boycott from within the panel, so he opted out after that. He was a huge loss because he was pencilled in for the number 14 spot. He was a big man, and with constant coaching, training and upgrading he would have made it. I mean, it took a couple of years for some fellas that came in to reach their potential, and Roche would have made it in time. He did well against Waterford in the 1994 championship and he actually was the man that changed that game, and played a big part in winning it for us.

He was intimidated off the panel by a player. There were rumours that Roche trained my horses, but that's bulls**t. I knew the family because I had trained Croagh/Kilfinny but that never came into his selection for Limerick. There are rumours, which are bulls**t, that go around the whole time. I enjoy that because it amazes me how people come up with these stories.

The John Roche situation developed without the knowledge of most of the panel but was given extensive coverage in the media. The holiday, on the other hand, was a real bone of contention with some players but of little concern to others. Perhaps the county board should have announced a holiday for the players – from county board funds – in the dressing room after the Munster final victory, regardless of what happened in the All-Ireland.

In an effort to resolve the holiday dispute, six players – captain Gary Kirby, Joe O'Connor, Mike Houlihan, Brian Finn, Ciarán Carey and Mike Nash – met with the county board. Nash explains the circumstances:

The holiday controversy was pure bulls**t altogether, and once the press got hold of it they ran with it. It was a thing of nothing. The county board were trying to get rid of Tom Ryan, that was basically what was happening with him. He resurrected Limerick hurling and brought them out of the doldrums. I don't know why they wanted rid of him, they obviously didn't like him and they kept going until they got rid of him in 1997. They were on about this holiday and it started about nothing and gathered momentum. At the end of the day, as far as I was concerned, the players didn't want it. They wanted their All-Ireland medals more than any holiday. Then it started with the county board versus the players versus the management. And what should have happened that time was that the whole team should have been taken away on a holiday by the county board, no more about it, and carry on because things were going well.

The holiday was a non-issue for Frankie Carroll:

A holiday would be lovely but it wasn't going to bring an All-Ireland medal to us. Some counties were getting holidays then but we were never used to getting holidays, so let's be honest – as far as I was concerned it wasn't as if we were losing anything. What you never had, you never miss. Some guys got irate over it, but I was more concerned with kicking onto 1995 and trying to win an All-Ireland.

Mike Houlihan feels the county board could have resolved the issue quite easily:

The holiday was a little bit of naivety on the county board's part, because in Cork, for example, every second year their footballers and hurlers were being taken on a holiday at that time. In 1992 we won the League, which was worth serious money at that time to the county board. We contested a semi-final in 1993, which was worth a lot of money to them too. We got a night in Killarney out of the 1992 League, that's all the expense they had out of that. They gave us two nights, they paid for one night and we had to pay for the second one ourselves.

And so the people of Limerick were denied an opportunity to witness the McCarthy Cup return to Shannonside. Many who longed to see that day have since gone to their eternal rest, their lifetime dreams in tatters, mentally scarred from the memories of that game. Bill Shankly's famous quote springs to mind, and can apply to hurling to: 'Football isn't a matter of life and death, it's much more important than that.'

☙

TEN

1995: HANGOVER

After the holiday row had settled down, another key battle took place that was to define the road ahead for Limerick. This was the bruising 1994/5 League encounter between Limerick and Clare in which Jim McInerney and Declan Nash were sent off.

Stephen McDonagh recalls a game that signalled the beginning of some intense battles between the counties:

The dirtiest game I was involved in was the League game against Clare that year. It was serious stuff, desperate stuff and there was serious belting. Clare came in that day with nothing only murder in their minds and demolished all before and behind them. It was lethal. Our milkman is still talking about it.

Jim McInerney gives his account of events:

We would have played Limerick a lot in 1992, 1993 and 1994, between challenge games and opening pitches. It wasn't just a case of meeting in the League and the championship. Different things had happened. There were comments passed at different times in different games, and a savage rivalry built up, meaning that it took very little to start a row.

That was a memorable day in Limerick. Some of the Clare lads stated since that it was the day we actually stood up for ourselves and it made us a better team as a result. Every time we met it was a tremendous battle; we were trying to get up the ladder and they were fighting to hold what they had.

I was centre-forward on Declan Nash and the ball went into the square and Joe Quaid cleared it. I followed in the ball, and when it was gone I got a bang on the head. I knew I would be going off, because it was a serious bang. There was blood spilling everywhere. I decided there and then that if I was going off, I wouldn't be going on my own.

All hell broke loose. It was Mike Nash who hit me, so I hit him back. Declan saw me so he went in to back up his brother. Declan and myself got the line but Mike got away with it.

I wound up getting stitches. I went into the Regional and there was this old man I knew on a stretcher with his arm in a sling. I said to him as I was passing, 'What happened?' He said to me, 'It's all your fault. When the row started on the field, a row started in the stand too and I got knocked and got my shoulder dislocated.' I was sorry I ever asked him!

After leaving the hospital I went back and got the dinner but the boys had left by then and were stopping at Setrights in Cratloe. I walked into Setrights and the place was packed but there was a hushed silence when I arrived. This lad from Tulla then spoke up. 'McInerney,' he said, 'I had a slash hook in the boot of the car and if I knew what you were going at today, I would have brought it in and given it to you so that you could have used it.' When he said that I got an almighty cheer from the crowd; you'd swear Clare were after winning the All-Ireland.

Declan Nash remembers it well:

Mike pulled on the ball but connected with Jim [McInerney] and the ball went into Joe [Quaid]. I was turned around and was going out the field but I heard a bang. The next thing I saw Mike was down holding his head, and I saw three Clare fellas around him and one of them was bleeding so I went for him. What I should have done was kept my hurley up, but I didn't. I got hit two belts of a hurley down on the head while I was there trying to hit him a few belts of a fist. I kept going and I just had him down and was trying to get a bit of retribution when Stephen McDonagh pulled me up. It was the only thing I ever held against Steve McDonagh: he pulled me off that bit too quick and I didn't even get a decent belt in!

McInerney did not lose any sleep over the suspension:

Declan Nash and myself got three months each but didn't miss any game because it was the last match before Christmas. We were back for the next League game in February. For the hearing, Loughnane said to me not to be saying anything about what happened, play it down, don't name any name. We went in and said a lot but said nothing. Nobody pointed the finger at anyone. It was over at that stage, there was no point in blaming anyone. I'd say it was the last time there was a League game held without cameras!

Mike Nash has a hazy recollection of events:

I barely remember Declan being sent off. If Joe called for the ball, I usually left it off and I kept out whoever was running in. I had to mind my patch. If McInerney ran into something he ran into it! Fellas love making stories out of these things. Jamesie O'Connor came out with a thing one time about someone squirting a water bottle into someone's face and starting a row that I was involved in. But sure, the Clare fellas make an All-Ireland out of these things, make legends out of nothing.

Stephen McDonagh remembers the squirting incident:

There was a League match in Limerick probably in 1997 when Mike Nash asked Fergie Tuohy for a drink of water and Tuohy squirted it into his face and all hell broke loose. There was murder again. Mike Nash might not remember it but I remember it. There was another League match in 1999 that I got the road in at the Gaelic Grounds. I got sent off with Tuohy.

Anthony Daly has an amusing recollection from that time:

I remember Liam Doyle slapping Houlihan in one of those League games with his open palm. It was the ultimate insult to Houlihan: 'Hit me a good lick so I can hit you back, but don't do that to me.' Doyle knew exactly what he was doing.

Joe Quaid has another memory:

In 1995 we played the opening of the field below in Broadford. Jim McInerney was after causing war in a club game against them the week before. He was running in along and John Flavin wore the hurley off him but McInerney kept coming. He struck the ball for a goal, and I said to myself, 'There's no way that you are scoring.' I turned it around the post, and all the supporters behind the goals applauded. Sure, they were all from Broadford.

The rivalry between Clare and Limerick during that period was intense, fascinating and not for the faint hearted. However, the determination to raise the bar to a level where they could beat one another led to silverware for both teams.

Despite the bloodshed, the wounds and the stitches – and there were many – both sets of players get along extremely well today when they meet, be it on the golf course, at matches, coursing meetings or even at the mart.

Some players who missed out in 1994 were given a chance in the League. Anthony Carmody was one, but his return was short-lived, as Tom Ryan explains:

We played Tipp in the League, second year out, and Carmody was picked at midfield. After a few minutes Carmody fell down and was taken off with an injured ankle. I was going home in the car afterwards and I got a phone call that himself and Ciarán were after playing soccer that morning behind in Pallaskenry. Carmody got injured in the soccer game and went onto the field injured for the Limerick game. Bang! Out the door he was sent. Never again seen while I was in charge.

Carmody recalls the circumstances:

Kilmallock were involved in the Munster club championship at that time. Their players were down to play on the Limerick team and I was listed as a sub. Ciarán and myself had played the soccer match and I had hurt my ankle. I couldn't let on a thing to anyone but it didn't matter, I was only supposed to be a sub anyway. Next thing it turned out the Kilmallock lads withdrew from the squad. Tom Ryan called me to one side and said, 'You are playing,' and I said to myself, 'Oh Jesus, how am I going to play?' My ankle was worse for wear in fairness.

In I went anyway and the same day I'd say I never played as good a game because everywhere I went the ball seemed to land into my hand. About fifteen minutes into the first half, the ankle was getting sore so I went down and said, 'I can't keep going.' Someone must have informed Tom, but I suppose he would have found out anyway. He brought us in and had a chat and obviously Ciarán was never going to be left off the panel, but he gave us a warning as to future behaviour. A couple of weeks later he was cutting the panel and one of us had to go.

In early 1995 there were personnel changes in the county board, including the sacking of chairman Gerry Bennis. Tom Ryan believes it was a political decision:

Brendan Danagher replaced Gerry Bennis who was after getting kicked out. Fine Gael elected Danagher. All the Fine Gaelers in the clubs all got together and they didn't give a f*** about Bennis.

Bennis acknowledges that his departure was not quite his own choice:

I was thrown out as chairman in early 1995, something I was very disappointed with. My position was contested and I hardly canvassed; I believed that I had no problem getting back in. I didn't recognise that Danagher had been chairman of Limerick County Council.

I felt I was doing a good job and that I had unfinished business. I would have loved to have had another two years to finish off the work that was started. We reorganised the county board under my chairmanship and delegated a lot of work to the other officers in the board. There were some people who may not have liked it. There was another wrong yarn that was put out, and that was that I was anti-football. That was not true. OK, I was a hurling man but I won two county championships playing football for Patrickswell. I liked football.

The one thing that did disappoint me about my tenure is that Tom Ryan fell out with me over the holiday. Perhaps I contributed to that, but we didn't have to fall out; we had a great year. My impression is that Tom may have cost me votes and sided with Brendan Danagher. Danagher ended up causing him a lot of problems as chairman afterwards.

I cannot emphasise enough that Tom and myself had a very happy year together. I honestly feel that I had enough experience gained from the mistakes that were made in 1994 and would have contributed to winning the All-Ireland in 1996. I would have changed the way we went to Croke Park for starters. We went up by plane in 1994. We met in UL and the wives and girlfriends went by bus directly to the hotel. We had to go through the city, out the Ennis Road to Shannon airport. The supporters made kings of us at the airport before we had won the All-Ireland. I thought it was crazy. We flew up to Dublin and drove across the city again. Before we arrived in Dublin, the wives and girlfriends were at the hotel.

Danagher insists it took plenty of persuasion for him to run:

A lot of people asked me if I would go for chairman. I had no notion of it, but eventually, after pressure from a lot of people, I did. The late 'Jap' Ryan was very instrumental in that and we were always great friends and he felt that with my experience I would be very efficient. I was also chairman of the county council. There were a number of clubs that approached me also.

Bennis challenged Danagher for the chairmanship a couple of years later, only to be denied by some suspect counting of votes:

At the start of 1997, I challenged Brendan Danagher. I did a proper canvass this time and the vote ended in a draw. However, there were two votes missing at the end. They couldn't find the two votes, and the rule was that when a tie arises the sitting chairman wins the casting vote from the vice-chairman. I would regret not canvassing the first time around and I was probably unfair in going against him the second time. The meeting was held up for ages because they were looking for the missing votes. A vote should have been retaken but I allowed the election to stand. I felt a bit guilty going against him even though I had looked for the nomination because I felt I had unfinished business. I had nothing against Brendan, I found him to be a gentleman, and I gave him more support than some of the people who should have given him support, but didn't.

Sandra Marsh joined the county board at this time, having successfully challenged the sitting PRO (Public Relations Officer), Harry Greensmyth:

I was very raw. I got involved by default in many ways even though I canvassed for it and was elected. I was a newcomer and wasn't well known. I was not very au fait with club politics. There's an enormous political element to the GAA. I have a professional attitude to things and I work very hard and am not happy if things aren't right or complete. I did a comprehensive job and never rested until my job was done.

In the 1995 Munster semi-final at Páirc Uí Chaoimh, Limerick beat Tipperary by 0-16 to 0-15, with Gary Kirby scoring a phenomenal twelve points. Turlough Herbert recalls a training session at the time:

In 1995 I actually made the team for the League matches, but I broke my thumb in a club match six week before the championship. I lost my place to John Flavin. Unfortunately for John he broke his leg and I got back in. I remember Pat Heffernan drove to Galway to collect me for a training session down in Páirc Uí Chaoimh prior to the Tipp game and he said, 'If we beat Tipperary, we are going to dominate Munster for the next few years.' He would have been right except for the arrival of Clare. That Tipperary game was played at an intensity I had never experienced before.

Flavin's loss was one of Ryan's biggest disappointments:

We were down two backs from 1994: we had lost Ger Hegarty to injury and Joe O'Connor retired. He didn't notify me of his retirement, he notified the county secretary. John Flavin was like John Roche, he had been in the camp for over a year and was being brought along gradually. He was going through what you would call our academy and he was ready. Before the championship he broke his leg. A disaster. He was never the same player after.

He was coming in 1995, and was a contender at wing-back a year ahead of Mark Foley, but he was better than Mark Foley at that time. He had more strength and he had a great temperament and could strike a ball on the volley like no other player. But I was always testing guys for a weakness, again showing the intensity and pressure of the selection process that players were being put through. They didn't know this themselves. Flavin had a weakness, which was the fact that he decided to go away and play junior football a fortnight before the championship. He broke his leg behind in Athea. That put a question mark over him. Had he the mentality, the mental strength that you need to say 'No, f*** off, I am not playing football, I have my place on the Limerick senior hurling team for the championship'? You need that as well, the missing ingredient in his case.

The fact that Flavin never came through would have been my biggest disappointment as Limerick manager. But the reason he never came through was his own fault. He went off playing junior f***ing B football with the club. He was a very good, nice fella like and then your man came looking for him, Davy whatever the f*** his name is, the secretary or chairman of Monagea, a small fella with a cap – he was a bollox anyway whatever his name was – and took him away to the football. He collected him and took him away and there were two years' work gone down the drain. We played Offaly quite a lot around that particular time and I remember their selectors had come in to me after a game. I think it might have been after the Jackie Power tournament. The Offaly selectors said he was the best they had seen, and wanted to know where he had come from. He was an awful loss to us. I was heartbroken over losing him.

Tom Ryan (*left*) and Dave Mahedy (*right*) assess their options
at training in the Gaelic Grounds.

Flavin did not consider himself an automatic selection:

It was tough at the time breaking the leg. To tell you the truth I didn't see myself as a dead cert for the team coming from where I had come from. I was after training as hard as any of the players and having a couple of very good challenge games but it was going to be very hard to go straight in and start against Tipperary in the championship. Realistically, I probably would have been wing-back although I played the opening of the field in Ahane at centre-back. Everything happens for a reason, I suppose.

Damien Quigley believes the player should not have been put in the position he was:

For Flavin himself and his place Monagea it would have been a phenomenal thing to play senior hurling. It was an awful shame. It shows how committed he was that he went playing for his club ten days before the championship. I would be critical of the decision to allow that fixture to go ahead. You can't blame a guy for playing with his club. He shouldn't have been in a position where he had to play that match. It was a Tuesday night ten days before a Munster semi-final. If Na Piarsaigh had a game ten days before my debut in the Cork game of '94, I would have played with Na Piarsaigh. You couldn't not.

Limerick met Clare in the 1995 Munster final. Stephen McDonagh recalls an odd comment from Ger Loughnane subsequently:

Loughnane said he saw me coming out the tunnel and that he wanted to hit me. I don't know if he was saying that just for the press. I had no visual recollection of seeing Loughnane anywhere. You could say a lot about Loughnane, but he brought a lot to it too. The scene is a bit duller when he is not involved. Say what you like about Loughnane, but when he was on the line back then he was in the zone. I think hurling in general needs those characters.

Frankie Carroll says Limerick failed to shake off the events of the previous year:

The forwards were functioning very well in 1994, everyone was contributing. But it wasn't the same in 1995. In my opinion there was a hangover there. In the media, meeting people through work, everything was revolving around 1994. There didn't a day go by for the next twelve months when someone didn't mention it to you. The team got to the Munster final but it wasn't the same team. You could put it down to complacency or you could put it down to a hangover, but the result was the same.

Clare hit the ground running, Limerick were a bit flat. To be fair to Clare they had been to Munster finals and were in the League final that year. They were no flat tyres. They had been consistently getting to finals, a bit like us when I was under-21. On the law of averages, if you keep getting to finals you will eventually win one, and to be fair to them, when they got to Croke Park they finished the job.

An option to make a 'behind the scenes' video of the Limerick dressing room was open to Tom Ryan in 1995. Such videos have become popular in the GAA, especially one that followed Galway's progress towards the All-Ireland football title in 1998. Ryan has major regrets over his decision not to allow the video to be made:

It's a pity we never videoed what went on in the dressing rooms; it's one regret I would have. It would have made a fabulous behind-the-scenes record. I slipped up there badly myself, but again it was my own stubbornness more than anything else.

Anthony Daly gives a Clare perspective on the 1995 Munster final:

I suppose that day a lot of us felt we wouldn't have hurled any more with the county if we had lost. We would have gone back and played a bit away with the club. While we were the first Clare team to get to three Munster finals in a row, we would also have been the first Clare team to lose three in a row. I just felt that day it was make or break for a lot of us. Players my age like 'Sparrow' and P. J. O'Connell and even some of the younger players were really beginning to feel it. And we were so ready for that game.

I remember George Power from my club went to Australia but came home for the Munster final. He said he saw us going in the gate and was just going to go up and tip me on the back and say best of luck when he took one look at my puss and said, 'No way, Jesus, I'll meet him tonight one way or another. F***ing hell, they are wired out of their heads.' And we were. We were wired in terms of focus that day. It wasn't just all bravado. It was focus on hurling the match and forgetting about all the shite that went with it like the parades and the tickets and all that.

We had probably got caught up in the history of being the first Clare team since 1932 to win Munster in the previous two years to a certain extent. I am not making excuses either; you either handle it on the day or you don't. I will say though that on that particular day we were very focused on the match itself.

If you look at the Limerick team with Houlihan and Ciarán and that, there were no shrinking violets playing for them. Anything Limerick threw at us that day we were going to fire back. We were very tuned and I honestly think they weren't as tuned as they should have been on the day. I honestly do believe that. At the back of our minds we were still very fragile if they were on the top of their game. Things could have gone against us and we might have dropped our heads. Even the way 'Fingers' took Ciarán apart that days says to me that obviously everything wasn't 100 per cent there. There were a few clashes in the Munster final that you knew they would be driving you back on your hole another day, whereas that day we were driving them back. Obviously they went out to win, but the body language wasn't as good as ours on the day I thought. When your dander is up, your dander is up.

Probably everyone in Limerick was telling them that they were unlucky in the All-Ireland and telling them you have beaten Tipp, ye will get back in it this year, and ye will sort it out this year. They were probably looking ahead a little bit. That can happen, it probably happened to us a bit in later years.

Rory Kiely says preparation was lacking:

We were too confident going into Clare in Thurles. I said to Tom that the three of us should take a day off and look at the video of the Tipperary game, that we were making mistakes. There was too much of an air of complacency and in my opinion that's what happened in 2008 as well.

Tom Ryan admits he got it wrong in that game:

I have no regrets about losing the All-Irelands, because losing them was a team factor, they were lost on the field. I blame myself totally for 1995 against Clare. I got it wrong there. I got the call completely wrong with our tactics. Leading up to the game it got very nasty and Loughnane started to spew out all sorts of s**t. I knew what they were going to do. I knew their tactics. I said these c***s are going to slate all around them, and you know their tactics were always questionable, and I have no problem saying that. They lived on the edge. I have no problem with that, but they went over the edge.

In the dressing room I said to the players, 'We will go out and we will f***ing hurl.' The team was flying – we were better prepared in 1995 than in 1994 and we were better because we had better men on the line before the injuries and we were improving all the time. There was no lack of focus. What Clare did in 1995 in Thurles was that they timbered us. They timbered Mike Nash, Dave Clarke, Declan Nash, Gary Kirby and Damien Quigley. They f***ing blackguarded us. I knew they were going to do that and I said, 'OK lads, we will hurl and we will get the frees and punish them. We won't get involved high up or low down.' And we played to the tactics, and stuck to them, there was no one taking a lease of themselves. Of course Clare f***ing timbered us out of it, timbered us off the field.

We lacked any kind of support in any boardroom; maybe it was our own doing, maybe we were too isolated, inwardly in ourselves. On top of that, the team never got f***ing recognition for f*** all – there and then, before or after. Never. Even Ciarán Carey's point didn't get on the top twenty score competition and we didn't make [Denis Walsh's] *Hurling: The Revolution Years* [Dublin, 2005].

Ryan says he prepared the entire panel – in a no-nonsense manner:

Turlough Herbert disappointed me – a great hurler at club level, and deserved his chance on the panel and got his chance on the team but didn't take it. He had a tendency to foul a bit much. You pay the price for that as well. There wasn't much mercy shown. It was a fairly ruthless regime. We hadn't any other option for wing-back that year because of injuries and Turlough Herbert deserved his chance.

We brought on Tadhg Hayes for Herbert. He wasn't going well enough, so we brought him off again. The idea that we had was that when you were on the panel, you were going to be called upon at any minute. And it didn't matter whether you were number 1 or number 30. Tadhg Hayes possibly went into Thurles for the Munster final that day thinking he wasn't going to be used and wasn't ready, but again he should have been ready because it was part of our team preparation that he and all players would be ready. The record under our management said that there were no certainties, everyone was played on form and were taken off and put on, there was no f***ing.

As well as that there was no question of me accounting for what I did. I picked the team, it was part of my f***ing job. That was it, good luck. I wasn't pulling any rabbits out of hats. They knew what I was thinking. They had been told that again and f***ing again. And they were being f***ed into an oil rag inside in that dressing room at meetings after training. There was nobody there only ourselves, and they knew what was expected and as a manager you must be able to impose your style on the team. We analysed games and performances the week after a game, and the roaring and the f***ing and abuse was unbelievable. The door was locked; we had no visitors and we worked it out between ourselves there and then. When and where players f***ed up they were told. There was no need of videos or anything. The video was in everyone's head.

Turlough Herbert feels management treated him harshly:

What Clare brought to the table was frightening; I couldn't imagine human beings being as fit as they were that day. We were cocky going into it, there was no doubt about it, and I would be quite sure about it. That time there was no back door and All-Stars could be earned from the Munster final. I remember saying to myself 'If I stand out in this, I could be in line for an All-Star', which was not the way to be thinking, obviously. Fergus Tuohy couldn't make the Harty team in Flannans and I felt I had it over him, but he was a handful that day. I felt that I was starting to come into the game before half time, I cleared a few balls but I was taken off at half time. I was very disappointed over that. I felt it was like a job where you are last in and first out. I felt I took the rap for that defeat that day.

Damien Quigley missed a goal chance at a vital stage of the Clare game, which he believes was the turning point:

I made a balls of the goal chance in the final. It would have made a massive difference to the game. In the first half I hit the crossbar, with the keeper beaten. In the second half the game was in the melting pot and I got clean through and f***ing kicked the ball and kicked it wide. I actually saw it in the eyes of Brian Lohan and Davy Fitzgerald, they knew it was going to be their day after that. When I missed it, they absolutely filled with belief. Whether we would have won the match or not if I scored I don't know, but certainly they were never going to lose after that miss. A goal at that stage was going to ask serious questions of them. I don't know how strong their character would have been, but it certainly wouldn't have been the saunter in the park it was afterwards. They may have timbered us but that's part of the scene. We wouldn't have spared them in 1996 when they were playing in the Gaelic Grounds.

Quigley has his own opinion on Hurling: The Revolution Years*:*

I was surprised when I saw that we weren't part of the book. It's not something I would take personally, but it's something that I have always been curious about. It's true to say that Clare and Ger Loughnane brought a lot of hype to the game, but it was in 1994 the colour really started when Limerick went bananas for hurling and there were Shaws jerseys everywhere. By 1996, at a time when there was still strong resistance to live games on TV, every Limerick game was shown live. Limerick were a box office draw. OK, you might say that Offaly, Wexford and Clare won their All-Irelands and that's why they were featured. I'm not sure what the criteria was, but just because you didn't lift the McCarthy Cup doesn't mean you didn't feature. Waterford were featured in the book without having won an All-Ireland.

Gary Kirby has harsh words for Jimmy Hartigan and the match referee:

Two incidents stick in my mind from that game. We were sitting into our cars to drive into the stadium after the warm-up and Jimmy Hartigan walks around with green t-shirts and throws them at each player: 'There's tops for ye all.' Here we were trying to get ready for a Munster final and this fella was trying to hand out t-shirts. Where were they two weeks earlier? And then at half-time we were in the dressing room and it was a very warm day and we had two sets of jerseys and were changing them. Hartigan was standing over us taking the jerseys off us in case we would put them into our bags. That's at half-time in a Munster final. All he was doing was aggravating fellas. That's what you were up against.

There were definitely a few decisions on that day that went against us. It wasn't the timbering as such, it was the decisions that were made by the referee. You can accept being timbered; if you didn't expect that in a championship match you may as well not be playing it. I was taken out after the puck-out from David Fitzgerald's penalty, but you accept that, because it was a free and it was given. It's hard to accept not getting the other frees. I would question the penalty they got.

Joe Quaid says Limerick took the game for granted:

I remember listening to Clare FM the night before and they were doing interviews. I got a call from another player and I said, 'These boys are up for this tomorrow,' and he said, 'Don't mind them, they are always like that.' I said it could be the rock we would perish on, and it was. Without a doubt it was over-confidence.

Mike Nash holds similar views:

We walked out thinking we were going to beat them. Some of them were thinking, 'This is only Clare.' We were expected to cruise it. I had too many experiences against Clare underage to know they were a banana skin. A lot of the players were sick of beating Clare and I remember [Dave] Clarke was asked a question in a programme interview, 'Who do you like beating the most?' 'Clare,' he said, 'because we always beat them.' They had that interview posted up inside the Clare dressing room as well.

Tom Ryan has strong views on GAA administation at the time:

The 1995 incidents in Thurles grieved me because they weren't commented on. Clare got all carried away in 'My Lovely Rose of Clare' and Biddy Earley and the 1932 thing and all that. I criticised the referee openly in the media. At that particular time criticism of referees was frowned on and I kept criticising him, I didn't give a f***. 'Oh ye are bad losers and sour grapes' and that kind of s**t came out of the lips of everyone, including our own c***s here.

I was hoping then that they would summon me to Croke Park. I had a barrister organised and a video of the f***ing match. And I would go up to Croke Park and I wouldn't give a f***. And I would say, 'I don't give one rattling f*** about any of ye here, the Munster Council or Croke Park or the county board or anyone. We will sit down and watch the video of this match here.' I didn't have to go up before any board. I had my apprenticeship served in hurling and the GAA. I never got my opportunity. The c***s below in Clare were running the GAA, you had Ó Laoire and Jimmy Smyth and all those f***ers that were there.

I never got my day in the sun in Croke Park. And I kept up the criticism any opportunity I got. I was willingly going out cutting up Johnny McDonnell in the press hoping I would be called before Croke Park and I never got it. They beat me at my own game. They were disciplining fellas and suspending fellas all over the country everywhere for every game that year, but not for this game. Seán Ó Laoire and all them c***s above in Croke Park probably said, 'We'd better leave this man alone.' The man I had lined up was Matt Shaw, who is involved with the DRA committee. He was my man. He is from Westmeath and he had a barrister and all lined up. I didn't care if they suspended me for life.

In September 1995 Tom Ryan's term as manager came to an end. He and Liam Lenihan were re-elected, along with Bernie Savage as third selector. Ryan recalls the contest:

The election took place in July and we were re-elected . . . Richie Bennis was kind of favourite to replace [Rory Kiely], and there were seventeen or eighteen nominations at the time. It was a pity in fairness that Richie didn't get in because I would have enjoyed working with him.

Richie Bennis remembers it differently:

Tom f***ing wasn't disappointed I didn't get in because he f***ing made sure I wouldn't get in! I didn't canvass at all but if I canvassed I would have got it. My attitude was they can take me as I am. If they want me they can have me. Tom didn't canvass against me but great friends of his did.

Mike Fitzgerald played an active part in the election of Savage:

I was very friendly with Bernie at the time, still am, and I canvassed for him because I thought he would make a good selector and he proved afterwards what a shrewd hurling brain he had.

Rory Kiely found it difficult to manage all his commitments:

I pulled out after two years; I was a senator also. I managed to keep it going but it was difficult. I could be missing an odd night, which wouldn't be fair either.

The new management structure was barely in place, however, when all hell broke loose, as Tom Ryan explains:

Straight away then there was f***ing uproar. We had a meeting with the county board at the Gaelic Grounds, which would be normal at the start of a campaign. They were hoping, of course, that I wouldn't be elected. When we met the county board, we normally met three people. We arrived anyway . . . it was Bernie's first outing, I always remember him inside. Brendan Danagher was the chairman with a big green tie on him at the end of the table. There were twelve of them there, the whole lot of them instead of just the three. It was like the f***ing Russian Politburo. It was very intimidating, especially after two years of hassle. I was elected. I had a mandate. These c***s had no say here.

Danagher said, 'We have a problem.' 'What problem?' 'We have a problem with the liaison officer Charles Hanley.' 'What problem have ye with him?' 'There's a bye-law stating that the liaison officer must be a member of the executive,' said Danagher. I had brought him into the setup, he was the main man in the whole scene, and held the whole show together. That's why it gave me so much time to build a team, sure, I had f*** all to do with anything only the hurling. Hanley did the arranging like a barrister, Mahedy doing the training, sure, we had a deadly setup. And I said to Danagher, 'Charles Hanley is not a member of the county board executive and the bye-law says he must be. Isn't it amazing that in the two years that was never made an issue of?' Charlie was getting a bit big for his boots in the eyes of Jimmy Hartigan, getting kind of popular and that, getting kind of known.

I said then, 'Would you tell me what position in the county board had Fr Tom Carroll, Phil Bennis' liaison officer?' I'd be quick to think on my feet, which is just as well because I didn't expect this, who would? Danagher was caught for words. He didn't know what he was talking about, didn't know Fr Tom Carroll or anything. He looked around him for answers. I said, 'What position had Fr Tom Carroll? It is a very straightforward question and in the circumstances very relevant.'

There was no answer forthcoming so I directed my response at Danagher because he was the spokesman. 'My dear man,' I said, 'whatever game you are at, you are taking the character of one of the best and one of the most efficient officials in the country. A man that has gained immense respect, people are very happy with him. He has respect up and down the country. You or any of ye c***s around the table will not get rid of Charlie Hanley. And whatever game ye are at ye better cough up.' There was silence for about ten minutes, because Danagher didn't know what to say . . . What they were hoping was that if they got rid of Charlie Hanley, I would have gone too. There was great sport and no one opened their mouth, like dummies. Then

Hartigan piped up. 'He overstepped his mark,' he says. And I said, 'So you are the gentleman that has the problem with Charles Hanley. But you are a bit short in your position. How, where and when did he overstep the mark?' 'Oh,' says he, 'I came in here tonight prepared to resign.' I replied, 'I couldn't give one f*** what you do, it's all the one to me if you resign or not. This is about a man's character. Has this man robbed money, misappropriated funds or broken rules? Come up with the answers, don't mind resigning, that's not an answer at all.' At that stage, Hartigan jumped up and said, 'I'm resigning,' and packed all his accoutrements into a f***ing bag and off he went. 'Off with you,' said I. About seven went with him, Rory Kiely, Eddie Wade, Dan Hickey and a few more.

Danagher stayed; he was stuck to the seat and couldn't move. He was nearly ready to have a heart attack. John Naughton didn't run out any door either, he stood his ground. I think there were four or five of them left. The Pudding [P. S. Ó Riain] stayed as well. So we had the resignation of the county secretary in the middle of the whole thing and that was the next bust up before any ball at all was pucked and nothing to do with hurling. 'Twas a f***ing terror, a big bust up before anything at all happened on the field. This was on a Monday night and a full county board meeting was due to be held the following night. 'I'll be at the county board meeting tomorrow night,' I said, 'and I don't give one f*** about ye. We will see about this thing, because ye won't f***ing get rid of Charlie Hanley.'

There was murder anyway about Hartigan and there was meetings and rows and fighting and f*** it, 'twas a terror and it was going on for about a month until Hartigan climbed down again and brought himself back like a bould child. And I'll tell you something – Charlie Hanley wasn't got rid of though.

The 2009 opinion of Brendan Danagher seems to differ wildly from that of the man who sat opposite Tom Ryan in 1995. Perhaps if this was also his opinion in 1995, he might have made a greater attempt at voicing it when acting as spokesman for the board executive:

I played low key in 1995, I was only just after coming in and when you are just after coming in you don't get involved. They tried to remove Charles Hanley, but I thought Charles did a great job. Charles and myself have been friends for years. I always believe that if a man is doing a good job he should stay there, regardless of whether he was a county board officer or not. You always have people looking for positions when a team is going well. We rarely had votes at county executive meetings, we always tried to smooth things out and get agreement.

Tom Ryan is adamant there were ulterior motives:

All Jimmy Hartigan could ever come up with was that Charlie Hanley had overstepped his mark. He could never come up with anything else. It wasn't Charles Hanley they were coming after, it was me. They didn't give a f*** about Charlie Hanley but they were thinking and planning and plotting. They weren't still f***ing finished because the following f***ing November didn't they change the rules for appointing the manager and the clubs and the PR system got f***ed. The executive would appoint the manager in future. Na Piarsaigh brought in a motion that the executive would pick the manager. Dan Hickey was behind that.

Mike Fitzgerald explains the rationale behind removing Hanley:

It was seen as a problem that Charles Hanley had too much of a say in running things. He was a top-class liaison officer, but was making decisions with Tom. The county board felt they should be involved in the consultation and they weren't.

Sandra Marsh has her own view:

Hanley wasn't a board officer and that was an officially appointed position, which held responsibility. If you weren't a board officer and you had control over something it probably wasn't seen as the best thing in the world. Control is the big word.

She also believes the change to the appointment process was based on sound business principles rather than a means to remove Tom Ryan:

When there was so much money being invested in team preparation and when there was so much at stake and when we had got so near in 1994 I can understand how the county board felt that they might have wanted a little more control over who was managing the county teams. There was a big financial responsibility upon the county board so I can understand why they might have wanted input into who was chosen as manager. I don't think the change of system was a 'get Tom Ryan' thing, but maybe I was outside the circle, maybe I was outside the loop. I wasn't involved in a number of things that went on because I was seen as a minor officer. There was a nucleus of senior officers that ran things, and in a way that's the most expedient way of doing things because it's too hard to control things within a larger group.

In his playing days Tom Ryan was abrasive, uncompromising, durable and teak tough. Opponents acknowledge that nothing soft was taken or given. Limerick County Board had a tougher proposition on their hands than they anticipated. 'Timber Tom' was going nowhere.

ELEVEN

ℭℬ

1996 (1): KINGS OF MUNSTER

*imerick began their League campaign in October 1995 in Division 2, having
been relegated from the top flight following what many believe was a
hangover from the All-Ireland debacle of 1994.*

*Limerick secured promotion after finishing third in Division 2 in what should
have been a comfortable campaign. Bernie Savage remembers the slow start:*

In the autumn of 1995 we lost the first two League games to Dublin
and Laois, and we were lucky to win the next match against Antrim in
Belfast by two points. I remember the Nashs' father got onto us and
f***ed us out of it. All the players turned up for training early in 1996
and you could see the change. We played Waterford in a challenge
game at Lismore and everyone put it together after that. There were a
couple of players who weren't great to train previously but they put it
in after that and trained every night.

Frankie Carroll says Limerick were looking beyond the League:

We mightn't have been great in the League but the League was
there to be played; the championship was there to be won, that was
the way we would have been looking at it. In 1992 the focus might
have been on winning the League, but we had moved on a few steps
from there.

Gary Kirby remembers a turning point in training:

We had a training session out in Maguires' Field near UL in
February of 1996. We were doing runs and I think only three-quarters
of the team got back within the time that was allocated. Dave Mahedy
wasn't happy and spoke to us. Half way around the next one we
stopped. Ciarán was the captain and then he decided to say a few
words. A few other people also spoke and we said, 'Unless we are
willing to do it now, there's no point.' So we forgot about that run, but

An anxious-looking Tom Ryan patrols the sideline in 1996 against Cork.

the following three runs were all done as a team within the time. That was a key moment.

The chances of beating Cork were dealt a huge blow when Mike Houlihan broke his jaw in a farmyard accident. However, Tom Ryan had ultimate faith in the healing powers of the man nicknamed 'Iron Mike':

Charlie Hanley took me to Cork to see Houlihan. He was in the hospital bed and looked like someone from Mars. It was like something you would see in a film, with a big thing over his head and all the wires coming out of it. His face was in s**t and this was the end of March or early April. The surgeon came out with a pencil and he was describing what was wrong with him. When I was going away I asked the surgeon, 'Will he be ready for the end of May?' 'This man might never play again,' was his answer. 'We'll see about that,' I said.

Ciarán Carey's availability might also have been in doubt but for the intervention of Tom Ryan:

Ciarán Carey had to go up to Dublin for one of them f***ing GAA launch things; he was captain, you see. I wouldn't go to any of them, I was too busy, I had no interest in media or f*** all, so he went. The county board wouldn't pay his expenses because they said he was misquoting them. Carey had no job at the time. We had to have an emergency meeting with them to get it sorted out. I had a right battle with Brendan Danagher. It was going on for three months and it was eventually only sorted a fortnight before championship.

Danagher is diplomatic:

These small things will always come up, but you generally resolve them. I would always prefer to resolve these issues behind closed doors. You get over all these things, it's a pity they become public, but we worked away.

The pre-championship challenge games were a huge asset to Limerick in the Tom Ryan era, and 1996 was no different. UCC Fitzgibbon star Eoin O'Neill emerged as a goal-scoring forward, Podge Tobin established himself as a full-forward, and Mark Foley served his apprenticeship as a wing-back having played all his League hurling in the forwards. The most important challenge game was against Westmeath, as Tom Ryan explains:

We got the team ready for the championship and trained away. Houlihan eventually came out of hospital. Westmeath rang looking for a challenge game so we went out to Ahane and played them. Mike Houlihan was togged, a brave man – and the hoor only out of hospital since the previous Thursday. There was blood coming out of his gums, and his jaw was still wired up. Seven f***ing days later we were going to Cork for championship. He had a big helmet on him with these big thick bars on the faceguard. 'Jaysus,' I said to myself, 'we will stick you centre-back, get you a bit of hurling and see how you go.' He got an awful roasting, got cleaned out, was missing balls, the whole lot. They were all there on the sideline, saying to take him off. I said nothing and let him hurl away.

Next thing, a big f***ing row started, a mother and father of a brawl. A Westmeath player came up and broke a hurley straight off the helmet and there was just a free for all, a bad row. Then they were saying, 'He will definitely have to be taken off now.' I would always wait, chance the f***ing thing as long as I could. And he pulled off the helmet and f***ed it into the next field. And, Jesus Christ, he started hurling like there was no tomorrow. The fear was gone, you see, the row was after getting him going, the jaw was forgotten about. Jesus Christ, he was driving balls 80 yards up the field, drop-striking balls and that. Houlihan was back. Sure, he went down to Cork the following week and walked all over the c***s.

Houlihan recalls his comeback:

One of their players hit me a belt of an elbow and maybe it didn't break my jaw again, but it shook it. I was minding myself, and I wasn't doing the normal things right. I wore the hurley off him, on the ball of course, and said I am not taking this any more. I was wired up for six weeks, I had two fractures. I had false teeth so luckily enough I was able to get some kind of food into me. There were no vibrations so I could train away while I was wired up and started running, when the boys were training. I was doing timed laps with Mahedy. I used to always grub well, but when that happened, I could only eat yogurts and use the blender and the pounds shed off me. I was flying, in as good condition as I was ever in. I went to the doctor in Cork and the doctor wanted to take out the wires, and I said no, I wanted to keep them in.

Seánie McCarthy was working as a rep for a company and I met him in a shop in Kilmallock about two weeks before the match. I

The Limerick team that dethroned the All-Ireland champions Clare in 1996 at the Gaelic Grounds. *Back row (l–r):* Seán O'Neill (Murroe/Boher), Owen O'Neill (Murroe/Boher), Mike Nash (South Liberties), Gary Kirby (Patrickswell), Podge Tobin (Kilmallock), Shane O'Neill (Na Piarsaigh). *Front row (l–r):* T. J. Ryan (Garryspillane),

Mike Houlihan (Kilmallock), Joe Quaid (Feoghanagh/Castlemahon), Declan Nash (South Liberties), Mike Galligan (Claughaun), Ciarán Carey (Patrickswell), Stephen McDonagh (Bruree), Mark Foley (Adare).

could talk through the false teeth. He said to me, 'You won't be playing in the game anyway,' and I thought in my own mind, 'That's what you think.' I ended up marking him in the game. The doctor wanted to take the wires out. He said to me, 'Look, if you break the jaw again I will have an awful job trying to get the wires out, but if you break it with no wires in, it's very easy to wire it up again.' That was the risk I was going to take. I took it. The very first ball that came, he nearly wrapped the hurley around my face, and I said to myself, 'This ain't going to happen again,' because they would put you away. Things worked well. We had only ever won a single match in Páirc Uí Chaoimh, the year before against Tipperary. Against Cork it was a fantastic day. Regardless of whatever else we won, be it Munster finals or whatever, Limerick supporters will never forget that one. Everybody was on song, it was a delight coming out of the park that day, the long walk up through the trees, Limerick supporters were doing cartwheels.

Nicky English's famous soccer-style goal against Cork in the drawn 1987 Munster final at Thurles has been shown many times. Podge Tobin side-footed a second-half goal to the top left corner of the net in Páirc Uí Chaoimh that any international soccer player would be proud of, yet that goal has rarely been aired since.

Limerick had lost to Cork many times down the years. There were injustices, there were poor performances, and there were days when Limerick were downright unlucky. Beating Cork in Páirc Uí Chaoimh in 1996 was sweet revenge for incidents such as Tomás Mulcahy's goal on the same pitch in 1992 and the excessive amount of injury time in 1987.

The one negative was that Damien Quigley broke his thumb and had to defer his final exams for a year.

Frankie Carroll missed out on the Cork game:

Houlihan had the broken jaw and I was playing midfield in the pre-championship challenge games. Shane O'Neill slipped into wing-forward in my spot, and then Houlihan got back. Shane O'Neill had been going well and they decided to leave him there. Houlihan was a must if he was available, so I lost out. I got caught in no man's land. I have to say it was frustrating at the time not being on the team because I was used to being on it. I knew there was a good team there that was going places, and I wanted to be a part of it.

Cork manager Jimmy Barry-Murphy was left wondering what he had got himself into:

That year was the start of my coaching career with the Cork seniors, and wasn't very illustrious. Limerick were a very seasoned team that time. I knew Tom Ryan and a few of the lads from when they played the 1994 All-Ireland final and I was with the Cork minors. I knew Limerick were good, but I didn't realise how good they were until we played them at Páirc Uí Chaoimh that day. It was some shock to the system realising how far ahead of us they were. It was an eye opener. Limerick had won with coaching and preparation and strength. I was really hoping they would go on to win an All-Ireland.

That was a humiliation for Cork; we weren't just beaten, we were annihilated. It was a humiliating defeat and led to a lot of soul searching. We had to readjust where we were going. We used that as a template, that it was finally time to move on from the players that had given great service and start with a young team of players and build from there again. It might take a couple of years but we knew there had to be a team-building process of a couple of years. We knew we weren't going to do anything in the short term.

The game had added significance for Stephen McDonagh:

You could never dream of going down to Cork and beating them down there by so much. I remember being inside in the Gaelic Grounds in 1984 on my father's shoulders watching the heartbreak of Leonard Enright flicking the ball into his own net. I grew up watching defeats like that and we never let up on the day when we got hold of them. I am living on the Cork border, and I spent my young years going out at weekends in Charleville. I rarely went out in Limerick; at that time the social scene in Charleville was as big as anything in Limerick. I would never have been one to gloat too much about defeating Cork or being triumphant, but that win was very satisfying. It was a great performance.

Three weeks later, Clare came to the Gaelic Grounds as All-Ireland champions, but were sent back out the N18 courtesy of a superb point by Ciarán Carey. The decision of RTÉ not to include the score among its 'Top 20 GAA Moments' in 2005 is a disgrace. Carey himself remains modest:

When I caught the ball, I had three options: 1. I was going to be fouled; 2. I was going to distribute it to someone else to score; or 3. I was going to create a chance for myself to put it over the bar. As it turned out it opened up and I had no choice but to have a go at scoring myself. I was waiting and hoping for a clatter, that someone would floor me and Gary [Kirby] would win the game with the free. When you are soloing, even though your eye is on the ball, you can see the field ahead of you, and I saw it opening up and kept going. The minute the ball went over the bar I knew the game was as good as over. But there was no time for cartwheels. I remember distinctly after scoring that my focus was on getting back into position to win the puck-out. You have to at that level.

From a Patrickswell point view there was a great sense of pride in winning that game. We were down three points. Barry Foley got a point, Gary got the free, Barry got another and I got the winner. My abiding memory of the game was that it was an extremely hot day. I have this thing about having steel studs on my boots. I had it in my head that I was able to turn quickly without slipping if I had steel studs on, but I went over the top that day, because the ground was like tarmac. I will never forget it, my feet were reefed with blisters afterwards.

Frankie Carroll wonders how Carey managed it:

Even after half of the Clare game I was shattered, so for Ciarán to make the run that he made after playing a full game was phenomenal. It was a real show of athleticism. I don't think anyone else in the team would have had the level of athleticism to do that so late in the game. As well as being an unbelievable hurler, Carey was an awesome athlete. That was a legendary score in Limerick. Fellas will always remember that whether it was in the top twenty scores or not. How many of the top twenty scores will be remembered in years to come?

The Clare defence had improved significantly from the 1994 Munster final but Mike Galligan believes there was nothing they could have done to prevent the score:

If you scored two points off the Clare defence you were doing well. They were winning all their matches with low scoring averages. They weren't giving away frees, even though they were hitting hard. The days of getting five and six points against them were over. Ciarán would admit his right side wasn't the strongest, and they couldn't foul him because Gary would put it over, so they did the right thing: they put Ciarán on his right side but he still got it.

Many Clare people were critical of Mike Houlihan following an incident involving Ollie Baker. Houlihan sets the record straight:

It's unfortunate for me to be so awkward! I tried to flick the ball off him and Carey ran into me, and the hurley went up and hit him on the head. Today it wouldn't happen at all because about 80 per cent of them are wearing helmets, which is great from a safety point of view. It was just one of those accidents.

Ger Loughnane was gracious in defeat, but must have been seething at the manner in which the game was lost. Clare may have won two All-Irelands but that defeat sticks out in his managerial career like a sore thumb. Jim McInerney believes Loughnane made a cardinal error prior to the game:

That game epitomised the evenness between us at the time, with only a puck of a ball between the teams. It was the only time I ever witnessed Ger Loughnane making a negative statement while I was involved with Clare. He said in the lead-up to that game that Clare had never beaten Limerick in the Gaelic Grounds in a championship match. I don't know if that's true or not, but true or not, he stated it and I suppose it created doubt in the players' minds. We were going to make history if we won it, and making history is a very hard thing to do. If he had his time back again, I don't know if he would have said it. I would have been one of the oldest in the dressing room, and the very fact that the record even existed in the first place was news to me. There were a lot of positives at the time and it was something we didn't need to know. Normally I would be very well up on the history of games, and I doubt if anyone in the dressing room would have known about that apart from Loughnane. I wouldn't say it was the reason we lost, but there may have been a certain doubt in the players' minds in the last ten minutes when the pressure came on.

Anthony Daly recalls the drive and passion of the Clare team:

If the previous year's Munster final was the most memorable victory, that [defeat in 1996] was the most memorable game of my time. The heat was unbelievable and the crowd and the atmosphere were electric. We passed Ivan's going into the game and all you could see was the street black with people. Loughnane stood up at the front of the bus and took the microphone and said, 'This is the stuff our fathers and grandfathers told us about. This is the Munster championship.'

The hair was standing on the back of my neck getting off the bus. I swear to God it was unreal. Were we wired going out onto the field! And we had maintained that Tom Ryan had whinged the whole year about us being dirty in the previous year's Munster final and Johnny McDonnell and the whole lot. I remember the national anthem was just about to start and I was marking Shane O'Neill from Na Piarsaigh and he kind of stood in front of me as we were turning around to face the flag and I remember saying into his ear, 'Get out of my f***ing light, young lad.' He looked back and I'd say he nearly got weak.

It's a game I found very hard to accept we lost. I really believed we hurled well on the day. Declan Nash's block on Éamonn Taaffe was a vital turning point. Another crucial moment was when Fergal Hegarty soloed through. They were after bringing on Ronan O'Hara as a sub, which none of us agreed with, and instead of putting it over the bar to put us four ahead, Hegarty soloed through and passed it into O'Hara who f***ed it up inside. It was the best game Fergal Hegarty ever hurled and he could have just put it over the bar. Ironically, he was the one who slipped at the very end when chasing Ciarán.

We mightn't have been quite as physically ready in 1996 as we were in 1995 with all the celebrating and that. Mike Mac would have said that he tried to cram too much into too little time, instead of maybe letting us go in a bit fresher and not quite as fit. Maybe he tried to push too hard for it and perhaps there was a tiredness that crept in near the end. I think they just came with a surge and sometimes teams can come with a surge, Offaly were very good at coming with that surge as well. I always thought Limerick were a surge team, and it was very hard to hold it off when it came, and it came just at the right time, the scores that won it were great scores. I have no problem in saying that Carey's score was the greatest I ever saw in the game of hurling.

Tom Ryan likens the Clare collapse to the 1994 All-Ireland final:

It was an unbelievable match. People talk about our loss in the 1994 All-Ireland final, but Clare had this match won. They were well ahead and they were laughing. I mean they even brought in Cyril Lyons. Next thing Barry Foley got two and Kirby got one and Ciarán got the winner. They didn't know what hit them.

Gary Kirby has fond memories of the game:

Passion and Pride: Frankie Carroll celebrates after scoring the equaliser against Tipperary in the drawn game of 1996.

I got a goal in the first half; Podge Tobin put me through with a great pass. That was the most satisfying victory because they were on a high. It's just the occasion, a roasting summer day, the terraces were packed so much you couldn't get any more in there, the buzz, the atmosphere in the ground, the atmosphere even going to the game. The whole build-up, the whole setup.

Here were the All-Ireland champions from the year before coming out against us who had been in the final the year previous to that again. And then to win it the way we won it, to get the last four scores. I don't think we got the recognition we deserved. I remember some said Clare were the ones that brought out the colour, but it was Limerick who brought out the colour, the sea of green when we won the Munster final in 1994 was unreal. And they go on and say the likes of Clare did it. Clare won their two All-Irelands and we lost our two. That's the only difference between the teams. I wouldn't say Clare were luckier; Clare got their chances and took them. We didn't. I wouldn't put it down to luck.

Damien Quigley recalls Loughnane's dressing room speech afterwards:

He spoke with great passion about the occasion, and the scenes before the game and stuff. It was a super speech, one of the best I ever heard in the dressing room. And he said, 'Lads, it's not worth a s**t unless you go off and do it.'

But the Clare boys would tell you they weren't ready for that match. It came a little bit soon for them, and their training was behind. Still though, Clare were unrecognisable from the team that beat us in the Munster final the previous year. The team that beat us in 1995 wasn't anywhere near as good as the team we beat in 1996. They had improved beyond all. They came through serious games outside Munster and were a far superior force. I couldn't see us being beaten by Clare in 1996, but that's because I didn't recognise how good they were, even though they were the All-Ireland champions. I couldn't see Limerick being beaten because we were so focused. We had blown Cork away. They had never been beaten since Páirc Uí Chaoimh opened, and we had blown them out of the water altogether. And we were really right, and despite them being All-Ireland champions I didn't think they would live with us. They had us on the ropes and they just didn't put us away. They hit three or four wides that would have nailed us.

At half-time in the Munster final against Tipperary at the Gaelic Grounds, Limerick trailed by 1-11 to 0-4. But in a thrilling second half they forced a draw and went on to win the replay in Páirc Uí Chaoimh a week later. Frankie Carroll scored the equalising point in the drawn game:

I didn't play in the first half but looking on, Tipperary gave an awesome exhibition of hurling. It wasn't that Limerick were that bad, it was just that Tipperary were awesome. Maybe Limerick stood off a bit but did Tipperary use the ball well, and gave a super supply to their forwards. It all changed in the second half. We got among them and upset them. To bring it back in points was most satisfying of all, rather than getting three goals and getting back into it quickly. Personally, I had come on and done well and had my place nailed for the replay.

Despite the huge deficit, Joe Quaid recalls a determined dressing room at half-time:

Ciarán stood up and gave a speech and said, 'We can either f*** off home or we go straight back out.' Nobody sat down, we were back out again after five minutes. We had been out a good few minutes waiting and some of the Tipp boys told me that when they were coming out onto the field there was some kind of an eerie feeling in the air. I would say it was like facing into an ambush. We dragged it back that day purely on points, with no goals. I remember being asked that night if we would win the following Sunday. I wasn't being cocky but I replied, 'We won today and we are going down to Páirc Uí Chaoimh next Sunday to collect the cup.' There was no way Tipperary were going to recover from that in the space of a week.

Stephen McDonagh remembers an incident in the tunnel in Cork:

In the replay Pat Fox was a sub, and whatever happened me, I went to go into the wrong dressing room, and I turned into Declan Ryan, and, of course, Ryan went for blood. This was under the tunnel. Houlihan came behind, and Fox was roaring, 'Come on Tipp' or whatever, and Houlihan planted the hurley across his arse and started another big hullabaloo. Houlihan then caught me by the collar; I didn't know where I was going. Deep down I knew we had them after drawing with them the first day.

Mike Houlihan explains it as he saw it:

The Tipp supporters were giving a bit of voice, and Fox came out geeing up the boys coming off, and I hit him a belt of a shoulder. His days of hurling were nearly finished but he still wanted to put the Limerick players down. I said, 'F*** you if you are trying to intimidate our players,' and I hit him a belt and drove him back and he hit me a belt of a hurley. He was a tough nut. I know he was on the way out that time, but he still wanted to put me away. It is still dog eat dog today; they still want to put you away today.

Gary Kirby was a serious doubt for the replay:

There was talk I had a fractured skull before the replay. But that was paper talk. I don't know where they got that because we didn't talk to anyone. The real story was that I had been getting fierce headaches and Dave Boylan sent me in to get a check-up because I couldn't even bend down to tie my lace without getting a headache. I got the all clear and once I got it, that was it. I remember the hospital staff said they would keep me overnight just to get the CAT scan the following morning so that I would be there in time ready to go first thing. I remember telling them, because they knew who I was, that there was to be no papers or anything like that. Next thing this photographer arrived the following morning to take a photograph of me. After we telling them we wanted nobody to know about it. I remember it well, but thankfully I got the all clear, I still get the headaches. It was severe to be honest. I couldn't stick it, but I got the all clear, thank God.

I remember the replay well because I used to drive to the matches. We had a choice between driving and going on the bus. Ciarán [Carey], Barry Foley and Carmel [Gary's wife] used to travel with me. It was prior to the construction of the Croom bypass and we were just gone past Croom village when the traffic was bumper to bumper. Sandra Marsh was there as well and she had the Na Piarsaigh guys with her, and she actually drove on the other side of the road. So I drove on the other side of the road going around the bends. That's how serious it was. If a car was coming we just pulled in, in front of another car. I remember at one stage Sandra pulled in and stayed in, but I kept doing it the whole way down to Mallow.

Once, when I pulled in, the driver nearest put down the window. He was wearing a Limerick hat, and he says to Ciarán, 'Look, we are all trying to get to the match, we are all trying to get there on time.' He didn't have a clue who Ciarán was. When we got as far as Mallow, all the traffic was gone. We were going to Blarney because that's where our training ground was. We used to meet there and get a garda escort in to Páirc Uí Chaoimh. We got to Blarney and the boys said, 'Do your puck around there and see how you feel and if you feel OK play away, and if you don't we won't start you.' I felt grand, sure, a replay of a Munster final . . . I wasn't going to say anything else!

Damien Quigley says the Tipperary back line was weakened:

Noel Sheehy was injured that year. Tipperary rarely conceded four goals when he was full-back. I had drawn out Paul Shelly and made the space. Sheehy was cuter and Tipp might have won the All-Ireland in '96 if he was around.

He goes on to sing the praises of Dave Mahedy:

Dave Mahedy is absolutely fantastic. Anyone that says anything negative about him doesn't know what they are talking about. He is a scientist of fitness and an expert on human behaviour by virtue of all the teams he has been involved in. He is a psychologist. Dave is seriously and unbelievably clued in. Incredibly experienced in all sports and brings it all to the game in a very balanced way. Mahedy was hugely central to everything that went on but he was not a hurling person and not a hurling coach. He did all the drills and stuff and was excellent at them but that's working on your skills, that's not coaching. Coaching is about improving weaknesses and learning how to play together as a team. Even now in Limerick we don't play to a pattern.

The final score was 4-7 to 0-16. Owen O'Neill joined a select band of those who scored two goals in a Limerick Munster final victory. Both were scored with the boot, a unique feat:

It wasn't that I had planned to kick them; the opportunities arose and were taken. Obviously you are conscious that someone may hook you, but hitting the net is what matters.

For O'Neill, however, it is the Clare game that stands out:

There was nothing soft and everything had to be earned. It was a game where the amount of hooking and blocking was phenomenal. There was no space. I remember going in training the following Tuesday night, and there were a lot of sore bodies. It wasn't from belts; it was because the ground was like concrete and a lot of ground had been covered by a lot of players that day. There was no doubt in the players' minds that we were going to do something that year.

Some credited a first-half goal to Damien Quigley, but Frankie Carroll has no doubt:

Winning that Munster championship was my most satisfying memory. I definitely got the goal in the replay, there are photographs and the video shows it clearly. I could feel it on the hurley. It was nice to be back on the team and scoring.

Nicky English believes Tipperary lost their chance the first day:

I think we should have won the game in Limerick: we were well clear at half-time. Liam Cahill had a goal chance after half-time. Had he put it away, the game was over. My big memory is that Joe Quaid made a massive save later in the half from Aidan Ryan who had struck a ground ball as clean as a whistle. When they got the draw the momentum had turned in their favour. I didn't go to Páirc Uí

Chaoimh with any great confidence that we were going to win. That's the way it turned out, even though we conceded a few soft goals. The goals were the difference, but we had shot our bolt in Limerick.

Winning a Munster championship by beating Cork, Tipperary and, for good measure, the All-Ireland champions Clare is a significant feat, and carries great significance in the history of the game. The show was not yet over though; another Croke Park occasion awaited.

TWELVE

ᛜ

1996 (2): DENIED ONCE MORE

*I*n the 1996 All-Ireland semi-final Limerick faced Antrim, as they had done two *years previously. Many of the players believed the team dropped a gear for those games. Mike Galligan gives his own perspective:*

We were lucky to play Antrim both years, because it gave us an easier passage to the final. I wouldn't consider it a hindrance, I feel what happened in 1994 had nothing to do with a weak semi-final.

Dave Mahedy's experience across a range of sports makes his views very relevant:

Playing Antrim didn't do us any favours both years as it meant that we effectively went eight weeks without a proper game. I hold the same view with Munster losing the earlier Heineken Cup finals. The Celtic League was in its infancy back then, and they were up against teams that had played cup finals in England the week before. You can say you are saving players from injuries, but you need competitive games. I remember Munster going over to play a friendly against Leicester in 2000 to try and get a game, but then they were going in against Northampton who had played an English cup final the week before. It's the same principle. That was one of the things levelled at Eddie O'Sullivan relating to the 2007 World Cup.

In 1996 we had the most competitive Munster championship ever. Then we had Antrim and then the All-Ireland final. We lost the momentum we had built up. It does make a difference in that the Munster championship was condensed, playing four games. You couldn't have got four harder games than in 1996. Then we played Antrim. After knowing what it was like playing them from 1994, we took time off training in 1996 to try and build it up again. You are going possibly seven or eight weeks with effectively a training game in between. In Kilkenny at the moment they are getting harder games in training than we got against Antrim that time.

Sometimes a team like Greece gets on a roll and wins a European Championship. We were on that roll in 1996, but once you get off it, it's impossible to get back on it. Wexford were also on that roll in 1996. That's just my opinion; it's not an excuse. Clare got on that run, Cork got on that run in 1999 and the whole thing opened up. As a trainer, you start in January, you have to have your team right for May and they have to maintain that level until September, whereas Kerry footballers have won All-Irelands by getting it right for mid-July for a Munster final, and it's a shorter spell to maintain that level. When you are trying to start in May and finish in September it's very difficult, that's why nowadays you see teams coming through late, through the back door.

Mahedy adds that maintaining momentum within games is also crucial:

If you relax in a game you can't bring it back up again, and that applies to any sport. That's why we attempt to train with match intensity. It's the same when we are on a run in the championship. I would imagine that a higher percentage of teams who won the All-Ireland in those days didn't play Antrim or Down in the semi-finals. The Offaly game in 1994, for instance, couldn't have gone any better in many respects; at half-time we were six points up and we maintained that and with five minutes to go were five points up. There was no evidence to suggest we would lose that game.

A change in the championship structure meant that 1996 was the last time an Ulster team appeared in an All-Ireland hurling semi-final. However, in seven of the ten previous years, the team that beat the Ulster champions failed to lift the McCarthy Cup, lending huge support to Mahedy's theory.

In an attempt to address the lack of competitive action, a challenge game was arranged with Clare between the semi-final and the final. Owen O'Neill picked up an injury but Tom Ryan says this did not affect him in the final:

The forwards were going well in training and I wanted the Clare backs to test them. I rang Loughnane looking for his backs and he said it was the whole team or nothing. Owen O'Neill picked up an ankle injury in that game but was passed fit to play in the final. But of course, John O'Connor planted him early in the game. It was that rather than any after effect of the injury which buried him.

Gary Kirby recalls the circumstances:

Tom said we were going down to Ennis. We didn't know if we were going training down there or what we were doing. We got to Ennis and all the doors were shut, and when we went into the ground, Clare were there warming up. 'F*** it,' we said, 'what's going on here?' Next thing Tom explained what was going on and in fairness to Clare all the big names were there to play us. That was two to three weeks before the All-Ireland. It was a good enjoyable game. If Owen O'Neill's ankle was sore from a twist, a pull in the final would make no difference to it. It might be hard on the shin, but that's a different issue.

Anthony Daly was surprised at the arrangement of the challenge game:

It was a bit stupid really, playing that challenge match. It was a bit unrealistic playing that time, we were the best and the worst rivals playing at the time, we were the two best teams in Munster. It was a bit far fetched. Can you imagine me now, if I was with Clare and we got to the All-Ireland final, picking up the phone and asking Liam Sheedy or Justin McCarthy for a challenge game before the All-Ireland final? I suppose that's the kind of zone we were in at the time with Loughnane; if he told us be there, we would be there. I know we were all looking at each other and wondering, 'What the f*** are we doing here?' When it was on then I suppose we were saying, 'We will meet these f***ers again next year.' There was a bit of that in it; it was dirty, but at the same time it was a bit false. It actually turned out to be a tough enough match. It kind of took on a life of its own.

The post mortem from the All-Ireland final itself began with a series of incidents that took place prior to the throw-in. Brendan Danagher gives his view:

My own opinion is that it was blown out of all proportion. If an individual player jumps on the spot or whatever, it's not the end of the world and I think it got too much publicity. If you win, everything is forgotten. If you lose, people tend to come back and pick out the worst points. Seán O'Neill got injured in a clash at the throw-in and Gary [Kirby] got injured soon after. It unsettled the team. Gary was our leading light and led with great dedication. He had an unusual style and centre-backs found it hard to handle him. I always considered if Gary was taken off that it would be detrimental to the team. He had been the leader in 1994, 1995 and 1996. He was a pure gentleman and a great man to have on any team.

Tom Ryan's views on the tussles between the O'Neill and O'Connor brothers early in the game are forthright:

Owen O'Neill was blackguarded, he was taken out. I had covered the jostling before the match with Seán O'Neill. I had gone into great detail about it. Again it comes back to the quality and intensity of our preparations with each player. We had a good session one Sunday morning above in Bruff coming up to the All-Ireland. I took him up the field and said to him, 'We can do without this tough man jostling, that's only the work of a f***ing eejit.' He was a good hurler. He had done a massive job for us since he came onto the scene in 1995, but he got drawn into that incident when I had specifically told him not to. I was very aggrieved about it. Discipline was a big thing for us, giving away frees, doing the f***ing eejit. We had no one sent off in four years of championship hurling. A major failing that day on his part.

Ryan is also unequivocal about the Gary Kirby incident:

Liam Dunne did a job on Gary Kirby, but in my opinion Gary Kirby's finger was not broken, it was severely cut. It was examined by the team doctor, Dave Boylan, whose competence was called into question by Kirby when he said the finger was broken. We had the Olympic physio with us. Kirby played on in the game and played for Patrickswell two Sundays later and scored 1-12. He was on *Laochra Gael* recently talking his bollox off about it. Dunne pulled but Kirby pulled as well. I didn't give a f*** about it, and it put Dave Boylan in a very compromised position over it, that we were not capable of recognising that a finger was broken. We received a lot of criticism for leaving him on the field injured but he played away and wanted to stay on the field. Our policy was that if a player was injured that he came off and that was it. If his finger was broken he wouldn't play away and he certainly wouldn't score 1-12 for Patrickswell two Sundays later.

However, Kirby maintains the finger was broken and that it was adrenalin that brought him through the game:

Tom told me I would be targeted, and told me to pull on the first few balls. Maybe it was a mistake I made myself. Normally I would try to catch one or two early on and I would have myself protected. When I was pulling, I left myself open too early in the game. The finger was broken. I didn't start the following week with the club, I only came on with five minutes to go. I started two weeks later all right. It was the little finger on the right hand. There isn't a lot you can do with the little finger, and in fairness it's starting to recover once it's broken. The x-ray showed that it was broken. I didn't play the GOAL match on the Wednesday night, though John O'Shea had asked me.

And as for the county board, Declan Nash and myself had to get a taxi from the hotel out to the hospital to get our injuries sorted out the following day. I was told not to hurl for four weeks. That match the following week was the only match of my nineteen years with the Patrickswell senior team that I didn't start. I wasn't going to go off in the All-Ireland final. I didn't even strap the finger. The adrenalin was going. They gave Liam Dunne the man of the match in the final, but if you watch that match you will see that very little ball came down between myself and Dunne. Everything bypassed us. I don't dwell on the incident too much, there's no point. People ask about it. They will always ask you. I asked the boys on *Laochra Gael*, 'Do we have to mention it?' and they said, 'In fairness, it's part of your life.' That's the only reason we did talk about it.

Mike Nash feels Wexford had to try something to negate the influence of Kirby:

Gary was playing outstanding hurling that time and was catching ball after ball. If you take Gary Kirby out of the equation, you are upsetting one of the main lifelines of the Limerick team. Everything was channelled through Gary. Dunne got his chance and he took it, and I can't say that I wouldn't do it myself if I was marking Gary, because you would have to. If he is putting his paw up there, you have to be taking the paw out of it, that's what has to be done as a back. OK, Gary played on – I didn't realise his finger was broken. I didn't realise it until the end of the match; he played on through the pain.

Stephen McDonagh has strong views on the referee's performance:

The pre-match stuff looking back was something that shouldn't have happened. Hindsight is probably twenty-twenty vision, but it wasn't a major deal. That final went pear shaped too. Having said that, I think we were the victims of the worst refereeing performance in an All-Ireland final. Éamonn Scallan should never have been put off. Both of us pulled high and I was left with a broken hurley too. It was ridiculous, stupid sending him off. The referee made up for it then, he totally switched. I thought we got a blackguarding in that All-

Ireland final, it was a disgraceful performance of refereeing. Because it was Wexford in the All-Ireland final and the fantasy of Liam Griffin and all the razzmatazz, the GAA put up with it.

Mike Nash believes the sending off was a hindrance to Limerick:

The referee sent Scallan off and spent the rest of the game making it up. Tom Dempsey ran through at one stage and Declan met him with a square shoulder, and there was a free. He gave free after free if you went near them. He was making up for sending Scallan off. Dave Boylan said to me afterwards that when he was a player with Midleton, their coach used to say that if they had an extra man, to go out and hit the opposition player as hard as you want. The reason for that is that if you get a player sent off we are still only level with numbers on them. The team with the man down will always get away with more. Wexford started diving and jumping and folding; every time they were coming through with the ball they would take ten steps before they would come at you. Storey came through at one stage and he must have had the ball in his hand for half a day.

After a fella being sent off everyone is kind of wary and saying, 'I don't want to be the next man sent off,' but what it probably needed was for me to get sent off. If I ran out and took Tom Dempsey or Storey out, it would have left Stephen McDonagh and Declan behind and they would have swept everything behind. That's what I was thinking afterwards, instead of us trying to play fifteen against fourteen. The extra man caused us too many problems. It upsets the game, the positions of the play and everything else.

Tom Ryan explains the use of the extra man:

We used Carey for a while as the extra man. He, by his own admission, didn't have his best game, he had a few bad wides. Clarke was extra man for a while as well. We changed it around a bit. The extra man can work in your favour and can work against you. History has shown that teams generally find it difficult to use the extra man in the biggest of games. You can put him in defence and might have a greater presence back there but it doesn't win you the match. I was aggrieved with the referee in 1996. Some of the decisions were diabolical; the standard of refereeing was poor. And I still question the standard of refereeing to this day. It's absolutely a disgrace that referees can make decisions that cost teams games and walk away.

Turlough Herbert remembers the preparations for the final:

We went up to Finnstown House hotel the week before the final for a sort of a dry run. I remember Dave Mahedy saying, 'The reason we are here is that everything that happens next Sunday, we are prepared for it. Nothing can happen next Sunday that we haven't planned for.' Except, of course, the extra man after Scallan was sent off. I can't recall that being planned for in training.

Damien Quigley says poor performances were the reason for defeat:

The game between Munster and Clermont Auvergne at Thomond Park in 2008 was a great example of the extra man not being made use of. Rugby is a game where the loss of a man can be very costly. Everyone has a different view of how the extra man could have been used in 1996. Could we have used it better? Of course we could, because we didn't use it at all. That said, the opposition usually dictates what happens with the extra man. The bottom line is that too many players didn't play on the day. And you can blame managers or anything but ultimately too many players didn't do it on the field.

Frankie Carroll agrees:

I don't think the second-half performance was good enough to win an All-Ireland. Galligan was a gifted hurler, well able to take a score and definitely had something to offer. It's fine coming in as a loose man, but it's up to Wexford who they leave loose and they decided to leave a defender loose. That point is overstated about Galligan being the loose man; they weren't going to let him loose for the second half. The loose man was probably down to a battle of wits, and we probably didn't push our issue enough.

Babs Keating believes Liam Griffin's greater planning stood to Wexford – and rues his own luck as Tipperary manager down the years:

Experience counts for an awful lot. The one year I believe Tipperary lost the All-Ireland in that era was in 1996. I believe Tipperary had a team good enough to win that All-Ireland. I was very unlucky with injury in 1993, and in 1994 we had a team prepared to win an All-Ireland. We hammered Galway in 1994 in the League final and the team disintegrated before my eyes in a matter of weeks before the Munster championship when we lost six players. Some of the best players were gone . . . John Leahy, Declan Ryan. However, they were all back in 1996 and the same team went all the way to the All-Ireland final the following year in 1997 when John Leahy, with the last puck of the ball, could have beaten Clare. That team in 1996 was probably better than the 1997 team. Nicky was still around, and Pat Fox was on the bench.

I'd be hard on the Limerick management in so far as it's gone to the stage now that when there's only a puck of the ball between the teams, it's the team that prepares the best that wins. I think Liam Griffin worked harder on Limerick, I know he did because I have a place in Rosslare and he sat down and discussed with everybody where they could neutralise Limerick. Certainly the two O'Connors worked well for him on the day and Liam Dunne certainly did his job. I know the hours that Griffin put in leading up to the All-Ireland final: I know people he asked; I know the amount of time he spent going around to people; and I know the amount of time he spent looking at videos and the options he worked on to cancel out Limerick's strengths.

Liam Griffin outlines in detail the intense preparation Wexford put in:

We were aware of the tradition between Limerick and Wexford, and 1910, 1918, 1955, 1958 and 1996 were the epics between the teams. There would have been massive planning put into that match because we recognised very early on – the players, the management team and the backroom staff – that we hadn't the best fifteen hurlers in Ireland, in fact, we went so far as to say that we didn't even have the best fifteen hurlers in Wexford on the field that day, but we had a very strong team spirit and we put a lot of planning into how we wanted to play our matches and how we were going to win them.

We had the advantage of playing Limerick in Kilmallock in the League that year, and we found them to be a robust and hardy team. We had the insight from playing them in that game and they had beaten us. They had been beaten by Offaly in 1994, and that was a match everyone in the country felt they should have won. Limerick had lowered the Banner and the Banner were the team of the century the year before because of all the hype of Clare winning and the hype surrounding Ger Loughnane. I played for Clare too, so I was delighted that Clare won the All-Ireland. Limerick had taken Clare down. They had taken them apart with one of the greatest and most important points seen by any of us, and then drew with Tipperary and beat them in the replay. Their stock was on the rise and we had to be 100 per cent prepared to try and play them. And we were. We never felt superior to Limerick but we felt we could beat them if we got everything right on the day. That's something we set out to do.

We had the advantage over Limerick and Limerick's backroom team of having had a complete microscope of their events since 1994 because they were a high profile team. We had come in under the radar in 1996 and nobody knew where we came from. I also felt that Limerick made a mistake breaking off at the parade that day because we had forecast that they would do it. We were never going to break away because we felt Limerick would try to intimidate us. Every team tries to set down a marker and make you follow their lead, but we were determined not to follow Limerick's lead that day. We were going up to Croke Park and do our own thing.

Éamonn Scallan was unlucky to be put off. There was still a bit of a residue from that Kilmallock game, and we felt that Limerick had roughed us out of it and that a few of our lads hadn't stood up and been counted. When that row broke out our lads all stood up because they knew they had to. Then the row spilled out of order a little bit and the next time it broke out, there was always going to be something done about it. Stephen McDonagh and Éamonn Scallan pulled on a ground ball, as you do. We always had great respect for McDonagh and we still would. McDonagh's hurley got caught in Gary Laffan's helmet so Éamonn Scallan pulled on his own and he got the line and Steve McDonagh stayed on. I believe that if McDonagh had been sent off it would have been a much more open game and it would have suited both teams better, but from that moment on we had to contain Limerick.

We had a plan in place in case we had a man sent off. We had discussed it and we had prepared it. It's not that we were expecting it, but we were allowing for every eventuality. We had a plan to isolate the extra man and we worked hard at that for the second half. We did isolate him and worked around him and our two players in the full-forward line really covered the ground. Gary Laffan and Tom Dempsey knew what to do, so we managed to get over the extra man situation pretty well. We had done our stats on all the matches and we knew that every game where we fouled more than the opposition, we lost. We had a game plan that nobody ever noticed. Tom Ryan had done a great job with that Limerick team for a couple of years but I think he felt hard done by that we didn't foul in the second half in our backs. We didn't foul and we used that system in the Leinster final against Offaly. We knew we couldn't afford to give away frees. We had studied Gary Kirby and we had known that he was one of the greatest free takers of all time and we had great respect for him. We had said that if we could hold Kirby to four points or less we would have a great chance of winning. He only scored two points and we only won by two. I don't subscribe to the theory that the referee gave Wexford handy frees. For example, there was a very brave decision made to put off one man in an All-Ireland final. We didn't let it shake our focus, because we had thought about it, we had planned for it.

We took control of that dressing room at half-time and we did not let it get out of order. We were saying, 'Hang on, we are still in an All-Ireland final, we have to leave all that behind us. We can't forget that we came up here to hurl. Now we have to revisit our game plan.' We had to hold our discipline. In hurling there is always a risk of losing discipline as players do when their blood is up after having a man sent off. They aren't going to come out after half-time and pull handy, they are going to pull hard. We had to make sure that we stayed in control and we put our lives on the line to make sure we stayed in control. In the second half we went out to stay in control, whatever else happened, because if we didn't stay in control we were definitely going to lose the match. The other thing we would have said was, 'These Limerick boys are hardy hoors, we don't want to get into a dogfight because there's only fourteen of us and there's fifteen of them.' We wanted to keep our heads down and try to hurl; we had set out not to foul.

I believe the Limerick public and Tom Ryan in particular got confused, and I can understand that because it seems to be unheard of that no team sets out not to foul in the backs in the second half of an All-Ireland final, but that was part of our game plan. We had done the same in the Leinster final against Offaly and nobody noticed. In the League semi-final and the quarter-final we had done the same. And nobody noticed that either. We had built in a culture of not fouling and we had built it into the team and after every single match we played there was always a post mortem about fouling. I felt we had the measure of Limerick the minute the ball was thrown in in the second half. I felt I had a job to do on the line. We had a system that I took charge once the team took the field. I had two selectors with me but there was only one person in charge. That's not being big headed. You can't have three fellows chatting on the sideline; if they felt we should do something they came to me with the suggestion. Sometimes they made a suggestion and I took it, and sometimes I didn't. I had to work my backside off in the second half to try and keep the rotation of the extra man going so they would not get to grips with us and also to make sure that no line was leaking in any way.

Two of the major talking points in the second half were the non-appearance of Mike Galligan and the disallowed goal by Brian Tobin. Referee Pat Horan offers his view on the goal:

There was a foul at the time, a push on one of the Wexford backs. It was away from the ball but not too far away. It wasn't shown on TV. I had blown and Damien Fitzhenry stood up and didn't even try to block it. The Wexford backs even stood up if you look at it on TV now.

Brian Tobin thought he had scored:

People were saying he had the whistle blown early but I didn't hear it. They were saying it was for a square ball, but he must have seen something.

Liam Griffin recalls the moment:

The whistle was blown beforehand. I didn't hear it myself, but I can remember Rory Kinsella saying, 'Free out!' and the next thing the ball was in the net. As far as I understood at the time, someone pushed someone in the back.

Tom Ryan feels the goal should have been allowed:

It shouldn't have been disallowed. There was no interference with any player; there was no incident. No forward, as I saw it, interfered with any back; the goalkeeper wasn't interfered with . . . The disallowed goal was a scandal, it was a disgraceful and outrageous decision. It was never caught on camera because it never happened. He made the decision from the middle of the field. It was a legitimate goal and the two refereeing decisions in my time that I have to highlight were the penalty decision in Thurles in 1995 and that decision.

The disallowed goal was the cause of Limerick losing that All-Ireland final. We would have won it by six or seven points. We had a lot of wides in the last eight or nine minutes. We had some very bad wides as well, everyone had them. Carey had one or two very bad wides. But that goal being disallowed finished us. It would have spurred us on if it had been scored. I have no problem contesting a game. Quality of hurling and image and discipline are very important to me and I have no problem with referees.

In this case we were dealing with a referee who shouldn't have been refereeing it because he was a Leinster referee, anyway. If Cork were playing he wouldn't be refereeing it, I guarantee you, because Frank Murphy would make sure he wouldn't be there. But again we had no representation in any boardroom anywhere. We were dealing with only wimps in the county board who were only penny boys. That's what they were and that's the way they acted, and that's what you have in the county board in Limerick and that's the way they are still. A pile of f***ing penny boys. There isn't a man in them. And they ask then why is Limerick hurling down. We are down because of the management, we are down because of the standards, we are down because of the whole makeup. It's further down we are going because rugby is going to clean away the whole thing in Limerick now and soccer is gaining ground by the day as well.

Declan Nash concurs wholeheartedly:

Against Wexford that day – and you can print this f***ing thing if you want – they had the toss and he [the ref.] didn't even remember who won it. When the man got sent off, he came down and gave out to us all for ruining the day and he seemed to be panicking. I can guarantee you that we were never going to win that day. Having sent off the man he wasn't going to be seen to be the man that beat Wexford. No matter what we did, we would have had to have been ten times better to beat Wexford that day. Can he see the foul for Brian Tobin's goal on video? It didn't f***ing happen, if that's what it was, and I sincerely doubt it, because I have been a long time waiting for an answer. I'd love to know if RTÉ have other pictures of what went on . . . Why wasn't that said at the time? Why wasn't the Limerick player who committed the foul spoken to?

It was the same with the Tomás Mulcahy goal in 1992 – Limerick seem to be prepared to take these decisions without arguing about them. It shouldn't have been up to the likes of Tom Ryan to question that; it should have been up to the county board, that's what they are there for. There should have been someone up there fighting and arguing about that straight away. It's a few more like Tom we need. There were incidents where every county have their grievances, but in

Limerick we would outdo a lot of counties for being sinned against. It's a pity the referee didn't highlight that foul on the day, because it would have eliminated a lot of doubt.

Mike Houlihan regrets that Limerick did not learn from previous Croke Park appearances:

At the end of the game I said to the referee, 'Do I score direct [from the free] or do I put it over the bar?' He said, 'It doesn't matter, time is up.' I said, 'Do I hit it into the stand so?' If that ball went directly to the net or was deflected in would it have been allowed? You have to say we didn't learn from 1994. The 1996 final was our fourth time playing at Croke Park, and we didn't really beat substantial opposition there. In the Offaly game we got hit at the very finish, but we had time to think about the Wexford game. You could sense on the field that it wasn't going to happen. It's a game that was torture to watch, and it was nearly torture to play in at times, and it didn't facilitate a great All-Ireland. Wexford won an All-Ireland but we didn't do ourselves justice and we can't keep blaming everyone else when we lose these games. What was not good enough on our part, I don't know, it might have been get rid of Mike Houlihan, it might have been get rid of Tom Ryan, it might have been get rid of someone else. Playing Antrim the second time didn't help. We didn't learn. Maybe there should have been a method of bringing the team back up to a different level for the final after the dip against Antrim. Perhaps we needed a different way of doing things. There's always something different needed to win an All-Ireland, and you hear the stories afterwards what extra things had been done to win the All-Ireland. It's like Griffin taking the team off the bus at the Wexford border. There's always something extra. What was that extra thing that Limerick should have been doing?

Liam Griffin says Wexford were relieved Galligan did not play:

From memory we knew prior to the game that Galligan wasn't going to appear. There was a lot of talk about it before the match. We were surprised because we always reckoned that Galligan was a very good loose wing-forward who picked up a lot of scores. We would have had to man-mark him to death. He was not into beating lads up, but D. J. Carey won All-Irelands and he never beat guys up either. I liked Mike Galligan, I always saw him as a tidy, nice hurler. The trouble for us was that we would have put Seánie Flood on Mike

Galligan, but we had no Seánie Flood; we lost him before the game. He was a brilliant hooker, very fast, a great stickman and didn't foul. We felt he would be ideal for Galligan.

Tom Ryan explains the background to the situation:

I had no problem with Galligan but he had not been going well in training coming into the final, and again the team was picked on form. Galligan knew himself he wasn't going well in training. If he didn't know, he should have known. Barry Foley had run out of steam in the second half, he started to founder. At that particular stage we had the play but we were not getting the scores. I was prepared to put Galligan in, but Jimmy Hartigan and the county chairman Brendan Danagher stopped it.

Galligan wasn't named on the official list of six subs that could be used. The year before, Éamonn Taaffe wasn't even named in the programme. Clare put him in, took the hit with the fine afterwards, £2,000 or whatever it was. I wanted to do the same with Galligan. They stopped him because of the fine. That was the actual fact of the matter. It's important to put it down because that did happen. And that's the way it happened.

When questioned on the matter, Brendan Danagher offered the following response:

I just can't pinpoint that exact moment, but the fact was that he wasn't on the list of six subs. That was an angle, that these things come up on the spur of the moment and you have to look at all of them. It's very hard to know if a mistake was made. I think really that the biggest mistake made that day was the disallowing of the goal. The one thing I will say to you now is that there are some things that click with me and some things that don't, and my recollection isn't as good as it was a few years ago.

Gerry Bennis says any fine should have been a non-issue:

They couldn't bring in Mike Galligan because Jimmy Hartigan and Brendan Danagher wouldn't sanction putting him in. The fine was worth it for an All-Ireland. If I was chairman I would have taken the chance, I would have sanctioned Galligan. The six subs rule was a stupid rule, and I would have no problem if the county board were fined £10,000 if it would win it. I thought they were very wrong not to leave in Galligan, and I made that very clear at the time. On the day, the way the game panned out, they needed him and he should have been left in.

Richie Bennis, who very nearly became one of Ryan's selectors, says he would have had no hesitation in putting Galligan on:

I was in the stand right behind the dugout that day. I could see that there was war. I remember the argument, and I presumed that was the reason for the argument. If I was on the sideline, I would have put him in and signed the slip of paper myself if I had to. They put in Taaffe the year before and he won the All-Ireland. Fines don't matter one f***. Wouldn't you pay it yourself to see Limerick win?

While the county board officers were acting according to the rule book, certain officers have had a history of hiding behind the rule book when it suited them and ignoring the rule book at other times. Some supporters believe the decision not to introduce Galligan had more to do with proving a point than adhering to the rule book. Based on the Pat McCarthy situation in 1987 (when McCarthy was not on the team list submitted to the referee for the League quarter-final but it transpired later that he would have been eligible to play), it was worth taking the risk and asking questions later. In Limerick GAA down through the years power has been more important than success.

The team management are not exempt from close scrutiny on the Galligan situation, however. Bernie Savage explains the dilemma:

In hindsight it was a mistake not to bring on Galligan, and we looked to bring him on but the rules stated that we couldn't. We could only name six – two backs, two forwards, a goalie and a centre field – on the list of six subs.

Galligan offers this take:

I didn't start the Antrim game. I was looking over my shoulder at that stage if I missed a ball. I had gone from being a certain starter, playing with confidence, to looking over my shoulder knowing that if I missed a ball I would be whipped off and maybe not started the next day. You need confidence to be hurling well. When you are a regular and are demoted after an average game it plays on the confidence. I was wearing the bicycle shorts at the time because I was carrying a niggling groin injury that I was getting treatment on. I was taking painkillers before and after training.

For the final, I was sitting down waiting to come on. I wasn't aware that I wasn't on the list of six subs. Owen O'Neill had an ankle injury going into the game and Dave Mahedy said to me to be ready. I remember the infamous Liam Dunne pull on Gary; I was thinking, 'I will be going in taking the frees now.' I had no nerves because I wasn't starting. I remember at one stage it appeared to me as if moves were being made to put me on and it was stopped. It's not a day I try to remember too much.

I just sat there waiting for the rest of the game and three subs went on and I remember thinking, 'I am obviously not going on now.' I was first into the dressing room after the final whistle and I wasn't happy, both at the fact that Limerick had lost an All-Ireland and that something was up. I went to tog off and, as it happened, I had left half my stuff on the bus. I was togging off on the bus and a supporter came in and said, 'What the f*** is going on? Why wasn't he brought on?' I didn't realise he was talking about me. I didn't even go back on the bus to the hotel. When I got to the hotel I met Donie Barry and he said that I wasn't on the subs and I was saying, 'What do you mean?' I wasn't even contemplating not being on the list of subs.

Then it became a bit of a tribunal and there were even rumours that I had refused to go on. I think that rumour was squashed fairly early. I never really got an explanation for not being introduced. One of the selectors came up later that night and said they felt I wasn't going well in training. I was going well though, because I knew I was playing for my place. You don't go from being on the team to not being even on the list of six subs in two games. What the motive behind it was, you will have to ask somebody else. There was no exchange of views leading up to the final with the management or anyone else. I was as surprised as everyone in the stand.

Dave Mahedy remembers the commotion on the sideline:

A discussion about Galligan was taking place and I didn't even know he wasn't on the list of six subs. The game was going on, and I was saying, 'Will ye get him on, will ye get him on?,' and the next thing, Turlough Herbert went on. I think there may have been an injury on the pitch and I went in with the water bottle. When I came out I was looking in and Turlough Herbert was inside and Mike Galligan was still on the bench. And I am there asking what happened. 'Did he pull a muscle warming up or something, or is there something else that I missed?'

Then some time after the final you find out that Clare did it with Éamonn Taaffe. In a way Jimmy was technically right but nobody is ever done for that. They were hardly going to come looking for the trophy back. Mike Galligan had played in every game; it wasn't like there was a transfer system where you were bringing in someone from somewhere else just for the final.

Turlough Herbert was introduced instead of Galligan:

I was brought on for Barry Foley who I thought could have been switched, and there was controversy about it because of the Mike Galligan situation. A ball broke to me and I took a snap shot and it went wide. To this day I get slagged about it, that the shot went into the commentary box in the Nally stand and nearly hit Michael Lyster.

Barry Foley felt he had more to offer:

I was called ashore, but there was certainly nothing wrong with me; I was willing to stay on and was fit and fresh. There was no injury. Things went unbelievably well in the first half; everything I hit went over the bar. In the second half I wasn't on the ball much, and was taken off. Losing was devastating for me but it was my first final. It was even more devastating for the older lads, Ciarán and Gary. I will never forget the homecoming; it was a fantastic reception, but it was very hard to take losing an All-Ireland final.

Ciarán Carey pulls no punches:

Losing the final in 1996 had nothing to do with 1994. From my point of view it's seldom you get the opportunity to go to Croke Park, but when you go, you must deliver the goods. No other excuse must come into it. To win an All-Ireland in Croke Park you must have three quarters of the team hurling well. Four or five, two or three holding their own is no good. You can possibly carry one or two not going well, and you can throw in a couple of subs, but you need to be hurling well.

As a team, if I picked three who hurled well against Wexford I am being generous. My opinion on Mike Galligan is that he had something to offer every day, he had legs and was able to score. But I am not going to say, 'If this was done, if that was done . . .' The bottom line is that whatever fifteen are picked must deliver the goods in Croke Park.

Joe Quaid made some unbelievable saves in the final but feels he had played better that year:

Probably one of the best matches I ever played in my career was against Antrim in 1996 yet nobody thought anything of it because it was Antrim. I would be friendly enough with George O'Connor and Tom Dempsey in Wexford and I keep telling them when I meet them, 'Ye were the worst team we met that year – and I include Antrim in that – however ye won it, and ye were never heard of before and ye haven't been heard of since.' What's worse, they actually agree with me!

Turlough Herbert believes Wexford did not get the credit they deserved:

That 1996 loss was devastating. The first time I watched it was in 2008 actually, and watching it I have to say Wexford were full value for their win. I thought Laffan got a few points from play in a low-scoring game, and other small unexpected things like that happened that we wouldn't have legislated for. Only a handful of our guys came out of that game with any credit.

Joe Quaid feels the game was lost long before the final whistle:

I don't think 1994 had any mental effect on us in 1996. If anything it should have made us stronger, but I don't think it did. I remember the 1996 match with fifteen minutes to go, there was only four points in it and there were fellas who had been there in 1994 walking around with their heads down. There was a break in play and I was out of the goals roaring at them to buck up, because with the Munster championship we had that year, the game was still there to be won. I remember the referee was about to throw the ball back in and I was outside on the 45 and had to run back into the goals.

Nicky English feels 1994 must have had an effect:

After 1994 I thought it was always going to be very hard for them to win one, because it became a holy grail for that team. We always believed in Tipperary that we would have beaten Wexford in 1996. Limerick underperformed in that final but we would have been quite relaxed going into it and I think we would have been able to deal with Wexford. We felt we could have won the All-Ireland if we had been in the position Limerick were in late in the game. I always believed they were carrying major scarring after 1994 and that cost them against Wexford. There's only a finite spell at the top for any team and Clare had come then. It's a very thin line and the mental side is huge.

Liam Griffin believes the two teams were well matched:

The scourging at the pillar? Seán O'Neill lies in a state of anguish as a single-minded George O'Connor prepares for more at the throw-in in the 1996 final. *(L–r)* Ciarán Carey (Limerick), Martin Storey (Wexford), Adrian Fenlon (Wexford), Mike Houlihan (Limerick), Pat Horan (referee), Seán O'Neill (Limerick), George O'Connor (Wexford).

It would be very arrogant of me to say that we were a vastly superior team to Limerick; we certainly were not. Were we the better team? I don't know, but on this particular day we managed to edge them out for a victory; it was no more than that. We weren't a poorer team than Limerick, we were of their equal and we just happened to get it right on the day. The underdog can often overturn the overdog.

You had the magic of Ciarán Carey and other names like him and he was regarded by every hurling man in the country as one of the all time greats and everyone wanted to see him with an All-Ireland medal but you don't get it handed to you and the bottom line is that it was a little bit to our advantage.

Turlough Herbert recalls the aftermath:

It was just an absolutely devastating experience. I remember bawling my eyes out for about an hour after the match and going back to the hotel and just going up to the room and starting again. I also remember a feeling, almost a sense of shame, for months afterwards, going out playing in club matches and having no appetite or desire at all. It was literally like a bereavement; it was a killer and I think people sensed that it was our chance and we didn't take it.

The game may have been over but the fallout was just beginning. In the days prior to their annual review with Tom Ryan and his management, the members of the county board executive held a meeting of their own, from which emerged the infamous 'twenty questions'. It was speculated at the time, and many still believe, that Pat Fitzgerald, the current full-time secretary of the Munster Council, was the man responsible. Dan Hickey was also believed to be influential in composing the list.

Rory Kiely remains coy:

The twenty questions, in hindsight, were a mistake. I was on the executive at the time and I wouldn't like to comment. Things were very emotional. It was very soon after losing the All-Ireland.

The chairman, Brendan Danagher, has little to say either:

The twenty questions have got enough publicity and have been turned in and out and it's time that they were buried for once and for all. My comment on the twenty questions is that they are gone and best forgotten.

His predecessor, Gerry Bennis, however, is forthright:

The twenty questions were crazy. The idea was that Brendan Danagher would have a list of questions in front of him to help him to structure the discussion. They weren't ever supposed to be handed out. It was an awful thing to do. I wasn't in the county board at the time but I was never far away, and while I wasn't privy to the twenty questions, I would have been very familiar with what went on. I think Pat Fitzgerald is being blamed in the wrong, even though it was circulated at the time that he was the brains behind them. They were definitely drawn up at committee level.

Mike Fitzgerald was part of the committee and gives an inside view of what took place:

The twenty questions arose only a week or two after the final. There was a county board officers' meeting and obviously it was decided to bring in the selectors to have a chat about it, which was a standard procedure anyway. It was felt, rather than having an ad hoc discussion, that there should be an element of control to the meeting and ask the management five or six questions. Some of the officers were missing on the night and when it finished up, it was felt that they should be consulted if they had anything to add. The list of questions finished up at twenty and some of them were sensitive. Some of them were a bit petty and they should never have been put down in print. They should have been summarised into four or five questions. They were never meant to be an official document. They may have been leaked. I am not saying that someone typed them out and gave them to someone, but they were probably verbally leaked over the phone. Tom knew in advance that there was a list of questions waiting for him and he took major issue with that. He most certainly fell out publicly with the county board and went to the media with his complaints.

The compilation of the twenty questions was not a one-man show, it was an executive decision. I am open to correction on this but from recollection Pat Fitzgerald was one of those who was not present on the night at the meeting. I think Pat Fitzgerald may have come up with three or four extra, which would have made ten, but it wouldn't be accurate to say Pat Fitzgerald was the man behind them. I will agree that his name was mentioned at that time, but I would say that it was purely because it was known that he hadn't been at the original meeting. I came into our meeting with Tom and there were twenty. It was a round, even number of twenty, which suggests to me that extra questions were added for the sake of it to get twenty, which is something like you would find in a table quiz. When I saw the list of twenty questions I couldn't believe it. I expected only six or seven. It was ridiculous really and it was something which became a joke in the media as well. Tom took issue. They were discussed on the night. He was well prepared and there was major bad blood after that, but he still had a year of his term to serve.

Sandra Marsh admits that the county board could have been more professional in their dealings with Tom Ryan:

I think the twenty questions could have been dealt with differently, more diplomatically and in a less confrontational manner. Obviously there was huge disappointment over the All-Ireland loss and the twenty questions could have come across as accusatory. That might not necessarily have been the best way of doing business.

The list grew and my take is that it was unfortunate in the way it was handled. I don't know how it grew so much. Submissions came through the secretary and I wasn't privy to that. I was only at the original meeting. I was aware of the dissatisfaction and that there were problems and that there was an interest in finding out what went on. Obviously you have to analyse two All-Ireland defeats in two years with the same manager, but my concerns would relate to the manner in which it was conducted.

I think a small group of the executive should have met the management first and then came back to the larger group. It was seen by Tom Ryan, with some justification, that he was being ganged up on. I am not saying that Tom Ryan was the easiest man in the world to deal with but I still had respect for him and I was disappointed that the relationship with the county board broke down.

We all willingly partook in the twenty questions. It was a sorry chapter in Limerick GAA history. The relationship broke down. The media started to run our affairs a little bit, which was very regrettable from my point of view. Our business was aired in public. The people who worked in the local newspapers ran with every piece of gossip that was in the public domain and the correct picture wasn't being portrayed. It was a bad way to do business and it was disgusting to see the relationship between Tom Ryan and the county board trashed out in the newspapers week in week out. It's not what I got involved in the county board for. It's about playing games on the field of play.

Tom Ryan gives what can only be termed a forthright appraisal:

The twenty questions were f***ing outrageous, scandalous. They were meant to force us out. We defended ourselves. Dave resigned because he was personally attacked in the questions. I met with Dave. We had a serious chat. I would rate his involvement with me with both Ballybrown and Limerick as one of the most important decisions I ever made. His work, his quality of work, his interest went beyond the call of duty. The use of the college facilities, his professionalism . . . I relied greatly on Mahedy for advice and an independent opinion. Mahedy was the key man. We had a meal and we sat down and I apologised because it was outrageous. It was an idea to push us out. But we weren't budging. Dave went because he had his wife to think of and his integrity was questioned. We were practically accused of taking money and much more. It was only the work of scumbags, and summed up who we were dealing with. Some members of the board didn't even know the questions existed. I only got them by accident.

Our meeting was called in late September, a review of the year, and Brendan Danagher rang me and we had arranged to meet. I looked up the calendar for a date. I was very busy at work and had more to be doing than thinking about them c***s. By chance one day, I looked at the paper and I think it was Tom O'Riordan in the *Independent* who had an article saying that I had been summoned to a meeting. I rang Hartigan, and said, 'Who is summonsing me to a meeting? What are you talking about? Where did the journalist get his information?' They had a propaganda machine that Stalin would have been proud of . . . The board actually met the *Limerick Leader* and they told them that if they printed anything more from me that would be in any way favourable to me that they would take all their printing work off them.

Dave Mahedy's departure was regretted by Sandra Marsh:

I was extremely sorry to see Dave go. He is extremely professional and I acknowledge his loss to this day. There was a breakdown in trust that arose from then on that was going to be almost impossible to recover from.

The players were also outraged at the twenty questions. Mike Nash was one:

The county board love to hold the torch over everyone else, that they are the boss and they don't want to lose the bit of power that they have. Small little men who get a bit of power, and aren't used to power, aren't able to handle it. That's what causes trouble in county boards, and that's what got rid of Dave Mahedy. Mahedy was way ahead of his time and very advanced. He started the Munster rugby team and he was behind starting to bring them to where they are, and hopefully he will get Limerick hurlers going again. They got rid of him then with stupid questions, twenty questions. Stupid men asking questions, men who would be well qualified to ask a stupid question. That's what you are talking about inside at county board level.

Joe Quaid says people always point the finger when you lose:

Nobody went up to lose the All-Ireland on purpose. It's like this thing in 1994 that Tom Ryan was sitting on his arse on the bench. If we had won that All-Ireland, Tom Ryan was the coolest man that ever won an All-Ireland. Tom Ryan sat on the bench for every match up to that. It was the same in 1996 when they gave out about us breaking from the parade. We left the parade at that stage before every game. Tom Dempsey said to me that we actually got the better start in the final and if they had lost the All-Ireland everyone would be saying, 'All the Wexford team wanted to do was walk around behind the band.' I got the same s**t with the quick puck-out.

Bernie Savage says the achievements of the time were too easily forgotten:

The twenty questions were ridiculous. The first question was, 'How did we lose the All-Ireland?', but nobody asked the question, 'How did we get there?'

Mahedy keeps the twenty questions as a constant reminder:

Whereas 1994 was a freaky game, 1996 was a final we should have won. We dithered with the extra man; we had five different extra men and it ended up as Ciarán Carey, the right man in the first place. We didn't plan for the eventuality of us having fifteen and them fourteen. We had covered for us having fourteen because we were used to that in previous years. That was one of the things we were criticised for in the twenty questions. I keep a copy of them on the wall of my office, because if ever I am successful with a team and I think I am getting too big for my boots, I look up and say, 'That's to remind me how close you are to winning, and how close you are to being the most useless bastard going.'

The twenty questions were:

1. Why did we lose the match?
2. Were Tom's fellow selectors privy to all plans associated with the team?
3. The exact role of Dave Mahedy?
4. Are the hurley carriers justified when players on the panel have to go up on the stand?
5. Why was Mike Galligan not included in the first 6 after it was indicated he could not play games prior to the All-Ireland and was told by Dave Mahedy that he may be on from the start if Owen O'Neill was not fit?
6. Were the players given any instruction with regard to decorum and behaviour for the Final? Dave Mahedy was present while it [the behaviour prior to the throw-in] was happening.
7. Why was it [the behaviour prior to the throw-in] allowed to happen? What happened on the Monday night prior to the final?

8. Players pestered for tickets – What was done about it?
9. Lack of punctuality during the weekend
10. Why did the team come out so quickly after half-time?
11. When Sandra asked Tom re: Shaws jerseys was referred to Dave Mahedy who said 'We are getting f**k all from Shaws.'
12. Is there a necessity for the two girls Cora and Sinéad?
13. Involvement of three selectors in Kilmurray Lodge re: Munster final and All Ireland final Monday?
14. Was there any pre-planning done in the event of a team losing a player on the day?
15. Do the selectors accept any responsibility for us losing the game?
16. Do they think that Dave Mahedy is the right man to train the team?
17. Does Tom [Ryan] feel that the best interests of Limerick Hurling are served by he continuing on as Manager of the Senior Hurling Team? This bunch of players having reached and lost 2 All Irelands. Would it not be better to make a fresh start under a new Manager?
18. Was there any instruction given to Joe Quaid to vary the puck-out and make use of the extra man in the 2nd half?
19. Do ye think the players were treated properly?
20. Have any monies been handed out to any member of the management that has not since been given to the Supporters Club?

Mahedy continues . . . :

I think the twenty questions were outrageous. We were after working our socks off and when they look back the 1994–1996 period was actually a good era in Limerick hurling. When I saw the questions I said, 'Look, I can't win here.' It was Tom who showed them to me, and when I saw them I said, 'That's it. Tom, I am gone.' There was no point continuing. People on the outside don't realise how you develop a spirit, it's a mutual thing, and if you have it together that's the secret. It's not someone coming in saying I am the boss and you are the lackeys, it's totally different to that. You work together and have a mutual respect. Those guys worked so hard and that helped the development of the team. Put those guys together and they would have the height of respect for each other. They died for each other . . . ten points down against Tipp and pulling it back without a goal, Mike Nash's block down on Nicky [English]. The shame of it is that that team didn't win an All-Ireland.

Administrators should administer. We on the ground respect their job but they don't respect our job. If you were an engineer, I wouldn't

9/9/96

Why did we lose the match ?

Were Tom'S fellow selectors privy to all plans associated with
the team.

The exact role of Dave Mahedy ?.

Are the hurley carriers justified when players on the panel have
to go up on the stand ?.

Why was Mike Galligan not included in the first 6 after it was
indicated he could not play games prior to the All-Ireland and was
told by Dave Mahedy that he may be on from the start if Owen O'Neill
was not fit ?.

Were the players given any instructions with regard to decorum and
behaviour for the Final. ? Dave Mahedy was present while it was
happening.

Why was it allowed to happen ?. What happened on the Monday night
prior to Final ?.

Players pestered for tickets — What was done about it ?.

Lack of punctuality during the weekend

Why did team come out so quick after half-time ?.

When Sandra asked Tom re: Shaws jerseys was referred to Dave Mahedy
who said   —   We are getting fuck all from Shaws.

Is there a necessity for the two girls, Cora and Sinead.?

RE

Involvement of Three selectors in Kilmurry Lodge going to Munster
Final and All Ireland Final Monday ?.

The official document containing the infamous Twenty Questions.

Was there any pre-planning done in the event of a team losing a man on the day ?.

Do the selectors accept any responsibility for us losing the game ?.

Do they think that Dave Mahedy is the right man to train the team.?

Does Tom feel that the best interests of Limerick Hurling are served by he continuing on as Manager of the Senior Hurling Team ?. This bunch of players having reached and lost 2 All Irelands. Would it not be better to make a fresh start under a new Manager ?.

Was there any instruction given to Joe Quaid to vary the puck out and make use of the extra man in the 2nd half?.

Do ye think the players were treated properly. ?.

Have any monies being handed to any member of management ~~would~~ *THAT* has not been handed over to the Supporters Club ?.

go to you and say you should approach it this way or that way. As a sports person, everyone will come to you and tell you what team to pick, what tactics to use, etc. And you will say to them, 'Well, what have you done?' You don't mind constructive criticism from people who know, like reading Tony Ward in the rugby, he is an international and knows what he is talking about. Others don't know what they are on about, making sweeping statements without knowing what they are on about. It's the same with the twenty questions. Looking back they must be saying to themselves, 'How did I write that?' Can you imagine them in smoke-filled dark rooms coming up with questions like 'Were the girls needed?'

They were all here in UL and they all assisted me. I try and include different people to give them experience. There are times when I need to be preparing for the next exercise, and rather than players standing around idle, they could be doing stretches or whatever. You need that sort of backup. Cora Fenton fitness-tested every one of those players in the lab, the likes of what DCU are doing now. She was doing it in 1994 and 1996 and the work she did was invaluable. She tested every single one of them down to VO_2 maxes, which we don't normally do because there are too many of them and you would have to spend so long on each person. You would do field tests, runs or shuttles or whatever. Sinéad Millea is one of the most respected players in camogie, the only one in that dressing room who had an All-Ireland medal. She is a qualified PE teacher, and the lads had great respect for them. Fergal O'Callaghan or Johnny Glynn were also involved but there were no questions asked about them because it was a girl thing. What are girls doing there? Nowadays there isn't a word; you have Angela Hogan in the dressing room doing masseuse, but things have changed now, which is good. The county board officials are thinking, 'We could be sitting on the bench or on the bus, but we are not, we are out in the stand.' Can you imagine a player bursting his bollox to try and make a panel, being devastated at not making it and then being handed the hurleys to carry. Wouldn't you think it was the greatest insult going? All the questions were like that.

The team was being announced on the tannoy on the Monday night as we were getting changed, before we went into the team meeting. We were in the Gaelic Grounds training, there was a huge crowd there and they were announcing the team over the loudspeaker while the players were sitting in the dressing room getting changed and ready to go into the meeting to be told the team. I don't know why that question is being asked of us, it's a mystery.

The Galligan thing was a mistake; I didn't know why he wasn't on the list. I would say to any player, 'Be ready,' because any player could . . . even in other sports . . . players that aren't necessarily listed can be introduced. I have always told players to be ready for that. Especially where there is a specialist position. Take, for example, Freddie Pucciarello, who was eating a burger outside the ground the day of the Heineken Cup quarter-final against Gloucester in 2008 and was called into duty.

The tragedy of 1996 was that the team failed to secure the McCarthy Cup. It is rare for a team without a winning record to lose two All-Ireland finals within a couple of years and finally reach the promised land. Kilkenny did it in 2000, but Kilkenny have a winning tradition and were backed up by a number of survivors from their last success in 1993. Galway managed it in 1987, but again had players from their winning team of 1980. Galway also won the title in 1980 having lost the finals of 1975 and 1979, but one wonders would they have beaten anyone other than Limerick that day.

As he left Croke Park in 1996, one supporter summed up Limerick's failure to perform on the biggest day of all. 'Limerick wouldn't have beaten Antrim in an All-Ireland final today.' Many would tend to agree.

THIRTEEN

෪

1997: BOARDROOM POLITICS

N*o sooner had the dust settled on the twenty questions when yet another dispute arose in early 1997. A holiday and spending money had been granted to the team for their efforts in 1996, but there were issues over spending money for the backroom team. Tom Ryan went face to face with the county board on the night Dave Mahedy's successor was confirmed:*

Mahedy left and I approached Brian Ryan who was with South Liberties at the time. I met him and we got on well, he was a very good trainer. We ended up winning the League with him that year. It was a good League to win playing against Tipperary and Clare with crowds of 30,000 at the games. We met the county board at the Railway hotel, and prior to our meeting Brian met with the county board and everything was arranged for him to start. We were due to go to Orlando on the holiday. They were well entitled to it and everything was above board and there were no problems. Bernie Savage had said to me in October 1996 that he wasn't going. Bernie used to travel with Mike Fitzgerald, the treasurer, and he was privy to all sorts of inside information. They would be soaking him and vice versa.

When we went into the hotel that night before the meeting Bernie was having a drink at the counter. I was surprised, because he had said in October that he wasn't going on the holiday. 'What are you doing here?' said I. 'It's all the one to you, sure, you aren't going on the holiday at all.' 'Ye are getting no expenses,' was his reply. Mike Fitzgerald had told Bernie in October that players were getting spending money but that the backroom team weren't getting any. Yet this was January and it was the first I heard about it. We were getting a holiday but we weren't getting expenses. 'Fine,' says I, 'we'll see.' We went up into the room and Brendan Danagher, Jimmy Hartigan and Mike Fitzgerald were above. 'Welcome gentlemen,' said Danagher. 'Tell me this,' said I, 'is it true that the management aren't getting any expenses?' 'It is,' said Danaher. 'Explain yourself,' said I. 'Sure, some of the backroom team have no jobs. Who exactly decided that?' I wasn't worried about expenses myself, I could afford to look after myself, but it was the backroom team who were my concern. 'Who made that decision?' I demanded. 'The executive,' replied Danagher. 'Where are the executive now?' I asked. 'Oh, they are not here,' was his reply. 'You better get them,' I said, 'and get them fast, because I will tell you one f***ing thing: no plane will leave Shannon on Wednesday morning and I will be on the radio and in the media in the morning.' By ten o'clock our spending money and our dollars were on the table.

The mentality of it all. It showed the vindictiveness of them and the low lights they were. We had brought the hurlers from nothing. They were £100,000 in debt when I took over the team. They were about £70,000 up by now and no McManus either. That was their thanks at the end of the day. Brian Ryan got a kind of a fright. The walls were nearly shaking in the room. I came down to Bernie and said, 'Oh, ye of little faith. You couldn't open your f***ing mouth, could you?'

Mike Nash was unable to go on the holiday:

We were after losing the All-Ireland. To be honest we didn't care about holidays. I didn't even go on the holiday that time because Barry was born around that time, and a year later I didn't travel either because my second son Brian was born. In one way I am sorry I didn't go, because it would have been good auld craic. It's on the field you want to be doing things, though. Players aren't worried about holidays, if the medals in are in their pockets. 'The Jap' was killed in an accident when the boys were away. It's ironic that, after so much trouble over the holiday. When it did happen it wasn't worth anything because they were coming home to carry 'the Jap's' coffin.

J. P. Ryan from Garryspillane, better known as 'the Jap', was involved with Limerick hurling as a selector and hurley carrier. He was widely recognised as one of the characters of the game – and was never shy when colourful language was required! Of the players in the squad, Frankie Carroll would have known him best:

'The Jap' had made the phone call to me when I started with the Limerick seniors. I was in the Golden Thatch nightclub in Emly one Saturday night before Christmas in 1990 and the DJ made an announcement: 'Phone call for Frankie Carroll'. It was 'the Jap', to tell me that the Limerick seniors wanted me for a challenge game against Waterford the following day. He came straight over, collected me from the nightclub and brought me home. I played well the following day in what was probably an unattractive match for the more established players, and made the panel after that.

He wouldn't go on the holiday to Orlando with us because he had a fear of flying. I was getting married in 1997 and was building my house. One evening I was working on the house and he called over to me. The craic was good. I was trying to persuade him to go on the holiday and he was trying to put me off going. He said, 'I went down to Shannon especially to see the plane and the wings are only hanging onto it with clothes hangers.'

He stayed at home anyway and when we returned he was dead. It was devastating. The craic we used to have going to the matches was unreal. He really wanted to be involved with Limerick hurling. I remember getting a car the year after I was called up to the Limerick panel. He told me not to tell them that I had a car, so that he could keep driving me. I kept my mouth shut and didn't let on a word to them. Even on the big days, like the Munster finals, you would be relaxed in the front of his car. 'The Jap' would be driving and it would be unbelievable craic, he would put on the Paddy Reilly tape coming home.

I remember coming home from the 1996 Munster final; we were stuck in traffic and 'the Jap' was weaving in and out of the traffic coming down along the road. Next thing a ban garda jumped out from nowhere. Sure 'the Jap' kept driving, but we were stopped about a mile further up the road. They were reading him the riot act. 'The Jap' got me to put my leg up on the dash and he said to the guards, 'This man was playing the Munster final today and I am rushing him to Limerick Regional hospital.' That was it; we were left off and we were laughing all the way home. He got away with it.

Micheál O'Grady too has fond memories:

I remember a funny incident at the very start of the Cork game in 1984. 'The Jap' was in charge of the hurleys on the line. Jimmy Carroll broke two hurleys in the first two clashes of the game. 'The Jap' decided to run straight across the field and into the dressing room. His cap blew off in the wind and there was an almighty cheer from the crowd.

Ger McMahon got on the wrong side of him on one occasion:

In 1982 we played Antrim in the League and we were staying overnight. A few of us were in the residents' bar until 2.30 a.m. and the next thing 'the Jap' arrived down and cleared us all up to bed.

P. J. O'Grady also has an amusing tale:

We played Laois in Rathdowney in the League in 1985. John Denton from Wexford was refereeing. 'The Jap' wasn't happy with him in the first half and hadn't been shy about letting him know coming off the field. The referee came into the dressing room looking for him at half-time but 'the Jap' couldn't be found. He had hidden inside in the toilets and was afraid to come out.

Another character was Tommy Casey, who drove players to training and games down the years. One of those was Mike Houlihan:

When I started hurling with Limerick first I was going in to training with Tommy Casey. He used to drive in Mick Mackey back in a different generation. You were sitting into a car that used to drive Mick Mackey, and Tommy would give us bullseyes going in to Limerick in the car. It was a privilege.

Frankie Carroll recounts a story Casey told him one time:

He was driving a few city players to a game and they were asking him about driving great players, so Tommy told them about driving all the greats – the Mackeys, Jackie Power, etc. They were starting to feel good about themselves in the back of the car, and feeling important. Then he turned around and sized up the boys and said, 'I drove an awful a lot of useless c***s as well.'

In 1997, the format of the hurling League changed; it began in the spring and ran right through summer, culminating in the final in October. It was a one-year experiment that was not retained, except for starting the competition in the spring rather than before Christmas.

It was always going to be hard for Limerick given the disappointment of the previous year's All-Ireland defeat, but in the League they defeated Kilkenny at Nowlan Park and shared the spoils with both Tipperary and Clare at the Gaelic Grounds before losing heavily to Galway in Athenry. Then, in a game against Laois in Kilmallock, Joe Quaid suffered a horrendous injury:

It was at the end of the first half and David Cuddy was taking a penalty. The sliotar hit the ground in front of me and bounced up and connected with my groin area. I went down immediately; I knew it was after hitting me somewhere. I didn't feel anything for a second. The sliotar rolled out so I tried to rise it. At that moment the pain kicked in. Mike Nash also hit me into the head trying to get the ball away. I finished the game and went to Dave Boylan and showed him the swelling. He said to me to go straight to the hospital. I knew then that there was damage done to the testicle. Looking back, I didn't realise it at the time, but the one thing I always prided myself on was being brave. I probably made more saves through bravery than with any hurley at times. It really only dawned on me in 1999 when Paul Flynn rounded Brian Begley and came through with the ball and scored a goal. He came in along the end line and I ran out and turned my back to it, which was something I never did in my life. Subconsciously the injury must have been the cause of that. If a goalie's nerve goes, he is in trouble straight away.

Quaid was unavailable for the start of the championship. His replacement, Albert Shanahan, had an impressive game against Waterford, which was settled by two Barry Foley goals early in the game following errors by the Waterford goalkeeper, Ray Whitty. Limerick advanced to play Tipperary but were well beaten, as Barry Foley recalls:

I had scored two of the handiest goals I ever got against Waterford in 1997. There were no soft goals against Tipperary though; there was a total collapse against them on the day. I remember we were confident enough after the way things had gone in 1996. We never hurled. Maybe we were a little cocky ourselves, I don't know, but we definitely didn't hurl that day.

Joe Quaid returned for the game:

I still probably wasn't 100 per cent against Tipperary. I remember diving across the goals at one stage to stop a shot and I fell on the ground and I was still sore. I probably shouldn't have come back that early. We never got going at all. I suppose when you have two All-Irelands lost in three years, it's hard to lift it again.

Frankie Carroll agrees:

The 1997 League was a good campaign, support-wise, more so than any normal League campaign. Expectations were high but things

(L–r) Haulie O'Brien, Frankie Carroll and Gary Kirby share a light-hearted moment after the 1997 League success.

went flat come the championship; maybe we were running on empty. A lot of players had a lot of hurling done and Tipperary beat us convincingly.

Tom Ryan did not see it coming:

We didn't play well, but during the week in training I never saw them in such order. The team was like poetry in motion. We did well against Waterford, put up a big score, and were winning by eleven points with fifteen minutes remaining. In the Tipperary game, Seán

O'Neill slipped and the ball went to John Leahy. He ran through and it was buried. We didn't recover from that. I often wonder why because we were never more ready, but at the same time we were lucky to have the League to fall back on. You had no back door that year unless you were in the Munster final, so we were glad of the League. We had great wins.

In other years the season would have been over for Limerick, but the new structure meant a League semi-final at Nowlan Park awaited in late August. It was billed as Tom Ryan's last match, but a weakened Limerick upset the odds. Ryan takes pride in the victory:

We went up to Kilkenny and were badly depleted. We had to go to our reserves to field a team but we had them ready because of the intensity of our preparations. Tony O'Brien, Jack Foley and Dave Hennessy came in and T. J. Ryan gave an exhibition at centre-back that night. It was one of the best hurling matches Limerick played in the four years I was involved. Nicky Brennan finished his managerial career that night; the supporters booed him and the Limerick team were cheered off the field by the Kilkenny players.

In early October, Limerick secured the League title with a gritty win over Galway, with Mike Galligan in fine form. The team had been recast after the championship exit, with both positional and personnel alterations. Many believed Tom Ryan was building for 1998, but the manager knew his goose was cooked, as Bernie Savage explains:

Tom had said to myself and Liam Lenihan that we were gone even if we won the League final. I suppose there was a lot of politics there that a lot of people didn't know about.

Since 1995 the power to appoint managers was in the hands of the county board executive, which gave the board the control it desired. Mike Fitzgerald provides an insight:

Limerick were beaten badly enough by Tipperary in 1997. Tom Ryan's days were numbered. There was such controversy over the four years, there was constant bickering, and I am certain the clubs were sick of it as well. I think the clubs wanted change and it was reflected in the 1995 vote to change the structure and that meant the end of Tom. He has tried unsuccessfully to be appointed a couple of times since then but he had burnt his bridges with the board from that time.

My knowledge is it was the clubs who decided to change the appointment process rather than the executive. A motion came from the clubs and the clubs wanted change. Dan Hickey was targeted because his club were involved in the motion. He was seen as being behind it because he was also a county board officer. I think the clubs were sick of the likelihood that Tom Ryan would be elected again, which would lead to more bickering, and they were handing back the power to the county board to come up with a system of appointing the manager.

Many believe only an All-Ireland title in 1997 would have saved Tom Ryan. However, given the antipathy in some quarters, even that might not have sufficed:

After I was elected for the second time in 1995, I knew I was gone as manager because the power was given to the executive to appoint the manager in the subsequent motion later that year. Éamonn Cregan participated in the gang-up against me and when he got the job he f***ed up the whole thing and made a bollox of it. Cregan wanted the job and he was the acceptable face, because he had been successful with Offaly – through no fault of his own. A couple of players participated in the final act of treachery against me. They didn't play in Nowlan Park. They knew I was f***ed. These players never really bought into our overall discipline plan. There was a conspiracy in the county board. They hoped I would resign, but I stayed, and forced them to sack me.

When the rule was changed allowing the executive to pick the manager, all the f***ing eejits in the county went in and voted for it. They didn't know what they were doing at the time. I was gone and Limerick hurling has paid a huge price for that. We would have won a series of All-Irelands. In 1998 and 1999 we were going to be one of the top teams in the country. We were always evolving and improving. We weren't always going to be denied an All-Ireland. All we had to do was to have patience and a bit of decency . . .

Limerick hurling is in the doldrums over the last ten years because of the incompetence of the county board, putting managers in place who couldn't coach teams and couldn't have a disciplined team. We are actually held up to ridicule and the indiscipline of our teams and the low standard of what they have achieved has to be placed on the shoulders of the administrators of the county board.

There was intense speculation at the time that Ryan did not have the unanimous support of the players. Perhaps in 1997 it was thought that Éamonn Cregan would deliver the ultimate prize.

However, speaking to some of those players in 2009, it seems their views may have changed with hindsight, with many expressing the opinion that the removal of Ryan was a mistake. It is also possible, of course, that, given Ryan's tendency to speak out in the press, some players may not be prepared, even today, to divulge their true opinions of the time.

In his speech after the League win in 1997, captain Gary Kirby was unequivocal in his support for the manager. Ryan was far from impressed, however:

That speech by Kirby was only bulls**t. They proved that afterwards when Cregan came in. Unfortunately we didn't reach the potential that those players had, because of me. My intensity didn't work well with certain players. And even with that, we still achieved an awful lot. What wouldn't we have achieved if we had the full support of those players? His big speech below in Ennis meant nothing. Words mean nothing. Those are the facts.

Kirby, however, stands by his speech:

I was fully in support of Tom Ryan. I don't think some of the players agreed, to be totally honest. I have heard rumours that one or two of the players didn't agree with what I said. We couldn't come out in the press and publicly criticise the removal of Tom; you are causing problems for the new manager even before he starts. You have to put your support behind the new man. At the end of the day we are only players, we are not administrators. I think it was a total disgrace; they treated Tom very badly. Some might say he was his own downfall for being outspoken, but that's what was needed.

Ciarán Carey held Ryan in high regard:

When Tom was there I rated him very highly; he had a lot to offer. He still has. You have to be very careful who you are talking to, and you have to be very prudent in your dealings with the media but Tom just let it out. At times some people would take off their hat to him for having a go at people, whether it's players or the county board, but at the end of the day there's a price to be paid for everything.

Declan Nash regrets that the players failed to take action:

To have won a National League and be thrown out days later is beyond me at this stage. There are reservations among supporters about every manager. But when you look at the Cork thing and how, maybe, we weren't strong enough to stand up at the time . . . perhaps players were beginning to think themselves that change was needed: it's hard to put your finger on it. When you look back on it, to see Tom Ryan being got rid of, the county board delegates should have stood up and said, 'Hang on one second, we haven't won many of those, what's happening here?' It was the best spell since I had been involved, even though we previously had coaches and trainers who had succeeded at other levels. He seemed to be able to put it right and he seemed to be able to take control. He took charge and I think, at the time, it's what Limerick needed.

To go into a championship [in 1994] with so many new players was some risk to take, but having said that he seemed to get the respect of the players, and part of that might have been fear. You couldn't dictate to Tom. That was possibly a part of it and certainly there's a lot to be said for it. I am not saying it's the way to go every time, as some managers can go overboard in that regard.

Éamonn Cregan took the job too early; we had won a League and suddenly nothing less than an All-Ireland would do. It would have been better for Éamonn Cregan's sake if Limerick had had a bad spell because he put himself under too much pressure to deliver, having been the manager that beat us in 1994. He was always going to get the job next anyway, because that time the county board had taken full control of who they would pick and so if they wanted Éamonn Cregan in they were going to get him. I think it might have been a prudent move to leave Tom there for one more year and just see how he would go.

There was never the remotest chance that Ryan would remain as manager beyond 1997, though Mike Fitzgerald denies that any business was done with Cregan prior to Ryan's departure:

Tom was there for four years, and there were a lot of issues over that time. The working relationship broke down between Tom and a member of the county board; they had major differences. Tom effectively started to run the team on his own, and there wasn't a proper unity there between the county board and Tom. The perception existed that certain county board officers weren't getting on with Tom. I think we suffered in both All-Irelands because of that, because there were controversies surrounding both.

I would have said that no business was done before the League final, certainly nothing was finalised, purely from maintaining the perception that the county board were doing their business properly. The dogs in the street know that there was a major rift at that stage and that there was a lot of resentment built up in the previous three or four years and that it was odds-on that the county board weren't going to pick Tom Ryan again as manager. You would have to be honest and say that. From a personal perspective, the relationship had broken down too much for any question of Tom continuing as manager.

Cregan was there, he was the obvious man and there was demand for him. The fact that he had been involved against Limerick in 1994, I think, he felt he wanted to win something with them to bury the ghosts. Even though there was no decision taken, it was quite obvious that he [Ryan] wasn't going to get another two years. There certainly would have been no decision made while Ryan was in charge but once Cregan had indicated that he would be available the job was always going to be his. It was definite then after the county final and he was duly ratified.

Brendan Danagher had announced that he was leaving in advance of the managerial change, and would ultimately be replaced by Donal Fitzgibbon:

I gave a commitment when I was elected that the maximum time I would serve in the position was three years. After winning the League, that evening I spoke with Tom Ryan and Jimmy Hartigan and said I would be vacating the chair. I explained that I was not going to be involved in the county board and that it's timely notice. In actual fact a lot of clubs encouraged me to stay for at least another year, but I made a commitment and that was that. The situation developed then that Tom Ryan departed. There were discussions about various aspects of the structure and there were people of the opinion that we should bring about a change; there were various views expressed among the committee and the result was that Éamonn Cregan became manager.

Sandra Marsh also says it is wrong to suggest Éamonn Cregan's appointment was rubber stamped well in advance:

The dogs in the street would have been saying that the League semi-final was Tom Ryan's last match, but there would certainly not have been anything discussed officially. What I will acknowledge is that his relationship with the county board was non-existent at that point and it would be a natural conclusion to draw that he was ending his tenure. No decision was made on the future of Tom Ryan until after the League final. Maybe there were approaches made to Cregan that I am not aware of. That's how business can be done sometimes. If you are inviting someone for interview in any walk of business, someone can be sent unofficially to suss out that candidate's availability. I remember the interview with Cregan. It was quite a straightforward thing and he was appointed.

Mike Houlihan believes Cregan was not the correct choice:

The manner in which Tom Ryan was gotten rid of was a very bad way of doing business. I was always of the opinion it was the wrong thing to do to get Cregan back. He obviously felt that he could contribute something. How he thought he was going to get a Limerick team to gel I don't know, after being in charge of Offaly in 1994. He had the king bit done, and trained a team to win an All-Ireland, and lost another, maybe the one he should have won. He was never going to be a winner unless he won an All-Ireland. The only thing he could have done coming in was win an All-Ireland; maybe he saw the potential for that. Tom Ryan had four years there, had his shot at it, he still had as good a record as anyone. The only blemish was that he didn't win the All-Irelands, and maybe he had his problems with the county board since the first day.

Ryan says he got no support from the main local paper:

I had a word with the then editor of the *Limerick Leader*, Brendan Halligan. Coming to the end of my term he printed in his editorial something like 'When Tom Ryan resigns as Limerick manager . . .' I rang him and f***ed him and asked him when I was resigning, and asked him where he got his information. 'Oh, I kind of understood it,' he said. 'Did you ever speak to me?' I said. 'Did any of your reporters ever speak to me?' 'Oh,' he said, 'I heard it.' 'Oh,' I said, 'is it kind of guess work?' I f***ed him from a pinnacle, and I f***ing called him everything. And then what did he do then, he started to engage with me, and the more he spoke, the more he released information. 'We were always supportive of you,' he said. 'I didn't want any support from you,' said I. 'It would be a sad day for me, the day I went looking

Babs Keating (*left*) and Tom Ryan (*right*) discuss hurling at a National League game in 1997.

for support from you. What the f*** did you do to support me? . . . He listened from start to finish, instead of saying, 'I am the editor. I will write what I like and this is my opinion.' All that sort of stuff was going on behind the scenes.

Reflecting on his time in charge, Ryan regrets not being able to establish a consistent forward line:

Our forwards were never great. It was the one area that tormented me the most. You were depending on Kirby and the free taking, Damien Quigley was prone to injury and T. J. [Ryan] was only coming and going. Frankie [Carroll] was in and out and not consistent, though he was a great hurler, but I found it hard to get the best out of him. When things went right for him he was a dinger, but when things went wrong it was a different story. He was an unbelievable hurler as well. The All-Ireland finals didn't go well for him but he gave an exhibition against Antrim. In the drawn game with Tipperary in 1996 he got two

Tom Ryan patrols the sideline in the 1996 Championship clash with Clare in the Gaelic Grounds.

great scores when we really needed them. I was disappointed with Shane O'Neill, he had been a successful under-21 player. We invested a lot of time in him, showed patience, but he never made the grade fully despite playing a lot of championship. Brian Tobin had excellent skills but he found the rigours of championship hurling difficult. David Hennessy broke my f***ing heart to make a county player out of him, because he wouldn't f***ing mix it. I tried everything with him, holding challenge matches, bringing the full squad to try one player. I always had Mark Foley pencilled in as a centre-forward, when his time would come. I had had him on the training panel since 1994 and it was as a forward he played in 1995 as a sub against Tipperary in the championship. If I had the luxury of playing him there always he would have been an excellent forward, but I had to move him to the backs in the absence of John Flavin. The first day I played Mark Foley in the League they booed him above in the stand. He fell all over the place. In Limerick you have a demanding following that expect instant success. A lot of these f***ers who want instant success forget that we haven't won a Munster championship for years, we haven't won an All-Ireland since 1973.

Success under Tom Ryan was won through commitment, hard work and a no-nonsense regime:

In all that time I missed no training session. Not one night. That was the level of commitment. There were no holidays. Another severe rule was that once you got injured, you went off the panel. You got the best of treatment; there was never a question mark over that, every injured player was always well looked after. But he was off the panel while he was injured, and a young fellow brought in straight away to keep the numbers up in training. When the player was back fit he had his chance to come back, but in the meantime there were other players trying to take the place from him. It cured a lot of injuries, I'll tell you that. It was better than any f***ing doctor, it was a kind of a miracle treatment. Because of that rule you didn't have that many fellows missing. They knew because of the rule that whoever was coming in had a chance. When any fella came into the panel it was explained to him that there was no such thing as being thrown in at the deep end. We tried them out, we coached them, we encouraged them, and every aspect of their fitness was looked at and they were put through it. The speed of their striking and the speed of the game we played was always being worked on. Because of that I had no hesitation in calling a fella off the bench. I am of the strong opinion that the mental strength, the mental readiness is as important as anything. Because in fairness they can all hurl.

And so the Tom Ryan era came to an end. Even though he delivered three trophies in four years – a feat yet to be repeated – he became known as the man who lost two All-Irelands. Some would have preferred if Tom Ryan had failed, as it would have made it easier to remove him, but ultimately it mattered little because he was ousted with the shine still on the League trophy.

Would Tom Ryan's success have continued had he stayed? We will never know. But what we do know is that he delivered for Limerick hurling two Munster titles and a National League. No one can ever take that away from him.

FOURTEEN

❧

1998–2002: NEW BLOOD

É̶amonn Cregan's reign as Limerick manager saw many changes in personnel over a five-year period. A lot of the players who were dropped have strong views on the issue, which is entirely natural. The manager who gives a player his debut is often remembered fondly, while the man who ends his career can be looked on with disdain, especially if the player deems it to be ahead of time. Cregan had difficulties when he began his tenure:

When I took charge of that team I found them ill-disciplined. I remember my very first training session being timed for 7.30 p.m., on the field. Some of these players strolled in at 7.35, 7.40, even 7.50 p.m. Some of them, though not all, were a law unto themselves, because they had been successful. They appeared to be able to get away with things that I didn't accept, that perhaps Tom was prepared to accept. Then, perhaps Tom didn't accept them and they were just testing me. There were problems like that which had to be sorted out. Some of them believed they were automatically entitled to a place on the team. The time eventually came to blood new players.

Tom Ryan disagrees:

I get on fine with Cregan today, and got on fine with Cregan then but he knows what I think of what happened that time. I would say that he dismantled the best team in the country. There was plenty of mileage left in them. We can get bogged down in winning All-Irelands but I am a believer in standards. Get the process right, have the base there. First of all, Cregan couldn't manage the players, and as I have often said, they weren't easy players to manage. Then when he wasn't able to manage them, he dropped them. And he brought back players that were finished – Ger Hegarty, Anthony Carmody and Pa Carey. Hegarty was gone. There was a huge move to get Hegarty back on the team when I was still in charge in 1997. We sat down and we judged it, and when a player gets injuries they take their toll and you have to call it then. I wouldn't be calling things wrong, I would be always justifying it myself. If Hegarty had anything to offer I would have brought him back in 1997.

There is a perception among supporters that Cregan set about dismantling the old team immediately in an effort to put his own mark on the side. However, in the 1998 championship game with Cork, Cregan started with fourteen of Ryan's team, and eleven of those that started against Tipperary in the 1997 championship, namely Joe Quaid, Stephen McDonagh, Declan Nash, Dave Clarke, Ciarán Carey, Mark Foley, Mike Houlihan, Gary Kirby, Barry Foley, Shane O'Neill and T. J. Ryan. In addition, Cregan sent out Mike Galligan and Jack Foley, the two stars of the 1997 League final, and Damien Quigley, who was unavailable in 1997 due to exam commitments. Indeed, the only non-Tom Ryan player to start the 1998 championship game against Cork was Pa Carey.

Carey, older brother of Ciarán, was seen as something of a hero in Limerick hurling throughout the 1990s, despite not playing an inter-county match or attending a training session. He had drifted from the inter-county scene, but was turning in impressive displays for Patrickswell teams that were winning county titles. Tom Ryan had little or no interest in Carey, however:

The one player I had an official deputation coming to me about was Pa Carey. He wanted to be part of the team when we were going well. He didn't turn up for the trials at the start of my tenure. The big success for me was Mike Nash. He was an unbelievable full-back but the public wanted to get rid of him. Cregan wanted to please the public and he brought back Pa Carey. The public were mad for Pa. He was the most popular man in the county. They said he was the best hurler in the country, but they were only seeing him a couple of times a year. I wanted a fella that would play well every Sunday, and maybe the odd Wednesday night as well.

A deputation came into me from Patrickswell to get him back on the panel. I didn't work with deputations. I said, 'Pa Carey, or Patrick as he likes to be called himself, knows why he isn't on the team.' I didn't say any more. It never came up in conversation with Ciarán but I was never worried about what Ciarán thought. They all had to look after their own business. There was no f***ing brotherly love in our setup. We were out there and we had matches to win and too much important stuff to do to be putting up with any pettyism.

Patrickswell Club men Eoghan Murphy (*right*) and Ciarán Carey (*left*) embrace following Limerick's victory over Cork in 2001.

Carey says he had other commitments:

I have no regrets about not being involved with the panel in the mid-1990s. My work commitments were huge around that time, because I was a sales rep for a company in Tullamore and I had to cover the whole country. That said, I probably could have applied myself better. If you really want to make time for something you will, but it's very hard to keep everything going.

His brother Ciarán saw the potential:

Every individual is different. Every manager, in my opinion, has to treat each person differently, and it's up to a manager to spot these things if he has the credentials to be a manager. Hand on my heart, if Pa Carey was dealt with right, treated right and approached right, he would have made a serious full-back. Tom was manager and was totally entitled to his views. From what I know of Patrick Carey, he was the type that would take a knock from a selector or manager to heart, whereas I would take it with a grain of salt and prove him wrong. Pa would take it to heart and go the opposite way, but if he was treated right and harnessed right he had the potential to be a Brian Lohan. Having said that, I never had a heart to heart with him about all that so I don't know how hungry he really was to make it with Limerick. I had a serious drive to be the best that I could be, and not only that . . . the most difficult thing when you set a standard for yourself is to maintain it. I don't know if Patrick had that mental drive to do that. How badly enough did he want to be the best full-back in the country? I never asked him.

Declan Nash saw no reason to drop his brother Mike:

I don't think we realised ourselves how influential Micheál was until he was gone and the unit was broken. Pa Carey came in and, to be honest, he had been away from it for a few years and we didn't have enough time to gel really. If something isn't broken, why fix it? If I was in trouble I could have Mike or Steve McDonagh on my shoulder just as easily, as I was there to help them out, and if you were under pressure there was always support and you got to know how one another played.

Mike Nash recalls an early trip with Cregan – and was none too impressed:

When Tom Ryan left, I was going to go as well as I was thirty-three at that stage. I met Cregan at Ballyneety golf course one day by chance. We had been playing golf separately but met inside afterwards having the cup of tea. He begged me to stay on another year. I said, 'Éamonn, my pace is going and you can't afford that. I know in my heart that I am lacking a bit of pace,' but he begged me to stay on.

That time, my wife Mary was expecting our second son Brian and he was due. Cregan took us up to the army barracks in the Glen of Imaal for a training weekend. We had to go, no excuses could be offered. I said to him that Mary was due, but he said there's nobody not going to be there. So I went and togged out and there was no signal in any mobile phone whatsoever. I got the number for the man at the game, and gave Mary the number to contact me. Everyone was there, except two players. They weren't there, but I was there. Éamonn Cregan brought us up there to knock the hearts out of us.

They had all these so-called experts up there; one fella could run up mountains, the other was there who could do press-ups with the backs of his hands on the stones. And they were challenging us to do it. Mike Houlihan went and did it and they were amazed.

That Glen of Imaal weekend was the greatest f***ing joke. All they wanted people to do was fail and your man doing these press-ups on the backs of his hands thinking nobody could do them. When Houlihan did it then, it f***ing killed them. And we were put running up and down the mountain trying to break your heart, break your spirit. It was supposed to be a team building thing and all they were trying to do was break lads' spirits. That night we were all inside in the one building and, having been through Templemore, I knew what to expect. I said to them, 'Barricade these doors now because these fellas will be in for us at 5 a.m. or 6 a.m. in the morning.' We barricaded all the doors and we slept and the next thing at 6 a.m. in the morning the bangs came on the door but the army couldn't get into us. The management got thick from that on.

Almost every player of the Tom Ryan era feels Mike Nash had more to offer, and that Carey and Nash should, at the very least, have been competing for the number 3 jersey.

For a League game at Tullamore Nash was named among the substitutes. The full-back line was Stephen McDonagh, Pa Carey and Tadhg Hayes. However, Carey got injured, and it was expected that Mike, being a natural full-back, would replace him. But when his brother Declan got the call instead, Mike knew his time was up. He informed Gary Kirby before contacting the manager:

I rang Cregan and said, 'Éamonn, you begged me three or four months ago to go back. Then you took me up to the Glen of Imaal when the young fella was born when other players weren't there. Yet I had to be there and I trained ever since. Obviously I am not in your plans. I am not going to be driving around the country acting the bollox. I wanted to retire last year and you wouldn't let me. What are you trying to do? Humiliate me?' He said that he wasn't.

I was working the next day. I had a gun in my hand because I was doing an armed escort and Mal Keaveney came out on the radio and says, 'Due to family and home commitments Mike Nash has retired from inter-county hurling.' I nearly left the gun off at the radio inside in the car. When I got back to the station I rang Mal Keaveney and asked him where he got the information. He said he got it from

Éamonn Cregan. And I said, 'Mal, we have been on the road long enough and you have done interviews with me before. If you wanted to know something off me, I would have told you. And what's more, I would have told you the truth.'

Mary wasn't very pleased because it sounded like she had forced me to give up inter-county hurling, which wasn't true. The *Examiner* had it, and I rang them up and I said, 'Your information is wrong. I want a statement on the paper tomorrow morning saying that I retired because I wasn't selected.' I don't know what sort of a half-hearted thing they came up with the following day but that was the end of my career.

Anthony Carmody and Ger Hegarty were recalled to the panel. Some of the casualties during Cregan's first year were fringe players who featured in League games under Tom Ryan. John Flavin was one:

After the change of management six or seven of us were all dropped who had been playing League games, including myself, Paddy Coleman, Brian Tobin and Frankie [Carroll], who would have been more regular. Different managers have different ideas, but to me he seemed to discard a lot of what was coming through, a lot of players coming up to the age of twenty-five, and kept on lads coming up to thirty.

Frankie Carroll was not overly pleased to learn that his career was over:

I was bitter enough at the time. I got married in 1997 and had decided to give it another two years and probably finish up at twenty-nine or thirty. At the time I thought I had something to offer and it didn't wear particularly well, but [laughs] I have moved on at this stage.

What sickened me was the way it happened. We were brought in to a meeting about how it was going to be a professional setup. Then I read in the *Limerick Leader* that I was dropped. I received a phone call from a buddy of mine to buy the *Leader*. It was not the way to do business. I rang Éamonn Cregan and we had a few words. Eventually I cooled down and he rang me to go in for a trial. They asked me to join the panel about six weeks before the championship but I declined. There were talks about calling me back a couple of years later, in 2001. There were soundings made, but there was nothing official. There were murmurs, but I didn't press any buttons to get back in. I was gone since 1998 and as far as I was concerned I was happy that I had given my bit.

Mossie Carroll (*left*) and Éamonn Cregan (*right*) rejoice after Limerick
beat Cork in 2001.

Winning a county with the club was my priority. It would have been
awkward with my brother Mossie being a selector by then.

*An emerging Cork team travelled to the Gaelic Grounds in 1998 and easily
disposed of Limerick at the first championship hurdle, thanks to a bagful of
points from Seánie McGrath. Two late Limerick goals gave the score some
respectability. Jimmy Barry-Murphy viewed the game as a significant step in
his team building process:*

The 1998 game was the day I really felt Cork were back on track,
that we were competitive again and wouldn't be blown away any
more. We had the mentality and assuredness, and even though Clare
beat us afterwards, beating Limerick in the Gaelic Grounds really got
that team going.

Following the defeat to Cork, Cregan began the search for new talent. In the process, some believe he discarded too many too soon, but this is an overly simplistic viewpoint. Others argue that, while a blooding process was necessary, a greater balance between youth and experience was required.

In 1999 against Waterford, twelve of the starting team and three of the substitutes introduced had begun the 1997 championship under Tom Ryan. A far from happy Gary Kirby was on the bench:

In 1999 I was injured for a while, and naturally, the older you get the slower you become, but I was going well. I knew myself I was going well. I remember I injured my hand and I couldn't do any hurling for four weeks. Derry Donovan asked me to try and run four miles and try to keep under seven-minute miles. I was doing them in six minutes fifty seconds. I was always able to get fit for championship. I used take it handy a bit for the winter, but once January came that was it; everything was taken seriously.

We played two challenge matches prior to the championship in 1999; one was in Claughaun against Offaly and I scored well in them. Before the team was picked I was told I wouldn't be playing, and the reason given, which I think was a stupid reason, was that they would prefer to put me on than take me off. That was the biggest kick in the stones over anything. If they had said that they needed me as part of the panel beyond 1999, told me that it was no longer a fifteen-man game, asked me to think about it to help the younger guys through my presence, I would have committed. He said to me, 'You know yourself when your legs are gone.' My legs weren't gone, I was able to go through two years with the club after that. I know it's a different level now and a different pace.

I remember saying to Cregan before the Waterford game in 1999 that we felt Brian Begley wouldn't do come the championship because he would be shown up on the faster ground. We told him Paul Flynn would run Brian around and that he wouldn't have the pace for him. Brian showed up well on soft ground in League matches; different story in the championship. They got rid of Mike Nash too fast; he was a fierce loss in 1999. It's only when he was gone that people realise what he was doing for you. Pa Carey was an unbelievable talent, was steady and was actually a better hurler than Ciarán. Even though he came back in for 1998, he had enough of it so wasn't there either in 1999.

Mike Houlihan terrorised the Waterford full-back line under the dropping ball in the second half of the 1999 game, scoring a goal in the process. He relished the full-forward role and had committed himself to Cregan. However, soon after he was told he was no longer required:

It didn't matter where I was playing, as long as I was on the team. The goal was a bit of a try but they all count. They were obviously looking for a target man. After that I got my redundancy letter in the post. I was after buying the bar, and Éamonn Cregan came out to Kilmallock and met me. He asked for a commitment and I said I would give it to him. I told him that I had a bar, that I was starting a business. I had the problem with looking after the bar while I was away at training and he said they would look after it. That was Éamonn Cregan's agreement. I didn't get any other answers about that and then I got the letter in the post. Kilmallock had two selectors at the time, and they called one day and told me that I had to ring Éamonn Cregan to give him a commitment. I said to one of them, 'Didn't the two of us already meet him at his house, and I told him that I would give him a commitment, even though my wife was expecting our second child?' I said, 'Aren't ye the two selectors, can't ye tell him?' but they said to me to ring him. Perhaps he had other news, I don't know. Maybe his hands were tied about getting the bar looked after. I got a letter telling me that my services were no longer required.

I had trouble with one ankle, I dislocated it. It was a problem, but a lot of hill training would always cause a problem. But still I played until 2005 with the club. I was thirty in 2000 and was prepared to give another year. Declan Ryan was older than me and was still playing for Tipperary in 2001. He was a different type of hurler, but he was seen as having a leadership quality. Did Mike Houlihan have a leadership quality? I don't know, that's not for me to say but that was the opinion.

Brendan Danagher pays Houlihan the ultimate compliment:

I always believed there was a second Ned Rea in Mike Houlihan. He was a big, strong man and he was always able to use his strength and was mobile. He should have been kept longer.

Ger Hegarty has no regrets over his own departure:

I remember Éamonn Cregan putting his panel together in October 1998, and I remember questioning the need to go back training in

October. That told me I was after losing the appetite to do the winter work, that maybe it was time to get out. I just felt that I had given it everything. I felt all emotions in 1996. Ultimately I am a Limerick man and a hurling man and I was thrilled to see Limerick doing well and getting back into All-Irelands. But obviously you are devastated not to be part of it. But again I took a step back and I said I am not going to be a hanger-on and basically I became in 1996 what I was in 1993 – a supporter.

I took it for granted in November 1987, with a good strong management and an enthusiastic and professional approach from the players, that Limerick would have picked up a couple of All-Irelands between 1987 and 1998. I took it for granted that the Limerick team would go on and win all major honours. I played under six or seven different managers with Limerick, and never played for any of them: I only played for Limerick. I never played for any manager, I played for the county but worked under the manager and was always happy to work under that manager.

Ciarán Carey believes too many players were released too quickly:

The players that hit me the most at the time were Mike Houlihan, Dave Clarke, Gary Kirby and Declan Nash, four rare breeds. You needed to be holding onto Kirby and making a Billy Byrne [of Wexford] out of him. From my point of view I think they made a major mistake. Having those four – whether they are playing, offering ten minutes or not even playing, perhaps carrying hurleys – would have been a massive lift. You can't bring out the axe like that.

Surgery was most definitely required following the championship exits of 1997, 1998 and 1999 but a better balance between youth and experience was needed. Mike Fitzgerald wonders how many of the experienced players would have accepted a back seat role:

The 1994 and 1996 team started to break up, and Éamonn was on record publicly as saying he wanted young blood. I remember an interview he gave where he said it was a young man's game and that caused a lot of resentment. It was taken as a direct reference to a good number of the lads that had been there in 1994 and 1996. Perhaps some should have been kept as panellists the same way Wexford kept the older players like Billy Byrne in 1996. On the other hand I doubt if some of the players would have been prepared to sit on the sideline

Éamonn Cregan (*left*) returns to sideline action after his dramatic u-turn in the national hurling league against Derry in 2002 watched by his predecessor Mossie Carroll (*centre*) and selector Mike Fitzgerald (*right*).

and train as subs. Gary Kirby's disappointment at being dropped from the starting team in 1999 would appear to indicate that.

Damien Quigley's career was ended through injury:

I have no objection to Éamonn culling me. I was gone. I got a spate of injuries then and I was working very hard as an accountant so my hurling days were gone. I was still able to play club hurling but that was it. I sometimes think that if Éamonn viewed my circumstances differently I might have played better under him. Éamonn only saw what was on the field. I broke my arm in a match in one of the first games back after the exams in 1997 and got a plate in it. I went back after that and one of my first games was a challenge against Tipperary the following February and I broke my finger and had a pin inserted. That was more surgery, that made it three surgeries in eighteen months. I didn't realise it at the time but I was a long time away from the game training-wise and I never got back to the pitch of the Cork game in 1996.

Éamonn Cregan is a coach rather than a manager, and you have to be a touch of a psychologist to be a manager, to be fair. Tom Ryan's way was 'my way or the highway' and I am not sure Tom would survive now, given where players are coming from nowadays. Jimmy Barry-Murphy was a god with the Cork players ten years ago in 1999, but he would have to prove himself to them again because it has evolved. Éamonn is lots of things; he is a most unbelievable hurler and a grand guy, but I felt he failed to realise that there was more to a hurler in terms of issues in their life outside hurling than what he saw on the pitch.

Quigley makes a valid point. In the modern era, with high mortgages and many other commitments, inter-county players are under enormous pressure to satisfy all masters. But can an inter-county manager afford to compromise in terms of attendance and punctuality, and still prepare properly for the championship?

Nigel Higgins of Wexford was a talented hurler in 2005 but walked away, unable to make the commitment. Éamonn Cregan offers his own explanation for releasing many of the experienced players:

I always remember Nicky English saying that the reason he retired was that when he was playing in the 1996 Munster final he ran for a ball two yards ahead of Stephen McDonagh but by the time he got to the ball McDonagh was two yards ahead of him. I always stood by that; if you cannot get to the ball fast enough, the time has come. You can see it in training. Houlihan had serious difficulty with one of his ankles; a great player but wasn't the fastest man in the world. His mobility was beginning to affect him. You can play through the pain but it's still going to limit you. Dave Clarke was certainly slow in the sprints and Gary Kirby was slow in the sprints and they weren't getting to the ball. You had other players there that were faster but wouldn't be as experienced. We did bring on Gary Kirby in the second half of the Waterford game, but players must accept when they are not getting to the ball. The game was getting faster and faster. I didn't accept it either when I was slowing down. I accept it now but I didn't accept it at the time. It was a changed era from 1994 and 1996. You were heading into 2000, which was six years on. A player who doesn't have speed in the modern game is in trouble. Gary used to play a game from within a certain radius of the centre but the game had changed. We kept him as an impact player in 1999 but Gary has his views on that and I have mine. Would any of them have been happy to remain on the panel? Now there are players better at coming on than starting. At that time it was different, it wasn't as fashionable to be an impact sub.

David Punch was a selector:

I probably would have differed with Éamonn regarding a couple of the mature players and would have felt that they had a year or two left, but Éamonn was the manager and he made the final decision. If things work out the following year, you are proved right, and if not, there is always a backlash.

For the 2000 campaign Declan Nash, Dave Clarke, Mike Houlihan, Gary Kirby and Mike Galligan were surplus to requirements, though Clarke and Galligan were recalled to the panel before the championship. Only four of the players who started in 2000 played in the 1994 All-Ireland final. In contrast, nine who featured in the 1994 final for an Offaly team of similar age profile also appeared in the All-Ireland final of 2000.

Limerick rattled Cork for long periods without ever looking like winning. It's a game that is remembered for Joe Deane's overhead goal and a deliberate blow received by Brian Begley early in the game. Barry Foley was not in Semple Stadium by the end of it:

I made s**t of my ankle after about fifteen seconds and hobbled away for twenty minutes. I came off and thought my ankle was broken. I listened to the end of the game in Cashel hospital.

Brian Begley, who played full-back the previous year, describes his transformation into full-forward:

I played in the backs all the way up along and was centre-back with the club in hurling and football. I enjoyed the backs, I was used to playing there, and I never thought about playing up front. I was marking Paul Flynn in 1999 and I got him on a good day. Éamonn Cregan asked me what I thought about playing up front, and I said I didn't mind as long as I was involved. There was a bit of pulling and dragging with Diarmuid O'Sullivan and the next thing there was a belt on the head; it was all in the heat of the moment. We have had a good couple of battles over the years, and I would have to say that he is a tough but clean full-back. You are always going to get it hard at that level with any full-back.

Much to his surprise, only days after returning to the panel Mike Galligan entered the game as a substitute:

I didn't think I would be brought in against Cork. I thought if we progressed in the championship I would get fitter and have more to offer. To be honest I was off the pace. You need to be on top of your game playing a Cork team in their prime. I met a selector the previous Christmas and I got the vibes that I wasn't going to be asked back and I wasn't until just before the championship. After that Cork game I announced my retirement to the county board and the *Examiner*. I saw the way things were going, even though I felt myself I had more to offer. I didn't put on weight and liked training, and I thought I would go on 'til I was thirty-five but every player thinks he can go on forever. I played against the likes of John Henderson and Lester Ryan in my first League game. It was a different generation. The only championship game I didn't play in was the All-Ireland final of 1996.

Joe Quaid had his tonsils removed in the spring of 2000 and did not play in the League that year. Timmy Houlihan did well in his absence and gave an excellent performance in the League semi-final against Tipperary. However, Houlihan was still eligible for the minors and, although Quaid returned for the championship, his days were numbered:

They brought me back for the Cork game, but I shouldn't have played. My head wasn't right, I had no confidence. I didn't have a run of games under my belt and had missed a lot of the season. I had enough at that stage because I knew I wasn't meeting the standards I had set for myself.

Limerick were in the minor Munster final that year and I went in to the Gaelic Grounds to collect two tickets for myself and my wife. I was handed one by Jimmy Hartigan. I said, 'What do you mean one, I am after playing in the semi-final,' and I asked him, 'How many tickets are you getting?' He replied, 'I am getting two.' I said, 'So you are telling me you can take your wife and I can't.' And he said, 'I am out seven nights a week.' And I said, 'Are you saying we don't put in enough commitment?' I lost it and I told him where to shove his tickets, that I would never put on the jersey again. I went home and I rang Donal Fitzgibbon [county board chairman] and I told him the story and he said he would get me two tickets, and I said, 'Donal, it's totally irrelevant.'

Then Cregan rang me in October. I was in the car park at the Red Cow in Dublin because I was staying there that night. He said, 'We are inviting you back on the panel but you are coming back as our number 2.' I said, 'Éamonn, I am delighted to know in the month of October you know what team you are fielding next June.' As I was getting out of the car, Marty Morrissey happened to be coming out of the Red Cow and he said, 'When are ye back training?' and I said, 'Would you believe I am just after tendering my resignation,' and I told him the story. And he said, 'Will you keep it quiet for a while until I get a camera down to the house?' So they came down the following week with the RTÉ cameras. And that was it. I had retired. The real reason, though, was the way I was treated by the county board earlier in the year.

The League campaign of 2001 is best known for a fateful Thursday night in which Limerick were beaten by Clare in a deferred game at the Gaelic Grounds. Three days later Limerick played Meath and were lucky to get out of Kilmallock alive. A dramatic improvement was needed prior to the championship. Mossie Carroll recalls the circumstances:

I remember there was a huge disappointment after the Clare game. It was an unbelievable occasion. It was like a championship match with the crowd and the buzz. We got an awful drubbing and things fell flat after that. As a selection committee and as a management team we decided that we had to try something different, and we put in the work over the next couple of weeks and got back on track.

Mike Fitzgerald was also a selector:

Éamonn decided to take a step back and allow Mossie and Joe Grimes take a step forward. He took more of a back seat role, observing while the boys did a lot of the training. The boys upped the tempo of the game, old style stuff with a lot of passion in training. I would say that the thing improved dramatically after that, and once the team settled into its groove Cregan took over the reins fully again.

All was not well between Cregan and the selectors, however, and while an encouraging championship run did help, cracks were evident beneath the surface. Cregan recalls a unilateral decision that may not have gone down well:

When Joe Deane scored the overhead goal in 2000, the heads dropped immediately. We were set to play Cork in 2001 again and I said to Derry O'Donovan that we needed to bring in someone to prepare the players mentally so that their heads wouldn't drop again in similar circumstances. I decided to bring in Niall O'Donovan and Mick Galwey to talk to the players and not tell anyone. If I had told the selectors, it would be all over Limerick that they were coming in. That caused problems with certain selectors. I kept it secret and it remained secret. Niall O'Donovan did the talking about organising and was very good. Then Mick Galwey spoke and I always remember his words: 'The opposition are going to score, accept it and be ready to move on.' Cork drew level at the end of the 2001 game in the championship and I remember thinking to myself, 'Will they remember now what Galwey said?' We also got a free near the end a long way out, and Ollie [Moran] came over to take it and I said, 'No, we have our free taker, Paul O'Grady.' There was an advertising hoarding for *The Star* newspaper in line with the uprights at the top of the wall at the back of the terracing. I said to Paul, 'Aim for the letter S on the word Star,' and he very nearly did, it went straight over. It was the most vital free he had taken and he split the posts. To beat Cork in Cork was a tremendous achievement.

Barry Foley scored the winning point from a sideline cut:

That game brings back good memories. I was captain as well, and getting the sideline near the end was special. I have very fond memories of that game; the approach was spot on from the players. We had a meeting on the Thursday night before the match and you could sense that we were going to win it. You would often get that sense, but it's another thing going out and winning it. I don't know if there was an All-Ireland in us, but the way the championship was that year, every team was capable of beating each other. If we had overcome Wexford in the quarter-final, we were certainly capable of beating any team on our day in 2001.

In the next round Limerick came back from the dead against Waterford but lost out to Tipperary in the Munster final. Ollie Moran and Brian Begley were key against Waterford. Éamonn Cregan recalls a late scare:

I was behind the goal in the Waterford game. Paul Flynn was able to hit a ball in such a way that it would go up and it would then dip. I was roaring at Timmy Houlihan, 'Don't let it dip,' and from 40 yards Flynn shot and it dipped and scraped the crossbar and went over.

A momentum-fuelled Limerick faced Tipperary in what turned out to be a dramatic Munster final. Owen O'Neill, who had been instrumental in the comeback against Waterford, went over on his ankle seconds after being introduced and had to be taken off. In the dying minutes Limerick missed a hatful of chances, including a Brian Begley shot that hit the post when a point would have given Limerick the lead. Tipperary cleared the ball downfield and Brian O'Meara scored. John O'Brien added a point to secure a two-point victory. Mossie Carroll rues the missed chances:

We were unlucky in 2001. I remember being behind the Tipperary goal for a while, and that goal led a charmed life because we definitely had opportunities to win that game.

Joe Quaid viewed things from a different perspective:

I went away and enjoyed a great supporter's year in 2001 and had a great time. Timmy Houlihan got the blame for the Munster final. I got up to go to the toilet when there was a break in play and someone roared at me to go away and get my boots. After the match they were lambasting Timmy. I wasn't playing, yet they were saying that I was the best goalie in Limerick.

Stephen McDonagh failed to last the full game:

I remember going in the car. Denis Carroll the PRO drove us in, and it was 28 degrees going into Páirc Uí Chaoimh. Compared to the emphasis on water now, I probably wasn't hydrated enough, and then you had the claustrophobic atmosphere in the stadium with the crowd.

I was gone mentally and physically by half-time but they said they would give me more time and I remember going off very early in the second half.

Nicky English was glad not to meet Limerick a second time:

Limerick came out of nowhere in 2001 and we were wary of them. I felt we were favourites for the Munster final, but for me it was a real pressure game because every year before that we had progressed a step. We would have had to win the Munster final in 2001 to continue the progression from the previous year. It was the warmest day I was ever at a match. It went down to the wire and could have gone either way. We got a relatively soft goal, but Limerick were right in it at the end. They fought hard that day and if they had beaten Wexford in the quarter-final, they would have been playing us for a second time. It would have been very awkward for us to beat them a second time. I was happy to see the back of Limerick in Croke Park that day because I felt we had a better chance of beating Wexford than beating Limerick a second time.

The quarter-final against Wexford was decided by a late Damien Fitzhenry goal from a free. Fitzhenry had scored a penalty earlier, and Paul Codd also scored a goal from a 21-yard free. To add salt to the wounds, Seánie O'Connor had a goal disallowed midway through the second half. There was a sense of déjà vu, the 1996 All-Ireland final all over again. Owen O'Neill believes the referee should have applied the rules more consistently:

I felt the referee was totally and utterly inconsistent. He blew on the foul where Seánie O'Connor scored the goal, but I had been fouled prior to that and after that and there was no free given. If consistency was applied we would have got three points from frees. But to blow for one and let the other two off was a wrong decision; anyone could see Seánie O'Connor going through.

Éamonn Cregan exonerates Clement Smith for committing the foul that led to the Damien Fitzhenry free:

The free that Clement gave away, I would have given away as well, because his man was always going to get around him. I felt sorry for the lads, because there's no point playing well in a Munster final if you don't win the All-Ireland quarter-final.

Stephen McDonagh has strident views on the game:

There was a bit of flaking in the game. Larry O'Gorman was mouthing, there would have been a lot of horses**t spoken on the field among the players. There would have been no love lost between Limerick and Wexford, to be honest, and that would have gone back to our clashes in the 1990s. There was a very messy League game in Enniscorthy in 1997 when there were a lot of nasty verbals. A lot of rubbish went on and Liam Dunne was talking that he would show his All-Ireland medal to Gary. Wexford were good at that.

The difference in class between the Wexford players and the Offaly players in my opinion was huge. Offaly were able to carry themselves. They had a bit of class about them off the field, a higher calibre of individual. We had a great relationship with Offaly. I would have had fierce high regard for the Offaly players, but I couldn't say the same about Wexford. There may have been fierce rivalry at that time between Limerick and Clare but at the back of it all there was fierce respect. In my case I wouldn't have that respect for Wexford. Certainly some of them were fine, but I wouldn't have any *grá* for the majority of them. Our paths don't cross that often but that suits me fine.

The following year a controversy arose over the issue of dual players. There were two dual players in the Limerick setup at the time, Stephen Lucey and Conor Fitzgerald. The pot had been simmering for a couple of years without ever boiling over, but the lid was well and truly blown off in 2002 when Éamonn Cregan resigned over the issue. Cregan outlines the background:

The seniors were in the Canaries on holidays with the under-21s and we spoke with Stephen Lucey and asked him to make a decision himself – Gaelic football or hurling. He wouldn't and he said the county board would make the decision. Lucey never trained, he played for twelve teams the first year he was with us. How can a player sustain that? He never did physical training with us and when he did a warm-up he lasted about six minutes. You cannot compete at the top level in hurling and football at the same time unless you are superman.

Cregan had been a dual player himself. But it was easier in those days, as Pat Hartigan explains:

In 1968, I played minor hurling and football, under-21 hurling and football, intermediate hurling and junior hurling and I played senior hurling and football in the League in autumn. It was quite common that time to play three matches on a Sunday. I remember playing both intermediate hurling and junior football for Limerick against Waterford one day and South Liberties had a League game against Patrickswell that night. So I stayed in the Gaelic Grounds until 8 p.m. that night.

They were different times regarding dual players. To be on top of your game now you have to be specialised. It was easy do both that time because football was very secondary. I would always have treated Limerick football as a training session. I never decided not to play football at any stage. I was a sub on the Munster team one year we were beaten by Connacht in Killarney. I would have liked to have won something in football and that was probably my best chance.

Éamonn Cregan explains how the dual player issue led to his resignation:

The selectors and myself had agreed in that year that the players would have to make up their minds. Then when we met the county board they had changed and one selector was the first to break ranks and said, 'We will have to accept it so.' The dual player issue at that time was a disruptive influence on the team and certainly was a disruptive influence on the selectors. I seemed to be in a minority, but I had the most vital thing of all – the support of the players. I felt I was outnumbered; I knew I had the confidence of the players but I felt I didn't have the confidence of the selectors. There was no point in continuing so I stood down.

I wanted to bring in Pat Herbert earlier in 2002 to assist me in the coaching of the team. I had spoken to him and he was interested. I went to a member of the county board one Friday and he said it was a great idea but by the following Monday it had become a bad idea. Then they wanted to bring in Dave Keane who was still with the under-21s and was doing well with them. But I wanted Pat Herbert. And I was shot down. That was the beginning of the end for me; I felt I was wanted out. The four selectors were against me. They did favour dual players. You can't please everyone. You are in charge of the team and you must do what is best for the team. If we had won an All-Ireland the year before, the dual player issue would have been forgotten about. One particular individual in the county board executive pushed and pushed for dual players continuously.

Donal Fitzgibbon offers his perspective on Pat Herbert:

The view at the time was that there were sufficient people on board rather than bringing in Pat Herbert. There was a general consensus among the selectors that there was enough expertise already available without having to add to it.

Mike Fitzgerald – selector, liaison officer and county board officer – says player power brought Cregan back:

I was liaison officer in 2002 and I was dealing with Liam Kearns, the football manager. Éamonn resigned out of the blue one night over an issue related to the players having to play a football match. None of the selectors were aware of his impending resignation. The hurling team were going well and had nearly all their matches won in the League, had just beaten Wexford, and then Éamonn resigned. Liam Kearns was quite happy that the hurlers would get the first call if there was a clash. Éamonn resigned and he didn't want any question of any dual players. He wouldn't come back under any circumstances and the county board consulted with him but he insisted that he wasn't coming back. Mossie Carroll was appointed on a caretaker basis until the end of the season, and he accepted it on the basis that Éamonn wasn't coming back.

The players revolted and my understanding is that key players had a meeting with Éamonn and persuaded him to come back. In his first meeting with the players at Kilmurray Lodge, Mossie was addressing players who were already aware that Cregan was on the way back. Mossie was badly treated and only found out the following day. The county board asked him to step back and he stepped down for the good of Limerick hurling so that there wouldn't be a serious split. I thought it was a great trial of the man. I would put that saga as the turning point in the downturn of Limerick hurling for the next four or five years because it was the advent of player power behind the scenes. The whole thing had broken. Mossie was now working with Cregan after having being ousted to allow Cregan back. We had no chance in the championship.

Unlike other experienced players of the Cregan era and subsequent managerial eras, Stephen McDonagh was there for one reason only – hurling – and took pride in the jersey. Behind-the-scenes manoeuvring was of no interest to him:

I stayed out of all the politics that time. I always saw it as a fierce honour to hurl for Limerick and I tried to do my best when I was there. When you are gone you will miss it but it's like the disappointment of the All-Irelands – you have to move on and you give the jersey to someone else. Other experienced players were involved. There was a couple of meetings at the time, I remember going to one of them.

Donal Fitzgibbon gives his view:

I have great regard for Éamonn, and he is very much his own man. I asked him why he didn't contact me before he made his decision to step down and he said because I would try to talk him out of it. I didn't know about it until I heard about the letter. Mossie Carroll was appointed, and he deserves credit because he stood aside again and made no issue of it. I think the players had a massive input. Éamonn would have had great regard from the players but it was he himself who actually made the final decision. There was a rump out there, in my opinion, who felt Éamonn had his time done, but the players were very much behind him and that would probably have had some influence on him but he definitely made up his own mind to come back. The biggest disappointment from his perspective was coming so close to winning a Munster title in 2001.

Éamonn Cregan describes the sequence of events surrounding his departure and return:

I was working at Newcastlewest golf club at the time and was coming back home from work one night. I had been working 'til 11 p.m. and got a phone call at 11.35 p.m. asking me to attend a meeting at the Gaelic Grounds. I said, 'I am in Adare at the moment,' and I went home and had a cup of tea and went out at about 12.15 a.m. to attend the famous meeting. They asked me would I consider withdrawing my resignation. I said no. They said, 'Thank you very much, we will be back in contact with you.' They rang me an hour later and thanked me for all I did. I was now gone and they appointed Mossie. They broke their own rules doing that, because they can't appoint a manager unless a full meeting of the county board ratifies the appointment. They may say now that he was made caretaker manager, but it appeared in the paper that time that he was the manager.

I had heard a lot of people had withdrawn their Mackey draw subscriptions in protest at my departure and that got to me. The following night I woke up in the middle of the night and said, 'I have to stop this,' so I contacted Donal Fitzgibbon at 2.15 a.m. and said, 'Donal, I am withdrawing my resignation.' Everyone at the time thought I was approached and asked to reconsider but no, I made the decision myself. Donal went back to the county board and I was reappointed. They couldn't contact Mossie Carroll, but it transpired that he was in Galway. He was met by two of the players up there. Eventually the whole thing was sorted out. I then got a sports psychologist in to meet the players, and I walked out and told them I was leaving the room for him to speak to the players on their own. We had him on a previous occasion in Killarney. Nobody was there, no selectors, only the players having their discussion. I got a phone call within half an hour to come back, and I was told what the players wanted.

They basically wanted me to pick the team on my own. I said that I wasn't sure I had the authority to do that but I would look into it. When I went to pick the team on the Tuesday night prior to the Cork qualifier game the selectors were walking off down to one end of the field. When I asked them about picking the team, they said, 'I thought you were doing that on your own.' That meant that one of the players had leaked to one of the selectors what went on at that meeting. I know who that player was.

There were three mistakes made that night in the Cork game, and I have grave concerns about the three mistakes, but it doesn't matter, they are history now. After that I said to Derry O'Donovan that it's time to step away from this, the selectors are trying to undermine me the whole time. A number of county board officers would have been quite delighted to see me step aside because I was a constant thorn in their side. Derry and I have always been basically pro-players provided they perform and do their best. I am anti-administration in many respects. But you have to have a happy relationship with all sides, they must all be working in the same direction pulling together. That second year there was always someone pulling against us.

Such was the level of controversy in 2002 that the games themselves have almost been forgotten. Limerick were beaten by Kilkenny in a League semi-final at the Gaelic Grounds, while in the Munster championship they lost to Tipperary by 1-20 to 1-13, with Eoin Kelly receiving a phenomenal supply of ball. In the qualifiers, a contentious refereeing decision by Barry Kelly handed a one-point victory to Cork on a Saturday evening in Thurles. Nicky English recalls the Tipperary game at Páirc Uí Chaoimh and sensed that there was something not quite right with Limerick:

The 2002 game was probably the peak of our team, the best performance we ever put together. The body language of Limerick that day wasn't great. I don't think they were gelling well that time and as a consequence the game was more comfortable for us than it should have been. Mark Foley was a key player for Limerick and Brian O'Meara was the type of player who we felt could cause him problems and pull him out of position. We named O'Meara at 12 and played him at 10, and that left things open, allowing us to deliver good ball to Eoin Kelly.

Mossie Carroll sums up the year in which he was the shortest serving Limerick manager in history:

2002 was an awful mess and things changed dramatically within twenty-four hours. That couple of weeks wasn't an ideal build-up to the championship. I was only interested in finishing out the year and disappearing at that stage. I had made my mind up to finish out the year and do as much as I could to be helpful and to move the thing along. Playing is the be all and end all, and if you get involved in your forties it's for the enjoyment of putting something back in. After that summer I felt life wasn't worth that sort of hassle any more. Things happened within a group and that's the way things worked out, circumstances were circumstances and I wouldn't blame anyone for that. That was the dynamic that the whole thing took on as the summer went on and it got to the stage when the buzz went out of it, and once that happened it was time to concentrate on working with my sons at underage club level. All you can give is a couple of years to it anyway. There is a lifespan. It would be a different story if you are successful, but it was one hassle after another and, at that stage, the breakthrough wasn't happening. I thought the county board were up front in my dealings with them and I would have no problem with the county board at all.

Éamonn Cregan has the final word:

It's amazing that when managers go into manage teams, the managers will always have problems with the county board executive. Anything good that came in Limerick came from the players. The famous commission that was formed in the 1970s came about as a result of the players approaching the county board looking for winter training. The executive officers of Limerick county board would never have come up with that idea. Executive officers don't want to go that far in case they are spending money. I met four inter-county managers in New Ross one day and they all had gripes with their respective county boards. Why are executive officers and managers at opposite ends except in Kilkenny and Kerry?

Cregan makes a very valid point. And one has to wonder if the immediate presence of silverware is merely a shield that temporarily prevents those county boards in Kerry and Kilkenny from meddling in team affairs.

FIFTEEN

ಛಿ

2003: HERO TO ZERO

imerick hurling has often been in the spotlight for the wrong reasons.
L*However, on 12 July 2000, something remarkable began, something that was to become a Wednesday night crusade over the following three campaigns. It became known as the 'three-in-a-row'.*

That night in Ennis, Limerick defeated Clare in an under-21 first round match – a Clare side that had won the All-Ireland minor title three years earlier. On 15 September 2002, Limerick won their third successive All-Ireland under-21 title. The circle was complete on a fantastic achievement.

However, before a sliotar was pucked at under-21 level, there were administration and coaching duties to be completed, as acknowledged by Donal Fitzgibbon:

Back around 1993 and 1994 we decided to pick the best thirty underage players in both codes to work with them in development squads. Tommy Quaid was heavily involved. His enthusiasm and passion for Limerick was demonstrated after he was dropped from the hurling panel in 1993. He could have walked away and become negative but he didn't, he completely caught himself up in youth development. There was great respect for him. His enthusiasm was contagious and spread throughout the underage structure. One of the original driving forces behind the five-year plan was Mick Tynan. Limerick CBS played their part also, along with people such as John Landers, Gerry Bennis, Pat Fitzgerald and Brother Philip Ryan.

John Landers is keen to stress that he was only one of a number of hardworking people. He says the lack of expectation helped enormously:

In the mid-1990s we went to Kilkenny, Offaly, Galway and Tipperary and assessed what structures they used for their underage competitions and incorporated that with the development model that suited Limerick. Competitions in Limerick weren't organised well and an under-16 player might average three games a year. We came up with an all-county structure that provided games. We were also fortunate that a lot of good players came along together. People outside of those holding board positions were given leeway to come up with ideas. We were coming from a low base and we had nowhere to go except upwards, whereas expectation can often be the greatest obstacle that we have to overcome in Limerick.

Donal Fitzgibbon deployed his business acumen in the quest for success:

In anything in life I have my own formula – vision, passion, discipline, character, team and teamwork. Any successful entity in life will have all these strands. If you are missing any one, you are going to lose out. Compare it to a rowing team. If all eight on a rowing team aren't pulling together you won't get to the finishing line first. The Irish rugby team brought the best people in from the right places and put them in the right positions. A vision without passion is only an aspiration, is only a dream. Character is based on trustworthiness, honesty, integrity and respect. You cannot do it alone, and you must identify the stakeholders in the team, having the best people in the right positions all working together towards the common vision.

While the three-in-a-row players did not achieve anything spectacular at minor level, they were certainly more competitive at that level from 1997 to 2000 than their predecessors had been from 1994 to 1996. However, Donal Fitzgibbon stresses that success at minor level was not paramount:

The objective was not on winning but on improving them as players. By the time they reached under-21-level, we decided to pick three men who had success themselves with premier level teams. I didn't really know Dave Keane but I approached him to take over the under-21 team for 1999 on the back of his success as a player with Cork and his association with Adare underage teams. The next piece of the jigsaw was John Mescall, who was also lecturing players of that age in his daily job, meaning that he could identify with them. Finally, we decided to get a link to the senior management and that was Dave Punch. Pat O'Callaghan joined as trainer in 2000 and also played a hugely important role.

The Limerick team that won the All-Ireland under 21-title in 2000. *Back row (l–r):* Paul O'Reilly (Patrickswell), Paul O'Grady (Patrickswell), Seánie O'Connor (Ahane), Brian Begley (Mungret), Stephen Lucey (Croom), Brian Geary (Monaleen), Eugene Mulcahy (Knockainey) Mark Keane (South Liberties). *Front row (l–r) :* Willie Walsh

(Murroe/Boher), Damien Reale (Hospital/Herbertstown), Donnacha Sheehan (Capt.)
(Adare), Timmy Houlihan (Adare), John Mescall (Ahane), Paudie Reale (Hospital/
Herbertstown), David Stapleton (Doon).

In 1999 Limerick faced Cork in the under-21 Munster championship at Bruff, a Cork side that was going for three All-Ireland titles in a row. In the previous two years Limerick had been well beaten by Tipperary, so a decent performance against the Rebels would have satisfied supporters. And they got it – a penalty by Diarmuid O'Sullivan saw Cork win by 2-15 to 2-10. Dave Keane, however, was not satisfied with defeat:

I thought the penalty was a harsh decision. Justin Daly was fouled outfield but the free was given against us. They ended up getting a penalty out of that free. We brought on Kevin Carey and he gave Diarmuid O'Sullivan a hard time in the second half but I wasn't comfortable at any stage of the game that we looked like winning it. It didn't matter a damn to the players, they didn't mind losing. They had played their championship and had seemed to take it in their stride. There was no expectation there anyway. That showed me what needed to change first of all. They needed to be devastated by losing.

Keane would never again taste defeat during his tenure as Limerick under-21 manager. They had their fair share of luck over the three years, something that has often eluded the senior team. Keane acknowledges that momentum played its part:

In fairness, if we had lost any one of those games at any stage during the three years, we wouldn't have progressed. It was the momentum that carried us. We won games that we should have lost and won games where the opposition were probably better than us. We still came out on top because of the team performance. We had players who didn't make it at senior level that we got the most out of. You expect your big names to play well all the time but we got players who weren't big names to give more than 100 per cent. The team was better than the sum of its parts.

Pat O'Callaghan (Scoby) remembers the night it all began:

We said we would give it a lash, which we did, and we won that night. One game led to the next and before we were finished we had played fifteen consecutive matches where we were unbeaten.

Dave Punch believes that first win was significant:

Timmy Houlihan came out and threw his body at a Clare player late in the game, and that won us the match. If that ball had hit the back of the net we might never have been seen again.

Paudie Reale, a star performer in the under-21 final of 2000, recalls the first round victory the previous year:

Clare had won the All-Ireland minor title in 1997 but there seemed to be a quiet confidence among us. A lot of that might have come from the dual players who had reached the All-Ireland under-21 football final against Tyrone early in 2000. There were also a lot of strong characters on the team, a lot of established senior players who had already played against Cork in the senior championship. It was a tight game against Clare. Timmy Houlihan made a couple of great saves near the end and we escaped intact. We celebrated at the final whistle that night like we had won the All-Ireland.

Limerick still had plenty to do, however – next up was a star-studded Cork in the Munster final at Páirc Uí Chaoimh. Limerick escaped with a draw following a last-gasp from 65 John Mescall. Paudie Reale recalls the manager's inspiration:

Dave Keane was a good man to talk and he always expected players to be confident. Within the environs of the dressing room he always played everyone up and played Limerick up. In an interview after the drawn game he was asked if he was surprised, and he said that he wasn't, that he thought we were going to win and was disgusted that we didn't. He was the same in the dressing room, that we should have won that game, and he kept saying, 'No more moral victories, that should have been a victory and it wasn't.'

Keane himself believes honesty played a big part in the system and uses the drawn Munster final as an example:

We took off Mark Keane, Dave Stapleton and Donnacha Sheehan. Between them they scored 3-14 in the replay and that might have been because they realised their places weren't secure. We were totally honest and there was nobody selected on club bias.

The replay at the Gaelic Grounds was the dream of all dreams, the night when nothing went wrong. It was also a night when no substitute was introduced, as Dave Keane explains:

We were put under pressure to play the game in Kilmallock and it was my first experience of traffic in the city for a midweek game. But I felt, 'Why should we accommodate Cork?' People didn't make the game, but all that helped us and we were now standing up to the Corks and the Tipperarys.

We didn't make a single substitution or a positional change, the fifteen that started stayed in their positions. It wouldn't have been fair to any of the players to take them off, having beaten Cork in the manner in which they did. Limerick might normally have been happy to give a good performance in Cork and accept defeat. That was the mentality that we had to change. It's normal for one team not to produce in a replay, and I drove it into them before the replay, 'Why should we be the team who doesn't peform?' That was the most complete performance over the three years. We did beat Galway comprehensively in the 2002 final but Galway still have a lot to prove at senior level. That Cork under-21 team contained players who won All-Ireland senior medals and All-Stars.

Pat O'Callaghan has good reason to remember the final score:

We won by 4-18 to 1-6. And those are still my Lotto numbers, 4, 18, 1 and 6. Unfortunately they haven't come up since!

Limerick played Antrim in the All-Ireland semi-final just three days later, as Paudie Reale recalls:

A few of the boys might have gone out celebrating but it was always going to be hard to make the journey up to Dublin and lift ourselves again. It wasn't a hectic performance by any distance; I remember Éamonn Cregan being very critical of certain players on 95FM and a lot of players weren't happy about it afterwards.

That Limerick team were seen as physically intimidating. Physically strong, tough and tenacious and that's what won it for us. In the final itself, Galway were the same so there wasn't much open hurling. Being part of one All-Ireland success and looking in at the other two, I think the first might not have been the classiest hurling team of the three but it had that doggedness and toughness to be able to grind out the wins. That team broke the mould. Limerick teams were used to being beaten. It was different for the teams that came afterwards, most of them had All-Ireland medals in their pockets and were used to beating the likes of Cork and Clare and Galway. To break the mould the first year, the team had to be extra strong, because there had been teams in previous years who were as good as Cork but weren't able to beat them.

The Limerick under-21 panel that completed the three-in-a-row in 2002. *Back row (l–r):*
Micheal Clancy (Granagh/Ballingarry), Eoin Foley (Patrickswell), Mark Keane (South
Liberties), Eugene Mulcahy (Knockainey), Paudie O'Dwyer (Kilmallock), Raymond
Hayes (Askeaton), James O'Brien (Bruree). *Second row (l–r):* David Punch (Selector)
(Patrickswell), Dave Keane (Manager) (Adare), Conor Fitzgerald (Adare), Michael
Clifford (Adare), J. P. Healy (Adare), Brian Carroll (Kilmallock and Staker Wallace),
Damien Reale (Hospital/Herbertstown), John O'Connor (Murroe/Boher), Dermot
Foley (Monaleen), Pat O'Callaghan (Trainer) (Adare & Hospital/ Herbertstown), John
Mescall (Selector) (Ahane). *Front row (l–r):* Donal Fitzgibbon (County Board
Chairman) (Mungret), Mike Fitzgerald (County Board Treasurer) (Kilmallock),
Andrew O'Shaughnessey (Kilmallock), Micheal O'Donnell (Garryspillane), Eoghan
Murphy (Patrickswell), Pat Tobin (Murroe/Boher), Peter Lawlor (Capt) (Croom),
Timmy Houlihan (Adare), Maurice O'Brien (Garryspillane), Niall Moran (Ahane),
Jimmy Hartigan (County Board Secretary) (Ballybrown), Michael McDonnell (County
Board Assistant Secretary) (Croom). *Seated on ground (l–r):* Patrick Kirby (Knockainey),
Mickey Cahill (Croom), Niall Curtin (Tournafulla), Thomas Carmody (Croom),
Marcus Cregan (Croom), Kevin Tobin (Murroe/Boher).

Pat O'Callaghan remembers the introduction of the then long-haired David Tierney in the All-Ireland final:

Eugene Mulcahy was marking Tierney and he went in and clattered the crossbar with the hurley trying to intimidate them. Eugene said to him, 'The next f***ing time you come in here I will give you a f***ing haircut.' That was Eugene, he was totally fearless, very reliable, did his business quietly.

Donal Fitzgibbon feels Éamonn Cregan's contribution should not be forgotten:

Nine of those players played in the League semi-final of 2000 and that has to be put down to Éamonn Cregan. He had a massive part to play in the first under-21 through his development of those lads. It was Cregan who recognised Brian Begley as a full-forward and Ollie Moran as a centre-forward. He was a great man to identify the right man for the right position. That League semi-final in 2000 was where they got their baptism of fire and their first taste of playing in front of 35,000 people.

In 2001 the run continued. Cork were first up, and led at half-time by seven points, having played against the breeze. Dave Keane remembers the circumstances:

We were missing Eugene Mulcahy who was suspended for playing in London. We didn't have a tested full-back and had to put Brian Geary back. We were five points down with the wind so we had to throw caution to the wind then and put Geary back out centre-back and bring on Brian Carroll. Donal O'Grady was midfield and he lost out for no other reason only to reshuffle the team. His sum total of hurling under us was that half an hour and we started winning again then and he was never back. He was almost sacrificed that night to put Geary out centre-back and we never got to see his potential, which he has since delivered at senior level.

Tipperary were defeated in a thrilling Munster final, and Galway were eliminated at the All-Ireland semi-final stage in Ennis, a game in which Andrew O'Shaughnessey made his debut at that level. Pat O'Callaghan remembers an incident during the game:

A Galway mentor charged down the sideline and met Dave Keane full force with his shoulder. We were never going to lose to them when they were up to that kind of rubbish.

In the final Limerick disposed of Wexford, having dictated for long periods but without ever opening up a big lead. Maurice O'Brien was a colleges star with St Colman's of Fermoy at the time and gave an unbelievable performance at wing-back. Wexford exploded into life in the final moments, but it was too little too late.

The 2002 Munster championship began with victories over Clare and Cork. Attendances regularly approached the 20,000 mark, and an epic two-legged Munster final saga with Tipperary captivated those who were present. Limerick were lucky to escape with a draw in Thurles the first night, as Dave Keane explains:

Eoin Foley scored the penalty for a draw when Conor Fitzgerald was fouled in injury time. We would have been willing to accept at the time that it was a dubious penalty. I had told Eoin Foley that if we got a chance I would be on the field to dry his hurley, and I was, and I also gave him a brand new sliotar. The Tipperary goalie was the only person who spotted it and was trying to come out with a wet ball and the referee stopped him, thinking he was the person trying to swap the sliotar. We definitely brought the attitude of win at all costs, without breaking the rules, maybe bending the rules slightly.

A common complaint over the years was that Limerick management teams lacked ruthlessness, decisiveness and cunning. Nobody can deny, however, that Dave Keane had that X factor, and proved it by doing to Tipperary what Donie Nealon had done to Limerick in 1971.

The replay was a fantastic contest, one of the most amazing games at any level. From the throw-in the pace was frenetic. But there was no settling down period, the pace never dropped until the final whistle blew after extra time. Dave Keane was concerned as the end of normal time approached:

I remember going into injury time we were four points down. Andrew O'Shaughnessey got the ball and hadn't done a lot all evening but he got the goal. Then Kevin Tobin got the equaliser. It's like running in a race, the psychological advantage is always with the person coming from behind and we had that advantage. Inside in the dressing room before going out for extra time I knew we were going to win. I remember Eoin Brislane got an inspiring point for them, but still I knew we were going to win. I remember one of our players clipped him on the way out and he reacted and the referee sent him off. We went on to win. That would be the game that would stand out across all the three years.

Pat O'Callaghan has fond memories of the game:

We had played the Waterford seniors in 2002 when we were going for the three-in-a-row, and they were preparing for the Munster senior championship. Their senior team beat our under-21 team by a point. There was hell for leather that night, no quarter given; that's what we had with the under-21s but it stood to us in the Tipperary games. The replayed game against Tipperary was another fantastic night. When Kevin Tobin equalised, I was on the far side with a water bottle. I remember racing down the field and I was about 10 feet off the ground. Before we came out of the dressing room for extra time, the atmosphere in the dressing room was unreal; they just knew, they were hopping off the ground waiting to go out and finish the job. Tipperary had us beaten four times and they still hadn't beaten us. Limerick were on fire. That's a night I will remember until I die.

Limerick completed the three-in-a-row by beating Galway comprehensively in the 2002 All-Ireland final. Pat O'Callaghan had his own worries:

My father was dying on the day of the 2002 final. And as the lads were coming onto the bus heading for the final they were asking, 'Scoby, what's up with you?' because I was always the one cracking jokes. And I was saying that things were grand. I couldn't tell them because if they heard Scoby's father was dying, the mood would have collapsed. He actually died that night and they didn't find out until the following day.

Dave Keane acknowledges the role played by the supporters, among others:

Donal Fitzgibbon to me was an excellent chairman and he set out his stall that the most important manager in the county was the senior manager and that everyone else had to fall in around that. I'd recognise that without having to be told and there wouldn't be any arguments. We played challenge games against the seniors and they were excellent matches. Without doubt it benefited many of the players to be involved with the seniors. There was also a core of dual players in 2000 and the under-21 football run generated good interest in the county. I was in Mullingar myself for the Tyrone game and but for Begley's shot that hit the crossbar after half-time they could have been dual All-Ireland under-21 winners.

There was a good core of winners involved and if you can get six or seven from any team putting peer pressure on the others to win, it's an

*(L–r): Paudie Reale (Limerick) and Damien Joyce (Galway) scramble for posession
in the 2000 under-21 All-Ireland final.*

ideal situation. While the under-21s gave great performances, there
was always a period in every game, even against Antrim, where I felt
the result could go the wrong way. People talk about the management
and the players but the supporters were also there, and that gave them
a great focus, a winning team; everyone wants to be associated with
winners. I remember going to the Galway versus Wexford semi-final
in 2002 and I would say there were no more than 2,000 at it, yet we
had 30,000 at our games.

*No sooner was the three-in-a-row in the bag when a dilemma arose – in late
2002 a replacement for Éamonn Cregan had to be found. Donal Fitzgibbon
stepped down as chairman and was replaced by Pat Fitzgerald of Doon. There
was only one logical choice for the senior manager's position, as Fitzgibbon
outlines:*

Nobody else was considered for the senior job apart from Dave
Keane, who was approached and asked if he was interested. He
indicated that he was, and we proposed him. Why wouldn't we? There

was no reason to knock him. He took on the job but it just didn't work out. He was very much the logical and obvious contender. There was a challenge in gelling players who hadn't had success and then perhaps you had players saying, 'I have my All-Ireland medals.' People have to take ultimate responsibility for their own actions. It looked like there were four or five strong personalities on the senior side and the same on the younger side. There will always be personalities and there will always be various interpretations among the different parties involved. My biggest disappointment was that we didn't take full advantage of the under-21 successes.

Some might say if I had remained as chairman that Keane would have remained as manager, which is a valid point. I had been chairman for five years and I had given my all. I think the new five-year rule regarding officers is good. The loss of Keane was enormous because he was a winner. He won games that were on a knife-edge that we might otherwise have lost. He took us over the finishing line. He was professional in everything he did and I worked very closely with him, building up a good friendship with him over his term. I had undoubted trust in Dave Keane.

Keane believed he was duty bound to make the step up to senior manager:

I suppose the possibility of a four-in-a-row existed but at the time you had to look at what was more important for Limerick; another under-21 wasn't going to do anything major. We were damned if we did and damned if we didn't by going with the seniors. It was about continuing the run, the rich vein of form, and if we didn't move up and Limerick lost at senior level the next year it would have been our fault. We felt obliged to step up but the fact that Limerick hadn't won at senior level meant there was massive expectation from the supporters, the county board and ourselves.

We drew with Waterford in 2003, but the second day Brian Begley got injured, Andrew O'Shaughnessy was doing the Leaving, and Niall Moran got clocked five minutes into the game, yet we were only beaten by two points by the Munster champions. I wasn't concerned about the League and would have viewed it as a competition to try out players. If you are looking at anything else from the League, you are using it for the wrong purpose. Looking back I believe you can't bring that many under-21s into a team together for their debut, but if we had more of a core of established talent at our disposal we'd probably have had to introduce only three or four under-21s. Limerick didn't have that core.

Pat O'Callaghan feels the togetherness of the under-21s never transferred to the senior camp:

There was great camaraderie in the under-21 dressing rooms and I used often mention the story of the three hundred Spartans and the Battle of Thermopylae. There was a great atmosphere. As the overage players left year after year, the younger players came in, and were warmly welcomed into the squad, unlike when the under-21 players amalgamated with the seniors. The same atmosphere wasn't there at all. There was something missing. I think myself that the senior players had a perception that the under-21s were full of themselves, that the attitude of some senior players was, 'F*** ye, ye are in with the big boys now.' My opinion, having worked with the under-21s, was that they weren't like that at all. There was no such thing as a superstar or 'I am better than you' attitude. If there was that attitude, we wouldn't ever have won a match at under-21 level. The under-21s were a fabulous bunch of players and I would compare them to the Munster rugby team, with their attitude, work ethic and togetherness. We didn't get that with the seniors. Given time with the same management team they would obviously have gelled, but we didn't get a chance to do that. The county board have made a balls of it by bringing in so many management teams since.

In hindsight it was a big mistake going with the seniors. Not having the same rapport with the seniors or the same camaraderie in the dressing room meant there wasn't the same dynamic on the field. You would imagine that the success at under-21 level would lift things more, but in fact it was the other way it went. I do believe given time that we would have got it right. People say we should have waited before getting involved with the seniors. You could consider it selfish on behalf of the management. If you allowed your three under-21 teams to go forward to senior with a new manager, and they won a senior All-Ireland you would kick yourself. That was the gamble and we firmly believed we had a strong enough panel at that stage, we had players that were used to winning. We knew them all, they were mad about us, had huge respect for Dave and we all got on well. There was never a row or a nasty word in the dressing room. Given another year we would have identified the senior players we wanted in a collective atmosphere, once they realised the younger players were down to earth. We would also have identified the senior players we didn't want. The seniors just didn't know the under-21 players well enough. If a team doesn't bond you are nothing. If you have two factions in any team, even within a club team, you are going nowhere.

If we had beaten Waterford the first day it would have changed everything. The senior players would have rowed in 100 per cent and said we are on a winning streak here, this is continuing from the under-21. It's seldom that there are conflicts in a winning dressing room, and if there are they are put to one side if the team is winning. We were lucky at times with the under-21s and there were drawn games that might have gone against us. If we had that bit of under-21 luck against Waterford, there would have been no questions of sackings or anything. All people would have said is, 'Whatever they are doing is working. Leave it alone.' But unfortunately we didn't get that win. We played Kerry in the qualifiers then in July 2003. Our boys weren't up for it. They reckoned Kerry were a second rate team. Kerry raised their game, perhaps because I had trained them a couple of years earlier with P. J. O'Grady. In fairness, Kerry had a good run that year. We were caught on the hop but still won by five points. People began to criticise and jump on the negative bandwagon then, saying that things were not right in the camp, looking for reasons as to why they weren't right, and looking for excuses that something was wrong.

Offaly defeated Limerick in an All-Ireland qualifier on Thursday 17 July 2003, arguably one of the worst nights in the history of Limerick hurling. Offaly had their own issues prior to the game though, as Simon Whelahan explains:

The three of us brothers walked away from the Offaly panel. [Mike] McNamara was treating us like s**t, we walked away on the Friday evening and we were back training the Monday before the game. We only missed one training session. He took a dislike to us because we had come back from winning the All-Ireland club title with Birr. I thought that win against Limerick would be a great stepping stone. We knew we could beat them, but on the night I thought that Limerick were getting on top of us. We were up a point but they were after getting two or three scores and then Ciarán Carey was brought on. They sprung me with about thirteen minutes to go to cancel the roar that was there when Carey went on.

His brother Brian was not entirely happy with the fixture:

It was awkward because it was on a Thursday night and the GAA were wrong to fix it for that night. I wouldn't care if it was switched for the pope coming to the country. Whether there was football or not, there's enough weekends in a year to sort these things out. What was done to both teams and both counties that day was a disgrace. At the end of the day both sets of teams and management are amateur people. We had lads, and I know Limerick were the same, who had to take a full day off work. We had lads in Dublin who had to come down that day to prepare for a game that evening and I am not 100 per cent sure but I think it's the only championship game ever played on a Thursday evening.

Limerick were a bit disjointed going into the game and after the first twenty minutes, when the battle was intense, they wilted a bit. I think we seized the opportunity. Mike Mac was in charge and we had put in a lot of work over the winter and probably our fitness stood to us. Limerick didn't appear to be a totally happy camp that year and it probably showed in the end because Ciarán Carey and Ollie Moran only went on as subs. If they were fit enough to play you would be starting them. You could sense it wasn't right. For our young lads it was a great win because it was their first win outside of a Laois or a Dublin side in the championship and they were thrilled with it. I was a little more realistic in that I knew Limerick at that time weren't coming up to the promise they had shown at under-21 and there was more to come out of them.

Although Barry Whelahan's views are tongue-in-cheek, they echo the perception surrounding the Limerick team at the time:

The Limerick boys were on the beer the whole week. That's how we won. We kind of knew they weren't going well. We had heard a few rumours that the boys weren't going training and were on the beer a lot. We were confident going in because we had heard that things weren't great down there.

Limerick had lost the Munster football final to Kerry the previous Sunday and were due to play Armagh in a football qualifier two days later. Pat O'Callaghan agrees that for the dual players to have to peak three times within a week without sufficient recovery was not ideal:

The Offaly game was a disaster. You have to be physically fresh and mentally tuned. Athletics was my area, and I know that if you had several races on the trot you wouldn't be fresh. As Sonia O Sullivan often says, that takes a few days. It comes down to mental freshness also. That Offaly game was our swansong. The rumour mongrels then went around saying that the players were drinking morning, noon and night in Scoby's bar, which was totally untrue. Once the rumours start it's very difficult to stop them. I have no problem saying that if Donal Fitzgibbon had been chairman of the county board that year we would not have been sacked and Limerick hurling might be a lot better for it in subsequent years. The replacement chairman wasn't up to scratch, in my book anyway. There was one particular individual from a neighbouring club who doesn't live a million miles away from Scoby's bar. I am led to believe that this individual was very vocal at county board meetings to get us ousted. I don't know where he was getting his stories from but they were wrong and totally exaggerated.

Paudie Reale has strong views:

Based on my experience, I can't recall drink being a problem. In 2000 with the under-21s we were only together from July to September, a relatively short period. It never affected the way we prepared. It's more of a problem when you are playing senior hurling because it demands that you train almost for twelve months of the year. I think everyone was well behaved in 2000 and had only one goal in mind and drink wasn't a problem with that team anyway. All the players have been tarred with the one brush, based on a minority. I know that Damien Reale is a model professional, and it annoys him and other players very much that they are perceived as doing this when they are not. The few that might have broken the rules have really blackened it for the rest of the players.

I am not sure if anyone is aware of the real facts. A lot of stories have been exaggerated and it's possible that managers have used it as an excuse as well. If managers don't achieve and win the matches that they were supposed to it can be easy to blame a so-called 'drink culture'. At inter-county level, if a manager knows that a player is drinking, it's very easy to cull him. It might be different at club level where you need everyone and are trying to encourage players. I can't see why it's such a big issue at inter-county level, especially when other committed players are available.

Dave Keane agrees that the stories were overplayed:

Drink wasn't an issue. People wanted to look for excuses and they put all these stories out. It was an excuse for everybody and that wasn't the case. You have to put it in context – it's an amateur sport, and they are young lads who are winning matches. We got three years from a core of the same players. To me, we didn't lose any match at senior level because of drink. The only way drink would have interfered was because of outsiders putting it in as an excuse.

Keane makes a fair point. The under-21 players that were part of the senior setup in 2001 trained at 7 a.m. on the bank holiday Monday morning, having lost to Wexford the previous day.

Tensions were high among club delegates at the next county board meeting after the Offaly defeat, and Keane was removed after a vote. Donal Fitzgibbon may have had the calmness and assuredness to save Keane for another year, but Pat Fitzgerald was less decisive and was swept along on a wave of public opinion. On the day Dave Keane was removed, a text message was sent from a key player to a county board official outlining that if Dave Keane remained as manager, he would no longer be available for selection for the Limerick senior hurling team. Some established players had made no secret of the fact that they were not happy with the make-up of the panel that year, particularly the inclusion of some under-21 winners at the expense of their own club-mates. Some established players even questioned the inclusion of players from within their own clubs ahead of what could be termed their own favourites. The tail was wagging the dog.

The majority of the team that lined out against Offaly in 2003 did not have an association with drink. It was a collective defeat, and all players have to accept responsibility for that. Granted there was speculation that one of those who started was seen drinking a few days earlier, but management cannot babysit players around the clock. If management had proof, that player could have been dropped.

While the stories were eventually confirmed, it was merely speculation at the time. For whatever reason, the team did not perform individually or collectively. Stephen McDonagh was withdrawn on the night:

I wasn't injured. I was marking Brian Carroll. Down through the years I had found it very difficult to get motivated for League games. The championship was different and you knew it was the championship with the buzz from the crowd. I remember going to Thurles that wet night and thinking, 'This is like a League game,' and my mind was not properly focused on what was happening. We were beaten and that finished Dave Keane. If there were 20 questions in 1996, there were 120 questions now.

Drink-fuelled celebrations in the immediate aftermath of success are common to all teams, and that was no different with the 2000 and 2001 All-Ireland winning under-21s. However, it is believed that most of the less disciplined players were on the 2002 team. For this, the supporters must shoulder the blame as much as anyone else. Having come back from the dead against Tipperary and demolished Galway, many supporters believed the team were invincible. Perhaps those players believed themselves to be invincible, but there was no shortage of people ready to buy them a drink at the time.

Over time, successive managers had no option but to drop any indisciplined players from the panel, and as a result Limerick lost some quality performers. Some returned periodically in later years but never had the same impact. Much of the indiscipline took place outside of the remit of management, and for that they cannot be blamed. In hindsight, perhaps some of the young players would have benefited from being protected in a way that top soccer players are shielded from undesirable influences. But how would the combined efforts of the county board, under-21 and senior management teams be received if they instructed teams not to celebrate victory? Hurling does not have the qualified personnel to deal with these issues the way professional soccer does.

Much of the fury vented by delegates the night Dave Keane was removed surrounded a drinking session in Charleville the night of the first round League game against Cork in 2003. The team was narrowly beaten but the performance was not hugely impressive. Joe Quaid travelled on the Limerick bus for the final time:

We stopped in Charleville for a few pints and they were organising house parties and having a singsong on the bus. I was sitting beside the driver at the front of the bus and said, 'I have enough. If after being beaten the way we were today makes them want to sing, I don't want any part of it.'

Stephen McDonagh was unaware of the session for some days:

I had to come home to milk cows so I didn't know what went on 'til the following Tuesday or Wednesday night. There was apparently a drinking session in Charleville, which happened. The story went around that there was a bottle on the bus. That story took a while to come out. I was a sub against Waterford in the championship in 2003. I wasn't injured. We were very busy here on the farm, asked Dave for a bit of time, he said 'no problem', that it was fine. He was very good about it. I played a couple of matches, and the form mightn't have been great. We trained inside in Mary Immaculate one night before the Waterford match and he came over and said that I wasn't going to be starting. I didn't like it at the time, being honest. After being there for eight or nine years, who was going to like it? I respected him an awful lot for being able to tell me, though. He could have just called out the team without saying anything, but he told me. I always thought it was good of him. It was a hard call for him. He was trying to put his own stamp on the team, but I took it on the chin.

McDonagh is philosophical about the waste of talent:

How many of those under-21s over the three years have consistently come on and made it as top class inter-county hurlers? Some of them showed massive potential and did unbelievable things in games at under-21 level and had so much to offer but never realised their full potential. They just had something. It's an absolute shame that some of them are no longer around who should be carrying the Limerick senior team at the moment. I think a lot of those lads will look back in ten years' time and they will cringe; they are only human at the back of it all. If I was to look back at my time hurling with Limerick, I can say I tried my best. Some days it worked, some days it didn't work but at least I gave it my best shot. If they are honest – and you have to be honest going through life – they will sit down there aged forty-five or fifty, they will have to have regrets. You only have a short span from twenty to thirty, but there are a lot of years to regret it afterwards.

Jimmy Carroll says the lack of progress in Limerick was not unique:

For the drawn game in 1981, Tipperary only sent out a handful of the old team, the likes of Paddy Williams, Peader Queally and Tadhg O'Connor. The majority of their team came from the three-in-a-row of under-21s that they won at the time. They damn near caught us that day, but Tipperary didn't go on and win anything afterwards for a long time either. Limerick are held up as an example where we had a three-in-a-row and didn't go on to win anything, but Tipperary were the very same back then. By 1987, when Tipperary did make the breakthrough, an awful lot of those Tipperary players were gone again.

His nephew, Paudie Reale, believes Kilkenny's lack of success at under-21 level in those years is something worth noting:

At the time, Kilkenny didn't figure in any of those three All-Irelands and were getting as many under-21s through onto their senior team as Limerick were. The problem was that Limerick had fifteen players on a similar level. We had too many good players whereas Kilkenny were producing a handful of excellent players. Limerick had an endless supply of very good hurlers. A lot of players were mature enough to play senior hurling at the time, and a lot of them did. It worked out for some and it didn't work out for others.

Éamonn Cregan had a good way with players, a good man to talk to them, and he made the transition fairly easy and straightforward. His drills were simple, and he was a big man for doing the simple things properly and doing them quickly. There weren't too many fancy cones lying around the place. He definitely knew what he was talking about.

Jimmy Barry-Murphy managed the Cork minors to All-Ireland victory in 1994, and built an All-Ireland winning senior team around the victorious under-21 sides of 1997 and 1998:

My own view, having been involved with underage teams, is that there is a huge step from minor and under-21 to senior. Some people don't realise that there is no guarantee whatsoever of success. You can win all the under-21s you like but it doesn't guarantee anything else whatsoever. It's a huge step, some players can mature and make that step up, others at twenty-one, having won a couple of All-Irelands at underage, think they have a lot won and can't be told any more or instructed any more.

Hunger is a big factor. In my experience in Cork some under-21 players, having won all Irelands, thought they had it all done. The hunger goes, while the bigger picture is to kick on and do it again at senior level. There's a huge step up, you are meeting hardier guys and more mature guys regularly and I think that's what happened to Limerick: that maybe too many of them didn't have the hunger when they reached senior level. I don't know what celebrations took place in Limerick but I can say that in Cork you wouldn't even know they had won anything; there would be celebration on the day, and it would really be it. There wouldn't be that big a deal made of it. I don't know the scene in Limerick, but given the lack of success I would imagine there was probably too much made of it by supporters as well. When you win underage All-Irelands, the responsibility is there to kick on and do it at senior level, and maybe some of the lads didn't maintain the level of discipline and training that they were supposed to do.

But while many associate the lack of senior success with a minority of indisciplined players, there were a number of committed players who did not make the breakthrough to senior level. Paudie Reale played in the National League for the senior team in 2001 but suffered a knee injury. The county board were reluctant to send him for keyhole surgery and so his club Hospital/Herbertstown took things in hand. Reale would never get back to the same level:

It was only when I was twenty-eight that it really hit me that I wasn't going to play senior hurling with Limerick. Up until then I always felt there was hope that I would get a break and I always believed I would play for Limerick. It hit me pretty hard at that stage realising that I had failed to do it. The club went down to junior for a couple of years also and that didn't help, because the step up was greater than when I had been playing with the under-21s in 2000. I had been with the under-21 panel in 1999 and I was also playing Fitzgibbon. Playing junior club hurling didn't affect Damien Reale though, and it's different when you are established as opposed to trying to get onto the panel.

Pat Hartigan was ahead of his time in terms of preparation:

Full marks to the under-21s for winning the All-Irelands but I always felt that there was a drink culture there that was going to affect lads when they advanced to senior level. It was a drink culture that was well known about and a lot of the players never distanced themselves from it when they became senior players. I think Dave Keane was an outstanding manager on the basis that he won three All-Irelands. I can fully respect him for letting sleeping dogs lie while the team was winning, but if that team happened to lose one of those matches everything would have been exposed. When the stepping stone to senior level came they weren't able to take it. The sacrifices are greater at senior level. It's not enough to be as good as your opponent at senior level. You have to be better. If you are satisfied to be as good as him, forget about it.

That's the attitude I would have adopted. It's hard to put old heads on young shoulders. At least, having got injured, I have no regrets; I didn't drink, I didn't smoke, I did a lot of weight lifting at the time in the garage at home. I weight lifted for myself. My level of conditioning was unequalled at the time. Doing five sets of thirty tummy crunches. We had a couple of other lads with us and it was a question of who could do the most. I would hate to have got injured and turned around and felt I could have done more when I was there.

The only thing I would have changed is my diet. In my time we were certainly eating white bread and red meat. We avoided water, now they can't get enough of it. My game suffered because of dehydration. Some nights I used go straight to training from work, without eating my tea, and I performed far better. On the evenings that I was home in time to have my tea before training, I couldn't run. I never realised the importance of diet. I am sorry that there wasn't more expertise in those areas that time. Injuries don't heal as quickly if you are drinking, and I feel that it's the same for diet. I feel I didn't maximise my own ability enough in terms of nutrition. It's a reflection that I never studied the fact that I could keep running all night on the nights I didn't eat before training. I remember coming out of Thurles after championship games and I mightn't urinate until Monday. There was a thought back then that water would weigh you down and that you couldn't run if you were full of water.

P. J. O'Grady replaced Keane as under-21 manager and the wheels duly came off, though there was no guarantee that success would have continued under Keane. None of the 2000 All-Ireland-winning starting fifteen were available in 2003; seven were available when the three-in-a-row was completed the previous year.

In 2003 Limerick beat Waterford at Kilmallock as they aimed for four under-21 titles in a row. However, they were defeated by a Setanta Ó hAilpín-inspired Cork in the next round. Pat Tobin and Maurice O'Brien were inspirational on the night, but Eoin Foley had gone on holiday the previous week. O'Grady explains the rationale behind some of the selections:

Andrew O'Shaughnessey took us out of trouble against Waterford as we could have been caught that night in Kilmallock. There were so many involved in the senior setup at the time it was very hard to get them for training or anything. In the Cork game we made a decision to break up the half-back line and put Paudie O'Dwyer on Setanta.

Setanta was playing well at the time, and in hindsight the idea should have been to keep the ball away from him, but purely from height alone we didn't really have anyone to take him on. The big problem that night was that Niall Moran should not have played. Niall was sick before the match; he was in a bad state. He didn't even know where he was, and finished up in Cork Regional afterwards. He had got a bang against Waterford in the replay of the senior game, and he might not have been fully right from that. We missed a few frees on the night and weren't beaten by that much. Setanta was causing problems at senior level and caused Frank Lohan bother in the Munster championship. If we had kept the All-Ireland-winning half-back line intact, who would have marked Setanta?

Micheál O'Donnell was a massive loss. He did his cruciate in 2002 and wasn't back in time. I have great time for that man as a player. He is nothing fancy but he is what you need on any county team. If you look back to Limerick teams in the John Flanagan era . . . if John Flanagan was on Seán Stack, Stack would say he couldn't get a touch of the ball, his hands and elbows would be in your mouth, and everything would go through him. And Micheál O'Donnell was the exact same, a typical example of that, an awful loss. A great grafter. Eoin Foley went on holiday the week before the match. We were annoyed with him, to put it mildly, but we couldn't afford to go out without him. He broke his hand in 2003 and he lost his confidence and his discipline.

2004 didn't go well. We brought in James Ryan and Eoin Ryan, who were still minor in 2005. To be fair our preparation was poor; the seniors were reluctant to release the players and we were lucky to survive against Kerry in the first round. But we thought we had a decent enough team going in against Tipperary, but the big players didn't perform at all. And when things go wrong they go very wrong. If you look back at the start of that game we had as many chances as they had but didn't finish and all of a sudden Scroope [Tony, Tipperary forward] had two goals in the back of the net. That was the most disappointing match I was ever involved in because you would expect a fight at least, but it never happened. We brought Paudie O'Dwyer back onto the panel; he wasn't involved against Kerry but, as was the case with Eoin Foley in 2003, we had to bring him back. You have to go out with your strongest team. I have no regrets about bringing the boys back. At the end of the day when you have a panel with players good enough to bring in you can drop guys. But you must put your best foot forward and put your best team on the field to have any hope. It would be different if you had twenty-four or twenty-five fighting for places, but let's be fair – we didn't have that.

The famous midweek under-21 nights were well and truly over and long forgotten. In many ways, by 2004 it was almost as if they had never happened. But such is the lack of depth of underage talent in Limerick that lackadaisical players receive the carrot rather than the stick approach. There is only one solution – the development of more quality players from the earliest age.

☾

SIXTEEN

2004–2006: FROM BIRR TO SHINRONE

The search for Dave Keane's replacement ended in Birr, County Offaly, when Pad Joe Whelahan was appointed Limerick manager – in name at least. Having had success at club level, he was used to being in control. However, in Limerick it became apparent that he was just one of a number of personnel in the management structure rather than the man with sole responsibility. It was not a system he was used to. Joe McKenna was appointed team co-ordinator, and assembled a management team that included Whelahan, along with two players from the Tom Ryan era, Declan Nash and Damien Quigley. Nash recalls his introduction:

Pat Fitzgerald was the chairman at the time, and Joe McKenna was the man who approached me to take the job. I actually said no three, if not four, times. I would have been very hesitant, and wasn't that anxious to take on the job. When I heard Pad Joe Whelahan was involved I began to reconsider because he had been successful at club level.

Dave Mahedy returned to the fold:

Going in under Pad Joe was a strange one. Believe it or not some of the people that co-wrote the twenty questions were involved in asking me back. I have been very lucky in the different sports but the one that I regret is Limerick hurling, not winning an All-Ireland. We were so close and that's why I am still there now in 2009. And I say to myself, 'What the f*** am I doing there now!' It's like an obsession in a way, I won't rest until Limerick win an All-Ireland. I know they will call me the biggest bollox under the sun but I don't care. I don't give a s**t and I would like to make a contribution to winning that and then I could retire gracefully. If that was ever achieved and I was part of it, I would probably never coach or train again. I would go off and do other things but you wouldn't see me on a sideline again. Ultimate fulfilment. I have won national championships in soccer, rugby, Heineken Cups, different things like that, Munster championships, county championships in different codes. The McCarthy Cup is the one glaring omission and the fact that we were so close twice, it's soul destroying.

Damien Quigley is very frank regarding his involvement:

My own personal view is that they approached me because they didn't have anyone else to give it to. I hadn't any previous involvement with any team. I wouldn't have had any experience whatsoever. There was a perception in Limerick at the time that there was fierce bias for lots of reasons. I suspect that they were trying to assemble a management team with no link to the under-21s, the established seniors, or to clubs with players on the panel. My understanding is that they literally disregarded people from Kilmallock and Patrickswell and all such places by virtue of possible bias. Not that there necessarily would be bias, but it was the perception of bias from outside. They had Declan Nash on board, because Declan was from South Liberties and they had nobody involved. I didn't know he was on board at the time.

There had been all sorts of stuff in the papers over the previous few years and I think the reality was that they just wanted to run a professional setup with no more nonsense. Whether the nonsense was ever there or not is irrelevant, but there was certainly a perception that there was nonsense. They wanted to eliminate that perception at all costs. I would assume they went through all the obvious experienced people, but they would have been associated with the big clubs. Joe was heavily involved in this, and he, along with Dave Mahedy, approached me. My suspicion – and it's only a suspicion – is that they came to my door for two reasons: 1. that I had no ties to any of the players; and 2. that I was an accountant working in a professional environment, and there was a presumption I would bring that professionalism to it. Pad Joe was from outside and in many ways he was being led. How could Pad Joe choose selectors when he knew so little about Limerick hurling? In fairness to him, he gave a huge amount of trust to guys he didn't know, to me, to Declan [Nash], to Dave Mahedy. Enormous trust, much more than I would have been able to do. It was a phenomenal thing to do when you think of it, coming into the cold, into that situation. It was a case of trying to put structures in place that were going to work.

Pad Joe Whelahan's first task was to establish a panel:

I brought in a couple of hundred for the trials and we cut it to fifty-five and we trained them and we cut it again. The trials were a success.

Damien Quigley was responsible for keeping records:

We had a meeting in the South Court, and a huge number of players turned up. We told everyone they would get a chance. I took the records of who played well in the trial games, when they came off, who did well, who didn't, what frees were conceded, etc. We kept records of who did everything and we whittled it down. We were chasing time, though. I had come in very late as a selector and we still had about forty-five on the panel in January. I'd have been very concerned myself because I had no experience. It would have been a big consideration of mine when accepting the job that players I had soldiered with were still on the panel. It was a big concern of mine.

Declan Nash outlines why former players were brought on board:

I suppose looking back we were taken in and seen as people who wouldn't be dictating our position as such. I think it was more to help communicate with players because we had played with some of them. Whether that's a good or a bad thing, in hindsight I think you are better off being away for a while longer after playing. It was felt that we could be trusted to do the job – because that's something that has failed Limerick – talking to players, telling them, 'I would have picked you, etc.' Players aren't stupid; we were listening to it for years when we were playing, selectors not wanting to be seen as the one who made the hard call. The hardest job of all is to fill the numbers 17 to 21 because these are the players who are missing out narrowly on making the team. I think we tried to be straight with players because players themselves know where they stand anyway. It's a tough job to do. I don't think one man should put himself in that position to do it. It's a job that needs to be spread between three or four people, but they have to be able to keep their mouths shut and get on with the job.

Pad Joe was depending on the selectors to bring him along. In fairness he wasn't as tuned in as he would have liked to be. He hadn't looked for the job; he was asked would he consider doing it. While he knew quite a bit about a number of Limerick players, he didn't have the in-depth knowledge of most of them. In fairness, he was left with myself and Damien to educate him about the Limerick players and he was also depending on Joe McKenna and Dave Mahedy. Dave Mahedy was probably the most knowledgeable of us all because he had seen and would have known a lot of players looking in from the outside.

In early 2004, the dual player issue returned. Whelahan, however, had no axe to grind with the dual players:

The footballers were going very well, and they were loyal to Kearns who had been with them since underage. If you are in training with a county team, a footballer comes in and does one or two training sessions, and gets picked ahead of you. Bar you are a f***ing eejit, you are going to turn around and tell me to f*** off. We had to stay loyal to the boys who were committed. We had meetings with the dual players and nothing came out of it. I had three or four people with me and we all stood together in what we were doing. We needed the full commitment of every player. We talked to the county board, and I had no problem with the county board.

Damien Quigley provides the logic behind the united decision by management:

It wasn't rocket science. I have had to juggle time in an awful lot of ways and the reality is that the GAA have probably shot the dual player in the foot. In 2003, Limerick had played a Munster football final on a Sunday, Offaly in hurling on the Thursday and Armagh in Hyde Park on the Saturday. That's a total of three games in six days. The two games have completely different skill sets. I mean hurling is a more skilful game than football, very different in terms of physical training; one is based on power, the other is based on short spurts, and that's one thing. Then you have this notional thing if you think it's possible to juggle a job along with full commitment to two inter-county teams.

At the time it was a media circus. There were six players talked about who were labelled as dual players. Mark O'Riordan had never played senior hurling for Limerick at that stage. Great guy, super fellow. Mike O'Brien, great guy. Mark Keane wasn't involved in the hurling panel at the time. Brian Begley was out injured. Stephen Lucey and Conor Fitzgerald played both. You were actually talking about two really, but there was this huge circus about six. It was ridiculous. A bit of common sense goes a long way. The boys wanted to do what was best for themselves as individuals. They wanted to play hurling and football – fair enough, that's their entitlement. We were trying to do what was best for Limerick hurling. I wasn't asked to be a selector on the football team, I wasn't asked to do what was best for one dual player. I was trying to do what was best for Limerick hurling.

I have every sympathy for the guys who were being put in the firing line during the whole thing because it was difficult. The Limerick footballers were going very well at the time, which said a lot of what the perception of the hurlers was, because in another time there would be no decision to be made, it would be hurling only. People make this song and dance over if we had the footballers etc. but in reality the dual players went off and played football because they perceived the footballers to have a better chance of winning something. Fair play to them. They had a choice, to play one or the other, and everyone would have been aware that they had a choice to make. It's impossible to play three games in six days. You have to have a bunch of guys who are willing to do everything for the hurlers. Would I have liked to have all those guys on board? Absolutely, if it was possible, but to our way of looking at it, it just wasn't possible

When we told the hurling panel of the final outcome regarding the dual players, they applauded. They wanted an end; they wanted closure. They [the dual players] made a decision to play football. We told the panel that and we were going forward from there. All the players have gone back playing hurling in the meantime, so it would be a huge slight on either set of players to say there was huge animosity between them. There might have been a small bit of short-term stuff but that happens all the time where there is a group of thirty players. They got to the final in 2007 together and became a different unit.

Joe McKenna agrees:

It's obvious, it's common sense. Supporters can want players to play both codes and that's fine, but if you want to win All-Irelands you can't play them. If you are playing Tipperary, Cork or Kilkenny, they aren't playing football. Most of them don't even play club football in Kilkenny. If you want to beat the big teams you have to at least train like them and be like them, and you might have a chance.

Declan Nash was unique in that he had prior experience of being a dual player:

I played part of a League with a Limerick football team back in the early 1990s. When I was under-21 in '87 we had to make a decision whether we would play hurling or football. I remember there was a chance of me captaining the Limerick under-21 footballers because South Liberties had won the under-21 football. It was between Pat Donnelly and myself for the captaincy. It would probably have been Pat anyway but I chose hurling.

In 2004 we were trying to bring Limerick hurling back up to where we felt it should be. From speaking to some of the players who were there, they didn't like to see players coming and going and, as one player said to me, 'what looked like training when it suited them'. All the players involved seemed to need to get every bit of hurling that they could. It would have been great to have them and it was great to see them return to hurling afterwards, but I think in this day and age, with the level of commitment that's needed, I don't think it's possible to play both. What can happen is that dual players will not make it at either one. What struck me when I was playing football was the level of physical fitness required. I thought I was as fit as I could be, and was used to marking the top forwards in hurling, but the physical aspect of the football was unreal. It was almost like rugby, and the amount of running was unbelievable. I don't know how anyone could attempt to play both at the top level in this day and age.

Brian Begley was one of the dual players but, as it happened, his playing career was interrupted soon afterwards:

We had played minor and under-21 in both codes and there was never a problem but at senior level it became a big issue at times. We were twenty-three or twenty-four and felt we were able to give a commitment to both teams. You can manage it for a couple of years – that's all I had planned to do it for – and as you move along in years the body isn't able to take the hits and the recovery takes longer. It was a pity the hurlers were without six panellists for a period of time. Limerick cannot afford to be without that many options. The three games coming together in one week in 2003 wasn't ideal. If there were only one or two involved they might have given a concession and worked around it, but the fact that there were six meant it was a lot of players from the hurling that would have been involved and might have missed the odd hurling session.

We were hoping the hurling management might have taken it on board that we wanted to do both. They didn't. They made it very clear at the time that it was either all hurling or nothing. We had been with Liam Kearns for a good few years and there was a great setup and a buzz. Liam had no problem with it. He was happy enough for us to give one night to the football and commit to the hurling after that. Having been involved with him for so many years it was very hard to turn your back on him. Maybe it would have been different if it had been another manager, but Liam Kearns had a lot put in. I remember around the time we committed to playing the football, my ankle was causing me trouble. I didn't play any football after that. I had three operations on the ankle; I went to Amsterdam for the third one. I didn't play any club. I went back training and it wasn't coming right. I missed out on 2004 and 2005, two years when I wasn't able to do a lot of fitness, and it was hard to get back. There were times when I thought I would never hit another ball again. When I came back then I had trouble with my knees.

Ciarán Carey can empathise with dual players but says the modern game has made it impossible to play both at the highest level:

My view is that if the man above gives you the skill and ability to play both, then more power to you. I saw nothing wrong with dual players in the old knockout system. At that time you could play both. Players are not bionic, and can't please everyone if games are clashing. I was no angel myself in that area; I have played soccer on the mornings of National League games, I have played soccer the week before important games – not to upset the applecart, but purely because of the love of the game of soccer. Obviously the dual players are mad to play football. But common sense must come into play. If there's a championship match on a Sunday, a championship match on a Thursday and a championship match on a Saturday, you have to ask yourself is that normal? I am probably contradicting myself as it's hard for them when they love both.

There was bits and bobs of hassle going on all the time there, there was lots of hassle. A lot of the time from 1997 up to when I retired in 2004 was probably wasted years because too many players during that period got the green and white jersey too easily. Although I didn't actually retire! I am still waiting for a phone call from Declan Nash and I never got it! As far as I am concerned you must deliver the goods with your club on a regular basis to merit even being looked at. You have to earn the right to a Limerick jersey. Previously players had to earn the right to the jersey. Too many Limerick players in the period 1997 to 2004 didn't deliver consistent performances with their clubs and didn't stand out on a regular basis.

Limerick hurling continued without the dual players and Pad Joe Whelahan was satisfied with progress:

I think the first year we did very well with no footballers, but people won't give you any credit for that. We had six footballers not playing in 2004, and Cork only beat us by three points and went on to win the All-Ireland. You get no credit for that. We hurled Kilkenny very well on the night of the official opening of the Gaelic Grounds. Patie Sheehan of Tournafulla was centre-back marking Shefflin and he got injured. He had hurled against Offaly in Birr in the League. A tough man he was, maybe not the best hurler in the world. But he hurled well in that game in Birr, and that was a vital game. In the League we lost to Cork. Tipperary won well but we beat Offaly, Wexford and Antrim well and got to the last six of the League, which wasn't too bad overall. I don't believe in League hurling. You don't base your year on League hurling; if you do that, you are at nothing. Championship is the game. We were very unlucky to lose narrowly to Cork and then Tipperary in the championship.

Stephen McDonagh was looking forward to the 2004 championship, but lack of League action left him disillusioned:

There were three games in the second phase of the League, and I felt I would have needed one or two of those games to try and get me up to speed. I was still very confident in my own self, that I would be right for Cork. I was a sub against Clare and Waterford, and didn't come on against Galway. I had a bellyful. I came home and told my wife Kay. My mother and father tried to talk me out of it for a while. A few of the players tried as well but I wasn't for changing. I made up my mind that I was going down to Jimmy Hartigan to tell him and that was it. I possibly would have got at least another year. It was an awful thing for all concerned – selectors who I had soldiered with, Joe McKenna who is a personal friend of the family. I can appreciate now where they were coming from, but at the time I was very cross. I knew in my heart and soul that there was at least another year in me. I sat in the stand watching the Cork game feeling I had something to contribute, but I would never say we would have won if I had been involved. You never know until you are out there. I would have felt that I probably gave it up a year too soon, but I have no regrets because I knew I was going nowhere. I would have no regrets about the decision I made when I made it, but I knew I had more left in me. At the time it might have been tricky but now it's water under the bridge.

I never spoke to Pad Joe Whelahan, who never rang me, which I found strange. It wasn't my choice to go in the month of April, but I felt there was no future for me. I have no regrets about never getting an All-Star. I would have preferred having another two years' hurling with Limerick, even though they weren't successful. It would have meant an awful lot more, but it wasn't going to happen. When you sit back and watch Tony Browne, who is probably the exception, I was probably a bit unfortunate in that I was playing in a position, when you move on a bit, that can be demanding. I wouldn't have minded trying wing-back.

Damien Quigley regrets the McDonagh situation, and called it a day as a selector after the championship exit:

I actually spoke to Steve before I took the job and asked him for his views. I would have huge regard for Stephen McDonagh. We burst each other for five years in training; I learned my trade off him. I asked him what his thoughts were on me taking it and on certain issues outside of that, and what the players' perception of me taking it would have been. It was a huge regret of mine that Stephen walked away after that League game in Galway. He had so much to offer us that year. Stephen knew what he needed matchwise and stuff. I felt that it wouldn't have been fair to throw him in that day against Galway because we were being absolutely destroyed. It would have been like a lamb to the slaughter. But in retrospect he needed game time.

I left at the end of 2004. I said I would give it a year and review it; it was too time consuming. I couldn't with young kids, and I probably gave it too much time as it was. The hardest thing about it was that, as a selector, you are involved the whole time; when you are a player you go training and you go home, that's it. Being a selector consumes you totally. There were lots of new lads and they were all mad for road and I thought they were a great bunch to work with. Michael McKenna did very well on Seán Óg Ó hAilpín against Cork. Everyone was saying he didn't hit a ball but Seán Óg didn't hit a ball either. Job done as far as management were concerned because Seán Óg was winning matches on his own for Cork that time, and he ended up player of the year. J. P. Sheehan from Tournafulla had raw material, as lots of players do. Lots of people have that potential, especially mentally, which is the main thing. He had the application and was very committed, which is the single most important thing. The Cahills from Croom were new on the scene as well and did very well.

J. P. Sheehan feels that not having hurled for the county at underage level affected his confidence:

I remember being able to outpace Ollie Moran in the physical training in UL in the spring. But I was probably at peak fitness at that stage whereas everyone else was only starting out. I was playing all my hurling in the League, and I remember going up to Antrim in March and scoring 1-3 or 1-4 and, to be honest, it was really the last good match I played for Limerick. I got one deadly chance of a goal in the championship against Cork that could have changed things too, because it would give you more confidence. When you come in without having played minor or under-21 for Limerick your confidence isn't at the same level as if you had that foundation behind you. It's a massive step up from club intermediate to senior inter-county. It takes more than a year and what happened me was that I pushed myself too hard training nearly every night of the week to get up to that level. Eventually it took its toll: I bolloxed up my knee and it took six months to come right.

Pad Joe Whelahan departed amicably in 2005 following heavy defeats to Tipperary and Cork. Declan Nash feels Whelahan was made a scapegoat:

Fellas weren't in the shape they needed to be in coming back after Christmas. In the spring of 2005 that had been a problem in Limerick; you are dealing with an amateur sport that is professional in many ways. What we found was that in 2004, and particularly in 2005, that there was a lot of fellas who had come back and it would take half the League for them to get fit. Even when we were going well that was the mentality, but you have teams like Cork and Tipp and Kilkenny who don't approach it like that and haven't been approaching it like that for years. They are athletes. In 2005 I remember Dave Mahedy getting the body fat tested. There were players that were over 20 per cent body fat and there were players who would have been classed as obese.

If you are preparing a team for an All-Ireland championship that began on the 15th of May as it did that year, what do you do? You do your best to get them fit and you encourage them to get fit. If it means leaving off some of your top players and putting them on a special training programme, you have to do it, just to get them fit. We tried that that year. In 2005 we were missing five of the team and we weren't strong enough for the first couple of games and the outcome was that Pad Joe was got rid of. I felt he was being made a fall guy. That's my honest opinion.

When Whelahan departed, Nash resigned in protest:

Another problem was there was expectation from 2004 and I think there were people who weren't prepared to take anything less than success straight off. Nobody was prepared to accept defeat, but when you were coming from a team that were missing five players you were always going to be under pressure because we didn't really have twenty-four or twenty-five players. If you take three or four players out of any team, it's a huge loss, if you don't have the backup.

There was nothing to be gained by Pad Joe Whelahan going that year, but it was put in such a way that I felt he was being sacrificed. That's what I picked it up as and that's why I wasn't prepared to agree to stand by this time, having seen what happened with the likes of Tom Ryan previously. I wasn't prepared to stand by and let it happen again without making some bit of an objection and I did. There was pressure put on me to go back in, which I did. I shouldn't have gone back, but I was told it would be all up in the air if I didn't. I was caught between a rock and a hard place, because of my love of Limerick hurling. I didn't want to be making myself out to be bigger than Limerick hurling but still I didn't agree with what happened. Even though I was supposed to be back as a selector at the time, I didn't feel my opinions were being taken on board. I felt he was definitely being made a fall guy, but who is to say we would have done anything different if he stayed. Fair play to Pad Joe for not coming out publicly.

Dave Mahedy offers his take:

There were a lot of issues, change of management, dual players. There were different things happening behind the scenes. There was no stability there. Declan was upset at Pad Joe going. Pad Joe was used to the club scene and had great success with Birr, but he wasn't used to dealing with the bigger organisation. He was used to doing the first aid, the coaching, the training, everything. He had five or six different people to do that in Limerick and he probably found it difficult to delegate and it was difficult. A modern manager needs to be pulling the strings, but Pad Joe wanted to be hands on. He was a hurling man but he didn't gain the respect of everyone because he was working off a different level.

It is acknowledged that, at the time of his departure, Pad Joe Whelahan was doing little, if any, of the training of the team. The time of year meant that little hurling was being done, and Dave Mahedy was looking after the physical side of things. Pad Joe looks back with regret:

The main regret I have is that I didn't stamp my own authority on Limerick, because Dave Mahedy was trainer and it was a little bit awkward. I find it very awkward working with a team that has a trainer, because I would normally train a team myself. I would have to blame myself for that. I am not saying I would have done all the training myself but I think I would have come to more of an agreement with Dave. You feel too left out.

It wouldn't be fair to say McKenna was after the big one, but I suppose when he saw his opportunity he took it. I thought that after 2004 in the championship, we were going places. I didn't get the chance to get the second year out of it. I'm too long on the road. You hear what goes on. There were things said and things done, and there's only one way to deal with that, and that's to go. There's no point in having a big row, the papers would pick up on that. They are always looking for something to say. I am not the only one to ever leave a county team. Why should I be on the papers blaming you and blaming him. I got the job, it was my job to do it, and I blame nobody else only myself. I felt if I got a second year in the championship, I would have had a right crack at it. League hurling doesn't bother me, I think League hurling is a joke. I parted on good terms and rang up all the boys before the All-Ireland final and wished them luck. Richie

Bennis got to an All-Ireland final, but he might have picked up a team that had a few years' work done with them.

Brian Whelahan offers the following perspective:

I know Pad Joe wasn't a happy camper, the way things were going with training, both physical and hurling-wise. From a physical point of view, he felt they were behind the other top teams. He had made up his mind after the second League game in 2005 to do the physical himself. Then the thing took another turn and he ended up walking away. I don't think there is a problem at county level getting someone in to do physical fitness, preparing teams and having them ready prior to a League. However, when you are doing that during the course of a League it's setting training back purely from a hurling point of view.

In that second year I remember talking to him and trying to steer him in the direction that Limerick needed, to be winning games or at least hurling well earlier in the League to give them confidence going into the championship. But unfortunately the programme that was being set out for them from a physical training point of view was that they were ready for the latter stages of the League and the first round of the championship. Results make or break you and the performances were very poor in the first two games of the League that year. I know myself he was very disappointed he didn't take control earlier that year, being his second year in charge. I do know that after that second League game he decided to take over the training.

They were beaten by Tipperary on the Sunday, and went for a recovery session on the Monday. He decided on the Monday evening he was doing all the training after that. But things took a turn and he was gone by the Wednesday night. The one regret we would have was that he didn't take control when he saw the way the fitness levels of his key players were a long way off championship level, which was maybe only ten weeks away. From that point of view he was very disappointed the way it worked out. Every time you take over a team, or every time you go coaching, you will always learn something. It's probably something that will always stick with him and will irritate him. I genuinely believe he holds no bad feeling but it's a regret of his because he feels he had a bunch of players that could definitely have done the business in Munster. At the end of the day he was the manager and the buck stops with him and that's just a regret he has.

That's life and that was it.

He was naive with the dual player issue; as far as he was concerned the boys decided to play football. When that was ongoing, because it was always an issue, the Limerick hurlers needed to be at a level of championship pace at the start of the League. Results at that stage would have quietened down that argument. There was definitely a naivety among the management in general about that in terms of stopping all this dual player crap going on. Every result that didn't go their way was perceived as going against them because there were six players playing football who weren't being picked. If the hurlers were winning that wouldn't be said. I think he could have underestimated the importance of the League in that situation.

Pad Joe Whelahan returned silently to Birr. It must be pointed out that, for a few seasons, key players in Limerick were embroiling themselves in politics. For example, it is widely known that certain players were not shy about attempting to dictate team selections and the makeup of the senior panel. Pad Joe Whelahan was a victim of this.

Supporters might have seen some of those players as heroes, based on their performances on the field. However, if they knew what went on behind the scenes, their opinions might change drastically. It is a bad situation when the tail attempts to wag the dog but unfortunately this is what happened in Limerick.

Joe McKenna took over when Pad Joe departed. Despite an illustrious playing career, McKenna was not an experienced hurling manager. However, he aimed for a professional outfit using business-like practices. Dave Mahedy explains how circumstances militated against him:

Joe McKenna was a fine manager and was used to managing from a work perspective. He wouldn't have been used to coaching and that's why he got in Ger Cunningham. Joe was nearly too honest and wasn't used to the day-to-day cut and thrust of teams and how things can be good and bad. He would find it difficult to accept someone wanting to do something else other than training, and it mightn't necessarily be work related, it could be social related. There was a drink culture, but that's across the board in society. It would be unfair to say that there's a drink culture in hurling or in Limerick hurling over any other sport. It's a society culture more than anything and it was part of the Celtic Tiger culture. I think people are only getting a reality check now with the tightening of belts.

I remember having the shock of my life reading Niall Quinn's book.

That was about professional footballers in England. That has changed with the foreign players and coaches such as Arsène Wenger, but back then they went to the pub after training and literally stayed there until the next training session. There is a drink culture, but it's not at the very top level and it's down to focus. If you want to be successful you know what's good and you know what's bad. Yes, the Munster rugby team, yes, the Irish rugby team, yes, Manchester United will have a blow out, but they will only have it every so often. They aren't going to be drinking on a Tuesday night and a Thursday night and a Friday night and then playing a game on a Saturday. The game of hurling has got so intense and you are putting so much effort into training three or four nights a week and a game at the weekend that you cannot do that. You physically can't.

Ger Cunningham recalls his first involvement:

My first session with Limerick was very early on a Tuesday or Wednesday morning. The lads needed someone to do early morning hurling sessions. Joe asked me to come on board a bit more. At the time I was full time with Thurles Sarsfields and I had committed to them and I didn't want to dishonour that commitment, so I was really only part time with Limerick but I was at as many sessions as I could. For the following year I went full time with Limerick, but for the first half of the year it was kind of a part time role. They asked me to replace Declan Nash as a selector. From a coaching point of view it's very difficult to spend so much time coaching players and not have a selection role. It made sense for the coach to be a selector at that level.

We probably didn't have the fitness levels and the group hadn't played together as a unit enough to beat Tipperary. I think that was the difference between ourselves and Tipperary. They were going well at that time, and they had played a lot more competitive games as a unit. We were still mixing and matching and trying to get the best fifteen out on the field and trying to get them to work as a unit. I think that's what might have caught us in the end. I will never forget the Galway game at the Gaelic Grounds [All-Ireland qualifier]; that came down to free taking and on the night we had no consistent free taker. We missed score after score. I think we had numerous free takers. We had Galway beaten if we had a free taker that night. That whole year for us was about finding our feet and I think for a lot of the players it was about getting a proper structure in place. I saw a different side to the Limerick hurlers I had been working with that day in Croke Park [versus Kilkenny in the All-Ireland quarter-final]. I think they realised then that the supposed gap that was there between the Kilkennys, the Corks and the rest of us wasn't actually as big. We had Kilkenny on the rack for certain periods in that game, but there wasn't sufficient belief there. I think even in the dressing room after the game they realised they weren't that far away.

A major talking point before the Kilkenny game was the selection of corner-back Mickey Cahill at wing-forward, which was based on the coaching philosophies of Cunningham:

A major component of the way I coach is the possession game. It's very rare in a match situation that one of your players has the ball in his hand for any more than ten seconds. An outfield player can't do that but a goalkeeper can. He has full control of where he is going to put that ball, and the object of the game is possession so we put major emphasis on our puck-outs and developing a system for them and Mickey had great movement. He had deadly pace, and we also picked James O'Brien from the physical point of view. We had success in previous games from winning high percentages of our puck-outs from that. The stats were there to prove that, so that's how the boys were selected, based on statistics from challenge games.

They hit the ground running in 2006. Training and pre-season went well. I suppose we may have changed the format of pre-season training and introduced an awful lot more hurling. We had a great run in the League but it was to the detriment of our championship looking back on it. We went to a League final two weeks before the first round of the championship. I suppose if we could have changed things . . . now that was something I would definitely have changed. That League final was a real occasion where the Limerick supporters got behind the hurlers again. There was euphoria even at losing the League final, but some supporters were probably overconfident in hindsight. People were delighted and there seemed to be a structure there and a system that people could buy in to and the lads were performing very well. It's just when you build the players up to a height of playing Kilkenny in a National League final, which they hadn't been in for a long time and then when you are not successful, the lads are on a downer and we just couldn't get them back up again in time. Two weeks was too short a period to get them back up.

However, there was naivety in the selection of the team to play Tipperary in the championship in 2006. Eoin Kelly scored 0-9 from play for Tipperary that day, and 0-14 in all. The man who had been a thorn in Kelly's side many times before and afterwards – Damien Reale – was not assigned to mark him at any stage during the game. Even before Kelly started to run amok, sections of supporters could be heard chanting 'Reale on Kelly, Reale on Kelly'. Cunningham explains the background:

It probably was discussed prior to the game, but the one thing I can remember us discussing was that we are not going to even consider Tipperary. That's not being naive or anything, we were after having a good League campaign, we were very confident in our ability and maybe in hindsight it was a fatal error but we disregarded the opposition from the point of view that 'We're going well for the first time in a long time, let Tipperary worry about us rather than us worrying about them.' The start of the game reflected that. The day we lost to Tipperary was two weeks earlier in the dressing room after the League final.

Babs Keating says it made no difference who marked Kelly that day:

I think the form Kelly was in at that stage, it didn't matter who was on him. At the end of the day Damien Reale is a right full-back, not a left full-back. When Reale switches to the other corner he is fouling the whole time. Reale can play at number 2 but not at number 4.

However, from a Limerick perspective, it was difficult to envisage Kelly scoring nine points – or anything like it – under the watch of Reale, given his record on the Mullinahone man. Richie Bennis feels the defeat was not as bad as it appeared:

They only lost by four points and Begley had a disallowed goal. I thought everyone over-reacted afterwards. The headlines in the *Limerick Leader* were unreal the following week. You could sense the mood wasn't great among the supporters; 'I'll never again follow them', that kind of an attitude. I couldn't understand why Damien Reale wasn't on Eoin Kelly. He wasn't told to go on Eoin Kelly, and he wanted to go on him.

Cunningham reveals how difficult it was to lift the players at that point:

We tried and we tried. Inevitably it took a change of voice or a change of manager to get that group of players lifted again. They had probably lost a bit of trust in us as a management team because we had convinced them they were going to win a national title and, all of a sudden, it didn't happen. From where they could have been, there was a massive fall and inevitably the players lost their trust in us as a management team. I found it very difficult as a coach – not speaking for Joe – but I found it difficult to get a response from the players for the rest of that championship campaign. We knew we were losing the players . . . maybe not losing the players, but the same interest and trust wasn't there. In order to gain that trust again we decided to shake things up a little bit when we picked the team for the Clare game. Obviously that didn't work. The players didn't respond to it, and going into Ennis, it probably wasn't the best place to try that.

In Ennis there was a terrible sense of déjà vu as the horrors of 1972, 1986 and 1993 returned. Lessons from history were not learned; the mistakes in team selection were identical to those made in 1972 – wholesale changes were made and a rookie full-back was selected out of the blue, Donal Manning in 1972 and Kieran Breen in 2006. In addition, Limerick named a radical dummy team, and the players must have been confused when they went to their positions on the field. After the Ennis debacle, the management stepped aside. Joe McKenna, however, says it was not the result in Ennis that led to his resignation:

I just stepped in. I had never really intended becoming manager. In 2005, we were unlucky against Tipperary in both the draw and the replay, and ran Kilkenny close in the All-Ireland quarter-final. I placed a lot of emphasis on the League in 2006, and we got into the League final against Kilkenny but we had played eight weekends in a row. We played very well in the League final. That was a hard game on us. It took a lot out of us. We were really drained going in against Tipperary two weeks later. We went down to Ennis . . . the whole thing of the League and Tipperary was down to tiredness. I found that to win an All-Ireland for Limerick I would need four years to do it, bringing in younger players and rebuilding. It had nothing to do with any game. I said to the county board at the time that I needed four years and I couldn't give that commitment. As with anything in life you have to have structures in place. We did a lot of good things; it was proven afterwards when the players realised what we did was right that, this was the way to do it.

Anthony Daly says the game was not as one-sided as the scoreline suggests:

We really drove it into the players that it was our own field and that we weren't letting Limerick into our own field to beat us. We were wired well, and we got the breaks early then. We had heard that there were going to be significant switches to the Limerick team that had been named. But I always treat those things with a pinch of salt. You can hear all those things and it can turn out that it's not the case, but we had heard that Geary would be up centre-forward. But look, when you have Seán McMahon centre-back, putting Geary on him was up our barrow. Geary was nearly a replica of McMahon, he was tough and strong, but that wasn't going to bother McMahon at that hour of his life. We did stats on it obviously, looking on where we would have won or lost it. We had thirty-seven scoring opportunities and Limerick had thirty-six. And we won by eighteen or nineteen points. It's amazing when you look at it that way. We converted 68 per cent of our chances from play and they converted something like 26 per cent of theirs. That will tell you it wasn't as one-sided as you would think. Fifteen minutes into the first half we got a goal, and that was sort of the turning point that got us to half-time.

Cunningham has his own views:

Every coach knows that when they have lost the dressing room or training ground there is no point. Anyone who has walked away will tell you that. When you know you have lost the players, when you know you haven't got them in the dressing room and you know you haven't got them on the training ground . . . it's only fair to the players. They have more or less told you without writing it out for you that this isn't going any further. Of course, the remaining games were very winnable and nobody will know if Joe McKenna and myself had stayed whether we would have won them or not, but from my point of view at that stage I finished with Limerick hurling because I had lost the training ground. That's where I spent most of my time with the lads and it's only natural that they didn't trust me any more because I had told them that we were going to go somewhere and all of a sudden we weren't there.

It would be very unfair to say that the players downed tools. I think the players were confused. I would like to believe that in Ennis everyone tried, that it was just one of those days when everything went horribly wrong. I don't blame any player individually for that, we have to take responsibility as a management team. Making the decisions we made, I couldn't blame any player. Yes, obviously, players were disgruntled because they were being played out of position and I know there were players taken off at half-time who weren't happy with those decisions, but they were all made for the good of Limerick hurling, not for the good of Joe McKenna or Ger Cunningham.

Cunningham believes his coaching philosophy is not suited to Limerick:

I would highly doubt that I will be involved with the Limerick senior hurlers after that short period. My only inhibition is that I would have certain principles on the way the game should be played. Some people have different terms for it, some people call it the running game. Personally, I don't think there's any name for it. I believe in a system of hurling that might not be conducive to the way that Limerick hurl. For the foreseeable future I think I will be outside Limerick circles, but nobody knows what's going to happen in the future. It was a huge honour for me. It was probably too early in my career, I didn't have enough experience at that level. I was out of my depth coaching an inter-county team. There were the two factors – a lack of experience at the time and an unwillingness to buy into my system. And that wasn't just the players, it was everyone – the supporters, management and players – because I believe the game should be played in a certain way and that wasn't conducive to Limerick at the time.

McKenna's reign will be remembered for that dreadful game in Ennis, but perhaps that is not a fair reflection on the strengths he brought to the role. McKenna introduced a business-like professionalism to the setup, and put structures in place that are necessary in the modern era to compete at inter-county level.

There was criticism of the manager when two players remained drinking in Wexford following a League game in 2005. But pointing the finger at McKenna in this instance is being blissfully ignorant of the problem. Many do not appreciate the efforts McKenna put in to help players whose discipline had left them.

Perhaps McKenna's greatest downfall was his absence from club games for a number of years prior to his appointment. Brian Cody, for instance, has been watching some of his panellists in club games since they were underage players, allowing him an insight into temperament, ability and character that cannot be bought. It must be said, however, that Cody's profession as a teacher allows him the necessary flexibility. McKenna, who did not have that luxury, may have erred in not appointing a shrewd selector who could do the job on his behalf.

But there is one thing we must learn from the McKenna era above all else — always tread carefully in Ennis, and never make those mistakes again.

☙

SEVENTEEN

2006–2008: PRIDE RESTORED

With the 2006 qualifier against Offaly looming, a replacement had to be appointed quickly. Salvation came in the form of Richie Bennis:

I often ask myself, 'How did I get landed with the job?' My brother Thomas had asked me to look at a septic tank belonging to his sister-in-law, the wife of the late Michael Kirby. This was the Monday after the Clare game and while I was working on it I got a phone call from a fierce hurling man who worked with my son in the HSE. We would often talk on the phone and he was asking me about the match. I said it was a disaster, and, to be honest, everyone said it was a disaster whether we liked it or not. He says to me, blackguarding, 'Would you be interested in the job?' And, of course, giving an auld smart answer, I said, 'I would if the money was right.' It was the furthest thought from my mind. But he said, 'I am serious.' I didn't know it at the time but he was also working in the same office as an officer of the county board, Tim Ryan, the youth officer. 'If they were stuck, I wouldn't let them down,' I said, because I knew the next match was coming up very quickly.

I got a phone call ten minutes later from Denis Holmes, the chairman. He said that Tony Hickey would go in as well and asked me would I work with him. I said, 'I haven't agreed to do any job, I was only blackguarding in conversation.' 'I know,' he said, 'but would you meet us?' 'When?' I said. 'We haven't much time,' was his reply, 'would you meet us this evening?' I said, 'I will meet ye anyway to see what this is about.' So we met in a car outside the Castletroy Park hotel, the three of us – myself, Tony Hickey and Denis Holmes. I knew Tony Hickey for years. I hurled with him underage. So the next thing Holmes asked would I do it, and Tony said, 'Come on, we'll do it.' 'Give me until the morning,' I said.

Séamus Hickey (*right*) dives full length to hook Diarmuid McMahon (*left*) in the 2007 quarter-final with Clare, as Niall Gilligan (*centre*) looks on.

Bennis already had his mind made up and immediately set about bringing his nephew, Gary Kirby, on board:

Stephen Lucey had been overheard in conversation saying something like 'Bring on Gary Kirby.' It was a kind of throwaway remark. So I went up to Gary and I asked him. 'Not a f***ing hope,' said Gary. 'Think about it until morning,' I said. 'It will only be a two match job, we won't let them down.' Gary rang me back within half an hour and said he would do it.

Kirby says it needed some thought:

When I finished the club scene in 2003 I decided that I would take a complete break from hurling for five years because of the kids. After that I would get involved in hurling again. Our circumstances had changed by the time Richie came along. I was working in 2003 but I wasn't in 2006. My wife, being the fire chief, needed as much time as she had for the job, so we decided that I would stay at home with the kids. She felt it would be good for me to get out some evenings. So she said, 'Why not do it?' I rang Richard back to talk about it and said, 'Look, if you want me to go in with you, I will.' The county board didn't want me as a selector, even though I was doing the selector's job.

Bennis then set about completing his backroom team:

I rang Bernie Hartigan, because we were always fairly close, and he went in as well. I had no trainer and Val Murnane was with the 21s with Tony Hickey, so Val came in with him. I rang Dave Mahedy but he said he wouldn't join us. The boys [the previous management team] walked out, and he felt he would be letting them down if he stayed.

Understandably, to join the new setup would have been difficult for Mahedy:

I didn't go in with Richie because it was too raw. I had worked with the lads for a few years and it would be a case of not wanting to be seen to turn my back on them. I had a long chat with Richie and told him that it had nothing to do with him and helped him with facilities and wished him well. It wasn't a case of hoping they didn't do well. I would love to have been on board if there were different circumstances.

With Mahedy out of the picture, Richie had to act sooner rather than later:

I rang Liam Kearns as I had heard about Dave Moriarty, who worked with Kearns for the Limerick footballers, and that's how Dave came on board.

Gary Kirby says they had first to lift the players:

I couldn't believe how low confidence was with them. We did very little training, no specialised stuff. Mahedy had them fit so we had no worries where fitness was concerned. We only went around talking to them. We only had ten days before the Offaly game and were quite pleased to see how they were, fitness-wise. We were quite pleased with their attitude. I remember the day we went up to play Offaly. I said we would let Andrew O'Shaughnessy take the close-in frees and let someone else take the longer ones. I said to Shocks, 'You are on the frees,' and he panicked and said, 'Oh Christ, I better do some practising.' 'What are you practising for?' said I, 'aren't you taking them all year for your club and putting them over?' He went over to the sideline to start taking them. I said to him, 'What are you taking frees from out there for? Go out there in front of the crossbar and take a few and put them over and then forget about it.' I knew from my own playing days that practising frees from the sideline is madness, because if a player misses a couple, the head drops.

Richie recalls a few hairy moments early in the game:

When Joe Bergin hit the crossbar I was thinking, 'What am I doing here, am I a bigger ape than I thought?' The game was over if that goal had gone in, we would have been ten points down, and I would have been history very quickly. First we brought back Donie Ryan as the extra man because T. J. was being taken to the cleaners. Bernie Hartigan came over and said, 'We are at nothing if we don't move Donie back up to the forwards,' so we moved him up anyway and he stuck a ball into the net before half-time. When I met the players first I said to them, 'I have no agenda or anything, I am just here to help out until something happens.' Lucey was centre field and he was moaning and groaning, so we decided to take him off. We didn't give a f***. 'Why me?' he said. 'Because you are injured,' we replied. 'I'll be OK,' he said. 'Come on, we are taking you off.' And we took off Geary too, he was carrying an injury but he wasn't hurling well either; there weren't too many of them hurling well, to be honest. We brought in Paudie O'Dwyer at centre-back and their centre-forward caught two balls. Mark Foley called me over and said, 'Richie, move me in centre-back and he won't catch any ball.' We moved Foley and their centre-forward didn't catch any other ball and Foley gave an exhibition that night. Niall Moran also gave an exhibition. The relief was unbelievable after the game. People were crying from the relief of it. People thought Limerick hurling was f***ed forever more after the Ennis game, and they definitely thought it was f***ed ten minutes into the Offaly game. Willie Walsh played very well against Offaly. We did so much switching against Offaly, I didn't even know myself what switches we made.

Brian Whelahan left the game with many regrets:

Limerick will probably thank Offaly for turning their season around. Joe Bergin got through and hit the crossbar. If that score either went over the bar or into the net the game was over as far as I was concerned. But fair play to Limerick; Mark Foley sent over a few long-range points from frees and they got the sucker goal before half-time. I was very disappointed going in at half-time. It probably summed it up for me that it was going to take another few years for Offaly to turn it around. The rebuilding process wasn't there. That game gave Limerick the confidence to go on and run the All-Ireland champions Cork to a point and gave them the strength to get to a final in 2007. From an Offaly point of view, I went home that night very dejected. I saw a lot of players around the field do something that should never be done and that was throw in the towel. To go from a seven-point lead to a ten-point defeat was a seventeen-point turnaround and was very humiliating.

Gary Kirby was always concerned about Dublin in the next round:

Brian Geary was injured but we had asked him to play against Offaly. Under normal circumstances we wouldn't have but we were only just after coming into the setup. His confidence had been destroyed from playing centre-forward against Clare and we wanted to play him centre-back. He trained hard to get fit for that match. His ankle was killing him and he didn't last, so we were without him for the Dublin game. Lucey was at midfield and we were struggling there. When those two players were taken off I think the other players said to themselves, 'These boys aren't afraid to make a move,' and we got more from them. It was a super victory against Offaly, but we had a potential downfall against Dublin. It wasn't all rosy in the garden. Naturally it was easy to raise the team for Offaly after the fallout from the Clare game, but the Dublin game was always going to be a banana skin. While it was always tight and touch and go, we never looked like losing it and we ended up getting through it.

Despite winning, Richie sensed dissatisfaction among supporters:

We went up to the Woodfield House after the Dublin game and I met individuals and they were constructive in a kind of abusive way. Get rid of this fellow, get rid of that fellow, get rid of the other fellow. We were lucky we didn't listen to them or we would have had to get rid of them all. Against Cork in the quarter-final we were five points down at half-time and Cork got a point that put us six points down. It was only then that we started hurling. The referee made a fierce bad decision against us. Brian Geary caught a ball overhead and a free in was given against him. We were only a point down at that stage. Ben

O'Connor took the free and while it went wide, it stalled our momentum.

We had a practice match among ourselves the weekend before that game. In the week prior to that, I went to Ollie Moran and Geary and told them that if they didn't tog for the practice match they would not be considered for the Cork game. The two boys were flying in the practice match. Mark Foley was supposed to take the long-range frees against Cork. There were two frees on Ollie's side and he took them, hitting one wide and the other out over the sideline. I wasn't happy with that. I called him aside and I told him if he did it again, I would take him off. Orders are orders, I had nothing to lose. If we had pulled it off we would have won the All-Ireland, we had momentum. That's what happened us in 2007 when we had the momentum. It's not that we were better than any other team but Limerick have always been a team down through the years that has to get the momentum going to do well. It's very hard to stop a Limerick team that has momentum.

Gary Kirby reveals county board meddling in team affairs:

Against Cork the county board wanted us to go by bus. 'No,' we said, 'we are going by cars and we are meeting in the hotel.' 'But that's not how to prepare,' we were told by the county board. Our response was, 'Lads, we are doing it this way and that's it.' We organised all the cars and we told them all to be there twenty minutes before we actually needed them to be there, to allow for any potential delays. Richard and myself arrived first. Jimmy Hartigan was there before the game saying, 'Lads, this is no way to prepare for a match,' and was saying it to the players as well. It ended up then that they couldn't organise one bus for us, they had to get two small buses to take us up to the field. We arrived at Semple Stadium as the Cork players were going in and we said to the driver, 'Make sure and park it in front of them and don't budge.' We got out in front of the Cork players and we told the boys to stand up tall and look strong. We were very unlucky not to pull it off in that game.

When we had met the county board originally they had no interest in winning the matches, they would nearly have preferred if we lost them just to have the season over. Yet we almost dethroned the All-Ireland champions. Richard was the manager and it's his nature to say a thing straight out. Sometimes he shouldn't, but he does. That's what county boards don't want to hear. The incident with Jerry O'Connor was harmless, a tap on the finger. I remember 'the Rock' went up the field for the penalty and Donal O'Grady met him a slap of a shoulder on the way. Limerick weren't going to be intimidated; the players prepared well for it, they worked hard, and it's a pity it didn't come off. Again you would be asking in hindsight how would it have gone. A Limerick team with momentum is a dangerous team.

Tom Ryan had been critical of the credentials of those on the interview panel charged with appointing the manager, a view supported by many in the county. Richie Bennis saw first hand how they operated. Although there was a flourish under his stewardship, it soon became apparent that he was not first choice on a permanent basis:

I went in for an interview for the full-time job but wasn't in the running at all. However, public opinion was swaying towards me. Tony Considine had the job and they wanted me to go as a selector. Jim Dooley asked the question, would I go as a selector? I said, 'Excuse me a minute, I am here to be interviewed for the manager's job and the manager's job only.' That's exactly what I said. I was interviewed and they told me wait outside, that they would have a decision made shortly. And I said, 'I'll head away home.' 'Don't, don't,' they said, 'stay there.' What I said to them then was, 'If ye do nothing else, make sure and get the right man this time.' They were dismissing me as a manager and I was prepared to walk out, and said to them, 'Just get the right man.' Public opinion had swayed towards me and a specific stumbling block meant the county board weren't in total agreement with Tony Considine.

Gary was a problem at the start because they didn't want two selectors from Patrickswell. I said, 'When nobody else would take it, he came with me, so either he is coming in with me now or I am not going at all.' I knew Anthony O'Riordan of old from when I trained Bruff and I rang him to come on board. I had Bernie Hartigan and Tony Hickey and Gary. I couldn't brush them aside, because they came with me at the very beginning when I had nobody. I wanted someone from the South or the West Division. I asked two people from the West, along with O'Riordan, Mike Houlihan and Stephen McDonagh. Houlihan was after buying a farm and was too busy with that. McDonagh said he intended hurling with Bruree for another year, which was fair enough, and O'Riordan was tied up with small kids. I rang Anthony again and said I would give him as much leeway as he wanted but that I would like him to come on board. It was actually he who got me to train the Bruff hurling team years earlier. 'Leave it with me,' he said, and he came back within half an hour and agreed to do it.

Kirby was infuriated by the lack of support from the county board:

At the start of 2007 we said we would get all the gear sorted out, which the players are entitled to. It's not as if they aren't entitled to it. So we said, 'Let everyone get the gear, backroom staff and all, and it's done and dusted for the year and we can take it from there.' But no, we were told that the backroom staff weren't entitled to it. The trainer and coach were entitled to get boots but nobody else was entitled to anything. We were looking to get the gyms sorted for the players as well and the county board were questioning that. We were trying to provide gyms for the players that were closer to where they lived. For someone like Mike O'Brien, a gym in Mitchelstown would be more convenient than dragging him into UL from Glenroe. That's what is wrong with Limerick hurling, the penny pinching. The players are entitled to meals after training and the county board got the steaks taken off the menu because they were costing an extra €5 each. This is what you are talking about dealing with a county board. I got wet gear and Dave Moriarty got wet gear with the Sporting Limerick logo stuck on over the Red Cow Inn logo. When the gear was given out the players didn't even get a 'Best of luck for the coming year, I hope things go well'. They were lucky to get even a grunt. You tell me if that attitude contributes to a happy atmosphere. It looks more like certain people are putting their own hands into their own pockets to buy the stuff, which the players are entitled to anyway. We got another guy to help us with the training, Fergal O'Callaghan, who was excellent. And again we were faced with questions: 'Why do we need him because we already have Dave?' From day one, you are fighting with the county board. Not once did the county board come to us before the All-Ireland final asking, 'What can we give you? What can we do to win this game? Is there anything ye need?'

In the 2007 League campaign the defeat to Kilkenny was a watershed, as Bennis explains:

Our aim in 2007 was to win a championship match and that match was against Tipperary on the 10th of June. That was our target. We felt the best preparation for the championship game was to beat Tipperary in the League. We put an almighty effort into the League game. There was a big crowd and a great day and we beat them. That game brought the appetite back for a lot of supporters. The next game was Galway in the Gaelic Grounds and we were beaten by seven points. Brian Geary and Ollie Moran were injured so we weren't too upset about that loss.

The Kilkenny game was a disaster. I stayed in the dressing room for about an hour after the match and I laid into them with the following: 'It's not about me, it's about ye. I will take the blame, no problem, for the defeat, but that's no good to ye. Ye have had eight managers in seven years and it can't be all the managers who are wrong. Unless ye get your act together ye are going nowhere.' They had a meeting the following night among themselves, and I believe it was fairly heated. I told them I didn't want to hear anything about the meeting, only a positive reaction on the field. Things moved on from there. We were short a number of players against Kilkenny. We started with Wayne McNamara at centre-back that day. I believe the only way you find out about someone is if you test him against the best. He was twenty-one, plenty old enough. The relegation matches in Nenagh against Offaly and Laois were great matches, much better than challenge matches. Challenge matches aren't worth a s**t to you.

Then we came into the championship. We were lucky enough the first day against Tipperary. The second day was a repetition of the 1996 drawn Munster final. The third day we played Kevin Tobin as a sweeper. It worked for a while and kept us in the game for a long time and allowed us to get scores on the board. But these things only work until the other team cop on. We should have put them away though. We had twelve wides in the game and they had only four.

In the first few minutes of the Munster final, Barry Foley and Brian Begley should have scored a goal each. It was 0-2 to 0-1 to us, and we would have been seven points up.

Babs Keating was always wary of Limerick on the hurling field. Tipperary's defeat in the 2007 trilogy confirmed his fears:

I don't believe we would have won an All-Ireland in 2007 but we had the team ticking over rather well, and Eoin Kelly was playing well. He hasn't played a game since in my opinion, but if we got to the All-Ireland final we would have put up a better show against Kilkenny than Limerick did. I feel we were good enough to go to the All-Ireland final if we had got over Limerick. I always believe we got the biggest riding we ever got in Thurles in the second game with the referee, right down to the very last decision for the 65 involving Ollie Moran. Number 1, the ball was wide; and number 2, it should have been a free out to Tipperary. I counted nineteen incidents where Brian Gavin went against us in the game, but that's history now. We were going as well as we could with the players we had.

I have often spoken about my fear of Limerick hurling and those three matches in 2007 sum it up. In my previous spell as manager we were too strong for Limerick in 1988 and 1989. In 1990 we had injuries but we still managed to beat them comfortably. In 1991 we were well on top against them. But despite our superiority in those games, I never lost the fear of Limerick hurling that I had held since the 1960s. At the end of the day, Limerick hurling finished my career as Tipperary manager in 2007.

Barry Foley recalls the confidence following the Tipperary trilogy:

They were three fantastic games with Tipperary, and even after the first game we were inside in training on a high, then, after the second one, it was the same thing again. Damien Reale was sent off in the first game and everyone put their shoulder to the wheel, meaning that it built up confidence and morale. To go on and win after three memorable games was unbelievable and that was proved with the scenes at the final whistle. You will get those scenes with Limerick; it meant so much to the supporters and the players. The Limerick supporters are crying out for success, and it was great for them to finally come out on top, because often in epic games like that Limerick come out on the losing side. I had a great chance after a couple of minutes of the Munster final. It still haunts me to this day that I didn't put it away. That's the difference between winning and losing, you have to be taking these chances in championship hurling.

Bennis explains how a blood injury proved costly in the Munster final:

With ten minutes remaining we were still in the game and Mark Foley got injured at the far side of the field. We sent across Maurice O'Brien as the blood sub but he had to come off before Mark was allowed back in. Dan Shanahan was loose for a split second while Foley was going back in, and Shanahan crept in and got the goal. We were chasing the game after that. Coming home on the bus the draw was made and there was huge silence. Clare. We weren't hugely disappointed because we were still in a quarter-final. We drew Clare in Croke Park, we couldn't ask for more. It was a chance to set the record straight from the previous year and there was no problem motivating them for that. One night we showed them the video of the match in Ennis but at half-time I went up to Gary and said, 'I don't think this is doing any good, I don't think it helps to show a bad performance,' so we turned it off. And they went out against Clare and played excellent hurling. I missed Donie Ryan's goal after half-time. I was in the sin bin up in the stand for that game and was making my way back out from the dressing room. My suspension arose because I encroached upon the referee after Mark Foley got the belt in the head in the third Tipperary game. Mark got injured and the referee never stopped play and Tipperary got a goal. That's why I was put up into the dog box as they call it for the Clare game.

Ironically, problems within the county board proved beneficial for the All-Ireland semi-final, as Bennis outlines:

Motivation wasn't a problem for the Waterford game. I never saw a setup so geared approaching the game. We had no county board. They were arguing among themselves at the time and Jimmy Hartigan was after resigning and coming back. Denis Holmes, the chairman, had announced that he was stepping down at the end of the year. Not having the county board definitely helped us with our preparations that summer because we were able to look after the pre-match arrangements ourselves. I drove up to Dublin at my own expense with my wife Mary and I got all the facilities sorted out in the right places. We did the warm-up in Parnell Park. It's the nearest thing to Croke Park. For the previous match against Clare, Jimmy Hartigan was putting us into a hotel with a nightclub until I found out about it and knocked it on the head. We were up by ten points against Waterford, but they brought it back to four at half-time. That wasn't a bad thing because if we went in at half-time with too much of a lead it would have been harder to focus the players for the second half. Then we got a penalty and Gary looked at me and I said, 'I don't know, go for the point.' 'Not at all,' said Gary, 'take everything that goes.' Shocks [Andrew O'Shaughnessey] looked up, we pointed for goal, and he stuck it.

James O'Brien being captain that year was an awful setup. He wasn't starting on the team every day, and you had Damien Reale who was a regular starter. I went to the county champions, Bruree, and said we wanted a captain that would be on the whole time. Bruree wouldn't change. The way the captaincy system operates was that in the event of James O'Brien being on the field he was captain.

The one thing we didn't want was the Waterford half-back line clearing the ball. Tony Browne had been doing that, but against us he didn't hit many. Even though Seánie O'Connor didn't hit that much of the ball either he did his job by stopping Browne. James O'Brien was a different type of player and came in and scored a point, but Browne scored a point and set up a goal. Seánie edged out James O'Brien for the final because he did that defensive job for us. Look at Ollie Moran, he didn't hit a ball that day but he still came in and did the job we wanted him to do. James O'Brien did a massive job in the Tipperary games for us, got great scores in the second game and did very well in the third game. It was between Seánie and James for a place on the team and we went for Seánie because he stopped Tony Browne and we were looking for the same job against Tommy Walsh of Kilkenny. But it wasn't that simple in the final. Kilkenny are Kilkenny. They are a different breed.

Gary Kirby explains the specific role given to Ollie Moran:

The management team will see that, while a player mightn't hit a ball, he would have the ability to stop his opponent from hurling. When we took over we looked through all the matches Limerick played for the previous two or three years. It was either the centre-back or the wing-backs who were getting the man of the match awards. We made up our mind that we would put someone in centre-forward who would stop the centre-back from hurling – we went for Ollie. Ollie exceeded expectations in terms of all the scores he got, but his main function was to stop the centre-back from hurling, which he did big time for us in 2007, particularly against Waterford. Sometimes the management team might do something that has supporters wondering, 'What the hell are they at?' If it works, it looks great, but if it doesn't work they are saying, 'What the f*** are they at?' Supporters are quick to knock guys.

Back to the future: ex-Limerick players Frankie Carroll, Shane Fitzgibbon and Mike Galligan and the under-15 team that participated in the Carrigdhoun tournament in 2008. *Back row (l–r):* Mike Galligan (Claughaun), Conor Sheehan (Cappamore), Liam Ryan (Doon), Mark Carmody (Patrickswell), Liam O'Dea (Pallasgreen), Jack Ryan (Croom), Colm Cummins (Doon), Nigel Mann (Ballybrown), Darren Sheedy (Coislea Gaels), Padraig Ahern (Adare), Kevin Mulcahy (Monagea), John Quirke (Croom), Darragh Treacy (St Kieran's), Barry Lynch (Deel Rangers), Brendan O'Connor (Croagh Kilfinny), Shane

Dowling (Capt.) (Na Piarsaigh), Joe Hannon (Adare). *Middle row (l–r):* Shane Fitzgibbon (Adare), George Lee (Ahane), Séamus Hartnett (Ahane), Andrew Minihane (Ahane), Jay Byrne (Knockainey), Dan Morrissey (Ahane), Patrick Drayne (Mungret), P. J. Hall (Adare), Brian Murphy (South Liberties), Stephen O'Riordan (Kilmallock), Brendan McCarthy (St Kieran's), Frankie Carroll (Garryspillane), Mike Ahern (Adare). *Front row (l–r):* Conor O'Brien (Mungret), Patrick Carroll (South Liberties), Tommy Hannon (Deel Rangers), Jack Ahern (Deel Rangers), Paul Reidy (Ballybrown), Luke Murphy (Monaleen).

Many supporters were critical of a photograph of Limerick players opening a supermarket that appeared in the Irish Examiner *the day before the final. It was a huge mistake by those involved and flew in the face of clear advice given by management, as Bennis explains:*

It was a new experience for me to be managing in an All-Ireland final so myself and Gary Kirby drove down to Cork to meet Donal O'Grady. He gave us great instructions on what to do, to make sure the players stayed away from this and that. We told the players exactly what he had told us and there were clear instructions on what not to do. The next thing I opened the *Examiner*! That was not good preparation. When you win an All-Ireland, then you can open up and launch as many things as you want. You can have all the distractions you want when you have the cup in your hand. The problem was that there was no point ridiculing the players at that late stage, it would have only distracted from the job in hand. It was done and that was it. I got offers to do things myself, and I didn't go near them. I turned down good money because I wanted what was best for Limerick hurling.

Barry Foley says Limerick never recovered from the early Kilkenny goals in the final:

Kilkenny are a level, if not two, above everyone else; they know how to win and they certainly have the hurlers. We had prepared for it to try not to concede goals, and yet again we conceded. Against Kilkenny, it's very hard to peg back two early goals. They are a very good team. Limerick didn't do themselves justice that day, the goals were the difference.

Richie Bennis feels the game plan disintegrated:

What we had set out to do at the beginning of the All-Ireland wasn't adhered to regarding how to deal with Eddie Brennan in particular. A lot of people questioned why Damien Reale wasn't switched onto Brennan, but people forget that Damien Reale had to mark Aidan Fogarty. Fogarty was the man of the match for the All-Ireland final the previous year. I also remember Eddie O'Connor's comments about our puck-outs setting the tone for that game. What actually happened was that we had asked our half-forward line to come out the field and create an extra centre field and let the ball from the puck-out go in behind them. Again Kilkenny were a level above all the other teams we had played.

After an encouraging 2007, things never picked up the following year, as Bernie Hartigan acknowledges:

We had a good run in 2007, and did better than we thought we would. The players weren't as determined at all in 2008. The same hunger wasn't there; players we expected to give more of themselves gave less.

Bennis sees 2008 as a missed opportunity:

You couldn't plan the year better with the decent draw. We went on holiday and had targeted three matches to win to reach the quarter-final of the League. We won those three against Offaly, Laois and Clare. We had Offaly beaten at half-time. We went down against Tipperary with a weak team, and I'm sorry I didn't put a stronger team out. We had five injuries and we said we won't beat them without the five, that we would throw in players and see what they were made of. I would have put in ten regulars with five newcomers in hindsight, rather than the opposite. They were all fringe players, and were entitled to get their opportunity, but not all together. They might have played better if they had more experienced players with them. We reached the League quarter-final against Cork and we lost by only five points despite losing Mark O'Riordan and Damien Reale in the one clash.

Bennis makes no apology for concentrating on the championship in 2008:

We would have run out of steam before the championship if we had targeted the League. We would have had to beat Cork, Galway, Tipperary and Kilkenny to win the League. We would have to put in an almighty effort and maybe have nothing to show for it and then be left flat afterwards. We said to ourselves we had a good draw in the championship, and we would target that.

Barry Foley feels the lack of spark in 2008 was not surprising:

Things were flat in 2008. After the hype of 2007 and the effort that was put in, it was always going to be very hard to match that. Things went a little bit stale, and training probably wasn't up to scratch. After the year before, we would have been mentally drained, making it harder to reach those heights again.

The Limerick intermediate team that won the Munster title in 2008. *Back row (l–r):* Denis O'Connor (Granagh Ballingarry), David Moloney (Blackrock), Paudie O'Brien (Kilmallock), Andrew Brennan (Caherline), Paudie McNamara (Murroe/Boher), David O'Neill (South Liberties), Peter O'Reilly (Patrickswell), Damien Moloney

(Effin). *Front row (l–r):* David Stapleton (Doon), Stephen Walsh (Glenroe), Gearóid
O'Leary (Dromin/Athlacca), Alan O'Connor (Ballybrown), Barry Hennessy (Kilmallock),
Tom Condon (Knockaderry), Ciarán Carey (Patrickswell), Peter Harty (Patrickswell).
Mascot: Donie Franklin (Knockane).

Prior to the championship, an undesirable headline pertaining to a breach of discipline by a Limerick senior hurler appeared in the **Limerick Leader.** *It is not something that lies well with Bennis:*

Everyone knew whom the allegation referred to. At the time, it was during a break from training. We questioned the man about it at the time. There was a great opportunity available to him on the field of play, which he didn't take. Another player would have appreciated it more.

Limerick lost to Clare in the first round of the championship at Thurles. Bennis says the concession of easy goals was Limerick's undoing:

Stephen Lucey was the cause of two goals, Brian Murray was the cause of one and Dodge was the cause of another. Brian Geary was a massive loss. We played against a strong breeze and were 0-4 to 0-2 up but we conceded a stupid goal. Stephen Lucey and Brian Murray were at fault for it. Then we came within four points again and they scored another goal and we were seven points down. I believe that if we got that one win we would have won the Munster final because Tipperary hold no barriers to Limerick, even going back to my time. Ollie scored a great goal in the second half and we came within two points again but they got another goal. Lucey was told not to leave the square but he did. Paudie O'Dwyer was caught inside, his man caught the ball and palmed it across the square for another Clare goal. We only lost by four points. It was a disaster. We had 65 per cent of the play but they scored four goals.

The players' attitude was as good as it had been in 2007 for the Clare match; they were spot on and mentally tuned in. That changed against Offaly and the problem was that losing the Clare match caused heads to drop. We thought we had the best draw of all in the qualifiers against Offaly at home. But after beating the s**t out of them above in Tullamore in both the League and the 2006 qualifier, it's hard to prevent players from being overconfident. It's hard to stop it seeping in. Our biggest problem is that many of our forwards who hurl well come in as subs but don't seem to perform when they start. During our reign, every sub who went on did well. But if they were started the next day, they had to be taken off.

Bennis rates Mike O'Brien as an unsung hero during his time as manager:

'Banger' was a great asset to Limerick. He might not have been a sophisticated hurler but he was a great man for us.

He is critical of the county board and wishes his successor well:

I was told I had an option of a third year but I don't mind being shafted because Justin [McCarthy] is a good man. I hope he is not coming to Limerick too late. He was unlucky with Waterford, they took us for granted in 2007 but I don't think they would have won the All-Ireland if they had beaten us. It was still too late for them by then.

In hindsight, he says it is unwise to have too many selectors:

Five selectors are too many, three is plenty. By the time you have the other four selectors consulted you have almost lost your train of thought. Circumstances dictated me picking mine.

Gary Kirby remains angry about the attitude of the county board:

People don't know what we had to put up with from the county board. They didn't even want us there in 2008; it was obvious by their reaction towards us. I'd say they nearly wanted to get rid of us after the 2007 All-Ireland. I know by the way they looked after us even. They weren't helping us anyway. There was no support at all coming. It was the same with Phil Bennis – he was demanding and if he felt he needed something, he said he wanted it. It was the same with Tom Ryan. Let's be fair, Limerick had done nothing all along. Next thing Tom wins us two Munster finals and wins a National League, gets to two All-Ireland finals in the space of four years – and gets kicked out. Why? Because Tom was outspoken, Tom was demanding.

Can every manager over the years have been wrong? Among certain members of the county board, having control has been more important than results on the field. Too often Limerick hurling has suffered because of tension – or indeed a complete breakdown of relations – between the county board and the management team. It is of fundamental importance that this be addressed for once and for all if real success is ever to be achieved.

The Limerick Masters team that beat Tipperary to secure the
All-Ireland title in 2004.

Back row (l–r): Seán Heffernan (selector) (Adare), Liam McCarthy (Ballybricken), Seán
Heffernan (Adare), Jim Fanning (Newcastlewest), James O'Donnell (Pallasgreen),
Gerdie McGrath (Doon), Andy Garvey (Hospital/Herbertstown), Mike Alfred (Adare),
Ger Moroney (Tournafulla), Maurice Curtin (Tournafulla), Murty Mulcahy (Killeedy),
Mike Kelly (Ahane), Jimmy Kearns (Old Christians), John Madigan (Feohanagh), Rory

Kiely (selector) (Feenagh/Kilmeedy), Mike Weekes (manager) (Bruff). *Front row (l–r):* Pa Doherty (first aid) (Adare), Danny Holmes (Doon), Johnny Gammell (Pallasgreen), Jack O'Connor (Capt.) (Kileedy), Donie Neville (Croagh/Kilfinny), Connie Connors (St Mary's Rathkeale), Ger Barron (Knockainey), Tomás Ryan (Ballybricken), Vincent Sheehan (Newcastlewest), Ray O'Leary (Bruff), Noel Sexton (Douglas, Cork).

EIGHTEEN

2009 (1): FUTURE VISION

There are many opinions on how best hurling can prosper in Limerick. While the county continues to strive for senior success, it is important not to lose sight of the fact that All-Ireland titles at other grades can have an impact. Mike Weekes was the manager of successful Limerick over-40 sides:

The masters brought new life to players who were going off hurling. The fruits were borne in that it renewed their interest in hurling and it inspired them to get involved in underage coaching. Most of them were former county players or exceptional club hurlers in their day. Their input towards coaching underage players is invaluable, in comparison to others who don't have the same level of hurling experience. The amount of enjoyment they got from putting on a Limerick jersey was unbelievable. Ger Barron, Andy Garvey, Mike Barron, were really proud to be wearing the Limerick jersey again. Even though it was meant to be fun, it wasn't fun. It's a serious competition. We were never properly acknowledged by the county board and we deserved that as a team who represented the county, were successful and won silverware.

The Limerick intermediate team won the All-Ireland in 1998, a success that led to Mike O'Brien and James Butler lining out for the seniors in later years. Tommy Quaid was a selector for the intermediate team, and died tragically on the day of the final. He had been injured at work in the week preceding the final, and was on a life support machine as the game took place. He died shortly after half-time. Limerick finished the game strongly to claim the title. Owen O'Neill played that day:

That was a difficult time for the players involved. Tommy had been very good to us that year, and as a panel we had got on very well together. When it came down to it we owed each other and the Quaid family to give it our best on the day. We weren't aware on the field that he had died. Games have different spells in them, teams have periods when they get the upper hand and that year we had a trend of finishing stronger in all the games. That year things had a habit of coming right for us.

Donie Carroll, who was also on the team, recalls a moment of reflection in the dressing room afterwards:

Henry Shefflin was wing-forward that day. He was a danger and scored all around him in the semi-final against Galway. In a way, we weren't able to handle him; there wasn't any of us able to take him on. Andrew Ryan got a lot of scores that day and Owen O'Neill got two goals. It was only coming off the field going into the dressing room that someone said it to me that Tommy had died. Perhaps there was a twist of fate at the time of his death when we came into the game. There was a bit of a downer in the dressing room afterwards when we had won it. I remember Ger Galvin starting a decade of the rosary afterwards, which was most unusual, but it was something that happened and was nice.

There is further sadness associated with that success – the untimely death of full-back William O'Brien in 2006. Donal Fitzgibbon pays tribute to both men:

William O'Brien was a colossus, and the word 'courage' and William O'Brien went hand in hand. He wasn't shy and he gave his all at all times, and that was reflected in his performances on the field. Primarily he was a huge and tragic loss to his family and also hurling in general.

It was at half-time in the intermediate final that the life support Tommy was on was disconnected. I was trying to keep it from the team and whatever happened, everything changed midway through the second half. I often think it was divine inspiration from Tommy. I would give credit to that team for the success we had subsequently, because that was the breakthrough in terms of winning All-Irelands after a barren spell of eleven years. Tommy was central to the progression of that team that year, and was a loyal servant to Limerick hurling in every respect.

Limerick also won the 2008 Munster intermediate final but were defeated by Kilkenny in the All-Ireland final. For a number of players the run acted as a stepping stone to the Limerick senior panel of 2009. Gerry Molyneaux was the manager and, despite the emphasis on youth, he recalled a former hero:

I made a phone call to Ciarán Carey, a legend in Limerick hurling, and asked him if he would make himself available. He told me he would think about it, and a week afterwards we were invited by Lixnaw to play the Kerry seniors in a tournament game to open their new pitch. Ciarán confirmed his availability for that and we were naturally delighted.

Carey was surprised to be asked, to say the least:

I was enjoying my hurling with the club and he rang me and said he was looking for a full-back. 'For what, Gerry?' 'The intermediates,' he replied. I got into knots laughing. I said, 'There's a lot more younger fellas out there besides looking for me.' 'We are badly stuck for a full-back,' he persisted. I said, 'Gerry, are you serious?' He said he was. I started laughing again. He said, 'I am serious, don't be laughing at me.' I asked him to give me time to think about it. I said I would play in a couple of challenges and if I was comfortable I would make a decision then. I would have approached those challenge games like Munster finals. At thirty-eight years of age, I had no choice. Going back to play intermediate wouldn't have been a fashionable thing to do. It shows a certain amount of humility and I know certain fellows could have played but didn't because they would have seen themselves as being beyond it. Patrickswell got to the Féile final and were beaten by James Stephens. I got talking to Brian Cody and he said, 'I see you are still hurling away,' and I said, 'I am.' 'You are dead right,' he said. 'Hurl for as long as you can, I will nearly go to the next match to have a look at you.' It's either in your blood or it isn't. Gerry Molyneaux can be described as the saviour of Limerick hurling [laughs]. Seriously though, he has contributed greatly to Limerick hurling over the years.

Donie Flynn believes proper refereeing in club games can help the development of players:

A recruitment process should be undertaken to encourage ex-players to become referees that will officiate in a manner that will allow players to develop to the maximum with full knowledge of the rules being applied using common sense. Limerick were the leader of the pack for producing excellent referees over an extended period . . . Steve Gleeson, Gerry Fitzgerald, Seán O'Connor, John O'Grady, Neilly Duggan, Terence Murray and Pat O'Connor, all of whom were previously involved in the game at every level. I also feel strongly that

The people who worked tirelessly for underage GAA in south Limerick received presentations at their final gathering in December 2008 from Pat Fitzgerald, the full-time secretary of the Munster Council. *Back row (l–r):* Denis Martin (Staker Wallace), Denis Crowley (Kilmallock), Ged Carey (Croom), Mike Meade (Ballylanders), Tommy Sheehan (Galbally), Séamus Murphy (Ballylanders), Ger Power (Garryspillane), Declan Murphy (Hospital/Herbertstown), Paddy Carroll (Staker Wallace). *Front row (l–r):* Pat Murnane (Camogue Rovers), Harry Greensmyth (Hospital/Herbertstown), Pat O'Dwyer (Bruff), Pat Fitzgerald (Munster Council Secretary) (Doon), Mark Reidy (Croom), Bill Fox (Ballylanders), Jim Hickey (Ballylanders).

hurling might be better served managed and developed at national level if a separate hurling board was appointed from within Croke Park. This board should have equal status and equal authority within the GAA to promote and develop the game as they see fit.

I have strong views on the admission by Nicky Brennan, prior to leaving office as president, that there is no vaccine to correct the epidemic scale of the problem that exists relating to managers and the amateur status of the game. In my view the vaccine is very straightforward: to ensure that every county board and club apply the rules that exist and do not allow any board or club to continually bring the association into disrepute, which means giving all personnel no more than the proper expenses legislated for the job by the association. I believe the management function may have served its time, and

Limerick's All-Ireland Intermediate Champions in 1998. *Back row (l–r):* Owen O'Neill (Murroe/Boher), Danny Murphy (Glenroe), Patsy Keyes (Camogue Rovers), Niall Murphy (Mungret), John Kiely (Galbally), Andrew Ryan (Ballybricken), William O'Brien (Knockainey).

Front row (l–r): James Butler (Murroe/Boher), Mike O'Brien (Glenroe), Ger Galvin (Feenagh/Kilmeedy), Pat Horgan (Tournafulla), John Cormican (Captain) (Monaleen), Paul Neenan (Dromin/Athlacca), Donie Carroll (Hospital/Herbertstown), Patsy Cahill (Croom).

possibly should be replaced by a solid management team of three or five selectors. It has become too easy to target one man, as happened in the Gerald McCarthy case, and I believe the legacies we have inherited from the management function have caused nothing but problems for county boards.

Pat O'Dwyer was secretary of South Bórd na nÓg for fifteen years prior to the boards' abolition in 2008. He worked effortlessly to promote underage development during that time and is now part of the county underage development structure:

I remember underage finals in the South division involving the three-in-a-row players, in front of large crowds. It was very apparent at under-12 level that there were quality players around, ever before they were brought into any county development squad. If credit is to be given to anyone for the three-in-a-row and the successes at other levels it must be given to the clubs where the players started. We are always hearing of the big names, but the true heroes in Limerick hurling are people such as Mark Reidy of Croom, Davy O'Keeffe of Granagh/Ballingarry, Breda Breen of Monagea, John Hayes of Pallaskenry, Jack Sheehan of St Patrick's, John Keane of South Liberties and Paddy Sullivan of Kilteely/Dromkeen. The four underage divisional boards also played their part, but it's the volunteers in the clubs who should be lauded for developing the talent. I feel the decision to disband underage divisional boards will prove costly in the long term. Limerick were capable of producing players who reached All-Ireland finals at minor, under-21 and senior level in the past fifteen years under the old system. The true test of the new structures will only become apparent in twelve years' time and I hope for Limerick's sake that things work out.

Kilmallock's Denis Crowley, a former Limerick hurler and county underage selector, says communication with underage players needs to be improved:

I am a firm believer that underage players will have more respect for and respond better to those in charge of them if they are treated with respect. Underage players are a lot more clued in these days than they would have been a number of years ago. They need to be communicated with, and spoken to at their own level. The traditional methods have no place in the modern society.

Turning back the years. Celebrating winning the Munster Intermediate Championship at Semple Stadium in 2008 are (l–r): Gearóid O'Leary, Ciarán Carey, Gerry Molyneaux (Manager), Gerry Murphy (Trainer), Stephen Walsh.

Another obstacle to the development of hurling in Limerick is the success of Munster rugby. Turlough Herbert, however, believes hurling is the game of heritage:

I have a certain amount of regret at my sojourn as a Limerick senior hurler, but at the same time I was lucky to be there and play in an All-Ireland final in 1996. I have my Munster medal but my uncle Seán hurled for Limerick and never won a Munster medal. I was very conscious of keeping the family name in there and Limerick hurling is the last thing we think about at night and the first thing we think about in the morning.

I have the ultimate regard for Munster rugby, what they have achieved and what they have done for Limerick, but I genuinely feel that hurling is the traditional game in Limerick regardless of what you might be led to believe. When Ahane were at the top in the '30s, you had Croom and then it was all city teams: Claughaun, Treaty Sarsfields, Young Irelands and St Patrick's. The Munster thing is phenomenal but it's a very recent thing and I don't think it is as deeply rooted in the Limerick psyche as people might think, and I think if Limerick won an All-Ireland that would become fairly apparent, that hurling is the treasure that runs through our veins in Limerick.

Limerick must learn from the success of others. Ned Rea was most impressed with the discipline of the Kilkenny players in the off-season some time back:

I was at a function a few years ago at Vicar Street in Dublin when Kilkenny were raising funds to go to South Africa. Éamonn Dunphy, D. J. Carey, Après Match and the Fureys were all there. It was a superb show at the end of November and there were about twenty of the Kilkenny panel there. There were only two of them drinking. They were after winning a league and a championship. This was the end of November, they weren't due into training until the New Year and there were only two drinking. That, to me, sent out a message. They were after winning a double, yet they still were able to hold back and that's the difference. Even at club hurling, if you want to be a serious club hurler now and win a county, you have to make sacrifices. When I was playing it was different and that applied to everyone, but now some teams take it so seriously that there's no more drink until the club is out of the championship.

Kilkenny are Kilkenny for a reason. The players are gracious and humble, live disciplined lifestyles off the field, and don't have a 'look at me' mentality. In Limerick we need to aspire toward players with that mentality. We need to be ruthless enough to cull players, regardless of their ability, whose lifestyle is not conducive to competing at the top level of intercounty hurling.

NINETEEN

CB

2009 (2): THE NADIR

Public *perception and image are areas that Limerick GAA needs to brush up on. For example, the excellent Noreen Lynch was associated with Phil Bennis' under-21 team in 1987. Yet, nine years later, one of the twenty questions related to the involvement of a couple of female professionals with the senior hurlers. This was in the same year when Niamh Fitzpatrick was closely associated with the Wexford hurlers. In many ways, this highlighted the need for modern thinking at county board level in Limerick. But in 2009, only two of the executive were under fifty years of age. Even at that, it is the opinion of many that one of the younger members, full-time secretary Mike O'Riordan, needs to learn a lot in terms of etiquette. There is resentment throughout the county at the huge expenses paid to county board officers annually. The 2008 balance sheet detailed a princely sum of €82,299 as the total expenditure on officers' expenses. In 2009, the Limerick underage teams had to take it upon themselves to raise funds to buy gear ahead of the annual intercounty underage tournaments. Given that €2,000 would have provided the necessary gear, the officers could have limited themselves to €80,000 and given the underage players the 'loose change'. In this day and age, club members in Limerick are entitled to a detailed breakdown of the expenses paid to each individual officer for 2008 and for all future years. Otherwise, the knock-on effect could be the refusal of grass roots members of the association to put their shoulder to the wheel for future county board fundraising activities. If individual officers are too much of a financial burden, then the number of officers on the board should be reduced.*

Tommy Cooke believes Limerick need to cater for their former heroes:

When Tom Boland was secretary of Limerick county board, he used to send me out two tickets for the All-Ireland final and I would send in the cheque to pay for them then. When Jimmy Hartigan replaced him in the 1980s, he would only send one and I would have to send the money in advance. I need two tickets, as I have no business going up to Dublin by myself at my age. I was going to write to the papers to protest in 2007 but because Limerick reached the All-Ireland final that year I didn't want to upset the team.

Cooke has a valid point. It's not too much to ask for such a legendary figure to receive a second ticket for someone to accompany him to a match.

Tom Ryan is unequivocal in his views of Limerick hurling:

The standard of coaching, standard of hurling and standard of discipline has been a disgrace. The drinking and the public image of the team is rock bottom. Really and truly, it has been a shameful period for Limerick hurling.

The drink culture has been highlighted in recent years, but it's not something new to Limerick hurling. It probably goes back to early in the twentieth century when a swig from a bottle during a game was commonplace. In 1974, anyone socialising at a well-known Castletroy establishment on the weekend before Limerick played Waterford in the Munster championship would have been in 'big name' company. Likewise, in 1982, there were rumblings of a session in a rural east Limerick village on the eve of the Limerick versus Waterford championship encounter. In 1993, a number of players would have found loose change from the night before in their pockets prior to the League semi-final and Munster championship games. However, regardless of their match preparations off the field, Limerick teams always gave 100 per cent on the field. A Limerick team playing with heart and not giving up without a fight is all that supporters ask for. In fact, a tunnel incident on the day they were hammered by Tipperary in the 1962 replay would appear to symbolise the reluctance to give up without a fight! While there have been some stirring comebacks in recent years, Limerick teams have sometimes thrown in the towel, which is a worrying issue.

The future generation of hurlers needs to maintain the traditional Limerick fighting spirit and steer clear of some of the habits of old. When the under-21s won their All-Ireland titles, a minority of players arrived at primary schools in an intoxicated state, despite having the honour of carrying the trophy. It is wrong to tar all with the one brush and the minority involved let themselves, their county, the schools and their families down. They don't need to be named: it's already common knowledge who they are. There were also issues involving the law when the under-21s and the seniors were on holiday abroad together in 2001. An innocent individual, who is a current senior player, carried the can for an incident where the law were involved and was punished. These days, hi-jinks seem to have become part and parcel of the holiday when a number of young friends go away together, However, when an intercounty panel takes a holiday together as an official party, there is a responsibility to lead by example and represent the county with honour and dignity. There is an old saying 'Ní thagann ciall roimh aois', *and as a county Limerick needs to learn the lessons of the three-in-a-row successes and take preventative measures in the event of any future success.*

On the field, 2009 brought more heartbreak as Limerick were knocked out of the Munster championship after a replay against Waterford. A ray of light began to shine through the dark clouds in the form of a decent qualifier run, as the team ground out victories over Wexford, Laois and Dublin. The influence of Justin McCarthy was beginning to show in the improvement of some of the younger players. But Croke Park brought its own misfortune yet again as supporters and players alike left the venue having experienced the most harrowing defeat in recent Limerick hurling history. The sight of an unmarked Lar Corbett finishing the sliotar to an open net is a moment that will remain painfully etched in Limerick minds forever more.

Limerick is now staring into an abyss. And how it responds to this defeat will say a lot about its character and its future as a hurling county. Clare did not forgot a similar humiliation by Tipperary in 1993 and used it to drive them on to victory in later years. Stephen McDonagh, as already outlined earlier in this book, never forgot an under-21 defeat to Tipperary in 1990. That's the mindset that Limerick needs the current crop to adopt. Limerick needs to strengthen its squad of players and while young blood is important, older players have a role to play. The mercurial Tobin brothers, while they provide their own difficulties, are players that Limerick cannot afford to be without. They may not always be starting options in every game, but they have delivered as substitutes. Can Limerick afford to have a player of Maurice O'Brien's calibre lining out for Dublin? Paul O'Grady of Patrickswell is a player that Limerick never got the most out of this decade, and many years were wasted being patient with ill-disciplined alternatives when O'Grady surely had something to offer. In recent times, injury has robbed the county of many three-in-a-row players such as Conor Fitzgerald, Brian Begley and Willie Walsh at various times and Limerick, of all counties, cannot afford injuries.

But, for all the heartbreak, it hasn't always been doom and gloom for Limerick. For Limerick hurling to prosper, it needs to return to the days when Anthony O'Riordan proudly raised the Irish Press trophy aloft in 1984, and raised the Munster under-21 trophy two years later, a feat that very few captains have achieved. There are other great memories that Limerick fans cling to, wishing they could occur more: Ray Sampson's winning point against Tipperary in the League final of 1992 will forever hold a place in Limerick hearts; Frankie Carroll's superb equaliser in the drawn Munster final in 1996 felt like it was a winning point, and in many ways deserved to be; Kevin Tobin's never-to-be-forgotten equaliser in Thurles in the replayed Munster under-21 final of 2002 shook the foundations of the Kinane Stand in Semple Stadium; Gary Kirby scoring 0-12 against Tipperary in 1996; James Butler's wonder goal in 2001 against Cork; Owen O'Neill's kicked goals against Tipperary in the replayed Munster final; Ollie O'Connor scoring the goal in the 1980 Munster final as John Horgan's hurley whizzed past his ear.

To finish, I think it is appropriate to repeat the words of Éamonn Grimes the man who provided the greatest memory of all by lifting the McCarthy Cup in 1973:

It would provide great joy for somebody else to take the mantle off me, of being the last man to captain Limerick to an All-Ireland victory. It would bring a sense of great elation to the supporters and I would love nothing more than to see the scenes of victory in 1973 re-enacted some day soon in Croke Park, with me looking up at the new captain from the field rather than looking down from the podium.

But for now, the heartbreak continues . . .

INDEX

Page numbers in *italics* refer to pages with photographs.

୯ଓ